PETER WAGNER

A SHORT
HISTORY OF
ENGLISH
AND AMERICAN
LITERATURE

PETER WAGNER

A SHORT HISTORY OF ENGLISH AND AMERICAN LITERATURE

ERNST KLETT VERLAG

For Charles and Joséphine Allain

Picture credits

Gedruckt auf Neoprint, hergestellt von Stora Papyrus aus chlorfrei gebleichtem Zellstoff, säurefrei.

First Edition   1⁶ 5 4 3 2 | 1996 95 94 93 92

The last figure shown denotes the year of impression.
© 1988 by Ernst Klett Schulbuchverlag GmbH, Stuttgart.
All rights reserved.
Printed by Druckerei Ludwig Auer, Donauwörth.
Printed in Germany.
ISBN 3-12-516140-1

Table of Contents

English Literature

American Literature

Preface

Literary histories are attempts to render more accessible the vast jungle called literature. Their problem lies in the fact that they are obliged to select, to simplify, and to establish an order of some kind in the face of diversity. The order that is finally achieved by a literary history is thus always an artificial one. The classification chosen here can be defended in view of the need of the student at the elementary level for guidelines and helpful suggestions.

The present literary history shares with others in the fields of English and American literature its arrangement by periods and genres, and its approach that gives preference to what time and literary judgement have proved to be great works of literature. It differs, however, in focusing mainly on the modern period, and in providing analyses of the novel, poetry, and drama, while paying less attention to literary criticism. Illustrations have been included to provide an idea of the original make-up of books and to stress the fact that in the past pictures were often an essential part of novels and books of poetry. In addition, the illustrations are also meant to demonstrate the important relations between art and literature in various historical periods.

This book makes no pretensions to comprehensiveness. Its aims are modest: to introduce the students to the major authors in English and American literature and kindle their interest in the land of literature that is introduced here.

It is a pleasure to acknowledge the help of several people in the preparation of this book. I am very grateful to Lila Richardson and Allen Gilbert for reading the entire text and for their expert advice on style and on several American writers. Professor Roland Hagenbüchle and Dr Ludwig Deringer have read the section on American literature and suggested a few additions and rearrangements for which I owe them many thanks. I also want to thank Richard Bonnin, who helped me – once again – with the locating and ordering of books and illustrations.

Above all, I want to thank Charles and Joséphine Allain, who made it possible for me to write this book. My wife Odile has borne with equanimity and patience my occasional periods of absence from family life.

Eichstätt, January 1987

English Literature

I. The Anglo-Saxon Period (449–1066)

1. General Background

Following the practice of linguists, literary historians have divided early English literature into the Anglo-Saxon (or Old English) and the Middle English periods. The Anglo-Saxon period began around the year 450 with the invasion of England by Jutes, Angles and Saxons from Denmark and northern Germany.

Among the earliest inhabitants of Britain were Celtic tribes. Subdued in the first century by the Romans under Julius Caesar and Claudius, they remained under Roman rule until the early fifth century, when the Roman legions were required at home to protect the capital. Traces of the Roman occupation can be found in English geographical names ending in -caster or -chester (Lancaster, Dorchester), which are derived from the Latin "castra" (camp). With the Romans gone, successive waves of Anglo-Saxons gradually conquered the south of England. The Celtic Britons were killed or forced into slavery; many escaped to Cornwall, to the mountains of Wales and Scotland, or across the sea to Brittany. It was during this period when the Celts retreated that the legends of King Arthur and his knights were invented. Celtic languages (Welsh in Wales, and Gaelic in Scotland and Ireland) are still spoken today, but the number of native speakers is steadily decreasing.

The Germanic tribes brought with them a common language called Anglo-Saxon or Old English, although different dialects existed in the various kingdoms into which the country was divided. The more important among these kingdoms were Kent, Northumbria, Mercia and Wessex. Under the Wessex **King Alfred**

Detail from the Bayeux Tapestry depicting the Battle of Hastings

(871–99) the West Saxon dialect gained a leading role. Alfred made his capital, Winchester, an intellectual centre in England and forced the Vikings (Danes), who tried to invade the country, to retreat to the northeast.

Roman and Irish missionaries brought England into contact with the Christian-Latin culture. **Saint Augustine** arrived in 597 and made Canterbury an important seat of Latin literature and learning. In Northumbria, Irish monks founded monasteries that became famous throughout Europe. The first religious poets, **Caedmon** and **Cynewulf,** lived in the northern half of England. Anglo-Saxon culture and literature came to an end with the Battle of Hastings (1066), when **King Harold** and his noblemen were defeated by **William the Conqueror,** Duke of Normandy.

2. Poetry

Anglo-Saxon poetry includes short and often witty riddles and magic formulas and the longer epic or elegiac poems telling of heroes and courageous deeds. *Beowulf,* a narrative poem of more than 3,000 lines, is the best known Anglo-Saxon saga. It contains elements of earlier sagas and blends the mythical and supernatural with the real.

Beowulf survives in a manuscript from the tenth century, but it was probably composed during the eighth century. The poem relates the deeds of Beowulf, a Danish hero, who sails from Sweden to Denmark to come to the help of his bother Hrothgar, king of the Danes. Hrothgar's castle and land are ravaged by a monster of human shape called Grendel. Beowulf fights the monster and tears away his arm. Grendel, although mortally wounded, escapes, leaving tracks of blood that lead to a cave in the sea. Hrothgar's court is overjoyed at Beowulf's victory, but Grendel's mother, determined to avenge her son, appears and carries off a Danish knight. Beowulf follows Grendel's mother into the sea-cave, kills her and returns to the court with the head of Grendel he has cut off. At Hrothgar's death, Beowulf is proclaimed king. Many years later, another fight takes place, this time involving an aged Beowulf and a fire-breathing dragon. The old hero slays the dragon but eventually dies of its fiery breath. Beowulf is then burned on a pyre, and his people lament his death.

The poem provides a vivid picture of the life and the way of thinking of the Anglo-Saxons. Interwoven with the pagan story are also some Christian elements.

The alliterative power of Old English poetry, which used head-rhymes (end-rhymes were introduced by the Normans after 1066), has had some influence on English and American poets in the modern period (see, for instance, the poetry of **John Donne** and of **Gerard Manley Hopkins**). **Ezra Pound** was considerably impressed by this kind of poetry and employed its techniques in his own verse. Pound translated into modern English the first half of an Old English elegy, *The Seafarer,* trying to preserve the poetic techniques of the original. Here is an excerpt from the poem, together with Pound's translation, providing an impression of Old English verse.

bitre breostceare   gebiden hæbbe,
gecunnad in ceole   cearselda fela,
atol yÞa gewealc,   Þær mec oft bigeat
nearo nihtwaco   æt nacan stefnan,
Þonne he be clifum cnossað.   Calde geÞrungen

wæron mine fet,   forste gebunden
caldum clommum,   Þær Þa ceare seofedun
hat' ymb heortan;   hungor innan slat
merewerges mod.

Bitter breast-cares have I abided,
Known on my keel many a care's hold,
And dire sea-surge, and there I oft spent
Narrow nightwatch nigh the ship's head
While she tossed close to cliffs. Coldly afflicted,
My feet were by frost benumbed.
Chill its chains are; chafing sighs
Hew my heart round and hunger begot
Mere-weary mood ...

The Seafarer is one of several elegiac poems in *The Exeter Book,* a collection of Old English verse from the tenth century. The monks **Caedmon** (d. 680) and **Cynewulf** (late eighth century) both wrote religious poetry in Old English. There are also many poems by churchmen written in Latin.

3. Prose

The Anglo-Saxon monks were the major authors during this period. They wrote in Latin, the official language of Medieval Europe. The outstanding writer among them has come to be known as the **Venerable Bede** (673-735). He left about 45 works, in which all the knowledge of his time is accumulated: medicine, arithmetic, astronomy, meteorology, music, rhetoric, philosophy and theology. The work for which he is best remembered is the *Historia Ecclesiastica Gentis Anglorum (The Ecclesiastical History of the English People),* which was finished in 731.

Two centuries after Bede, English prose received a splendid impetus through the activity of **King Alfred** (871-901). He defended his country against the Danes and then gathered round him scholars and educators from England. Alfred founded an abbey at Winchester and promoted the use of written English rather than Latin, initiating the first historical record of English laws in the *Anglo-Saxon Chronicle.* Alfred also arranged for a number of Latin works, including Bede's *Ecclesiastical History,* to be translated.

Sermons in Old English prose have come down to us from the pens of **Aelfric,** a Benedictine abbot, and **Wulfstan,** Archbishop of York, who lived in the late tenth and early eleventh centuries.

II. The Middle English Period (1066-1500)

1. General Background

The Duke of Normandy's victory over King Harold in 1066 meant radical and painful changes for Anglo-Saxon culture and customs. The new masters, the Normans, were descendants of the Vikings but spoke Norman-French. They did not trouble to learn the language of their subjects. Therefore, until the fourteenth century, three languages (and many dialects) were spoken in England: French among the nobility and at court, Latin among the learned clergy, and English among the ordinary people (nine tenths of the population). The mixed character of the English language as spoken today, with its Latin and Germanic bases, goes back to this period when the better sort of people called the meats on their table "beef, veal, pork, and mutton" (from the French boeuf, veau, porc, mouton); the meats came from farms where the respective animals were called ox, calf, swine/pig, and sheep.

The Normans not only forced their French language upon the English but also introduced the feudal system and martial rule. In literature, they brought new models and subjects from France and changed the Anglo-Saxon system of versification (the end-rhyme became the poetic standard). While the Old English language gradually discarded most of the flexional endings, Norman-French added new lexical and grammatical elements to what became Middle English, the language of the great poet Chaucer.

The kingdoms of England and Normandy, ruled by William and his successors, including the Plantagenets (1154-1485),[1] became a powerful force in Europe. In 1205 England lost Normandy, and a new nation began to take shape in England. Toward 1400 a language had developed that was neither Norman-French nor Anglo-Saxon. English, the language of the people, had absorbed French vocabulary and grammatical rules. It became the official language of the country, now spoken in schools and courts of law.

There were also a number of historical and political events with far-reaching consequences. The crusades began in 1096 and exposed Christian Europe to Arab culture. The Magna Carta[2] of 1215 established that taxes had to be levied with the consent of the barons, not by the King alone, and that nobody could be detained

---

1. The English kings of the Anjou-Plantagenet family ruled, in a direct line, from 1154-1399 (Henry II, Richard I, John Lackland, Henry III, Edward I, Edward II, Edward III, Richard II, Henry IV), and, in the Lancastrian and York lines, from 1399-1485. The Lancastrians included Henry IV, Henry V, and Henry VI; and the House of York, Edward IV, Edward V, and Richard III.
2. Under King John Lackland, the English barons were granted the liberties of England. The new Magna Carta or Great Charter (1215) was revised several times. It introduced the idea of law as something that is above the King's power, and it protected and guaranteed the freedom of the English Church and the feudal rights of the barons. Although the mass of the people were not very much concerned, this charter was a first step towards individual liberty.

illegally. It was a first step towards representative government. Under the Plantagenets, the Hundred Years' War (1337-1453) saw the English monarchy fighting
for, and eventually losing, its French possessions. The Wars of the Roses (1455-
1485) locked the House of York (the white rose) and the House of Lancaster (the
red rose) in a fierce and bloody civil war. It was ended by the marriage of Henry
VII, which united the feuding families and founded the Tudor[1] line.

For readers and writers, and for literature generally, the establishment in 1476
of Caxton's printing press brought a revolution heralding the beginning of the
modern period. A much favoured form of literature was the romance, consisting of
tales of heroic knights who sought adventures and battles in order to prove their
courage to, and love for, the ladies of the courts. Many of these romances were
translations from the French. It was Chaucer who broke with this tradition, and
his marvellous *Canterbury Tales* remains the outstanding work in the literature of
the Middle English period.

2. Latin and French Literature in England

In his *Historia Regum Britanniae* (c. 1136) the monk **Geoffrey of Monmouth** (d.
1155) recorded the legendary stories of the Celts, including those of the illustrious
King Arthur and the magician Merlin. The Anglo-Norman priest **Wace** (who is
also the author of the *Roman de Rou,* a chronicle history of the dukes of Normandy) turned Geoffrey of Monmouth's history into a French poem of 14,000 lines
entitled *Geste des Bretons* or *Brut d'Angleterre* (1155), representing King Arthur as
a blameless and victorious sovereign sitting with his knights at a round table.
Wace also added to this semi-mythical life of Arthur the legend of the Holy Grail.
In 1205 another priest, **Layamon,** translated Wace's *Brut* into English, employing
the Old English method of alliterative verse but also rhyme as in the French original. This book became a major source for English poetry, prose and drama.

The French metrical romances (tales of chivalry[2] mingled with love stories and
magic) were known throughout Europe. Thematically, they deal with the deeds of
Charlemagne,[3] Arthur and his knights, and the Roman and Greek heroes celebrated in the classical epics. The poem with the strongest influence throughout the
Middle Ages was the *Roman de la Rose,* an allegorical romance written between

---

1. The Tudor line ruled from 1485-1603 and included Henry VII, Henry VIII, Edward VI, Mary I, and
Elizabeth I. The term "Tudor" also signifies a style of architecture.
2. Chivalry refers to the qualities of courage and honour associated with medieval knights; also the
knightly system with its religious, moral, and social codes that demanded the defense of the weak and
of the (Catholic) faith.
3. Charlemagne (742-814) was King of the Franks and of Germany (768-814), and Emperor of the
Holy Roman Empire (800-814). He introduced Frankish political institutions in Saxony, and made
Christianity compulsory. He improved the administrative institutions and promoted education, the arts,
and commerce. One of the great literary works dealing with his campaigns in Spain is *La Chanson de
Roland* (The Song of Roland), a medieval French epic describing the annihilation of the rear guard of the
Frankish forces at Saragossa.

1256-1275 by **Guillaume de Lorris** and **Jean de Meun**. The almost 22,000 lines of this work abound with personified virtues and vices and analyse love in its various aspects. With its didactic and satirical passages (including many verses against women) and its presentation of the courtly and philosophical discussions of love, the *Roman de la Rose* is the most eminent literary work before Chaucer, who translated a part of it into Middle English.

3. Literature in English

The first truly English literature emerged in the fourteenth century, when an English language, Middle English, had developed. Religious literature from this period is best represented by **William Langland's** (c. 1330-86) *Piers Plowman*, written and revised between 1370-1390. It is an allegorical poem which, like the *Roman de la Rose*, is told in the form of a dream. Composed in alliterative and unrhymed verse, *Piers Plowman* records much of the indignation the common people felt at the many abuses in Church and State. **John Wyclif** (1324-84), a scholar and reformer, tried to abolish some of the bad conditions by training a group of unselfish priests and by translating the Bible.

In addition to the popular adaptations of French romances, of which *Sir Gawain and the Green Knight* is the finest example, literary genres that prospered were tales, such as those of *Gamelyn*, the young knight cheated out of his property but regaining it with the help of outlaws, and ballads, such as those about Robin Hood, the kind-hearted outlaw of Sherwood Forest. There were also travel reports (e. g. *The Travels of Sir John Mandeville*, 1375) and didactic poetry, the verses of **John Gower** (1325-1408), in Latin, French and English, being the best known examples.

But no poet writing in the English tongue in the fourteenth century could surpass the work of **Geoffrey Chaucer** (c. 1340-1400), the son of a London wine merchant. He had an interesting career that included positions at court in the service of King Edward III. As a soldier under this king, he was taken prisoner in France. Later, Chaucer travelled abroad on many occasions on diplomatic missions and may have met Boccaccio[1] and Petrarch[2] on a journey to Italy in 1372-73. He also worked as a customs official for the port of London, and his last official position was deputy forester in the King's forest in Somerset. He was buried in the Poets' Corner of Westminster Abbey. Chaucer was initially very interested in French poetry. He translated a third of the *Roman de la Rose (The Romaunt of the*

---

1. Giovanni Boccaccio (1313-1375), an Italian poet and humanist who is best known for his collection of stories or "novellas" entitled *Decamerone*, first printed in 1470 and written between 1348-53. This work, which is concerned with the morality of love, exerted a great influence on European literature.
2. Petrarch (Francesco Petrarca, 1304-74) was an Italian writer and humanist whose poetry, especially the sonnets, established the motifs and comparisons for many poets in several European countries until the end of the seventeenth century. Petrarchism is a special kind of love poetry in which comparisons are made between the beloved (woman) and beautiful things.

Rose) and wrote *The Book of the Duchess* (c. 1370), a dream-poem on love in the French tradition. Thereafter he was for some time attracted to Italian literature, the most important of his Italian-influenced works being *Troilus and Criseyde* (c. 1385), a love story set during the Trojan War and for which Chaucer was inspired by Boccaccio. Shakespeare also treated the subject in a play bearing the same title. During the last period of his poetic career Chaucer turned to English themes, and in 1386 he began *The Canterbury Tales* which he left unfinished at his death. It is in this work above all that he proves a masterful poet, a shrewd observer, a kind-hearted satirist and an excellent painter of characters and customs. The following lines from the opening Prologue (in which the major characters are introduced), given in Middle English and a modern translation by R. M. Lumiansky, refer to April, a new season and the renewal of life. A number of modern writers have alluded satirically to this important section in their own works (see, for instance, T. S. Eliot's reference in *The Waste Land,* 1922, and David Lodge's opening in his novel *Small World,* 1984).

"The Knight" from Caxton's edition of *The Canterbury Tales*

Whan that Aprille with his shoures sote
The droghte of Marche hath perced to the rote,
And bathed every veyne in swich licour,
Of which vertu engendred is the flour;
Whan Zephirus eek with his swete breeth
Inspired hath in every holt and heeth
The tendre croppes, and the yonge sonne
Hath in the Ram his halfe cours y-ronne,
And smale fowles maken melodye,
That slepen al the night with open yë,
(So priketh hem nature in hir corages):
Than longen folk to goon on pilgrimages
...

When April with its gentle showers has pierced the March drought to the root and bathed every plant in the moisture which will hasten the flowering; when Zephyrus with his sweet breath has stirred the new shoots in every wood and field, and the young sun has run its half-course in the Ram, and small birds sing melodiously, so touched in their hearts by Nature that they sleep all night with open eyes – then folks long to go on pilgrimages ...

The Canterbury Tales is a collection of stories told by pilgrims who have met at a hostelry in Southwark. In order to pass the time as they travel from this part of London to the shrine of Saint Thomas à Becket[1] at Canterbury and back, the accompanying host convinces them to tell four stories each, two on the way and two on the return trip. But the work is incomplete: instead of 29 tales (by the 29 pilgrims), there are only 24 stories told altogether.

---

1. Thomas à Becket (1118-1170) was Chancellor of Henry II and later Archbishop of Canterbury. In his clerical office, he was forced to oppose the king and tried to defend the rights of the Church. Becket was exiled to France. When he returned to England, Henry had him assassinated in the cathedral at Canterbury. Becket was canonized in 1173, and his shrine at Canterbury became famous as a place where miracles were performed. The story of Saint Thomas à Becket has been the subject of plays by Tennyson and T. S. Eliot.

In the "Prologue" Chaucer introduces the pilgrims in gentle humorous descriptions. Their tales cover a wide field of subjects, from the Knight's romantic story of chivalry to the Monk's complaint about the evils of the time, from satirical tales about marriage to downright erotic adventures told by the Miller and the Reeve. The stories are linked by narrative exchanges between the pilgrims and by prologues and epilogues.

The major part of the work is written in rhyming couplets of various metres. It shows Chaucer at his best as a gifted versifier and a humorous satirist who provides a vivid and sympathetic picture of medieval clerical and lay society.

The fifteenth century did not produce a poet of Chaucer's stature. But it would be misleading to label it a barren age for literature. Although poets such as **Thomas Hoccleve** (or **Occleve**, c. 1369-1426), **John Lydgate** (c. 1370-1449) and **John Skelton** (c. 1460-1529) did not go beyond the imitation of Chaucer, popular poetry (songs and short verse) flourished, especially the Scottish ballad. Poems worth remembering are **William Dunbar's** (c. 1456-1513) *The Thistle and the Rose,* a political allegory in rhyme royal, and **John Barbour's** (c. 1320-95) *The Bruce,* a verse chronicle of the deeds of Bruce, a Scottish king, and his follower James Douglas.

One of the first prose works **William Caxton** (1422-91) printed after establishing a printing press at Westminster was **Sir Thomas Malory's** (d. 1471) *Morte d' Arthur* (1485), a long cycle of Arthurian legends divided into 21 books. It is a free translation in prose from the French and from other sources and records the major romances of chivalry of the Middle Ages: those of King Arthur, the adventures of the Knights of the Round Table, and the legend of the Holy Grail. The collection is one of the most important prose works in English written and published before the sixteenth century.

Some decisive developments also took place in drama during this time. Between 1200-1400 the medieval church plays, brief scenes based on the Bible and the lives of the saints, were acted by the clergy in the church buildings. Gradually, the plays were secularized, a process that is mirrored in the removal of the theatrical scenes from the church to the streets. In the fourteenth century these Miracle and Mystery Plays, as they were called, also introduced comic characters. They were rivalled by the very popular Morality Plays, in which the characters are allegorical figures representing vices and virtues. *Everyman* (c. 1509-19), which is still performed each year at Salzburg, Austria, is the best-known example in this genre of didactic drama. The play shows how Everyman, called by Death, is forsaken by all his former companions and is left alone with his Good Deeds that ensure his going to heaven. In addition to the originally religious church plays (Miracles and Mysteries) and the Moralities, there were Interludes, i. e. short and humorous scenes or dramatic dialogues often performed in the houses of the better educated gentry. The characters in these plays were mostly drawn from real life and enjoyed a great popularity.

III. The Sixteenth Century

1. General Background

Politically and ideologically, this century saw alternating periods of stability and radical changes. Henry VII (1485-1509), the first king in the Tudor line, ended the Wars of the Roses and passed on to his son Henry VIII (1509-47) a monarchy that had gained in power and respectability. It was under the energetic Henry VIII that a new age began and that England opened to the influences of the Renaissance: Italian art and culture (see the influential works of Petrarch and Boccaccio in literature, and of Donatello, Leonardo da Vinci, and Michelangelo in art, architecture, and the sciences)[1] provided the whole of Europe with new forms, ideas and themes. Man reached out to explore the world around him in science and philosophy, and, beyond the horizon, in the voyages of discovery.

But the rule of Henry VIII, wich had begun in splendour, ended in despotism and in a separation from the Church of Rome, when the Pope refused to grant the King of England a divorce from Catherine of Aragon. Henry got rid of her anyway and founded the Anglican Church[2] in 1534, with himself as the Supreme Head. The story of Henry's wives, who succeeded each other to the throne and the Tower of London, has been told many times and once even in an excellent TV series. With his new church, Henry, like his daughter Elizabeth I, pursued a middle way between Catholicism and Protestantism.

After Henry's death England experienced several religious wars and much bloodshed. Edward VI (1547-53) tried to make England a Protestant country; his sister, Mary Queen of Scots (1553-58), beheaded in 1587 for alleged treason, intended to return it to Catholicism. Elizabeth I (1558-1603) was a true follower of her father, Henry VIII, whose politics she continued. She persecuted Catholics not because of their faith but as enemies of the state, a state that was to have a unified Anglican Church.

---

1. On Boccaccio and Petrarch see notes on page 12.
Donatello (Donato di Niccolò di Betto Bardi, ?1382-1466), the most versatile Italian sculptor of the early Renaissance who introduced secular themes into the art of sculpture and decoration.
Leonardo da Vinci (1452-1519), Italian painter, sculptor, architect, scientist, and technician. He was the outstanding genius of the Renaissance. He worked in Italy and France, leaving several magnificent works of art and studies in the natural sciences and in mechanics that were far ahead of his time.
Michelangelo (Michelangelo Buonarroti, 1475-1564), Italian sculptor, painter, and architect. He was the major artist of the high Renaissance and is famous for numerous paintings and buildings in Italy, such as the Palazzo Farnese and Saint Peter's in Rome.
2. The Anglican Church (also called The Church of England) was established by Henry VIII, in 1534, when the Pope refused to grant him a divorce. The archbishops, bishops, and deans of the Anglican Church are appointed by the Sovereign (who must be a member of the Church) on the advice of the Prime Minister. The clergy are required to take an oath of allegiance to the Crown and are not allowed to sit in the House of Commons. The Church has two provinces: Canterbury and York, each comprising several dioceses; and it can regulate its own worship.

Queen Elizabeth I
The Ditchley Portrait

The defeat of the Spanish Armada in 1588 proved beneficial for England. It established the country as a major political power in Europe and ensured a period of flourishing intellectual and cultural life. Social changes during Elizabeth's rule included improvements of the Poor Laws, but bear-baiting and cock-fighting, those remnants of the Middle Ages, remained remarkably popular.

The predominance of the Italian Renaissance is particularly obvious in the English literature of the sixteenth century: the introduction of the Italian sonnet form and the Italian locations and themes in drama are just two examples of the strong Mediterranean influence on England.

2. Poetry

Nowhere is the Englishman's fondness for Italian themes and forms more obvious than in the poetry of **Sir Thomas Wyatt** (1503-42) and Henry Howard, **earl of Surrey** (c. 1517-47), the major poets in the reign of Henry VIII. Wyatt introduced the Italian sonnet form (two quartets and a sestet or two tercets) into English literature, and it remained popular until Shakespeare gave preference to the final couplet, the English form, first devised by Surrey. Surrey's durable innovation was the use of blank verse, another poetic form Shakespeare owes to his predecessor.

Edmund Spenser (1552-99) and **Sir Philip Sidney** (1554-86) were the dominant figures in English poetry toward the end of the century. Both proved especially important in the development of the sonnet form. Sidney was a glamorous personality at the court of Elizabeth I. His cycle of 108 sonnets was published in 1598 as *Astrophel and Stella.* This is essentially the monologue of a lover discussing aspects of love, virtue, and beauty during his own love affair. With his rhyme pattern (abab abab cdcdee; or abba abba etc.) Sidney leaned more toward the French tradition, though he shared with Spenser the typical closing couplet of the English sonnet. Spenser's sonnet collection, *Amoretti* (1595), consists of 88 sonnets in the English manner. But this is not Spenser's best poetry. His major work with a lasting influence is *The Faerie Queene,* a giant fragment published between 1590-1608. It is a monumental poem far too long for many modern readers. Modelled to some extent on the *Orlando Furioso* of Ariosto[1] (published in 1532 in complete form), it tells of human virtues, such as love and faith, in the form of allegory, each virtue being personified as a special knight or protector. The chief beauties of this epic lie in the particular episodes with which the allegory is varied, and in the descriptions of fights, temptations, and battles. The "Faerie Queene" represents the glory coming from the possession of virtue, though she also signifies Queen Elizabeth. Spenser's epic is full of noble ideas, patriotism, profound learning, and chivalry. What he bequeathed to later poets was a stanza form of his own invention, the Spenserian Stanza. Thomson, Keats, Shelley, Byron, and Tennyson were to use this form. Here is the beginning of *The Faerie Queene.*

> The Patron of true Holinesse,
>   Foule Errour doth defeate:
> Hypocrisie him to entrape,
>   Doth to his home entreate.

> A Gentle Knight was pricking on the plaine
> Y cladd in mightie armes and siluer shielde,
> Wherein old dints of deepe wounds did remaine,
> The cruell markes of many a bloudy fielde;
> Yet armes till that time did he neuer wield:
> His angry steede did chide his foming bitt,
> As much disdayning to the curbe to yield:
> Full iolly knight he seemd, and faire did sitt,
> As one for knightly giusts and fierce encounters fitt.

Some of the Elizabethan dramatists proved themselves great poets outside the drama. **Christopher Marlowe** (1564-93), for instance, wrote the love poem *Hero and Leander* (1598); Ben Jonson produced numerous lyrics inspired by Horace, Virgil and Pindar[2]; and **William Shakespeare** (1564-1616) wrote outstanding narrative poems such as *Venus and Adonis* (1593) and *The Rape of Lucrece* (1594) that appeared in countless editions and show the influence of the love poetry of Ovid[3].

---

1. Ludovico Ariosto (1474-1533), Italian poet and dramatist who wrote the first regular Italian comedies. He has gone down in literary history for his *Orlando Furioso* (1516-21, enlarged in 1532), an epic poem in 40 cantos that combines the Frankish saga of Roland with the tales about the knights of King Arthur.
2. Horace (Quintilius Horatius Flaccus, 65 BC-8 BC), a Roman poet an writer best known for his satires and odes, which were much read in the eighteenth century. He also wrote a book of criticism which deals especially with poetry. Literature, according to Horace, must be "dulce et utile", i. e. sweet and useful. Virgil (Publius Vergilius Maro, 70 BC-19 BC), the most famous of the Roman poets. His *Aeneid,* an epic dealing with the fall of Troy, served as a model for all the Latin epics of the medieval period and for the new classical epic of the Renaissance. Virgil influenced eighteenth-century English poets as well as Wordsworth and Tennyson.
Pindar (c. 520 BC-445 BC), a Greek poet whose verse was inspired by myth, and characterized by high pathos and formal logic. His poems were first printed in 1513; his odes impressed many subsequent poets because they are distinguished by bold metaphors and an elaborate prosodic structure. Dryden, Pope, and Gray were among those who tried to imitate Pindar.
3. Ovid (Publius Ovidius Naso, 43 BC-AD 17), a celebrated Roman poet who spent much of his life in exile. His major works were widely read throughout the Middle Ages and were especially popular between 1600-1800. They include love elegies *(Amores),* mock didactic verse *(Ars amatoria* and *Remedia amoris),* and verse narratives in a historical-mythical frame *(Metamorphoses).*

3. Drama

Sixteenth-century English drama is indebted to the Miracle and Morality Plays and to the late medieval Interludes. The influence can be studied in the comic characters of **John Heywood's** *The Play of the Wether* (1553), an early example of a play drawing heavily on elements of the popular Interludes.

Equally important was the influence of Latin examples, both in comedy and tragedy. The first true English comedy, for instance, **Nicholas Udall's** *Ralph Roister Doister* (c. 1553), shows traces of classical Latin writers like Terence and Plautus. Elizabethan drama began with tragedies written by lawyers who copied Seneca, the philosopher of Nero's time. The first extant tragedy in English, *Gorboduc* (1562) by **Thomas Norton** and **Thomas Sackville**, owes everything to him. Five of Seneca's plays were translated, published and performed between 1559 and 1581, and his influence was still noticeable in Shakespeare's *Titus Andronicus*.

From 1580 to 1596 more than one hundred different plays are known to have been performed in London. Of the immediate predecessors of Shakespeare the most influential writers were two masters of tragedy – Thomas Kyd and Christopher Marlowe – and the playwrights better known for their comedies – Lyly, Peele, and Greene. **Thomas Kyd** (1558-94), unlike the other authors discussed here, did not belong to the group known as the "University wits". His fame rests upon one play, *The Spanish Tragedy* (1592), which remained popular all through Shakespeare's lifetime. Written in blank verse, this play accepted as much as was convenient of the Senecan tragedy and became the model for later tragedies of revenge.

Christopher Marlowe (1564-93) was born two months before Shakespeare. A young Cambridge dramatist, Marlowe had a tempestuous short life and found a tragic death when he was stabbed in a tavern brawl. Had he lived longer, he might have become as important a dramatist as William Shakespeare. Marlowe's most important work is contained in four tragedies written between 1587 and 1593: *Tamburlaine the Great, Dr. Faustus, The Jew of Malta,* and *Edward II.* Although there are obvious faults of construction, youthful carelessness, and other flaws in his works, Marlowe gave to tragedy a sound conception of character and the magnificent instrument of his blank verse.

Frontispiece of *Doctor Faustus*

Comedy developed in the hands of **John Lyly** (1554-1606), **George Peele** (c. 1556-96), and **Robert Greene** (1587-91). **Lyly** was a politician and courtier who is better known for his prose work *Euphues* and mainly wrote what is essentially high comedy for an educated audience. He combined the realistic farce, the Latin comedy, and the allegory of the Morality Plays into a new design, as in *The Woman in the Moone* (1597), which also has attractive lyrics. **George Peele** was the most notorious of the rakish University wits and produced a mythological play, *The Arraignment of Paris* (1584), which is written in verse and was performed before Queen Elizabeth, and successful comedies like *The Old Wives' Tale* (1595), a satire on the romantic dramas of the time. However, Peele was not as influential as **Robert Greene**. Greene's best play is a comedy in verse and prose, *The Honorable Historie of Friar Bacon and Friar Bungay,* which was acted in 1594. It has characters from high and low life and shows an amazing freshness, charm, and humour.

In 1592 the London stages had to be closed because of a plague, and when theatrical performances resumed about two years later, there was a new celebrity called **William Shakespeare** (1564-1616) who began to make himself noticed as actor, playwright, and shareholder in theatrical entertainment. Many of his plays were written before 1600, although complete editions of his works did not appear before 1623.

4. Prose and Prose Fiction

The work of **Thomas More** (c.1477-1535) embodies the classical scholarship of the century. More was a friend of Erasmus[1] and the author of *Utopia,* first written in Latin (subsequently also in English) and published in 1516. It is a speculative essay on the best possible form of government. More's creation of the name 'Utopia' in this work passed into general usage and has been used to describe ideal projects and fantasies of the future.

Some critics have seen the beginning of the novel in two late sixteenth-century romances that remained popular until the eighteenth century. The first is *The Arcadia*, by **Sir Philip Sidney,** begun in 1580 and first published in 1590. Written for an educated aristocratic audience, this is a complex romance, with generous intermixtures of verse and prose, which is set in an ideal pastoral world (an island suggesting More's *Utopia*) where shipwrecked princes and beautiful princesses engage in chivalric adventures. The other influential prose romance was written by **John Lyly** (1554-1606). It was published in two parts, the first in 1578 as *Euphues, or The Anatomy of Wit,* and the second in 1580 as *Euphues and His England.* The work reduces story and plot to a minimum and concentrates on the discussion of love, manners, sentiment, and moral reflection. *Euphues* is famous, if

---

1. Desiderius Erasmus (Erasmus of Rotterdam, c. 1466-1536), an important humanist, scholar, and social critic. His satirical attacks on the Church and on theology paved the way for the Reformation, but he never joined the Protestants and argued against Martin Luther on the issue of free will.

not notorious, for its peculiar style, "Euphuism", which is characterized by an excessive use of alliteration and antitheses, allusions to historical and mythological personages, and a predilection for far-fetched similes.

A second group of Elizabethan and Jacobean[1] writers lived much lower down the social scale. Unlike the courtiers Lyly and Sidney, they depended on their pens for a living. Their descriptions of the low life of Elizabethan London bubble with life, and the realistic elements of their tales helped to create a new literary form – the novel. Thus **Robert Greene** (c. 1560–92), **Thomas Lodge** (1558–1625), and **Thomas Deloney** (1560–1600) wrote occasionally improper narratives replete with incident, crime, and love. The major characters in these short pieces were not knights and noble ladies but the London thieves and rogues, and their victims. Deloney also gave us more homely stories in *Jack of Newbury* (c. 1600), which shows the life of the weavers, and *The Gentle Craft* (c. 1600), which deals with shoemakers. Realistic though these tales were, they had little artistic form. It was **Thomas Nashe** (1567–1601), a pamphleteer, poet, satirist, and moralist, who made some progress in this direction with his picaresque *The Unfortunate Traveller, or The Life of Jack Wilton* (1594). This is a tale of a rogue in the army of Henry VIII, containing adventures galore and gruesome descriptions of torture and death. The book is the nearest approach to the realistic novel produced in the late sixteenth century.

---

1. The Jacobean age was that of James I, king of England from 1603 to 1625. He insisted on the divine right of kings.

IV. The Seventeenth Century

1. General Background

With the death in 1603 of Elizabeth I (1558-1603) the reign of the Tudors came to an end. Momentous political and religious changes had taken place during her rule. The reign of the Stuarts[1] under James I (1603-25) ushered in the end of regal enlightened despotism and foreshadowed the revolutions. When the Scots James VI succeeded to the throne of England as James I, England and Scotland were united. The year 1605 saw the "Gunpowder Plot", an attempt to blow up the English Parliament, and thereafter the Stuarts began their battle with the House of Commons[2] and the Puritans[3]. In 1629 Charles I (1625-49) dissolved his Third Parliament and, for the following eleven years, ruled according to the "Divine Right of Kings". In domestic and foreign politics, Charles was as unsuccessful as his predecessor. He became the arch-enemy of the Nonconformists[4]. In 1640 the "Long Parliament"[5] was established, and two years later the Civil War broke out. Charles surrendered to Parliament in 1647 and, after two years, was executed. The ensuing period of the "Commonwealth" did not last long. In 1651 Charles II attempted an invasion of England. When it failed, he was forced to return to his exile in France. In 1653 Oliver Cromwell dismissed the "Rump Parliament"[6] to become Lord Protector of England. Four years later, he declined the English crown. He died in 1658. His feeble son, Richard, was unable to hold office for a full year. From then until the Restoration of the monarchy in 1660 England was governed by Parliament.

Charles II (1660-85) brought from France worldliness, wit, and a court circle of artists, poets, and writers who infused new life into England's art and literature. But political upheaval continued. Under Charles II the Act of Uniformity[7] was

---

1. The Stuarts: the English kings James I (1603-25), Charles I (1625-49), Charles II (1660-85), and James II (1685-88).
2. The House of Commons is the "Lower House" of the legislative body of the United Kingdom. The Parliamentary Act of 1911 established the dominant role of the Commons. The House now has 635 members who are normally elected every five years.
3. The Puritans were an extremist Protestant group who believed in Calvin's doctrine of predestination and tried to abolish Catholic elements in the Church of England. They refused to accept bishops and preferred presbyterian or congregational forms of church organizations. Many emigrated to New England in the 17th century; those who remained in England joined the opposition against the king under Oliver Cromwell. In 1689 they were given religious equality.
The Puritans were known, and often ridiculed, for their strict morals, their Bible reading, their fundamentalist attitudes, and their objection to frivolous entertainment, such as the theatre or dancing.
4. Protestant groups or Churches, such as the Puritans and Methodists, that do not recognize the authority of the Church of England, are referred to as Nonconformists.
5. The English Parliament between 1640 and 1649 was called the Long Parliament.
6. In 1648 Oliver Cromwell excluded the Presbyterian Protestants from Parliament. The "Rump Parliament" continued until 1653 when Cromwell became Lord Protector of England.
7. The Act of Uniformity was passed in 1662. It abolished Cromwell's Presbyterian Church organization and strengthened the hierarchy of the Church of England.

passed, depriving the Nonconformist clergy of their positions. England and Holland were at war between 1665-67 and again from 1672-74. There were catastrophes, too: hardly had the Great Plague subsided (1665) in London, when the city was struck in 1666 by the Great Fire.

James II (1685-88) attempted to re-establish Catholicism. But when the Protestants appealed to William of Orange in Holland, he set sail for England and forced James into exile in France (Glorious Revolution)[1]. On James's abdication, William and Mary were proclaimed King and Queen. In 1690, James made a last desperate attempt to regain the throne by landing in Ireland and raising forces. But William defeated him and ruled until 1702.

The social and political conflicts of these troubled days have left their traces in philosophical and moral writings, defending either body or mind, reason or faith, worldliness or religiosity, rationalism or empiricism. **René Descartes** (1596-1650), the French mathematician, physicist, and philosopher, made man the centre of the universe with his famous phrase, "cogito, ergo sum". He relied exclusively on reason and distinguished between spirit and matter. His influence on the development of philosophy and science was immense. **Thomas Hobbes** (1588-1678) published his *Leviathan* in 1651, defending materialism and explaining both ideas and sensations as the result of matter in motion. Hobbes explained man as a selfish animal interested merely in self-preservation. Order, according to Hobbes, can only be established by the granting of absolute power to a ruler or a body of rulers. It is obvious that both Cromwell and James II interpreted such ideas as a justification for their claim for absolute rule. The philosophy of **John Locke** (1632-1704), however, stressed the importance of the contract in government. Unlike Hobbes, Locke believed that the ruler of a state was responsible to the people. With his *Two Treatises of Government* (1690) Locke pointed to the modern democratic way; and in his *Essay Concerning Human Understanding* (1690) he formulated the "faith" of the Age of the Enlightenment.

The seventeenth century was an age of exploration in many areas. America was colonized: Jamestown, Virginia, was founded in 1607, and the Pilgrims landed in New England in 1620, to be followed by the Puritans a decade later. In science, the establishment of the Royal Society in 1662 proved important. By 1687 **Isaac Newton** (1642-1727) published his *Principia Mathematica*. The seventeenth century was thus marked by upheaval, revolutions, and great changes. It was an age of contradictions and contrast, seeing both the publication of the vastly influential *Authorized Version of the Bible* in 1611 (commissioned by James I in 1604), and the unabashedly hedonistic works of the libertines and rakes at the court of Charles II.

---

1. The Glorious Revolution: In 1688 the Anglican Church and the supporters of Parliament united against James II and, in a bloodless revolution, offered the English crown to the Dutch Protestant Prince William of Orange. When William arrived, James fled to France and William and his wife Mary (daughter of James II) were declared King and Queen. Before they became sovereigns, they agreed to the Bill of Rights which regulated and established constitutional monarchy. Catholics were now excluded from succession to the English monarchy.

2. Poetry

One of the first major works to be published after 1600 was William Shakespeare's collection of sonnets. It was published in a pirate edition by Thomas Thorpe in 1609. Shakespeare had written poetry before 1600, but his new collection showed that he had broken with the tradition of sonnet-writing. In his own sonnet no. CXXX he satirized it by mocking Petrarchan comparisons.

> My mistress' eyes are nothing like the sun;
> Coral is far more red than her lips' red;
> If snow be white, why then her breasts are dun;
> If hairs be wires, black wires grow on her head.
> I have seen roses damasked, red and white,
> But no such roses see I in her cheeks;
> And in some perfumes is there more delight
> Than in the breath that from my mistress reeks.
> I love to hear her speak, yet well I know
> That music hath a far more pleasing sound;
> I grant I never saw a goddess go;
> My mistress, when she walks, treads on the ground.
> And yet, by heaven, I think my love as rare
> As any she belied with false compare.

As always, Shakespeare was different. The first 126 of his sonnets are addressed to "Mr. W.H.". This person has been identified as (among others) Henry Wriothesley, earl of Southampton. Held in terms of warmest affection, these poems express

William Shakespeare

John Donne

the love of a man for another man. The first seventeen (the so-called "procreation sonnets") urge the friend to marry in order to preserve his beauty in his children. The last twenty-eight poems of the collection are addressed to an unidentified "dark lady". These sonnets express the joys and pains that love can offer, for the lady is unfaithful to her husband and to her lover, the poet. Shakespeare's sonnets outlived the Elizabethan period. They belong to the best poetry in the English language and influenced generations of later poets.

John Donne (1572-1631) is beyond doubt the poet whose powerful verse set the tone in the first decades of the seventeenth century. His life was adventurous: a Catholic in the early part of his life, he was educated at Oxford and Cambridge and was notorious as a gallant and courtier, running away and marrying his master's niece, Anne Moore. However, in 1615 he took Anglican orders and began to preach sermons, sometimes before Charles I, that rank among the best of the century. From 1621 to his death he was the Dean of St. Paul's. Donne's poetry combines the two sides of his character, that of the passionate soldier, lover, and drinker, and that of the great preacher and devout person. Interweaving passion and reasoning, Donne was the first of the "metaphysical poets", a term invented by Dryden and adopted by Dr. Johnson to describe Donne and his school (i.e. Herbert, Crashaw, Vaughan, Carew and Marvell). Their work is characterized by witty conceits (striking metaphors) and far-fetched and impressive imagery. A lover and a sensualist, Donne never abandoned intellectual speculation – when he saw beauty, he also saw the corpse and the skeleton. His passions were at the service of his thoughts. He avoided accepted verse forms, creating new rhythms and images that startled readers. The first stanza of the "Canonization" shows him as the analytic sensualist.

> For God's sake hold your tongue, and let me love,
>   Or chide my palsy, or my gout,
> My five gray hairs, or ruined fortune, flout,
>   With wealth your state, your mind with arts improve,
>   Take you a course, get you a place,
>   Observe His Honor, or His Grace,
> Or the King's real, or his stampéd face
>   Contémplate; what you will, approve,
>   So you will let me love.

In the elegy "To His Mistress Going to Bed" he compares his lover to a "new-found land."

> License my roving hands, and let them go
> Before, behind, between, above, below.
> O my America! my new-found-land,
> My kingdom, safeliest when with one man manned,
> My mine of precious stones, my empery,
> How blest am I in this discovering thee!
> To enter in these bonds is to be free;
> Then where my hand is set, my seal shall be.

As only a few of Donne's poem were published during his lifetime, it is difficult to categorize his work. Some critics have divided it into three periods: the early years of the court life, the later time of introspection, and the last years of his life. Most of his love poems are collected in the 50 *Songs and Sonnets* (which contain no actual sonnets). His sonnets are collected in the two series, *La Corona* and *Holy Sonnets*. No. XIV of his *Holy Sonnets* shows the typical application of the terminology of love and erotic passion to God.

> Batter my heart, three-personed God; for You
> As yet but knock, breathe, shine, and seek to mend;
> That I may rise and stand, o'erthrow me, and bend
> Your force to break, blow, burn, and make me new.
> I, like an usurped town, to another due,
> Labor to admit You, but O, to no end;
> Reason, Your viceroy in me, me should defend,
> But is captived, and proves weak or untrue.
> Yet dearly I love You, and would be lovéd fain,
> But am betrothed unto Your enemy.
> Divorce me, untie or break that knot again;
> Take me to You, imprison me, for I,
> Except You enthrall me, never shall be free,
> Nor ever chaste, except You ravish me.

Until the Restoration, Donne's poetic style remained dominant in English literature. It can be traced in the works of a number of his followers. Among these, Herbert, Crashaw, and Vaughan were profoundly religious. **George Herbert** (1593-1633), one of the better known Anglican metaphysical poets, poured forth his quiet and sincere verse in *The Temple,* which was published posthumously and contains 160 poems. **Henry Vaughan** (1622-95) was also an Anglican poet. He was born in Wales and called himself "Silurist" after the ancient Silures. Influenced by Donne and Herbert's pronounced devoutness, Vaughan recorded his mysticism in such poems as "The Retreat", contained in *Silex Scintillans* (1650). **Richard Crashaw** (1612-49) started off as an Anglican and an admirer of Herbert's poems. He later became a Catholic and worked in Rome, where he came under the influence of Italian poets like Marino and Spanish mysticists. Like Donne, he employed erotic metaphors in the description of religious ecstasy.

A few other poets remain to be mentioned, most of them followers of Donne or influenced by his poetry. Closest to Donne was **Andrew Marvell** (1621-78). His poem "To His Coy Mistress" celebrates the pleasures of erotic love in an exhortation (carpe diem) to his lover.

> Had we but world enough, and time,
> This coyness, Lady, were no crime. [...]
> But at my back I always hear
> Time's wingéd chariot hurrying near;
> And yonder all before us lie
> Deserts of vast eternity.
> Thy beauty shall no more be found;
> Nor, in thy marble vault, shall sound

> My echoing song; then worms shall try
> That long-preserved virginity,
> And your quaint honor turn to dust,
> And into ashes all my lust:
> The grave's a fine and private place,
> But none, I think, do there embrace.

Surprisingly, Marvell was a Puritan, an admirer of Cromwell and tutor to Cromwell's ward. After the Restoration Marvell's poetry assumed a satirical and bitter element. **Thomas Carew** (c. 1595-1639) is one of the more important poets of the so-called Cavalier School. Carew was a disciple of both Jonson and Donne. A master of the heroic couplet, he wrote fine elegies, numerous songs, and licentious amatory poems like "The Rapture". **Robert Herrick** (1591-1674) is more indebted to Ben Jonson and stands a little apart from the Cavalier lyricists. He spent his exile as a cleric in Devonshire, producing secular and divine poems. To Jonson's art of brief expression he added his own fanciful and melancholic outlook in verse expressing the transience of human life. **Sir John Suckling** (1609-42), **John Cleveland** (1613-58), and **Richard Lovelace** (1618-58), also Cavalier poets, wrote mainly licentious love poems. **Abraham Cowley** (1618-67) was the last of the metaphysicals and already very much of a Restoration poet. As a precursor of Dryden, he started off with poems in the manner of John Donne and ended up as a poet of cool reason, an intellectual who ignored the heart.

John Milton (1608-74) was the last great poet of the English Renaissance. He was a Puritan who, both in verse and prose, dwarfed his contemporaries. Coming of a moderately well-to-do London family, Milton never had to earn his own living and could afford the leisure Shakespeare never had. He received a remarkable education at Christ's College, Cambridge, and very early developed an interest in poetry while studying the ancient literatures. During the six years he spent at his father's country-residence at Morton in Buckinghamshire, Milton wrote his early poems - *L'Allegro* and *Il Penseroso* (i.e. "Mirth" and "Melancholy"), which blended the artistic spirit of the Renaissance and the graver mood of Puritanism. They show his descriptive gifts and a highly individualistic musicality. *Il Penseroso,* for instance, celebrates the pleasures of solitude and contemplation while personifying and addressing "melancholy".

> But hail thou Goddess, sage and holy,
> Hail, divinest Melancholy,
> Whose saintly visage is too bright
> To hit the sense of human sight;
> And therefore to our weaker view,
> O'erlaid with black, staid Wisdom's hue.
> Black, but such as in esteem,
> Prince Memnon's sister might beseem,
> Or that starred Ethiope queen that strove
> To set her beauty's praise above
> The sea nymphs, and their powers offended.
> Yet thou art higher far descended.

Comus, a morality play, was also produced during this period, as well as an elegy to a friend, Edward King, which is entitled *Lycidas* (1637). In 1638 Milton undertook a voyage to France and Italy, visiting the Vatican and Naples and writing a few poems in Latin. But he was soon back in England and stepped into the arena of political controversy, siding with the enemies of the King. In 1643 he married a girl of 17 who left him within a month. Milton immediately wrote a treatise on divorce and soon began publishing political pamphlets, such as *Areopagitica* (1643), which defended the liberty of the press, and some works against the monarchy.

Milton's eyesight was by this time steadily declining, and about the middle of 1652 he became completely blind, a fact which he recorded stoically in his most famous sonnet.

> When I consider how my light is spent
>   Ere half my days, in this dark world and wide,
>   And that one talent which is death to hide
>   Lodged with me useless, though my soul more bent
> To serve therewith my Maker, and present
>   My true account, lest he returning chide;
>   "Doth God exact day-labor, light denied?"
>   I fondly ask; but Patience to prevent
> That murmur, soon replies, "God doth not need
>   Either man's work or his own gifts; who best
>   Bear his mild yoke, they serve him best. His state
> Is kingly. Thousands at his bidding speed
>   And post o'er land and ocean without rest:
>   They also serve who only stand and wait."

With the Restoration of 1660 Milton retired from public life. He barely escaped imprisonment. Blind, half-fugitive, and disillusioned, he turned to compose some of the most powerful poetic works in the English language, *Paradise Lost* and *Paradise Regained. Paradise Lost* was completed in 1665, but held up by the Great Plague and the Great Fire in London, it did not appear until 1667. The subject of this epic is the fall of man. Milton created a new kind of English for this poem, a blank verse which is highly artificial and removed from everyday speech. Yet the diction, however Latinized it may be, is appropriate for the subject and contributes, together with the wealth and freshness of Mil-

John Milton

ton's imagination, to the magnificence of the poem. An excerpt from Book IV (Satan's address to the sun) follows here.

Sometimes towards *Eden* which now in his view
Lay pleasant, his griev'd look he fixes sad,
Sometimes towards Heav'n and the full-blazing Sun,
Which now sat high in his Meridian Towr:
Then much revolving, thus in sighs began.
  O thou that with surpassing Glory crownd,
Lookst from thy sole Dominion like the God
Of this new World; at whose sight all the Starrs
Hide thir diminisht heads; to thee I call,
But with no friendly voice, and add thy name
O Sun, to tell thee how I hate thy beams
That bring to my remembrance from what state
I fell, how glorious once above thy Sphear;
Till Pride and worse Ambition threw me down,
Warring in Heav'n against Heav'ns matchless King:
Ah wherefore! he deserv'd no such return
From me, whom he created what I was
In that bright eminence, and with his good
Upbraided none; nor was his service hard.
What could be less than to afford him praise,
The easiest recompense, and pay him thanks,
How due! yet all his good prov'd ill in me,
And wrought but malice; lifted up so high
I sdeind subjection, and thought one step higher
Would set me highest, and in a moment quit
The debt immense of endless gratitude,
So burthensome still paying, still to ow.

Like *Paradise Lost, Paradise Regained* (1671) is a religious epic. It is a shorter poem (there are only four books while *Paradise Lost* has ten books) dealing exclusively with the temptation of Christ in the wilderness. Milton's last work was *Samson Agonistes* (1671), a tragedy following classical Greek procedure.

After Milton came the new literature of the Restoration period. Poetry was now less passionate. The Restoration poets mistrusted feeling and imagination. Reason, coupled with culture and city manners, governed literary taste. The Puritans, now ousted from power, were ridiculed in a wave of satires, ranging from the burlesque to the obscene. **Samuel Butler** (1612-80) wrote a mock-heroic poem, *Hudibras* (1663-78), denouncing all the hypocrisies of Puritanism. Butler's tale of Sir Hudibras, the fat and quarrelsome knight, and his squire Ralph, is reminiscent of Cervantes,[1] and, in its coarseness, of Rabelais[2] and Scarron,[3] both vastly influential

---

1. Miguel de Cervantes Saavedra (1547-1616), Spanish writer whose major work in fiction, *Don Quijote* (1605-1615), became the prototype of the picaresque novel. This masterpiece has proved influential for

Frontispiece and title-page
of Butler's *Hudibras*
(edition of 1744)

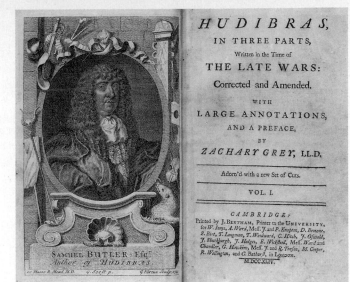

French writers. With the help of burlesque, travesty, and parody, Butler ridiculed
the Puritan mentality, as in this description of Hudibras's religion.

> For his religion, it was fit
> To match his learning and his wit.
> 'Twas Presbyterian true blue;
> For he was of that stubborn crew
> Of errant saints, whom all men grant
> To be the true church militant;
> Such as do build their faith upon
> The holy text of pike and gun;
> Decide all controversy by
> Infallible artillery;
> And prove their doctrine orthodox
> By apostolic blows and knocks;
> Call fire, and sword, and desolation,
> A godly thorough reformation,
> Which always must be carried on,
> And still be doing, never done;
> As if religion were intended
> For nothing else but to be mended.

---

many European writers. Cervantes also wrote outstanding stories (*Novelas ejemplares*, 1613) and a
number of comedies.

2. François Rabelais (c. 1494–c. 1553), French writer, humanist, and doctor. He published many works
on archeology and medicine but is mainly remembered for his satirical and fantastic books about the
popular giants Gargantua and Pantagruel (1532–52). Rabelais's comic realism ranges from obscenity to
parody. His influence on English literature was widespread after the first good translations had appeared
in 1653. Samuel Butler, Jonathan Swift, Laurence Sterne, and James Joyce are among the writers who
have drawn on Rabelais's humour and wit.

3. Paul Scarron (1610–1660), French writer who wrote satirical verse epics, comedies, and an outstanding novel, *Le Roman comique* (1651 and 1657), with convincing realistic descriptions.

The Restoration wits, many of them also notorious rakes and libertines, left their traces in the poetry of the closing decades of the century. Among them were **Charles Sackville, earl of Dorset** (1638-1706), **Sir Charles Sedley** (1639-1701), and **John Wilmot, earl of Rochester** (1647-80). Rochester, like his dissolute friends, was a brilliant satirist equally able to write fine misanthropic pieces like "A Satyr on Mankind" as well as daring amatory poems which most modern anthologies prefer to ignore. The shocking if not obscene verse produced by these poets was a reaction against the severe and often false morals the Puritans demanded and tried to enforce during their rule. The erotic and libertine poetry of the Restoration rakes was naturally welcome in court circles, though the London middle class condemned both the poets and their lyrics.

Donne and Milton were the outstanding figures in the first half of the century. **John Dryden** (1631-1700) was the most prominent poet in the forty years following the Restoration. Unlike Milton, Dryden identified himself with official opinion, even changing sides during the first half of his life. Thus he wrote an elegy on Cromwell's death, but when Charles II came back from exile he celebrated the King in "Astraea Redux". Dryden was the chronicler of his age, recording catastrophes like plagues and fires as well as military victories in his *Annus Mirabilis* (1667). He selected contemporary themes and fashioned them into poetry, often of the satirical kind. Thus he mocked the politician Shaftesbury in his *Absalom and Achitophel* (1681), in which Shaftesbury is Achitophel.

> Of these the false Achitophel was first:
> A Name to all succeeding ages cursed.
> For close Designs and crooked Counsels fit;
> Sagacious, Bold, and Turbulent of wit,
> Restless, unfixed in Principles and Place,
> In Power unpleased, impatient of Disgrace.
> A fiery Soul, which working out its way,
> Fretted the Pigmy Body to decay:
> And o'er informed the Tenement of Clay.
> A daring Pilot in extremity;
> Pleased with the Danger, when the Waves went high
> He sought the Storms; but for a Calm unfit,
> Would Steer too near the Sands, to boast his Wit.
> Great Wits are sure to Madness near allied;
> And thin Partitions do their Bounds divide:
> Else, why should he, with Wealth and Honour blessed,
> Refuse his Age the needful Hours of Rest?
> Punish a Body which he could not please;
> Bankrupt of Life, yet Prodigal af Ease?
> And all to leave, what with his Toil he won,
> To that unfeathered, two-legged thing, a Son.

Like Swift and Pope, Dryden was a master of poetic irony. He made the heroic couplet the classical form of poetic expression which would be used by his successors in the eighteenth century. Yet he also wrote religious poetry, such as *Religio Laici* (1682) and, after embracing Roman Catholicism in 1685 (at the accession of

James II), *The Hind and the Panther* (1687), a poem of 2,500 verses defending his new faith. Dryden is remembered for his odes, too, such as "A Song For St. Cecilia's Day" (1687), and for his translations of classical poetry and the adaptations of Chaucer and Boccaccio in heroic couplets, published as *Fables, Ancient and Modern* (1699). Dryden depended on the money he got for translations, for the Revolution in 1688 deprived him of his pensions and of the office of Poet Laureate. It must be said to his credit that he did not turn away from his adopted faith.

Thus the seventeenth century boasted a number of great poets. The development from Donne to Dryden mirrored the momentous changes in taste, philosophy, and manners. It was a movement from passion and religion to intellect and urban wit. And reason, wit, and good manners were to dominate the poetry of the early eighteenth century.

3. Drama

The beginning of the century was dominated by William Shakespeare. The works written about his life and work are legion. We know that he was born in Stratford-on-Avon, made an unwise marriage there, went to London, amassed a fortune, came back to Stratford a wealthy citizen, and died there. He needed money and wanted property, and he got both by writing his plays. Shakespeare was not interested in leaving exact versions of his works, nor did he think of his plays as literature: he wrote for the audience in the playhouse, not for the reader in the "closet".

The publication of his plays is a story by itself. In Shakespeare's time, regular and authorized publication was the exception rather than the rule and plagiarism was rampant. Some of his works were published in his lifetime as Quartos (so called because they are printed on a quarto size page); and they were often faulty copies. After his death two of Shakespeare's fellow players, John Heminge and Henry Condell, brought out the first collected edition of his plays, the so-called Folio edition (1623).

As a young dramatist, Shakespeare wrote comedies and historical plays, some of them in collaboration with contemporary playwrights like **Beaumont** and **Fletcher.** His early comedies show him as a lyrical writer imbued with exuberant mirth, buoyancy, and imagination. In *Love's Labour's Lost* and *The Comedy of Errors* Shakespeare resorted to the popular ingredients of comedy, such as mistaken identities, surprises, imbroglios, puns, and quibbles. But he was also capable of writing in different veins, producing romantic comedies like *The Two Gentlemen of Verona* and boisterous plays bordering on farce, such as *The Taming of the Shrew.*

Written around 1594, this comedy is presented as a play within a play. Christopher Sly, a drunken tinker, is spirited to a castle, where he is assured he is a lord and attends a play performed by strolling players.

This play deals with the taming of Katherina, a termagant and the elder daughter of a rich gentleman of Padua. Petruchio, a gentleman of Verona, who has determined to marry

Katherina, cannot be deterred by her rude rebuffs, pretends to find her courteous and gentle, and manages to tame the "shrew" by several rude actions, such as keeping her waiting on the wedding-day, appearing clad like a scarecrow, and refusing to attend the bridal feast. At his own home, he distresses Katherina further by several mad pranks and finally takes her back to her father's house. Katherina's sister, Bianca, has also found a husband, and another suitor has married a widow. The bridegrooms make a wager as to which wife shall prove the most docile, and Petruchio wins triumphantly when Katherina turns into a quiet, obedient wife.

Shakespeare's early history plays appealed to all the diverse elements of his audience, which, filled with national pride by the defeat of the Armada, wanted pageants and patriotic speeches. Shakespeare provided these, and more, in the three parts of *Henry VI,* in *Richard III* and *King John.* Contemporary playwrights, especially the University wits **Greene, Peele,** and **Marlowe,** did not always like the versatility of the newcomer from the provinces. They saw in Shakespeare a clever and ruthless opportunist hobnobbing with the rich and mighty, such as the earl of Southampton, and giving the public what it wanted, not what it ought to have. There was much self-interest behind such reproaches. William Shakespeare did satisfy public appetite for theatrical crime and violence in his first tragedy, *Titus Andronicus,* which provides a remarkable mixture of massacre, rape, torture, and cannibalism. In everything he did, whether it was poetry, comedy or tragedy, Shakespeare tried to outdo his predecessors.

The most glorious period of Shakespeare's activity began with *Romeo and Juliet,* a lyrical tragedy. The play has everything to please the kind of audience he wrote for – fights, low comedy, philosophy, romantic love, and untimely death.

Based on an Italian romance by Bandello that was often translated into English, *Romeo and Juliet* was probably written around 1595. It focuses on the bitter enmity between the two chief families of Verona, the Montagues and the Capulets. Romeo, the son of old Lord Montague, falls in love with Juliet, and she with him, when he attends in disguise a feast given by Juliet's father, Lord Capulet. Romeo wins Juliet's consent to a secret marriage, and they are wedded the next day by Friar Laurence. Complications ensue when Romeo's friend, Mercutio, quarrels with Tybalt, of the Capulet family, and Romeo, coming on the scene, kills Tybalt. Romeo is then banished from Verona, and Capulet proposes to marry Juliet to Count Paris. Friar Laurence advises Juliet to drink a potion before the wedding which will render her lifeless for 40 hours, and he also promises to inform Romeo of this trick so that he can rescue Juliet from the vault and carry her to Mantua. Juliet does as the friar tells her, but his message to Romeo miscarries, and Romeo hears that Juliet is dead. Equipped with poison, he comes to the vault to have a last sight of Juliet. Outside the vault, he happens upon Count Paris; they fight and Paris is killed. Romeo drinks the poison and dies, and when Juliet awakes she guesses what has happened, stabs herself and dies. The friar and Count Paris's page tell the story to Montague and Capulet who, when confronted with the tragic results of their hate, are reconciled.

A variety of comedies followed in quick succession. *A Midsummer Night's Dream* revealed Shakespeare's poetic genius in drama, combining mythical Athens with his own Warwickshire. The clown becomes a complex and important character in Shakespeare's next three comedies: Touchstone in *As You Like it,* Feste in *Twelfth Night,* and Falstaff in *The Merry Wives of Windsor* are all examples of this. *Much*

Ado about Nothing is another entertaining comedy while *The Merchant of Venice*, written about 1596, is one of Shakespeare's most peculiar plays, mixing tragic elements with comedy and romance. The play follows Marlowe's *The Jew of Malta* in its conventional antisemitism and has in Shylock, the Jewish usurer, a complex character better suited for tragedy than comedy.

During the period 1594–1600 Shakespeare wrote a number of historical plays, returning to English history with *Richard II,* which has often been interpreted as a work of propaganda in favour of Robert Devereux, earl of Essex. This was followed by the two *Henry IV* plays, which are more than mere histories, for Sir John Falstaff holds up the action gloriously and also plays out his wit in *Henry V.*

A certain sense of gloom then seems to enter the plays that followed, even the comedies. Antonio in *The Merchant of Venice,* and Jacques in *As You Like It,* show a bitter pessimism that was now to come to the fore. The comedies written between 1600 and 1608 are not meant primarily for laughs. *Troilus and Cressida* is a dark comedy of Greek myth that failed as a play in Shakespeare's day because it preached too much about order and the need to maintain it. *Measure for Measure* and *All's Well That Ends Well* are still romantic comedies, full of improbabilities and bathed in a light of exquisite fancy, yet they contain undeniable notes of melancholy. Gloom and melancholy also pervade the great tragedies from that period: *Julius Caesar, Hamlet, Othello, Timon of Athens, King Lear, Macbeth, Antony and Cleopatra,* and *Coriolanus.* They picture the world as full of evil forces, and man as either thoughtless and dominated by passions or – in the case of *Hamlet* – meditative and unable to take action. Shakespeare took his plot for *Hamlet* from the thirteenth-century Danish historian Saxo Grammaticus and an earlier version of the play that may have been written by Thomas Kyd.

The story opens with Claudius on the throne of Denmark. He has murdered his brother and with indecent haste married Gertrude, the king's wife. Hamlet, the dead man's son, is urged by his father's ghost to take revenge. But Hamlet's melancholy, introspective and scrupulous nature makes him irresolute and paralyses his will. In order to escape Claudius's suspicion, he feigns madness and treats rudely his former lover, Ophelia. Hamlet has a play acted before Claudius reproducing the circumstances of the murder, and Claudius betrays himself. In the following scene, Hamlet accidentally kills Polonius, Ophelia's father, and is then sent by Claudius on a mission to England.

THE
Tragicall Historie of
HAMLET,
Prince of Denmarke.

By William Shakespeare.

Newly imprinted and enlarged to almost as much againe as it was, according to the true and perfect Coppie.

AT LONDON,
Printed by I. R. for N. L. and are to be sold at his shoppe vnder Saint Dunstons Church in Fleetstreet. 1604.

During that journey Hamlet is supposed to be killed by order of the king, but the ship is captured by pirates and Hamlet returns to Denmark. There, he finds that Ophelia, crazed with grief, has committed suicide. Her brother Laertes, the complete opposite of Hamlet's character, has come home to take vengeance for the deaths of his father and sister. Claudius arranges a fencing match between Hamlet and Laertes, in which the latter uses a poisoned sword, and kills Hamlet; but only after Hamlet has mortally wounded Laertes and stabbed the king. Gertrude drinks from a poisoned cup intended for her son.

Othello, the Moor of Venice was written between 1602 and 1604. It is a study in jealousy, a theme Shakespeare also treated in his comedies.

The first act is set in Venice. Othello, a moor in the service of the state, has secretly married Desdemona, the daughter of a Venetian senator. When Othello is accused of having abducted Desdemona, he justifies his deed, and the Senate then orders him to lead the Venetian forces against the Turks.

The plot continues on Cyprus, where Othello has landed with his wife and soldiers. His friends include Cassio, a young Florentine, who has helped Othello when he courted Desdemona, and Iago, an older soldier, who is bitterly disappointed at Othello's decision to promote the young Cassio. Iago decides to take revenge on all and everyone: he arranges for Cassio to get involved in a fight, so that Othello deprives him of his lieutenancy; and he suggests to Othello that Cassio is Desdemona's lover. With the help of his wife Emilia, who is Desdemona's waiting-woman, Iago manages to have Othello see Cassio in possession of a handkerchief which Othello had offered to Desdemona. Giving in to Iago's promptings, and almost mad with jealousy, Othello strangles Desdemona in her bed. Both Iago's guilt and Desdemona's innocence are finally revealed to Othello. Iago is arrested, and Othello, trying unsuccessfully to stab him, kills himself.

King Lear and *Timon of Athens* are near-hysterical condemnations of ingratitude. Shakespeare exploited a chronicle play, *King Lear* (printed in 1605 but performed much earlier), and collections of histories and sagas for his tragedy about the unwise old Lear, king of Britain, who is victimized by two of his daughters.

Intending to divide his kingdom among his daughters Goneril, Regan and Cordelia, Lear asks them to say which loves him most. Goneril and Regan declare their love without hesitating, and Cordelia, disgusted with their falsity, merely speaks of filial duty. Infuriated with Cordelia's answer, Lear gives two thirds of the kingdom to Goneril and Regan and divides the remaining third between them, leaving Cordelia with nothing. But he soon finds out about the true character of his daughters when Goneril and Regan refuse to maintain the old king and turn him out of doors in a storm. Meanwhile, Cordelia has become the wife of the king of France. The earl of Gloucester takes pity on Lear and is blinded by his enemies. Gloucester's son Edgar, who has been cheated by his bastard brother Edmund, tends his blind father until the latter's death. Lear, now insane with rage and ill treatment, has been conveyed to Dover, where he finds Cordelia. Goneril and Regan fall in love with Edmund and finally turn against each other; Goneril poisons Regan, and then takes her own life. Commanded by Edmund, the English forces defeat the invading French; Lear and Cordelia are imprisoned; and by Edmund's order, Cordelia is hanged. Lear dies from grief, and Edgar eventually proves his brother Edmund's treachery.

While Othello and Lear become victims of their jealousy and imprudence, Macbeth is overpowered by destiny and the entreaties of his wife. The tragedy of *Macbeth* was first performed at the Globe Theatre in 1606.

Shakespeare's Second Globe (drawing by Walter C. Hodges, 1973)

The play opens with Macbeth and Banquo, generals of Duncan, returning from a victory over rebels. The two friends meet three witches who prophesy that Macbeth shall be "thane of Cawdor" and then king, and that Banquo shall beget kings. When Macbeth learns that the Scottish king Duncan has indeed created him thane of Cawdor, he gives in to the arguments of his wife and kills Duncan, who is visiting his castle. Further bloodshed follows, as Macbeth orders the murder of Banquo and his son Fleance. But Fleance and Duncan's sons escape, and Macbeth, haunted by the ghost of Banquo, again consults the witches. They tell him to beware Macduff, the thane of Fife. Thereupon Macbeth has Lady Macduff and her children murdered and learns that Macduff has joined Duncan's son Malcolm. Lady Macbeth becomes insane and dies, and Macduff, returning with Malcolm's newly gathered army from England, kills Macbeth and thus makes the prediction of the witches come true.

Many of Shakespeare's tragedies figure heroes embodying common human faults, such as pride, jealousy, ingratitude and prodigality, and it is their weaknesses, however slight they may be, that ruin them. Thus Brutus, in *Julius Caesar,* may be the most righteous of Romans, but Cassius knows his weak points and persuades him into killing Caesar.

Shakespeare's last plays, written after his retirement to Stratford in 1610, are of a very different character. *Cymbeline, The Tempest,* and *The Winter's Tale* show a soul at rest with itself and with the world and may reflect something of the comfort Shakespeare found in his daughters Judith and Susannah. *The Tempest* is a romantic drama that has inspired numerous other works of art, including an incomplete opera by Mozart and music by Berlioz and Tchaikovsky.

The play is set on a lonely island where Prospero, formerly duke of Milan, has spent twelve years with his daughter Miranda. By his knowledge of magic, Prospero has released several spirits imprisoned by a witch. He is served by the spirit Ariel and by Caliban, the witch's son. When the play begins, Prospero's magic wrecks a ship on the island carrying his brother Antonio, who ousted Prospero from the throne, and some of Antonio's friends and their children. As is usual with Shakespeare, a series of misunderstandings and aborted schemes for treachery follows, and all turns well in the end through the guiding benevolent art of Prospero: Miranda falls in love with young Ferdinand, Prospero gets back his dukedom and renounces his magic, and they all embark for Italy, leaving Caliban alone on the island.

These romantic comedies, together with *Pericles,* which Shakespeare probably wrote in collaboration with another writer, have a new and delicious vein of lyricism – the tragic bitterness has gone. Shakespeare wrote his last historical play, *Henry* VIII, with John Fletcher. The Globe Playhouse burned down during its first performance, and the end of the Globe also marked the end of Shakespeare's career: he died three years later.

Why, one may ask, is Shakespeare's work considered so great? To begin with, there is his verbal genius, which is even more striking than his almost cinematic scene-changes. The meaning and the sound of words were all-important to Shakespeare. Thus he displayed a lyrical and musical gift in his early plays, backed up by beautiful poetic imagery. This imagery reached extraordinary heights in the great tragedies and later plays, in which language became compressed and at times harsh. His versatility as a writer of various types of comedy, tragedy, and history plays is unparalleled in the world's literature. No other playwright achieved his consistency of quality, and his dramatic excellence allowed him to match the specialists in almost any area of drama. It is just because Shakespeare ignored contemporary dramatic rules – the famous unities of action, time, and place – that he was superior. His sole aim was to divert and to move his audience. In Shakespeare's plays tragical, romantic, humorous, and farcical elements are often interwoven: the coarse competes with the sublime, and the serious with the humorous. One of the reasons why this should be so is that Shakespeare wrote plays for, and was aware of writing them for, an Elizabethan audience made up of aristocrats, gallants, thieves, sailors, soldiers, and apprentices. This "mixed bag" of people wanted a variety of things, and Shakespeare gave them action and blood, beautiful phrases and wit, thought and debate, subtle humour, boisterous clowning, love stories, songs and dances.

Admittedly, Shakespeare, like Molière,[1] was a great borrower, copying previous plays and quarrying for subjects in Holinshed's *Chronicles,* Plutarch's[2] *Lives,* William Painter's *Palace of Pleasure,* and Boccaccio's *Decameron.* But he almost always produced something better than his sources, and his unique gift for charac-

---

1. Molière (pseudonym of Jean-Baptiste Poquelin, 1622-73) was the outstanding French comic playwright of the seventeenth century. He was the creator of French classical comedy and has left a gallery of portraits and human types. His plays were exploited by Dryden, Wycherley and Vanbrugh, and by many other writers during the Restoration period. Molière's most influential plays are *L'Avare,* 1669, *Le Tartuffe,* 1664, *Le Malade imaginaire,* 1673, *Le Bourgeois gentilhomme,* 1660, and *Le Misanthrope,* 1666.
2. Plutarch (Plutarchos, 50-125), Greek philosopher and historian. His 44 biographies of great Greeks and Romans are written in a lively style and contain many anecdotes, but they are not accurate historical records.

terization, with which he created unforgettable types, makes up for the lack of verisimilitude in some of the plays. No other dramatist has given us so vast a gallery of unforgettable characters.

Shakespeare's fame overshadows the merits of a group of dramatists who were his contemporaries. Elizabethan und Jacobean drama was immensely rich, and writers of talent were numerous. After Marlowe, **Ben Jonson** (1572-1637) was Shakespeare's greatest contemporary. Jonson was a classicist, a moralist, and a reformer of the drama. His plays generally obey the rules of the unities of time, place, and theme. Ben Jonson created abstractions, types of characters controlled by the medieval theory of the "humours", i. e. sanguin, choleric, phlegmatic, and melancholic. Thus his comedy *Every Man in His Humour* (1598) is little more than a demonstration of the humoral theory, which defines characters as influenced by one quality, such as avarice, cowardice, or boastfulness. Despite his limiting theory of characters, Jonson was an outstanding playwright in the area of comedy. By studiously observing and ridiculing the types of men of his day, Jonson became a sort of Dickens of the seventeenth century. His best plays were written after 1600: *Volpone* (1607), *The Alchemist* (1610), and *Bartholomew Fair* (1614). The first two focus on the same theme – rogues getting rich on the credulity and stupidity of the ignorant. Since Jonson was a realist, he made Elizabethan London the setting of his dramas. Thus *Bartholomew Fair,* which is concerned with contemporary low life, presents in a farcical light various scenes of the most popular fair in London; its most important character is Zeal-of-the-Land Busy, one of several hypocritical Puritans.

The element of realism was pursued by a number of playwrights, notably **Thomas Dekker** (1572-1632); **John Webster** (c. 1580-1625); **Thomas Middleton** (1570-1627); **George Chapman** (1559-1634); **John Marston** (c. 1576-1634); and **Thomas Heywood** (c. 1573-1641). Collaboration between these playwrights was common and frequent. Heywood apparently participated in the writing of 220 plays. Among the important dramatists providing living pictures of London were **Francis Beaumont** (1584-1616) and **John Fletcher** (1579-1625). Working together on several plays, they achieved a common style and produced their best work with the tragi-comedy *Philaster, or Love Lies A-Bleeding* (1608-10). In *A Woman Killed Kindly* (1603), Heywood adapted tra-

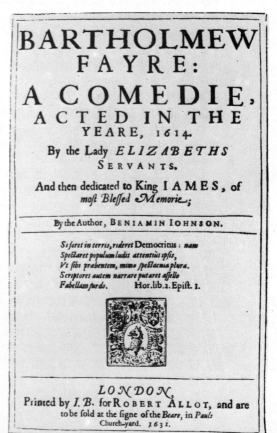

BARTHOLMEW
FAYRE:
A COMEDIE,
ACTED IN THE
YEARE, 1614.
By the Lady *ELIZABETHS*
SERVANTS.

And then dedicated to King IAMES, of
moſt Bleſſed Memorie;

By the Author, BENIAMIN IOHNSON.

Si foret in terris, rideret Democritus : *nam
Spectaret populum ludis attentius ipſis,
Vt ſibi præbentem, mimo ſpectacula plura.
Scriptores autem narrare putaret aſello
Fabellam ſurdo.* Hor.lib.2.Epiſt. 1.

LONDON,
Printed by *I. B.* for ROBERT ALLOT, and are
to be ſold at the ſigne of the *Beare,* in *Pauls*
Church-yard. 1631.

gedy to the sensibilities of the middle class. Yet the most profound of the tragic dramatists was John Webster, who is still known for his revenge play *The Duchess of Malfi* (1613-14). **Cyril Tourneur** (1575-1626) further developed the tragedy of horror and revenge and displayed a strong taste for the perverse in *The Revenger's Tragedy* (1607). This is also true of **John Ford** (1586-1639). His *'Tis Pity She's a Whore* (c. 1625-33) deals with incest and murder. Finally, **Philip Massinger** (1583-1640) and **James Shirley** (1596-1666) followed Ben Jonson's example in comedies and tragedies. Massinger's finest play is a comedy, *A New Way to Pay Old Debts* (c. 1625), in which he portrays in Sir Giles Overreach a miser who can easily compare to Volpone or Molière's Harpagon. Shirley wrote about 30 plays and produced some of the best comedies before the closing of the theatres.

When the Puritans finally prohibited stage plays and closed down the theatres in 1642, they did not stop English drama at its height. At this time there was little new development and much imitation of earlier examples. Still, with their decision the Puritans destroyed a tradition of writing and acting. When it was revived two decades later, English drama was not the same. The break between 1642 and 1660 was not absolute, as some sort of theatrical entertainment in private houses continued, **Sir William Davenant's** "entertainments" being the best-known example.

With the return of Charles II both the drama and its audience changed. Theatre-going now became a monopoly of the upper class and the court. The fashionable Restoration audience wanted wit, humour, and sex, but little else, and the playwrights catered to these narrow tastes. The new theatres brought some changes affecting productions, such as a reduction in size of the platform-stage – which meant less contact between the actors and the audience – and the introduction of women players. The old intimacy of the Elizabethan stage was lost (see illustration p. 35), but the actresses (women's roles were formerly played by boys) introduced a more realistic sexual atmosphere. Charles and his court had spent their exile in France, at the splendid and frivolous court of Louis XIV, and the new English drama absorbed some of the French spirit in language (correctness and lucidity), manners, and attitudes toward love.

It was in comedy that the Restoration found its peculiar excellence. Typically, **Shakespeare's** comedies were now disliked, but those of **Jonson, Beaumont, Fletcher** and **Shirley** found imitators. The main ingredients of the new comedy of manners were lust, cuckoldry, and intrigue, covered by a smart veneer of wit. It was in the work of five dramatists, who belong to two different generations, that the comedy of manners was evolved: **Etherege** and **Wycherley** produced their plays between 1665-1676, and **Congreve, Vanbrugh,** and **Farquhar** between 1692-1707. **Dryden,** too, tried his hand at comedy, yet his *The Wild Gallant* (1663) and the slightly more popular *Marriage à la Mode* did not hold the stage. **Sir George Etherege** (1635-91) was the senior Restoration comedian. He discovered the new formula for successful plays with *The Man of Mode* (1676). Dispensing with morals and romanticism, Etherege provided witty portrayals of elegant ladies and educated gallants in their dissipations, love-affairs, and intrigues.

With **William Wycherley** (1640-1716) the comedy of manners progresses to satire and even cynicism. In his first plays, *Love in a Wood* (1671) and *The Gentleman Dancing-Master* (1672), he was still experimenting, reaching the full potential of his powers with *The Country Wife* (1674) and *The Plain Dealer* (1676), the second influenced by Molière's *Le Misanthrope*.

The Country Wife is one of the wittiest of his plays. The plot illustrates the folly of excessive jealousy and credulity in lovers. Mr. Pinchwife comes to London for the marriage of his sister Alithea, and brings with him his innocent country wife. His exaggerated jealousy puts ideas into her head. Sparkish, who was to marry Alithea, has too much trust and confidence in her, losing her to a new wooer. The central figure of the play is Horner, an ironic libertine who pretends to be impotent in order to seduce his victims the more easily. Horner is eventually able to convince Pinchwife of his wife's "innocence." The theme of cuckoldry is thus dominant in this play, as in many other Restoration comedies.

Wycherley's satire is founded on his cynical mockery of human puppets pursuing illusory pleasures.

The following decade saw some plays by **Thomas Shadwell** (1640-92), who rejected the principles and conventions of the Restoration comedy and tended more to Jonson's comedy of humours. His best plays are *The Squire of Alsatia* (1688) and *Bury Fair* (1689).

The Restoration comedy reached its zenith with the works of Congreve, Vanbrugh, and Farquhar. **Sir John Vanbrugh** (1664-1726) was the least skilled of these dramatists, though he was an important architect who designed and built Blenheim Palace for the Duke of Marlborough, and his own Haymarket Theatre. Vanbrugh's major comedies, *The Relapse, or Virtue in Danger* (1696) and *The Provok'd Wife* (1697), suffer from faulty style and plot; yet the plays were successful for a while. It was definitely **William Congreve** (1670-1729) who contributed most to the development of the later Restoration comedy. Congreve returned to the surface gaiety of Etherege in dealing with the world of fashion, courtship, and seduction, yet he conducted his comedies with a brilliance of dialogue and wit which Etherege never achieved. Congreve concentrated very consciously on the formal and artistic aspects of comedy and saw himself as the reformer of the stage. With *The Old Bachelor* (1693), he made his reputation suddenly and early in his life. Modelled on Etherege's *Man of Mode,* the play portrays the chase for erotic pleasures, the cynical despise of marriage, and the desire for money and property. Technically, the later comedies - *The Double Dealer* (1694); *Love for Love* (1695); and *The Way of the World* (1700) - are even better, though they all conform in theme and strategy to the model of the successful Restoration comedy of manners.

Restoration drama produced few important tragedies. **Sir William Davenant** (1608-68) introduced what came to be called heroic drama. His *The Siege of Rhodes* (1656; enlarged in 1662) impressed Dryden. Like Davenant, Dryden exaggerated the "love versus honour" theme, and in his tragedies he gave his characters grandiose and ranting speeches declaimed in regular heroic couplets (see *Aurengzebe,* 1675, and *The Conquest of Granada,* 1672). In his later tragedies, such as *All for Love* (1677), Dryden gave up the heroic couplet for blank verse. The more important writers of tragedy were **Thomas Otway** (1652–85) and **Nathaniel Lee** (1649–92). Both stood under the influence of Elizabethan heroic tragedy and the plays of Corneille[1] and Racine.[2] Otway's best tragedies are those in blank verse: *The Orphan* (1680) and *Venice Preserved* (1682). They contain strong elements of sentimentality, but it was Lee who gave in completely to sentiment and bombast. *The Rival Queens* (1667) was perhaps the most acceptable of his eleven tragedies.

The witty and immoral comedy of manners was thus the outstanding achievement of the Restoration period. But now the great names in European drama were French – Molière in comedy, and Racine and Corneille in tragedy. They influenced English drama considerably and not always for the better. As England now had no Shakespeare, English drama slowly began to decline. After 1700, this decline was hastened by literary attacks on the theatre and the increasing importance of middle-class sentiments and taste.

4. Fiction

Poetry and drama took pride of place throughout the seventeenth century. It was left to the Age of Enlightenment to consolidate prose fiction as an acceptable and respectable form of literature. Seventeenth-century English prose was fed by three different sources: the prose romance, the realistic and picaresque tale of low life, and spiritual autobiography.

Surprisingly, the beginnings of fiction were not further developed. The religious debates, with their pamphleteering wars, and the many wars of the seventeenth century may be responsible to a certain extent. If anything flourished, it was the prose romance that came from France with the interminable books by **Madeleine de Scudéry**.[3] Her *Le Grand Cyrus* was translated in 1655 and enjoyed great popularity.

A new type of fiction did not emerge for several decades. It came with **John Bunyan** (1628–88), the son of a Bedfordshire tinker. Bunyan received little education and knew only one book really well – the Bible. Both his style and imagery depend heavily on it. John Bunyan was a soldier in the Republican Army, a preacher, and a mystic who defended Puritan principles. At the time of the Resto-

---

1. Pierre Corneille (1606–84), French playwright and creator of the classical French tragedy. *Le Cid* (1637) is one of the plays that exerted a powerful influence on the English dramatists of the Restoration, especially on Dryden. Corneille portrayed the conflict between passion and duty at a crucial point of moral crisis, and the heroism of his protagonists is grounded in social and psychological facts.
2. Jean Racine (1639–99), French dramatist who wrote at first under the influence of Molière and Corneille but then found his own style of tragedy. His most important play is *Phèdre* (1677). Racine was inspired by Greek and Roman literature and history, and his plays were often translated into English.
3. Madeleine de Scudéry (1607–91), French writer of heroic romances that were extremely popular. Such works as *Artamère, ou le Grand Cyrus* (1649–53) extended to 10 volumes and combined stories of love and war, set in ancient countries, with allusions to contemporary French society.

Frontispiece of the third edition of *The Pilgrim's Progress*

ration he was sent to prison for twelve years. Released in 1671, he continued to preach until his death. Bunyan's work shows that religious fervour had not died with Milton. Of his several works it is *The Pilgrim's Progress,* begun in Bedfordshire jail and fully published in two parts in 1684, which has left a lasting impression. Bunyan used as a basis for his book neither his education nor literary tradition but rather his own religious experience and the prose of the *Authorized Version of the Bible.*

The Pilgrim's Progress is an allegorical story in the form of a dream. The hero, Christian, travels from the City of Destruction to the Eternal City, leaving behind his wife and children who will not heed his religious advice. Part I describes Christian's arduous pilgrimage through such allegorical locations as the Slough of Despond, the Valley of Humiliation, and Vanity Fair. Among the various personages he encounters are Mr. Worldly Wiseman, Faithful, and Giant Despair. Part II of the book relates the journey of Christiana – his wife – and their children to the same celestial destination.

Despite its Puritan and biblical allegory and overt didactic-religious tendencies, *The Pilgrim's Progress* is remarkable for the beauty and simplicity of its language. Bunyan possessed great narrative skill and his book has been translated into over one hundred languages.

Bunyan's spiritual autobiography and the realistic description of low life by Nashe, Greene, and Deloney were soon united by another dissenter, **Daniel Defoe** (1660–1731), a contemporary of Bunyan and the father of the English novel.

5. Nonfiction

The masterpiece of early seventeenth century prose is the *Authorized Version of the Bible.* Undertaken at the request of James I, it was brought to completion by some fifty scholars and first published in 1611. There is hardly an English writer who has not been influenced by it, and few books have exerted a more beneficial influence on the style and grammar of the English language.

Two writers stand at the beginning of seventeenth-century prose. **Francis Bacon** (1561-1626), a learned, worldly, and ambitious nobleman with a powerful mind, wrote most of his works in Latin, but what he has left us in English also proves his excellence. His *The Advancement of Learning* (1605) described the conditions of knowledge and the ways in which they might be improved. However, his fame rests upon his brilliant *Essays* (1597), published in enlarged editions in 1612 and 1625. These essays (58 in the latest edition) are compact in style and balanced in their phrasing. They discuss moral and political issues in a precise and almost scientific manner.

In *The Anatomy of Melancholy* (1621) the Anglican clergyman **Robert Burton** (1577-1640) analysed Hamlet's disease, the mental ailment we would now call neurosis or depression. Like many other Elizabethan writers, Burton was fascinated by the issue of melancholy and wrote a huge, strange, yet enthralling work full of the most bizarre stories, recondite learning, and curiosities. It has given pleasure to many writers since its revival during the Romantic period.

Sir **Thomas Browne** (1605-82) was a deeply religious and learned physician standing between the modern and medieval ways of thought. In his major works, *Religio Medici* (1635), *Pseudodoxia Epidemica* (1646), and *Hydriotaphia* (1658), he enquired into the meaning of life and the search for truth, discussing the relationships between science, authority, and faith.

The sermon was an important seventeenth-century prose form. **John Donne** and **Lancelot Andrewes** (1553-1626) were famous preachers, and so was **Jeremy Taylor** (1613-67), who is remembered for the passion and splendour of his sermons. The Puritans had a whole phalanx of clergymen who wrote sermons. They developed a particular kind of hortatory sermon, the jeremiad[1] (the best examples of which come from New England). **Richard Baxter** (1615-91) was one of their outstanding preachers.

The ideological and religious controversies of the age drove many authors to write prose, such as **John Milton's** *Areopagitica* (1644) in defence of the free press. One writer, however, stood apart from these tendencies, and his work has made the greatest appeal to posterity: **Izaak Walton's** (1593-1683) *The Compleat Angler* (1653) has seen hundreds of editions. The

Being a Difcourfe of
FISH and FISHING,
Not unworthy the perufal of moft *Anglers.*

Simon Peter faid, I go a fifhing : and they faid, We alfo wil go with thee. John 21.3.

London, Printed by *T. Maxey* for RICH. MARRIOT, in S. *Dunftans* Church-yard Fleetftreet, 1653.

---

1. See p. 182.

book is a gentle praise of the sport of angling and of the English countryside.

The philosophical influence of **Thomas Hobbes** and **John Locke** has already been discussed in the introduction to this chapter. In literary criticism **John Dryden** played the role which **Dr. Johnson** and **T.S. Eliot** fulfilled in subsequent centuries. Dryden stated his classicist philosophy, which was to bear fruit in the early eighteenth century, in the *Essay on Dramatic Poesy* (1668), the *Preface to the Fables* (1700), and his *Essay on Satire* (1679, sometimes attributed to the earl of Mulgrave). For Dryden, literature was to give a picture of truth and to imitate nature in the manner of the ancient Greek and Roman authors. According to his principles, literature must appeal to reason and obey rules.

Finally, the diaries of **Samuel Pepys** (1633-1703) and **John Evelyn** (1620-1706), covering the years 1660-69 (Pepys) and 1631-1706 (Evelyn), recorded history in terms of its immediate impact on people. Both diaries are fascinating prose documents of the Restoration period.

V. The Eighteenth Century

1. General Background

Many terms have been used to describe the eighteenth century: the Age of Reason and Revolution, the Augustan Age or Neoclassicism, and the beginnings of Romanticism. These terms indicate philosophical, political, and literary trends, and they also provide an idea of the varied facets of an epoch that saw the advent of modernity, of democracy, progress, and alienation, though hierarchical and hereditary patterns remained. Change occurred, but at a pace people could adapt to.

The century began with the reign of Queen Anne (1702 - 1714), heralding a time of relative stability after the social and political upheavals of the seventeenth century. Great Britain was created in 1707 when Scotland joined the Union of England and Wales. The four Georges gave little more than their name ("Georgian England") to an era dominated first by the Whigs[1] (1715 - 1761) and then by the Tories[2] (1783-1830). Under the Georges - George I, 1714-1727; George II, 1727-1760 - it was Robert Walpole who ran the government, guaranteeing economic growth and peace at home, even though he had to resort to bribes and blackmail. As the outstanding political figure of the first half of the century he was followed by William Pitt the Elder in whose time as Foreign Secretary (1756-1761) Great Britain became the leading power in Europe and the colonies. Between 1783-1801 William Pitt the Younger guided Britain as Prime Minister through a much more difficult time into the nineteenth century. Throughout the century, France remained England's arch-enemy and both countries were engaged in a series of wars. From the 1760s on, revolutionary forces began to make themselves felt. Parliament emerged as the most influential political power, with John Wilkes and Charles James Fox acting as the outstanding figures among the opposition. Amazingly, the two major revolutions of the century left Britain almost unscathed, though the reverberations of the American War of Independence (1775-1783) and the French Revolution in 1789 also caused a few tremors in England.

The most spectacular social phenomenon was the growing influence of the middle class and the decline of aristocratic power. Although the landed nobility remained in power until the nineteenth century, the plutocracy of the trade "barons", the merchants and the shop owners, was eventually the driving force behind the national economy. In religion, the influence of the middle class was noticeable in

---

1. The Whigs were an English political group or party which, from 1679, was opposed to Catholics on the throne. The Tories were their political opponents. The Whigs defended parliamentary and individual rights in the Glorious Revolution (1688) and helped the House of Hanover to take over the English monarchy in 1714. For several decades, the Prime Minister came from their ranks. The modern British Liberal Party developed from the Whigs.

2. Initially (1640) the term "Tories" was used to refer to Irish Catholics and the opponents of the Long Parliament and the Commonwealth. From 1679 the Tories supported the monarchy and became the opponents of the Whigs. They controlled the government between 1710-14 and between 1784-1830. After 1832 the modern Conservative Party emerged from their ranks.

the rise and spread of Methodism,[1] founded by John Wesley (1703-91) and his brother, Charles.

England preserved her agrarian character, for even toward the end of the century, when the "Agricultural Revolution" was followed by the Industrial Revolution, seventy-five per cent of the population lived in the country while the population of London doubled. The contrast between city and country – always a favourite subject of eighteenth-century literature – deepened in the last third of the century, accompanied by more rapid economic and social changes. Slowly but steadily, the growing proletariat began to organize itself, finding radical spokesmen among the intellectuals.

To a certain extent, these were the consequences of the Enlightenment. In England, where the middle class and the aristocracy set the tone in culture and philosophy, nature and reason were essential terms based on the belief in man's benevolence and common sense. In his *Essay Concerning Human Understanding* (1690) John Locke had established a psychological and empirical theory of cognition which focused on the individual and demanded religious and political freedom. And David Hume's *Enquiry Concerning Human Understanding* (1748) carried further into skepticism the theory of impression and association. It was the pursuit of happiness, here and now instead of hereafter, which occupied moral philosophy from Shaftesbury[2] to Jeremy Bentham[3] and was codified as a human right in the Declaration of Independence beyond the Atlantic. Deism,[4] the child of the union between religion and the Enlightenment, was supported by the French "philosophes", above all by Voltaire,[5] but in England Methodism began to rule the field

---

1. An evangelical Church founded in 1729 by John and Charles Wesley and dissenting from the Church of England. In the eighteenth and nineteenth centuries it had a large following among the poor. Methodism stresses grace through faith. The use of lay pastors who travelled around the country and practised open-air preaching proved successful for recruiting new members. The Methodist Church has a powerful voice in Britain and the United States.

2. Anthony Ashley Cooper, 3rd earl of Shaftesbury (1671-1713), moral and aesthetic philosopher, greatly influenced by Deism and Platonic ideas. Strongly opposed to the selfish theory of conduct propounded by Hobbes, he argued that man has "affections" for himself but also for the creatures around him and that man, in order to achieve rectitude and virtue, must respect society and the public. His principal work is *Characteristics of Men, Manners, Opinions, and Times* (1711, rev. in 1714).

3. Jeremy Bentham (1748-1832), English lawyer and philosopher. He formulated the political and ethical theory of utility in his *Fragments on Government* (1776) and *Introduction to Principles of Morals and Legislation* (1780 and 1789). According to Bentham, the greatest happiness of the greatest number of people must be the measure of right and wrong both in everyday conduct and in legislation.

4. The religious-philosophical belief, held by many philosophers of the Enlightenment, which rejects the supernatural doctrines of Christianity and advocates a "natural religion" with a Supreme Being who created, but does not interfere in, the world. Its major spokesmen in England were Charles Blount (1654-93) and Matthew Tindal (1657-1733), and in France, Voltaire and Diderot.

5. Voltaire (François Marie Arouet, 1694-1778), French writer and philosopher and one of the major spokesmen of the Enlightenment. He left an enormous number of works in the fields of literature, journalism, politics, history, and philosophy and was respected, and even feared, by the sovereigns of his age. Voltaire was opposed to any kind of fanatical or doctrinal religion. His guidelines were reason and the empirical sciences, and he never tired in defending the rights of man. Outstanding among his publications are his witty and frivolous epics directed against the French monarchy and the Catholic

after mid-century. If hedonism and materialism also survived, it was mainly among the aristocracy. Noblemen still went on the customary Grand Tour (a tour through Europe) as part of their education, and in France they became acquainted with the theories of d'Holbach, Helvétius, La Mettrie[1] and Voltaire. Some English rakes, notably Sir Francis Dashwood and John Wilkes and the members of the Hell Fire Club, put into practice the French philosophy of pleasure and enjoyment. It found literary expression in Wilkes's parody, *An Essay on Woman* (1763), and John Cleland's notorious *Fanny Hill* (1748/9). The English libertines, however, imitating French examples, were a minority and certainly not as influential as the Frenchmen they tried to emulate.

2. Poetry

In poetry, as in literature generally, the eighteenth century was a time of transition and new beginnings. After the end of the Restoration period, the principles of Neoclassicism as exemplified by Pope and Swift ruled the field until well into the second half of the century when sensibility and sentimentality announced Romanticism. Neoclassicism, also called the Augustan Age, derived its rules from antiquity (Aristotle, Horace, Longinus)[2] and French Classicism (Boileau),[3] considering

---

Church (e. g. *La Henriade,* 1728, and *La Pucelle,* written in 1733 and published in 1762), his comments on England and the English (*Lettres philosophiques sur les Anglais,* 1734), his novels (e. g. *Candide,* 1759) and tales. He also wrote several excellent histories and a brilliant *Dictionnaire philosophique* (1764).
1. Paul Heinrich Dietrich Baron von Holbach (1723-89), a German-born philosopher who moved to Paris in 1735 and belonged to the circle of the "encyclopédistes" and the "philosophes", a group of writers and thinkers who advocated skepticism in religion, materialism in philosophy, and hedonism in ethics. The group included Montesquieu, Voltaire, Diderot, Rousseau, Buffon, d'Alembert, Condillac and Helvétius.
Claude Arien Helvétius (1715-71), one of the *philosophes* who developed a moral philosophy based on mechanism, materialism, and the senses.
Julien Offray de La Mettrie (1709-51), French philosopher, atheist, and materialist. He was persecuted because of his materialist view of man (*L'homme machine,* 1748), and, like Voltaire and a few other men of the Enlightenment, was welcomed by Frederic the Great in Berlin, who provided him with an income.
2. Aristotle (384-322 BC), Greek philosopher and scientist and a disciple of Plato. His extensive works in logic, ethics, metaphysics, physics, rhetoric, and poetics shaped the development of medieval thought. His writings were then harmonized with Christianity and were central in the teaching of higher education from the 13th to the 17th centuries. Aristotle's treatise on poetics came into prominence rather late (in the 1550s) and was instrumental in the rise of Neoclassicism.
Horace: See page 17, note 2.
Longinus was the author of a Greek critical treatise (*On the Sublime*) written in the first century A. D. Locating the sources of poetic skill in the intensity of the writer's emotions and thought, the work was translated in the seventeenth century and had a marked effect on eighteenth-century critics and writers. The idea of the "sublime" paved the way for Romanticism.
3. Nicolas Despreaux Boileau (1636-1711), French critic and poet, whose *Art Poétique* (1674), a poem in four cantos, established canons of taste and poetic form that achieved international importance. In England, Dryden, Pope, and Addison considered Boileau as a literary and critical authority.

social conventions more important than individual convictions and seeing reason as superior to emotion. Form often determined content, while the imitation of nature was to reflect an order combining the general, Horace's "dulce et utile" ("sweet and useful"), reason, wit and common sense. Originality in form was not asked for, rather the masterful use of prescribed literary genres, such as the epic, the ode, the verse satire, and the numerous imitations of classic authors. In the poetry of the first part of the eighteenth century reason and emotion no longer work together. In fact, emotion is almost despised as inferior. Hence it is understandable that after 1760 emotion began to displace reason. In many ways, sentimentality, the Gothic, and Romanticism can be explained as a reaction against the intellectual rigour of Neoclassicism, as the individual rebelling against society and conventional artistic forms. Eighteenth-century poetry, then, had two strong currents fed by reason and emotion; the latter came to the fore at the time of the French Revolution.

The poets one associates most with Neoclassicism are **Jonathan Swift** and **Alexander Pope**, the latter being the most influential figure. **Swift** (1667-1745), who is better remembered as a prose-writer, was an outstanding humorist and a savage satirist whose tales and satires in verse have left a lasting impression. In 1711 he published several *Miscellanies in Prose and Verse,* among them "Baucis and Philemon", a verse tale and parody of Ovid's metamorphosis, and the two "town eclogues", "A Description of the Morning", and "A Description of a City Shower", both parodies of classic originals but also satires on London's dirt and confusion. Perhaps unjustly, Swift has acquired the reputation of being a misogynist. As a modern follower of Juvenalis[1] and Ovid,[2] however, Swift did not put down women, but rather human vanity, falsity, and pretension. Thus, in "A Beautiful Young Nymph Going To Bed" (1734), he shows the miserable reality of a prostitute's life, a far from glamorous aspect that eighteenth-century males preferred to ignore. Swift shocked his readers with his mock-heroic couplets hiding an essentially moral message about Corinna:

> *Corinna,* pride of *Drury-Lane,*
> For whom no shepherd sighs in vain;
> Never did *Covent-Garden* boast
> So bright a battered, strolling toast;
> No drunken rake to pick her up,
> No cellar where on tick to sup;
> Returning at the midnight hour,
> Four stories climbing to her bower;
> Then, seated on a three-legged chair,
> Takes off her artificial hair:
> Now, picking out a crystal eye,
> She wipes it clean, and lays it by.

---

1. Juvenal (Decimus Junius Juvenalis, c. 60-136), Roman satirist, who attacked the vices of his age. His works were translated and adapted to English conditions in the seventeenth and eighteenth centuries. John Dryden was one of the principal translators and was influenced by him.
2. See page 17, note 3.

Her eye-brows from a mouse's hide,
Stuck on with art on either side,
Pulls off with care, and first displays 'em,
Then in a play-book smoothly lays 'em.
Now dextrously her plumpers draws,
That serve to fill her hollow jaws.
Untwists a wire; and from her gums
A set of teeth completely comes.

The description of Corinna's undressing not only reveals a decaying body but also ridicules and exposes the erotic interest of male readers. In the tradition of Ovid's *Remedia Amoris,* Swift wrote a number of poems on the folly of love, such as "The Lady's Dressing Room" (1732), "Strephon and Chloe", and "Cassinus and Peter", both published in 1734. They stress the need to be sensible, even when in love, and are thus typical examples of Neoclassical poetry which puts reason above emotion.

Alexander Pope (1685-1744) was the outstanding poet of the first half of the century. In many ways Dryden's heir, Pope was dwarfish, weak, ugly, and venomous, but elegant and strong in his work, which shows a rare singleness of purpose. In his early 'teens, Pope wrote his "Ode to Solitude" and the "Pastorals", and at twenty he produced the *Essay on Criticism,* a work in Dryden's tradition that preaches correctness in literary composition and the filing and polishing of phrases and lines until perfection is reached. If this was literary criticism in verse, Pope also tackled philosophy in verse in his *Essay on Man,* published pseudonymously in 1733. This didactic poem owes much to the philosophies of Viscount Bolingbroke and the Earl of Shaftesbury (1671-1713), the former a Deist and the latter propounding rationalism and tolerance. Pope's pithy couplets contain moral precepts summing up the rational notions of the early decades of the century. In the history of poetry, however, Pope has gone down for two other works he wrote, both of them delightful satires - *The Rape of the Lock* and *The Dunciad.* It was in *The Rape of the Lock* (1714) that Pope was at his best as an effective satirist, mocking the whole of the fashionable society of the eighteenth century, while nevertheless indicating that he had some attachment to its elegance. The ironic description of Hampton Court in canto iii is typical of the attitude and tone of this poem:

Close by those meads, forever crowned with flowers,
Where Thames with pride surveys his rising towers,
There stands a structure of majestic frame,
Which from the neighboring Hampton takes its name.
Here Britain's statesmen oft the fall foredoom
Of foreign tyrants and of nymphs at home;
Here thou, great Anna! whom three realms obey,
Dost sometimes counsel take-and sometimes tea.

Hither the heroes and the nymphs resort,
To taste awhile the pleasures of a court;
In various talk the instructive hours they passed,
Who gave the ball, or paid the visit last;

One speaks the glory of the British Queen,
And one describes a charming Indian screen;
A third interprets motions, looks, and eyes;
At every word a reputation dies.
Snuff, or the fan, supply each pause of chat,
With singing, laughing, ogling, and all that.

Influenced by Boileau's *Le Lutrin* (1683), Pope's satirical story of the theft of a curl from the hair of a young lady of fashion develops to its full potential the absurdly dignified style known as mock-heroic, in which irony is created by the disparity between the trivial subject and the highflown language. In *The Dunciad* (1743) Pope made a severe attack on dullness in general, and the contemporary dunces from Grub Street (minor poets who wrote aggressive satires) in particular.

Pope certainly set the tone and standards for his age, and for his followers to take up the heroic couplet meant also taking up Pope's diction, his epigrams, and his wit. Some poets, though, had enough individuality not to be dominated by Pope's authoritative figure. Thus **Matthew Prior** (1664-1721) is remembered for the formal elegance of the songs, philosophical poems, and verse tales collected in his *Poems on Several Occasions* (1718). **John Gay** (1685-1732), after imitating Pope for a while, found his own style, too, in the parody of pastoral poetry, *The Shepherd's Week* (1714), and the popular versified *Fables* (1727). The heroic couplet as a poetic form remained influential. **Oliver Goldsmith** (1730-1774) chose it for both his long poems *The Traveller* (1764) and *The Deserted Village* (1770). In these works he turned away from the city and lamented the decay of English village life. This was an achievement in itself, for Pope kept the reader's attention fixed on urban society. Goldsmith, and **George Crabbe** (1754-1832) with his harsh and bitter images of the country in *The Village* (1783), were thus indebted to Pope only in form, but their preoccupation with nature indicates an independent theme of eighteenth-century poetry that came to the fore with the precursors of Romanticism. Like many others in his time **James Thomson** (1700-1748), a Scot, sought fame in London. He turned away from the heroic couplet and imitated Milton's powerful blank verse. Thomson's great cycle of poems about nature is *The Seasons,* completed in 1730. It became popular throughout Europe and also had an audience among ordinary people, whom Pope's elegant satires never reached. *The Seasons* is a minute description of the changing countryside under snow, rain, or sunlight, but its diction is still conventional and too much indebted to Neoclassicism to make it a Romantic poem. Thomson's other great poem is *The Castle of Indolence* (1748) in which he attempted the Spenserian stanza while describing pilgrims enticed by the magician Indolence into a castle full of sensual joys. The inhabitants of the castle gradually lose all initiative and are thrown into a dungeon to perish. Two knights, however, storm the castle, capture Indolence, and set the prisoners free. Thomson's revival of Spenser's heritage, his preference for blank verse and dislike of the heroic couplet, characterize him as a poet between Neoclassicism and the growing current of Romanticism which, around mid-century, was also fed by Young, Gray, Collins, and Cowper.

In the second half of the eighteenth century, English poetry had no domineering figure like Dryden or Pope. However, a number of poets produced a most interesting and diverse body of verse that gave more room to sensibility, though this also meant the development of an exclusive poetic diction as an expression of refined taste. The poets' focus gradually shifted from moral and social aspects to the more personal and individual, and to emotion. The first reactions against the long rule of reason were beginning to show in melancholy poems, visions of the dark and of death, and in the obvious inclinations of some poets towards the grotesque, exoticism, and the subconscious. The very titles of the published poems and collections indicate the poetic preoccupation. Between 1742-1745 **Edward Young** (1683-1765) had his *Night Thoughts on Life, Death, and Immortality* published, evoking a sombre atmosphere of night, tombs, and loneliness in some 10,000 lines of blank verse. Young's work set a fashion for gloomy lyrics like Harvey's *Meditations among the Tombs* (1745-1746); Robert Blair's *The Grave* (1743); and Thomas Warton's *The Pleasures of Melancholy* (1747). **Thomas Gray** (1716-1771) wrote only ten poems, almost all of them melancholic in tone, which were nevertheless vastly influential. The opening of his *Elegy Written in a Country Churchyard,* first published in 1751, and written in the masterly form of Dryden's heroic quatrain, captures the sentiment of the precursors of Romanticism:

> The curfew tolls the knell of parting day,
>   The lowing herd wind slowly o'er the lea,
> The plowman homeward plods his weary way,
>   And leaves the world to darkness and to me.
>
> Now fades the glimmering landscape on the sight,
>   And all the air a solemn stillness holds,
> Save where the beetle wheels his droning flight,
>   And drowsy tinklings lull the distant folds;
>
> Save that from yonder ivy-mantled tower
>   The moping owl does to the moon complain
> Of such, as wandering near her secret bower,
>   Molest her ancient solitary reign.

In Gray's poem, every effect is worked for, creating a carefully chosen harmony of sound and imagery.

Significantly, **William Collins** (1721-1759) poured his poetic energy not into an adoration of the rising sun or the dawn of day but into an *Ode to Evening* (c. 1747), which became a successful poem. It opens thus:

> If aught of oaten stop, or pastoral song,
> May hope, chaste Eve, to soothe thy modest ear,
>   Like thy own solemn springs,
>   Thy springs and dying gales,
> O nymph reserved, while now the bright-haired sun
> Sits in yon western tent, whose cloudy skirts,
>   With brede ethereal wove,
>   O'erhang his wavy bed:

Now air is hushed, save where the weak-eyed bat,
With short shrill shriek flits by on leathern wing,
    Or where the beetle winds
    His small but sullen horn,
As oft he rises 'midst the twilight path,
Against the pilgrim borne in heedless hum.

Indebted and inspired by the form of Horace's odes, Collins, who became insane at the age of 30, attempts in this poem a combination of dream-like effects, a musical expression of emotions, and of formal elements still reminiscent of Neoclassicism – there is pastoral and mythological personification, adoration of "Fancy" and "Friendship", and a distinct poetic diction.

William Cowper (1731-1800) was the poet of nature and is mainly remembered for *The Task* (1785), a poem of more than 5,000 lines of blank verse pitting friendly nature against the wicked town in rural scenes foreshadowing the work of Wordsworth.

The quest of the ancient and the exotic, a characteristic trait in eighteenth-century English culture, also left its traces in poetry. Although fabrications, **James Macpherson's** *Fragments of Ancient Poetry Collected in the Highlands of Scotland, and Translated from the Gaelic or Erse language* (1760) and his "episodes" from the Gaelic epic *Fingal* took Europe by storm. **Thomas Chatterton** (1752-1770) attributed his poems to the fictitious fifteenth-century poet, Rowley, and they too were rather successful. Chatterton, however, disappointed and humiliated at the early discovery of his forgery, committed suicide when he was eighteen and thus became the hero of the later Romantic poets. Bishop **Thomas Percy's** *Reliques of Ancient English Poetry,* published in three volumes in 1765, is a mixture of folk ballads and poems from his own pen. His collection opened up the forgotten world of the ballad. Percy adapted its wild and coarse vigour to eighteenth-century taste.

Finally, two poets remain to be mentioned who are better described as individual figures, if not misfits, than within any particular literary period – **Robert Burns** and **William Blake.** Scotland's bard, **Burns** (1759-1796) was a farmer at Mossgiel until the publication of a collection of his poems opened for him the doors of fashionable society in Edinburgh where, for a brief period, he was admired as a peasant poet. In his personal life, he was the paradigmatic poetic rebel, revolting against the restraints of conventional morality and Scottish Presbyterianism[1] by indulging in drink and love affairs. Burns was capable of writing in two distinct styles: that of a cultivated English poet – he had read Pope, Gray, Thomson, and Shakespeare – and the rougher and more earthy style of his own land, although he obviously manipulated what are only seemingly naïve dialect pieces. A man of the land, Burns wrote about what he liked, including women and drink. His famous songs were greatly influenced by popular Scottish poetry. Ploughing up a mouse's nest, he wrote a perfectly serious ode "To a Mouse".

---

1. A Protestant form of church organization that has its origin in the teaching of John Calvin and was popular in Scotland and America. It implies the election of members of the church community who then serve as representatives of the church at general meetings called synods.

Apart from his songs and short poems, Burns went down in poetic history for his *Tam O'Shanter* (1791), a satirical poem written after his return from Edinburgh. It tells the story of Tam's encounter with witches and his breathtaking flight, described in a mixture of ironic distance and compassionate humour which make this satire a unique poem in English literature.

William Blake (1757-1827) has been called a Romantic poet. Some critics have interpreted his work, together with that of Wordsworth and Coleridge, as that of a member of the first generation of the Romantics. While his poetry is not devoid of Romantic themes and elements, it would be misleading to see him merely as a proponent of Romantic ideas and ideals. In fact, Blake's work as a painter, engraver, and poet – he tried to combine both the visual and the literary in his poems – is original enough to make it stand alone in English literature. Admittedly, he straddled the turn of the century and was a contemporary of several Romantic poets, yet only *Milton* (1804-1808) and *Jerusalem* (1804), his great prophetic books, appeared after 1800; the main bulk of his poetry was produced during the French revolutionary period. Using the twin arts of drawing and poetry, Blake depicted his visions and mystic views of life in a system of carefully created symbols and cosmic figures derived from various traditions. Blake printed most of his poetry himself, with the text in his own handwriting and illustrations commonly intertwined, by a method of etching he invented for the purpose. Modern editions of his lyrics, mostly type-set, cannot compete with the clarity and beauty of the original illustrated books produced by the poet. His widely known "The Tyger" – from *Songs of Experience* (1794) – is a good example. In this poem he juxtaposes beauty and fear, energy and terror, in a simple form and in symbolic allusions to contemporary events in France. William Blake saw himself as a prophet whose duty it was "to open the immortal Eyes of Man inwards into the Worlds of Thought, into Eternity" (*Jerusalem,* I, 5).

The Tiger

Tiger, tiger, burning bright
In the forests of the night,
What immortal hand or eye
Could frame thy fearful symmetry?

In what distant deeps or skies
Burnt the fire of thine eyes?
On what wings dare he aspire?
What the hand dare seize the fire?

And what shoulder and what art
Could twist the sinews of thy heart?
And when thy heart began to beat,
What dread hand? And what dread feet?

What the hammer? What the chain?
In what furnace was thy brain?
What the anvil? What dread grasp
Dare its deadly terrors clasp?

When the stars threw down their spears
And watered Heaven with their tears,
Did he smile his work to see?
Did he who made the Lamb make thee?

Tiger, tiger, burning bright
In the forests of the night,
What immortal hand or eye
Dare frame thy fearful symmetry?

If he is to be believed, Blake actually communicated with the angels and beings his pictures portray. His contemporaries misunderstood or ignored him, *The Examiner* dubbing Blake "an unfortunate lunatic," a term that stuck with him; and it was only in our century that the greatness of his visionary poetry has been recognized. Trained as an engraver, Blake developed a taste for Medieval and "Gothic" art which his imagination reworked into a huge mythology of his own making. In this he portrayed symbolically the forces always at war with each other in the soul of man. In his early *Songs of Innocence* (1789) and *Songs of Experience* (1794) he showed "the two contrary states of the human soul" that later took shape in the cosmic figures of Orc and Urizen. His *Marriage of Heaven and Hell* (1793) demonstrates his philosophic-visionary ideas in a world that is upside-down. God, in this book written mainly in prose, is a tyrant destroying his rebellious children, while Satan stands for energy and freedom. It is Satan who is cast into the role of Messias, and Hell offers truth. In the first of his mythical poems, *Visions of the Daughters of Albion* (1793), Blake exemplified what he saw as the disadvantages of laws and conventions. A rebel at heart and in his mind, and a prophet in words, William Blake wholeheartedly embraced revolutionary thought and action. He celebrated the events in France in *The French Revolution* (1791); he saw it not only as the liberation from political oppression, but also as the liberation of human imagination. In the same exuberant terms he welcomed the struggle for freedom of the American colonies. In his *America. A Prophecy* (1793) the American fight for independence appears in visions alluding to the Last Judgment. The hero of this poem is Orc, a rebellious Prometheus who puts to death the dragon of English tyranny. The action is set in the fabled continent of Atlantis. Blake's vision of history and life as a cycle appears in his symbolism, which draws on numerous European and Eastern

myths. His essential message is the identity of God and man, and the rejection of the mysterious God of the Church, of Deism, and of natural religion. But he also rejected the "common sense" of the Enlightenment and tried to pour his philosophy into one great epic: between 1795-1804 he worked on it, first calling it *Vala* and then *The Four Zoas,* developing the themes of the fall and the subsequent rise of man and the world. These themes are also significant in his final works, *Milton* and *Jerusalem.* In view of his visionary world view – Blake saw nature as the fallen world, not as God's magnificent creation – he must be seen as a poet at variance with his Romantic contemporaries. For when Wordsworth and Coleridge published their *Lyrical Ballads* (1798), a sort of manifesto of Romanticism, they defined nature as a central and positive force, as the great teacher of words and the prime bringer of happiness. William Blake, then, was an original and highly idiosyncratic poet and painter who carried eighteenth-century English poetry into the nineteenth century.

The bizarre and vastly fascinating world below the "genus grande" of eighteenth-century poetry is usually ignored by literary histories. Throughout the century Grub Street writers – poor hacks, journalists, and impoverished poets who catered to public taste and were badly paid by avaricious publishers – produced popular poetry, parodies, skits, and ballads that, more often than not, were as successful as the works of the great poets. Bawdy travesties of classical works became good sellers, such as Charles Cotton's *Scarronides* (1664), a scatological satire on the first and fourth books of the *Aenaeis* featuring a storm of farts. *Scarronides* went into more than ten editions and remained in demand for half a century. In a similar way, many of the century's great works were ridiculed in burlesque parodies ranging from the ribald to the obscene. Pope's *Rape of the Lock,* for instance, was mocked by Joseph Gay's *The Petticoat* (1716) and Giles Jacob's *The Rape of the Smock* (1727). John Wilkes's obscene *An Essay on Woman* (1763) made more headlines than its target, Pope's *Essay on Man.* The eighteenth century saw the end of the tradition of erotic bawdry, for the taste of the rising middle class forced coarser stuff – which had been publicly accepted in earlier centuries – underground. In their private clubs, aristocratic libertines continued the Restoration custom of writing erotic and comic verse (the **Earl of Rochester** remained popular in erotic poetry throughout the eighteenth century, but he found no true successor) and obscene songs, yet they were hardly heard of in public. But even without them, the average reader had great choice in the area of the "genus medium" or "genus humile" of poetry. One author writing in these genres was **Thomas Stretser**, who was employed by the notorious publisher Edmund Curll. In the manner of Charles Cotton's *Erotopolis. The Present State of Bettyland* (1684), Stretser produced a number of bawdy poems exploiting the established tradition of geographical or topographical allegory. In his *A New Description of Merryland* (1740) and *Merryland Displayed* (1741) Stretser describes the female body as if it were an unknown land. Both titles became best-sellers. Such poetry gradually disappeared after midcentury as the guardians of morality ushered in an unprecedented prudery in taste and manners to which Queen Victoria would later contribute her name.

3. Drama

The beginning of the eighteenth century saw the end of the boisterous, ribald, and witty Restoration comedy. In 1700 **William Congreve** (1670-1729) wrote one of the last and most brilliant plays of this genre, *The Way of the World,* which despite its initial failure still holds the stage. The central characters are Mirabell, an experienced and refined man of the world, and Millamant, a proud and beautiful coquette yet also intelligent and capable of love. The plot develops around Mirabell's successful attempt to win both Millamant and her fortune, and the unsuccessful intrigue of Fainall and Mrs. Marwood, who are after Lady Wishfort's money. The play presents an excellent combination of social criticism, comedy, and witty dialogue, and something quite unique in Restoration comedy – serious love and genuine affection. The two lovers, Mirabell and Millamant, are pitted against their corrupt enemies, and there are also a number of comical types, such as Witwould and Sir Wilfull Witwould, and the nymphomaniac Lady Wishfort. Congreve's greatness lies in the accuracy with which he shows the values of a shallow world. The elegant triumphs over the inelegant, and the witty over the dull. Sentiment hardly ever intrudes, and the closed doors of fashionable society keep out morality, too.

If *The Way of the World* is less coarse than previous comedies of manners, it is because criticism had set in against the "immorality" and "sinfulness" of Restoration society and its comic reflection in drama. In the prologue to his play, Congreve made a mocking allusion to an attack that had "reformed" the Londoners and their theatrical tastes. This was **Jeremy Collier's** *A Short View of the Immorality and Profaneness of the English Stage,* first published in 1698 and often reprinted and enlarged on in the eighteenth century. A clergyman and strict moralist, **Collier** (1658-1726), and some other writers, produced scholarly and elaborate accusations that brought the weight of the Church and middle-class society to bear against the drama.

The Puritan hostility towards the stage was one of the reasons why eighteenth-century drama produced only a few works of value. Congreve, for one, felt the impact of moralism. His *The Way of the World* was not well received and he renounced any further writing for the stage. The few comedies that appeared in the first decade of the new century express the gradual change of taste. Thus **George Farqu-**

Portrait of William Congreve
by Godfrey Kneller, 1709

har's plays are not true Restoration comedies; they indicate the transition to sentimental drama. In 1706 **Farquhar** (1678-1707) wrote *The Recruiting Officer,* a play not set in London – like previous comedies – but in Shrewsbury where Corporal Kite and Captain Plume demonstrate intricate problems of recruiting in a provincial town. The province, this time Litchfield, is also the setting of Farquhar's *The Beaux' Stratagem* (1707). Though he wrote it on his deathbed, the play is brimming with humour and action.

Aimwell and Archer, the penniless gallants known as types from earlier plays, arrive at an inn in Litchfield, in search of adventure and money. They hide their identities, Archer passing as Aimwell's servant. Boniface, the landlord, concludes that they are highwaymen. Dorinda, daughter of the wealthy Lady Bountiful, falls in love with Aimwell – in church – and the latter manages to get admitted to Lady Bountiful's house, together with Archer who has fallen in love with Mrs. Sullen, the wife of Lady Bountiful's son. Aimwell and Archer rescue the ladies during an attack by rogues, and they both intend to cash in on the advantage thus gained. But Aimwell, who has posed as his elder and wealthy brother, confesses the fraud in the presence of the trustful Dorinda. Good news arrives of the death of Aimwell's brother and of the accession of Aimwell to title and fortune. Sullen agrees to the dissolution of his marriage, and all ends happily with Mrs. Sullen free to marry Archer, and Aimwell his Dorinda.

With the plays of George Farquhar, the comedy of manners came to an end. Drama in general, and comedy in particular, then suffered a sad decline. A number of causes contributed to this development. To begin with, the moralists gradually achieved their aims, which meant that comedy became less shocking, less witty, and much duller. Dramatists no longer wrote for the nobility, the audience of Restoration comedy, but more and more for the middle class. Sentimentality was substituted for wit, and the Italian opera,[1] pantomime, and "entertainments" stole much of the limelight from drama. In 1737 the Licensing Act[2] restricted dramatists' freedom of expression, driving a number of good men out of the theatre – among them Henry Fielding who turned to the novel as a more exciting field. The Licensing Act was the government's answer to political allusions and slander on the stage. By 1747, when theatrical activity was completely halted, the theatres had to resort to clever advertising if they wanted to survive. To evade the law, patrons were now invited to attend "exhibitions", "coffee and pictures", etc. It is hardly surprising then that the outstanding work in the early decades of the cen-

---

1. Italian opera became a very popular form of theatrical entertainment in the eighteenth century. Italian singers, such as Senesino, worked in London and were known throughout the country. Significantly, the German-born Georg Friedrich Händel (1685-1759), who settled in London and became a naturalized Englishman, had the libretti of his operas written in Italian (e. g. *Rinaldo,* 1711).
2. Many plays in the early eighteenth century contained social and political satire and obvious allusions to such politicians as Walpole, prime minister from 1715 – 17 and 1721 – 42. Matters came to a head when Walpole was satirized in Gay's *The Beggar's Opera* (1728), and in some of Fielding's farces (e. g. *Pasquin,* 1736). In 1737 Walpole introduced the Licensing Act. This made the Lord Chamberlain licenser of theatres in London and Westminster. All plays were now censored before they could be performed. The Act brought Fieldings's career in the theatre to an end and has been blamed for the decline of English drama in the 18th century.

tury was not a traditional comedy but John Gay's musical play, *The Beggar's Opera* (1728). This burlesque arose out of a suggestion by Swift to Gay that a play set in Newgate would be an "odd pretty sort of thing."

The main characters are Peachum, a fence and informer; his pretty daughter, Polly; Lockit, warder of Newgate prison, and his daughter Lucy; and Captain Macheath, highwayman and lighthearted winner of women's hearts. Polly falls in love with the robber, who marries her. But when her father informs against Macheath, Polly's husband is arrested and sent to Newgate. Here he conquers Lucy's heart, and both women have a spirited conflict. Lucy overcomes her jealousy and makes possible the escape of Macheath.

A great success, this play was the English response to the Italian opera that was beginning to flow into London. As it contains numerous satirical allusions to the Whigs and Walpole, the latter managed to have the sequel to the play, *Polly,* banned. The great charm and deliberately unromantic setting of the *Beggar's Opera* attracted Bertolt Brecht in our century who brought it up to date in *The Threepenny Opera.*

The gradual intrusion of middle-class values into drama is also obvious in tragedy. **Joseph Addison's** *Cato* (1713) is very much a rigid Neoclassical play in blank verse and with the strict observation of time and place. **Nicholas Rowe** wrote *The Fair Penitent* (1703), an extremely successful tragedy in blank verse which is much concerned with emotions and sentiment. But it was with **George Lillo** (1693-1739) that domestic tragedy arrived in plays with great moral emphasis and melodramatic themes with a wide and immediate appeal. Very little is known about Lillo, who was possibly the descendant of Flemish refugees. With *The London Merchant, or the History of George Barnwell* (1731) he wrote a play whose influence extended beyond English literature.

In this drama, for the first time, the lives of ordinary people are portrayed with all the seriousness which had been formerly restricted to the upper strata of society. It is based on an old ballad and deals with the seduction of Barnwell, an apprentice, by the heartless courtesan Millwood. Barnwell becomes so infatuated that he not only robs his employer, Thorowgood, but is even induced by Millwood to murder his uncle. For this crime Millwood and Barnwell are executed.

But tragedy was not as popular as the new sentimental comedy. The plays of **Richard Steele** (1672-1729), for instance, such as *Grief à-la-Mode* (1701), *The Lying Lover* (1703), and his successful *The Tender Husband* (1705), and *The Conscious Lovers* (1722) are a sort of propaganda of bourgeois virtues, and dramatic presentations of moral lessons. The depths of sentimentalism were reached in Hugh Kelly's *False Delicacy* (1768) and Richard Cumberland's *The West Indian* (1771), both obscuring human issues in a welter of emotions. A few playwrights like **Colley Cibber** (1671-1757) and **George Colman the Elder** (1732-94) tried to stem the tide of sentimentality with more humorous plays. But they were less successful than **Henry Fielding** whose plays from the 1730s are the only ones worth remembering from this period. Refusing to write in Steele's manner, Fielding made comedy the vehicle of social satire. There is a great resemblance between his plays and his novels, which both attack the moral corruption of the

high and mighty. In *The Modern Hus-band* (1732), for instance, the protagonist lives on the proceeds of his wife's prostitution. Fielding was best in the area of burlesque farce. His greatest success in this genre was *The Tragedy of Tragedies, or the Life and Death of Tom Thumb the Great* (1731). Ridiculing contemporary playwrights and heroic tragedy in particular, it tells the story of Tom Thumb at the court of King Arthur, where he kills millions of giants, falls in love with the princess Huncamunca, and is swallowed by a cow. In a sort of Hollywood show-down, the members of the court then kill each other.

By mid-century, however, when Fielding and others had turned their backs on the theatre, drama had become so feeble that a blood-transfusion was needed. Two Irishmen, **Oliver Goldsmith** (1730?-74) and **Richard Brinsley Sheridan** (1751-1816), breathed new life into comedy. Goldsmith attacked the sentimental drama, calling it "bastard tragedy", and praised the virtues of what he termed "laughing comedy", the kind of comedy of manners Sheridan and he wrote. His early play, *The Good-Natured Man* (1768), is not a particularly good example of his principles; but with *She Stoops to Conquer* (1773) he wrote a masterpiece. Its plot, though highly improbable, adds appreciably to the humour of the play by creating hilarious situations.

The major characters are Hardcastle, his wife, and their daughter. There are also Mrs. Hardcastle's son by a former marriage, Tony Lumpkin, an ignorant, idle, and mischievous drunk who is spoiled by his mother; and young Marlow, a womanizer posing as a bashful young man. Marlow and his friend are on their way to pay the Hardcastles a visit, since Sir Charles Marlow has proposed a match between his son and Miss Hardcastle. However, young Marlow loses his way and ends up in Tony Lumpkin's favourite pub, where he is directed to a "neighbouring inn", which is really the Hardcastles' house. The resulting misunderstanding – Marlow treating Hardcastle as the landlord of the "inn" and taking his daughter for one of the servants – contributes to the fun of the play. It is with the arrival of Sir Charles Marlow that the misunderstanding is cleared up, and all ends well.

Sheridan's achievement is even greater than Goldsmith's. His fame rests upon three comedies, *The Rivals* (1775); *The School for Scandal* (1777); and *The Critic* (1779). Sheridan was early distracted from his career as a dramatist and in 1780 became a successful politician. He brought back to comedy something of the brilliance of Restoration dialogue, tempered with a more genial and romantic atmosphere. *The Rivals,* written when he was only 24, shows him as a master of comical situations, good characterization, and elegant dialogue. The play exposes the foibles and preoccupations of the fashionable society at Bath, with several love-affairs and intrigues. It features, among other characters, Mrs. Malaprop, who has gone down in theatrical history as the stock type misapplying long words. Sheridan's *The School for Scandal* has become a classic English comedy.

Sheridan's best play contrasts two brothers, Joseph Surface, a hypocrite, and Charles Surface, a kind though reckless spendthrift. Charles is in love with Maria, the ward of Sir Peter Teazle, and Maria returns his affection. Joseph courts her for her fortune, and at the same time declares his love for Lady Teazle. Sir Peter suffers from the frivolity of his young wife, which provides the conversational topics for the scandal-mongers, Sir Benjamin Backbite, Lady Sneerwell, and Mrs. Candour. When Sir Oliver Surface, the rich uncle of Joseph and Charles, returns from India, he decides to test the characters of his nephews before revealing his true identity. The following scenes prove Joseph's wickedness while Charles wins his uncle's heart. Finally, Charles is united to Maria, and Sir Peter is reconciled to Lady Teazle.

Sheridan's third comedy, *The Critic,* is a farcical satire on the pretensions of contemporary tragedy and sentimental drama, but also on the aggressive literary criticism of the day. With its verbal dexterity and sarcastic humour, it is brilliantly funny. However, Sheridan was exceptional, and eighteenth-century drama was a rather dry stretch relieved by only a few oases. Literary greatness was achieved in other areas.

4. The Novel

The appearance and quick success of the novel fluttered the literary dove-cotes of eighteenth-century England. Until well into the second half of the century, many critics regarded the novel as a new and inferior invention. Poetry remained in high esteem. It is significant that Henry Fielding, when he turned to prose fiction after 1737, called his novels "comic epic poems in prose". Despite the bad reception the novel was initially given, its victorious advance could not be stopped.

The rise of the novel owes much both to the increasing importance of readers and authors from the middle class and the introduction of an element of realism in prose fiction. The man who experimented most with the representation of realism in prose writing was **Daniel Defoe** (c. 1660-1731). A dissenter[1] from the lower middle class, Defoe had a bizarre career that mirrors his interests and achievements: he was in turn shopkeeper, journalist, and government spy; he was a bankrupt, an inventor, and a traveller; and he stood in the pillory and was on several occasions imprisoned. Daniel Defoe was a bigot and hypocrite at heart. At the age of forty he added the genteel French prefix "de" to his name, Foe; and he

1. Dissenter was another term for Nonconformist (see page 21, note 4).

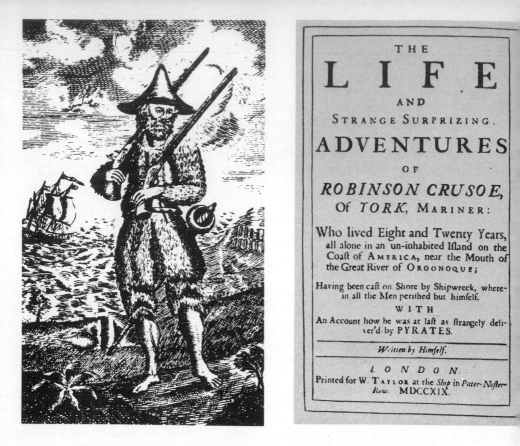

was capable of writing pamphlets against prostitutes, recommending to send them to the workhouse or to the colonies. But his factual fiction, his new way of writing, "the circumstantial method", helped to create what has come to be known as the novel. As a journalist, Defoe thought little of art and literary theory. He was fifty-nine when he wrote the first part of *The Life and Strange Surprising Adventures of Robinson Crusoe, of York, Mariner.* Before this successful book appeared, he had been publishing all sorts of journalistic, political, and moral tracts, among them *The Shortest Way with the Dissenters* (1702), a satire on the Church of England that was at first misunderstood; and *A True Relation of the Apparition of one Mrs Veal* (1706), a fictionalized ghost story based on actual contemporary events. Defoe enjoyed trying out new forms of prose in the border area between fact and fiction. *Robinson Crusoe* (1719), with its semblance of a travel report, its simple language, "authentic" narrator, and wealth of details, is just another example of his method. It became the first influential novel of the century. The story of the book is generally well known, having its basis in the true adventures of Alexander Selkirk, the sailor who lived alone for several years on the island of Juan Fernandez. Defoe supported it with his wide reading in travel literature, and with his own experiences. Crusoe embodies the practical and religious Englishman who makes good because he is diligent and pious. Cast in the autobiographical form of a diary, this novel, and others Defoe was to write, tried to create the impression of authenticity.

The reader was to regard it as true, not as fiction. Defoe avoided all stylistic decoration and fine writing, concentrating instead on the semblance of reality and on moralizing. *Robinson Crusoe* had an immediate and permanent success. It was translated into many languages and led to numerous imitations. Defoe exploited its success with two sequels, *The Farther Adventures of Robinson Crusoe* (1719), and the *The Serious Reflections ... of Robinson Crusoe* (1720). He then turned to stories with stronger picaresque elements. In *Captain Singleton* (1720), the hero, like Robinson, recounts his exotic adventures in Africa and as a pirate in the Pacific. *Colonel Jack* (1722) features a criminal, tracing the stages of his life as a thief, a servant, and as a slave owner and soldier in Europe and America. The structure of these novels is always the same: they are fictitious autobiographies with picaresque episodes. This is also the case with Defoe's best works, *Moll Flanders* (1722) and *Roxana* (1724). Both develop the theme of the single woman who is left to fend for herself. *Moll Flanders* shows Defoe at his best.

The protagonist of the novel, Moll, is born in Newgate prison, the daughter of a woman who is to be transported to Virginia for theft. Thus abandoned and left in ignorance of her origins, Moll grows up in the household of the compassionate mayor of Colchester. Although she is seduced very early in her life, she makes her fortune through a respectable marriage. However, upon the death of her husband, she goes through five marriages, some of them bigamous, and enters into all sorts of liaisons to earn money. When she visits Virginia, she discovers that her current husband is her half-brother. Leaving him behind, she returns to England and, for want of money, becomes a highly successful pickpocket and thief. When she is caught, she ends up in Newgate Gaol where she meets her future husband, James, a highwayman. They are both transported to Virginia, but they manage to take their gains with them. In America, Moll finds that she has inherited a plantation from her mother, and she and her husband spend the remainder of their lives in prosperity and penitence.

Roxana, also termed *The Fortunate Mistress,* presents a similar story but is set in a higher social class. The heroine is a kept woman who amasses wealth during her career in England and on the Continent. The novel has a rich social and cultural background but, like Defoe's other works of fiction, suffers from a lack of literary art. Defoe was too much interested in his themes and his moral message to care about the development of the novel as a literary genre.

In this he resembled Swift. If Daniel Defoe was a moralist, **Jonathan Swift** was a merciless satirist who believed that man had hardly advanced beyond the stage of barbarity. As a writer, Swift did not cherish the novel but rather short prose fiction and poetry. Like Defoe, Swift tried his hand at a number of literary and journalistic forms. He preferred to write prose satires or satirical essays. His target was the corruption he perceived in politics and the Church in particular, and in society in general. In *A Tale of a Tub* (1704) he tells the farcical and wildly funny story of three brothers – Jack, Martin and Peter, who represent Calvin, Luther, and the Catholic saint – and what they do with their inheritance, the Christian religion. Queen Anne was so shocked at this satire, which she considered blasphemy, that she would not allow the clergyman Swift to be made a bishop. In the most bitter of his prose satires, *A Modest Proposal* (1729), Swift defended

Ireland and ironically suggested that the terrible famine could be eased by canni-balism, and that the Irish children should serve as food for the rich. *Gulliver's Travels* (1726) is by far his greatest book, though it is not a novel in the usual and modern sense of the term.

Its form indicates Swift's debt to Defoe, for the preface tries to establish authenticity by declaring that Richard Sympson, the "editor" of the "book", had received documents from Lemuel Gulliver.

Gulliver begins his report with a factual record of his education and training in medicine and navigation, and of his first voyages as a ship's surgeon. In the same sober manner he introduces his first adventure, the sinking of his ship, and his struggle ashore as the sole survivor. Up to this point, the book reads as if it were written by Defoe. So the reader is lulled into confidence and credulity.

But then the tale takes a different turn in the scene of Gulliver's awakening, when he finds himself the prisoner of the Lilliputians. The description of life in the kingdom of Lilliput is one of the most devastating and painful satires in literature, once one realizes that Swift is really talking about English public life which he effectively lampoons. With the description of Gulliver's services for the Emperor, Swift parodies English politics – he even has Gulliver urinate on the palace in order to put out a serious fire. After some further adventures in the Empire of Blefescu, Gulliver returns home to England, but only to finance another voyage by exhibiting Lilliputian cattle he has brought with him.

'A Voyage to Brobdingnag' has the same introduction as part I. This time, Gulliver is cast among the giants and suffers from the huge animal world around him. The King's unex-pected and disgusted reaction to Gulliver's proud report on eighteenth-century English social and political institutions mirrors Swift's anger and contempt. An eagle carries off the hero and drops him into the sea, where an English ship eventually picks him up.

To the modern reader, part III of the book, entitled 'A Voyage to Laputa, Luggnagg, Glubbdudrib and Japan', is perhaps the one that is the most difficult to understand because it is a satirical attack on targets of Swift's own period. The most fascinating voyage Gulliver undertakes is the one which leads him to the land of the wise horses known as Houyhnhnms and contrasted with the dirty, man-like creatures called Yahoos. A good deal of this section of the book consists of conversations, debates, and general descriptions of the Houyhnhnm view of life; this creates an atmosphere of grave discourse and also sets the satirical tone, showing the eighteenth-century Englishman as vastly inferior to intelligent, clever and reasonable horses. Every question the horses put to Gulliver elicits answers that inexorably reveal the evil uses to which men have put their much-praised faculty of rea-son.

Gulliver returns to England. This time, his readjustment takes much longer, and the process is brilliantly shown by a great number of details.

With this book Swift conveyed terrible truths about human nature and civilization, so much so that many critics see misanthropy as the predominant element in *Gulliver's Travels.* This is certainly too exaggerated a view, for Swift's rich satirical resources and his wit tone down his sarcastic message and show an amazing vitality of imagination. It has been argued that *Gulliver's Travels* is not a novel but rather a string of loosely connected adventures. But there is an undeniable purpose of arrangement in this book, and an organic unity which helps create the total impact. *Gulliver's Travels* is thus an early example of the fable type of novel, with such modern descendants as Butler's *Erewhon* (1872), and Orwell's *Animal Farm* (1945), to name just two examples.

Daniel Defoe believed in common sense and in the advancement of civilization, and he created prototypes of the realistic novel. Swift, however, was a skeptic; his *Gulliver's Travels* is to be seen within the tradition of the Utopian travel report distorted by exaggeration and parody. Defoe was simple, serious, and moralistic; Swift was ironic, complex, and satirical. What they had in common was a disregard of formal aspects – they were more interested in what they had to say.

Robinson Crusoe and *Gulliver's Travels* have the rare merit of appealing to both old and young, and the versions for children are still being widely read. This is not the case with the novels of **Samuel Richardson**. But it was Richardson who, after the death of Defoe, did most for the flowering of the novel in England. **Richardson** (1689–1761) was the son of a joiner and was trained as a professional printer. Asked by a publisher to prepare a series of model letters for those who could not write for themselves, he composed love-letters and others for use on various occasions. Thus he discovered that he had the gift of expressing himself in letters. His three major works – *Pamela* (1740), *Clarissa* (1747/8), and *Sir Charles Grandison* (1754) – are all novels in the form of a series of letters. It was with *Pamela* that he had an instant and spectacular success.

Pamela is the first example of the modern English novel of character. Pamela Andrews, the heroine, tells her story in a series of letters while she is employed as a lady's servant. When the story opens, Pamela's mistress has just died, and the young servant girl is pursued by the lady's son, Mr. B., who takes dishonourable advantage of Pamela's position. He attempts everything he can to force her to his will, even imprisoning her in the charge of two villains, Mrs. Jewkes and Monsieur Colbrand. At one stage, Mr. B. is on the point of raping her, but he is scared off when she swoons. Pamela indignantly repels all his advances, and finally B., being much in love with her, decides, despite her humble birth and position, to marry her.

In 1742 Richardson added a second part, showing Pamela and Mr. B. in happy married life, which is merely interrupted by a brief interlude when he becomes involved with a widowed countess at a masked ball. With dignity and sweetness, Pamela suffers the burden of an occasionally profligate husband. This second part, to a modern reader, has an almost unbearable moral tone.

Pamela's victory is a strange sort of reward, and the morality of the book is somewhat dubious nowadays, for it is obvious that her fight for virtue is also governed by downright calculation. Her chastity is a commodity to be bargained for, and she never considers Mr. B.'s true character, which is that of a vicious, cruel libertine. The novel has a number of unpleasant aspects, such as a prurient inquisitiveness about women, and a combination of stern morality and a secret interest in sexual matters. Ian Watt, in *The Rise of the Novel* (1957) rightly called *Pamela* a striptease in the form of a sermon.

But the novel has some positive aspects. For the first time in the history of prose fiction, a writer put the war of the sexes and the class war at the centre of a novel. Pamela's story of success naturally appealed to exploited servant girls, and above all to middle-class women. Yet *Pamela* is more than just an eighteenth-century social document, for with this novel Richardson gave a new dimension to prose fiction. The technique of letter-writing, which was not invented by Richardson, was not as awkward and restricting as it might seem at first glance. Of course, seen in a realistic light, Pamela - an eighteenth-century servant girl - is unusually well educated and writes an unnaturally large number of letters of interminable length. The novel as a genre, however, profited from this technique. Introducing an element of control, it led to a tightening of plot through a strong organizing principle that was lacking in earlier works of fiction. The new method also enabled Richardson to describe immediate impressions, thus providing analyses of conduct and consciousness. In many respects they are prophetic of the modern "stream of consciousness" in the novels of James Joyce and Virginia Woolf. Thus *Pamela* was an important breakthrough in the development of the English novel. For the modern reader, though, its negative aspects, such as the priggish morality and the lengthy and boring didactic passages, are too obvious, and more often than not too much stressed. It has more historic than artistic value.

Richardson's second novel, *Clarissa, or the History of a Young Lady,* was published in seven volumes and is probably the longest novel in the English language. A sort of pendant to *Pamela,* the novel has as its major character a young lady of wealth and beauty, virtue and innocence, who, in order to avoid a marriage her parents are trying to arrange, seeks help from Lovelace, a handsome yet unscrupulous young man. Lovelace drugs and rapes Clarissa. Repentant, he asks her to marry him, but she refuses. Worn out by shame, she dies, leaving Lovelace to his remorse. Though this sounds like the plot from a cheap modern novelette, *Clarissa* offers close analysis of character, and a complexity of make-up in some figures that is most unusual in the literature of the age.

Sir Charles Grandison introduces a hero full of the highest virtues, and so moral that, to the reader, he becomes unbearably perfect.

It is undeniable that Richardson influenced later novelists - even those, like Fielding and Smollett, who consciously wrote in reaction against him. What he introduced into fiction were the analysis of emotion and motive, introspection, and the belief in the value of feeling. Richardson's combination of emotion, sensibility, and morality, presented in a form accommodating psychological realism, touched the hearts of European readers. From this point in the history of the novel, it was only a short step to the sentimental as it was demonstrated by Sterne's *Tristram Shandy* and, later, by Dickens and Thackery.

Henry Fielding (1707-54) disliked Richardson's work, and both writers waged literary war almost continuously, Fielding satirizing *Pamela* with his *Shamela* (1741) and *Joseph Andrews* (1742), and Richardson creating Charles Grandison as a counterpart to Fielding's *Tom Jones* (1749). Like Richardson, Fielding was very conscious of the literary genre, the novel, but his approach and viewpoint were fundamentally different from Richardson's mixture of Puritan-bourgeois morality and sensitive psychology. Fielding developed a type of novel that is comic and realistic, and which features not ideal protagonists, but men and women with typical human faults. Fielding's plots are characterized by the picaresque and by comments from an ironic and understanding author. Educated at Eton and in

64

Gin Lane, an engraving by William Hogarth, 1751

Leyden, Henry Fielding came from an upper middle-class family with aristocratic branches. Until Sir Robert Walpole's Licensing Act of 1737 drove his plays from the stage, Fielding was a moderately successful playwright. He became a lawyer and then a political journalist before being appointed Justice of the Peace for Westminster and Middlesex. As such he was indefatigable in his duties and the originator of many reforms. His novels may be a by-product of a busy career, but they also express his first-hand knowledge of the social conditions in eighteenth-century England. It was Fielding's friend, William Hogarth,[1] who gave pictorial expression to the social problems of the age, and Fielding voiced his own criticism and moral message in novels whose social panorama, humour, and literary finesse make them masterpieces of eighteenth-century fiction. Essentially, Fielding saw himself as a moralist and satirist; and it was as a satirist that he launched into his novel-writing career.

With *Shamela*, Fielding ridiculed the content and method of Richardson's *Pamela*. The pun of the title ("sham") indicates the heroine's hypocrisy. Her virginity and innocence are merely means to an end, the end being the property of the man she wants to marry. Fielding also mocked Richardson's epistolary form by having Shamela write in impossible situations and in a style that is studded with grammatical and lexical mistakes. His first major work in fiction, *Joseph Andrews* (1742), also started out as a parody of *Pamela:* Joseph was devised to serve as Pamela's brother, but Fielding then developed his novel into something far bigger than a mere skit.

Joseph is the brother of Richardson's Pamela, a role which provided Fielding with a useful device for exposing the priggish and calculating elements in Pamela's behaviour. As a hand-

---

1. William Hogarth (1697-1764), an important English painter and engraver. He provided the illustrations for several works of literature, including 12 engravings for Butler's *Hudibras.* Hogarth became immensely popular with his series of engravings on what he termed "modern moral subjects": *The Harlot's Progress* (1732) describes the career and the death of a prostitute; *The Rake's Progress* (1733-35) traces the steps of a libertine toward ruin and madness; and *Marriage à la Mode* (1743-45) depicts the tragic consequences of a marriage arranged by greedy parents. Fielding and Smollett were two writers who cherished the art of Hogarth and compared characters and scenes in their novels to his prints. Hogarth's moralism is obvious in the series mentioned above, and in his later engravings, the *Industry and Idleness* series (1747) and the two prints *Beer Street* and *Gin Lane* (1750-51).

William Hogarth, *The Rake's Progress* (1735)
Plate 1: The young heir takes possession of the miser's effects

Plate 3: Tavern Scene

Plate 4: Arrested for debt as going to court

Plate 6: Gaming House
Scene

Plate 7: Prison Scene

Plate 8: Scene in Bedlam

some young footman, Joseph has to fight for his virtue against the amorous advances of his employer, Lady Booby. Joseph resists, mainly because of his sweetheart, Fanny, and is dismissed from Lady Booby's service. On his way home he is attacked by robbers who leave him half-dead by the roadside. Discovered by the passengers of a passing stage-coach, he is carried to an inn and there he meets an old friend and mentor, Abraham Adams, a curate. Parson Adams decides to accompany Joseph on his journey. They encounter all kinds of characters and meet with numerous adventures, Adams getting into a number of hilarious situations. Finally arriving in Joseph's home town, they prepare Joseph's wedding. Unfortunately, however, Lady Booby has also arrived at her country seat in the same village, and she tries to avenge herself on Joseph by having him and Fanny arrested for stealing a hazel twig. Just before being sent to prison, they are saved by the arrival of Lady Booby's son, Squire Booby, and his newly-wed wife, Pamela. The Squire rescues both Joseph and Fanny, and when it turns out that Joseph is really the son of gentlefolk, he can finally marry his Fanny and live on a property given him by his new-found parents. Parson Adams gets a comfortable living by Squire Booby while Lady Booby sets off for London to find solace in the arms of a young captain of dragoons.

For this novel, and for the others that followed, Fielding drew on ancient classical authors as far as style and narrative method are concerned. But he was also indebted to medieval satires and morality plays, and to the works of François Rabelais and the dramatist Molière. The greatest influence was exerted, as Fielding himself admitted, by Cervantes's *Don Quixote* (1605) and Le Sage's *Gil Blas* (1715-1735), the most influential picaresque novels for eighteenth-century writers. From drama, Fielding took the idea of types. In Lady Booby and her amorous maid, Mrs. Slipslop, but above all in Abraham Adams, he created some of the most significant comic characters in English literature. Parson Adams, however, is not merely a figure of fun. Like Cervantes's Don Quixote, he demonstrates the vast difference between the ideals of Christianity and its practice in contemporary society. More often than not, Fielding contrasts Adams's genuine Christian charity with the harshness and superficiality of people who live by materialistic standards while paying lip-service to those of Christianity. Adams is thus in many respects the real hero of the novel, which shows that Fielding was as much a moralist as Richardson, for beneath the lively comedy of *Joseph Andrews* there are the ever-present themes of charity and justice.

Henry Fielding's theory of the novel as put down in the preface to *Joseph Andrews* helps one to understand his work, even though in practice he did not always abide by his rules. His experience as a writer of comedies and burlesque plays often shows in the characterization and the structure of his novels. In his satirical novel, *The History of the Life of the Late Mr. Jonathan Wild the Great* (1743), he produced a fictional biography of a thief and organizer of robberies who had been hanged at Tyburn, London, in 1725. Fielding describes Wild as the superman of crime, a man beyond good and evil, and demonstrates the small division between a great criminal and a great soldier – or a politician like Sir Robert Walpole, who is one of the satirical butts of the novel. With *Jonathan Wild* Fielding also parodied contemporary history writing and the popular epic celebrating great personages.

It was with *Tom Jones* (1749) that Fielding came nearest to the realization of his own concept of the novel. *Tom Jones* is three times as long as *Joseph Andrews,* but it has a better coherence of plot.

The hero of the novel is discovered as an infant in the house of the wealthy and benevolent Mr. Allworthy, who lives in a country house in Somerset with his sister Bridget. Allworthy, who assumes that a nurse, Jenny Jones, is the mother of the child, takes a fancy to the boy and decides to bring him up. Jenny and the alleged father, Benjamin Partridge, leave the neighbourhood.

Tom Jones grows up with the son of Bridget Allworthy. Bridget's husband, Captain Blifil, dies a few years after the birth of young Blifil. It turns out that Tom is good-natured and easy-going while Blifil is clever, hypocritical, and nasty. Several times, Blifil tries to get Tom into trouble. Blifil ingratiates himself with their tutors – Square, the philosopher, and Thwackum, the parson – and Tom has to endure many beatings at their hands. The situation is not eased when Tom finds Square in bed with Molly Seagrim, the gamekeeper's daughter.

Tom now makes the acquaintance of Sophia, daughter of Squire Western, the owner of a neighbouring estate and a hard-drinking, hard-riding, and hard-swearing man. Squire Western likes Tom because of his manliness, and Tom and Sophia fall in love.

Meanwhile, Blifil also has his eye on Sophia, and when her aunt arrives from London, a marriage is prepared between Blifil and Sophia, the aunt misunderstanding Sophia's feelings. Blifil manages to convince Allworthy to banish Tom from his house, and Sophia Western, refusing to marry Blifil, sets out for her aunt's house in London. The following part of the novel traces Tom's picaresque journey to London, during which he quarrels at an inn, meets his future companion, Partridge, and rescues a lady named Mrs. Waters. She lures him to bed in an inn at Upton, where Sophia has also arrived. Furious at Tom's infidelity, she departs with Mrs. Fitzpatrick. In London, Sophia is introduced to several important people, among them the sophisticated and lecherous Lady Bellaston, who takes the naive Sophia under her wing.

When Tom arrives in London, he is seduced and kept by Lady Bellaston; but when he meets Sophia in her house, the two lovers are reconciled. More adventures now follow. It is discovered that Mrs. Waters is none other than Jenny Jones, which shocks Tom, for he thinks he has committed incest. But eventually the truth is revealed – Tom's real mother is Bridget, Mr. Allworthy's sister. The odious Blifil is banished, though, at Tom's insistence, with a yearly stipend, and all ends happily, with Tom and Sophia married and living on Squire Western's estate.

It is quite obvious that the story of the novel depends on the stock theatrical contrivances of the day, such as tag names (Allworthy, Thwackum, etc.), missing heirs, incredible coincidences, and accidental meetings. Yet Fielding handles his plot with great dexterity, and even the minor figures contribute directly to its unfolding. The structure is also quite impressive: the first section, consisting of six books, deals with events in Somerset (the country); the second section, also six books, takes us to the road; and the third section, again divided into six books, carries the action to London (the city). Thus the formal structure of *Tom Jones* adheres even more to classical models than that of *Joseph Andrews.* Fielding also introduces into the narrative numerous allusions and what he calls "similes" – most of them derived from the ancient classics, such as mock-heroic battles. As an author, Fielding constantly interferes in the narrative, holding up the action and weakening the illusion of the reader. What he wanted to achieve with this method was to counteract the dangerous falsities and evasions of reality of romantic illusion. As a matter of fact, Fielding becomes a member of the cast, so to speak, discussing the philosophical and moral issues arising from the actions of the characters. Seen in modern terms, this moral commentary may be a deficiency – moderns like Henry James believe that the art of fiction demands that everything should be conveyed through the words and actions of the characters. But Fielding attempted a combination of story, character, and authorial comment, a combination that is not altogether unconvincing.

Compared with other eighteenth-century novels, *Tom Jones* offers superb characterization, including not representatives of virtue but almost unheroic figures. Tom, for instance, is brave and generous, but he also has no control over his impulses and instincts; he is, in other words, an ordinary human being. Weak and even immoral as he may be on occasion, Tom does not enjoy his sins, and he is able to learn and to repent. *Tom Jones* is thus not an immoral book because Tom goes to bed with several women and indulges with Lady Bellaston. The novel is, in fact, moral insofar as Fielding suggests that there are worse sins than those of the flesh. Tom regrets his immoral behaviour, and he makes amends. By contrast, Richardson's Pamela is too angelic to be a realistic character and to convince the reader.

In *Tom Jones* Fielding addresses himself to a wide range of moral and social issues that include his satirizing of pretension and hypocrisy and his appeal for tolerance and Christian charity. In essence, his authorial comments are meant to carry these issues to a higher intellectual and philosophical plane and thus to educate the reader.

If *Tom Jones* is still a popular novel today, it is because of its rich variety of characters, each with his own individualistic idiom, and its acceptable philosophy of man's nature. These aspects are ideally complemented by boisterous humour and good sense.

Fielding's most fully drawn heroine is Amelia, in the novel of that name published in 1751. As Fielding idealizes the main woman character, this leads to an excess of pathos depriving *Amelia* of the balance which *Tom Jones* possesses. From a literary viewpoint, the domestic novel *Amelia* is not quite successful. It lacks Fielding's earlier lively spirit and exhibits deficiencies in plot and characterization. So *Tom Jones* remains incomparably his finest novel. As far as plot and character are concerned, Fielding dominated the English novel for more than a century.

Henry Fielding's influence can perhaps best be studied in the novels of **Tobias Smollett** (1721-71). Born in Scotland, Smollett studied medicine and later became a ship's surgeon. To the novel he brought nothing that was new in form, but he introduced a background of realistic and picaresque descriptions of low life. To this he added a superficial element of sentiment. Smollett's most characteristic novel is *Roderick Random,* published anonymously in 1748.

Roderick Random is closely modelled on Smollett's early career. The hero, a Scot of gentle birth and much neglected during his youth, sets out for London together with his friend

Strap. There, Roderick is cheated by a succession of rogues. After serving as the assistant of a French apothecary, he falls into the hands of a press gang, and so joins the navy, though not in the role he had imagined for himself. He is present at the siege of Cartagena (like Smollett himself), is shipwrecked and robbed and, as the footman of an eccentric poetess, falls in love with her niece, Narcissa. Other adventures follow thick and fast. After his return to England, Roderick is kidnapped by smugglers and even joins the French army. Back in London, he tries unsuccessfully to marry a rich heiress, but losing all his money in gambling he is thrown into prison for debt. He is saved by the appearance of his uncle, and embarks on a journey to South America, where he meets his long-lost father, now a rich trader. Together they return to Scotland. Roderick's father buys back the family estates and helps his son to marry Narcissa.

The plot of the book is much like those of Defoe's novels in its disjointed series of adventures among sailors, soldiers, and city scoundrels. Also, the influence of *Don Quixote* and *Gil Blas* is quite obvious. Thus *Roderick Random* belongs firmly to the old picaresque tradition, showing society from below in realistic descriptions and caricature-like figures. Smollett's strong points are fast and furious action and muscular prose, and he provides vigorous pictures of naval life.

The picaro's series of comic travels is the basic pattern in all of Smollett's novels. *Peregrine Pickle* (1751), though stressing erotic aspects, relates the adventures of a swashbuckling sailor on land, who meets with all sorts of adventures in England and on the Continent. And Smollett's last novel, too, *The Expedition of Humphrey Clinker* (1771), which reverts to Richardson's technique of telling the story in the form of a series of letters, is fundamentally a picaresque novel. Smollett translated the novels of Cervantes and Le Sage. His own *The Adventures of Sir Launcelot Greaves,* published between 1760 and 1761, tried to transpose Don Quixote to English soil. But Smollett also developed themes and methods that were to influence later writers. His *Ferdinand Count Fathom* (1753) features an utterly evil character, and the book foreshadows the horror scenes of the Gothic novel toward the end of the century. With his gallery of curious characters, Smollett gave important impulses to his own countryman, Walter Scott, and to the early Dickens. Smollett is remembered not for his literary art, but for his gift as a fabulist.

The most eccentric novel of the eighteenth century ist **Laurence Sterne's** *The Life and Opinions of Tristram Shandy, Gentleman* (1759-67). It breaks all the rules, including those of language and punctuation, and deliberately avoids even the idea of a traditional plot. Although written in the first person, the novel arrives at the hero's birth only half-way through the book. It may not be easy to pidgeonhole *Tristram Shandy,* yet as a novel it is indebted to both Richardson and Fielding. From Fielding, **Sterne** (1713-68) borrowed his method of authorial intrusion and ironic yet lenient commentary, and from Richardson he took the seemingly spontaneous dialogue between a writer/speaker and his addressee. Essentially, Laurence Sterne tried to show with *Tristram Shandy* the difficulties involved in writing a novel and in communicating with language. His achievement consists in the development of both ironic distance and emotional subjectivity.

Characteristically, there is very little of the "life", and even less of the "opinions", of the hero in this book. Instead, there is a group of humorous figures: Walter Shandy, the hero's father,

The Siege of Namur (detail) by Bunbury, 1773

who is wrapped up in all kinds of fantastic and paradoxical notions which he defends with an impressive parade of pseudo-scientific learning; "my Uncle Toby", his brother, wounded in the groin at the siege of Namur and, though a gentle and modest man, a dedicated follower of the science of fortifications and military attacks; and Corporal Trim, Toby's servant and assistant in his "war games". Behind these three major figures, Yorick the parson, Dr. Slop, an incompetent local quack, and the widow Wadman play important roles, and there is a gallery of minor characters.

The first three volumes of the novel are mainly concerned, besides many digressions, with the circumstances attending the hero's birth, such as the precise date and manner of Tristram's conception. Eventually, the narration arrives at the night of Tristram's birth. The incompetent Dr. Slop is summoned, and he manages to flatten Tristram's nose with his forceps, mistaking the infant's hip for its head. After the birth, Sterne finds time to write his preface, and then Tristram's story is resumed, with numerous digressions and discussions of noses, the naming of babies, and with the unfortunate incident in which Tristram is "unmanned" by a closing window. Much of volume VI of the novel is concerned with the breeching of Tristram; and volumes VII and VIII abandon the story altogether to describe the author's travels in France and to relate the story of the King of Bohemia. The last volume is concerned mainly with Uncle Toby and the amorous advances of the widow Wadman. Featuring a naive and bewildered Toby, and an enterprising widow who is curious to find out where exactly Toby was wounded, this is one of the high and bawdy points of the book. Finally, when Corporal Trim enlightens his master as to the real intentions of the widow, Toby makes a hasty retreat from the danger of marriage.

Tristram Shandy is a parody of many things, among them the methods of telling a story, and the various types of learning and pedantry. Like Swift, Sterne ridicules pseudo-scientific lore. Much of Sterne's humour, when it is not erotic or bawdy, is based on the parody of the theory of the association of ideas as expounded by John Locke in his vastly influential Essay Concerning Human Understanding (1690). Language in Tristram Shandy is always ambiguous, which leads to great misunderstandings and hilarious situations.

Sterne's psychological approach in this novel marked an advance in sophistication – like human beings, Sterne's characters are strange and unpredictable, and the novel shows that behaviour is governed as much by heredity as by environment. Sterne's notion of time, and its handling, are extremely modern. Based on Locke's theory, time is shown to be both subjective and objective; Sterne employs time on several levels, always playing with eighteenth-century conceptions of how man notices the passing of time. Tristram Shandy is a far more coherent book than its apparent formlessness would suggest. Despite Sterne's constant play with formal elements, such as typography, his novel possesses an inherent unity, which is, however, not that of normal chronological sequence. The story of the book, if story it can be called, is closely bound to the narrator and his method of telling his tale, which is the association of ideas. It is this principle which allows Sterne great variation in plot and chronology.

Tristram Shandy made Sterne a literary celebrity in the whole of Europe. Some critics objected to his frequent use of "double entendre" and bawdy humour. The sentimental passages of the book were generally preferred to Sterne's rough humour, which often borders on the obscene. In his second book, *A Sentimental Journey Trough France and Italy* (1768), he tried to accommodate critical voices and contemporary literary taste by stressing sensibility and sentimentality. Portraying a journey through France – typically, the author never reaches Italy, which is promised in the title – Sterne allows tears to flow freely. Unlike the popular travel reports of the factual and fictional types, he concentrates on trivial and accidental meetings and observations. *A Sentimental Journey* offers a much quieter mood as well as moral and philosophical reflections, but it is not without ironic humour, erotic incidents and allusions, and occasional parody. To some extent, these elements counterbalance the sentimental aspect of the novel. The very title of Sterne's last novel announces a new current in the development of the English novel: the rise of sentimentalism. It grew out of sensibility, and its offshoot, the Gothic novel.

Fielding died in 1754, Richardson in 1761, Smollett in 1771, and Sterne in 1768. In only four decades the English novel had made some giant steps forward. After the work of these four great writers, a relatively barren period followed. Though the stream of fiction broadened continually, nothing of intrinsic literary value was written in the form of the novel. For the novelists writing in the closing decades of the century, "heart" and "feeling" became central terms. **Oliver Goldsmith,** who was also a poet and playwright, contributed to the field of the novel a country idyll called *The Vicar of Wakefield* (1766). Goldsmith had a great deal of sentiment to offer, but unlike later sentimentalists he did not drown his tale in it; his gift for comedy and characterization, and his dramatist's eye for effective situation, are equally noticeable in his book. Sentimentalism thrived with such Richardsonian successors as **Henry Mackenzie** (1745-1831) and **Fanny Burney** (1752-1840). Mackenzie's *The Man of Feeling* (1771) features a hero who is forever weeping under the stress of some pathetic scene or emotion. In one tearful exposition this novel unites the influence of Richardson and Sterne, but also of such foreign fiction as Marivaux's[1] *Le Paysan parvenu* (1734-35) and *Marianne* (1731-42), and Rous-

---

1. Pierre Carlet de Chamblain de Marivaux (1688-1763), French writer and playwright. He is known for his 30 comedies dealing with intrigue and love, and for several novels (many of them unfinished) whose refined and subtle analysis of sentiment became known as "marivaudage" and ushered in the wave of novels concerned with sensibility.

Satire on *The Man of Feeling* by Thomas Rowlandson, 1788

seau's[1] *La nouvelle Heloïse* (1764). **Fanny Burney's** *Evelina* (1778), a novel in letter–form modelled on *Humphrey Clinker,* took London by storm. With admirable illustrative incidents, it describes the entry of a country girl into fashionable London society. *Evelina* is a sentimental love story, but there is enough irony and humour to interest even a twentieth-century reader. **Henry Brooke's** *The Fool of Quality* (1766-70) is an educational novel that was written under Rousseau's influence, but its sentimentalism is overdone.

The popularity of the Gothic novel (also called the novel of terror) in the last three decades of the eighteenth century is a fascinating phenomenon. In a way, this type of fiction, with its mystery, emotionalism and horror, is a reaction against the rationalism of the Enlightenment, and it also foreshadows the very real terrors and the bloodshed of the French Revolution. A number of sources have been identified for the Gothic novel, among them Elizabethan drama, pre-Romantic poetry from England and Germany, the sentimental novel, and the popular Oriental tale. **Horace Walpole's** *The Castle of Otranto* (1764) is generally regarded as the prototype of the Gothic novel. "Gothic" is above all an architectural term, denoting the kind of European building which flourished in Medieval times and showed no classical influence. Toward the middle of the eighteenth century, Gothic architecture began to become popular again in England. Horace Walpole himself built a sort of "Gothic castle" at Strawberry Hill, near Twickenham, London. Through its associations with medieval ruins, this kind of building suggested mystery, wildness, and romance.

The Castle of Otranto is set in Italy and deals with a gigantic helmet that can kill people. There are also tyrants, supernatural events, and secret terrors. **William Beckford's** *Vathek* was first written in French in 1781-82 and translated into English in 1786. It shows both the influence of the tale of terror and the Oriental

---

1. Jean-Jacques Rousseau (1712-78), Franco-Swiss writer and philosopher and one of the dominant intellectuals of his age. His influential works include studies of art and culture; a plan for a new scheme of education (the novel *Emile,* 1762) in which the child was to develop its talents in natural surroundings; a theory of politics (*Du Contrat social,* 1762) advocating equality before the law and a more democratic distribution of wealth; and a novel (*Julie, ou la nouvelle Héloïse,* 1764) which provides a critical view of contemporary manners and ideas within the framework of a love story. Also of interest is his autobiographical *Les Confessions* (1781-88).

74

tale. This last type had become popular with the translation at the beginning of the century of *The Arabian Nights*. As early as 1759 Dr. Samuel Johnson had published his *Rasselas* (not a Gothic novel but rather an Oriental tale written for didactic purposes), and Beckford's *Vathek* eventually combined Gothic horror with Oriental mystery. His novel relates the story of a caliph who pursues his sophisticated cruelties and intricate passions, aided by his mother and supported by an evil genius. The main impression of the book is of a fantastic world of lavish excesses. The most able and popular of the later practitioners of the Gothic novel were **Mrs. Ann Radcliffe** (1764-1823) and **Matthew Gregory Lewis** (1755-1818). Radcliffe produced five novels, of which the best are *The Mysteries of Udolpho* (1794) and *The Italian* (1797). The first links the novel of terror to the Enlightenment by providing a rational frame for the action - everything can be explained. There is also no shortage of sentiment as well as sentimental descriptions of scenery in the story of an innocent and sensitive girl fallen into the hands of a powerful and sadistic villain named Montoni, who owns a grim and isolated castle where mystery and horror stalk in lonely chambers and haunted corridors.

Matthew G. Lewis perfected the novel of horror in *The Monk* (1796). Influenced by Goethe and the German Romantic writers, he used a modification of the Faust theme for a portrayal of seduction and sensuality. The hero is a monk who gives in to his passions and fantasies, indulging in sex, perversion, murder and black magic, until he is finally punished for his treaty with the devil. Lewis was nicknamed 'Monk Lewis' after the great success of his book, which offended contemporary taste and was subsequently published in a cleaned-up version. In the nineteenth century, this type of novel was continued with **Charles Robert Maturin's** *Melmoth the Wanderer* (1820), which also features an evil hero who is Faust, Prometheus, and Don Juan in one person. Finally, **William Godwin's** *The Adventures of Caleb Williams* (1794) combines elements of social criticism and themes that were to become important in the crime novel. Godwin, the father of Mary Shelley (the author of *Frankenstein*, published in 1818), concentrates on a sort of psychological horror in the story of Caleb Williams, who has witnessed a murder and is chased by the murderer, Falkland. Man destroys man, and the rich and powerful torture the poor, both physically and mentally.

The flowering of the Gothic novel indicates that in eighteenth-century prose fiction, as in poetry, there was a vast underground of popular literature. Most of these works have gone unrecorded in literary histories. One of the most underrated novels is *Chrysal, or the Adventures of a Guinea*. Written by **Charles Johnstone,** it was published in 1760 and met with great success. The hero is not a person but an inanimate object, a piece of gold. This literary device was not original; yet it allowed a wide range of scenes and profound social satire that is of the calibre of Swift and Fielding.

However, the most successful, and equally the most neglected, novel of the eighteenth century is **John Cleland's** *Memoirs of a Woman of Pleasure* (1748/9), better known as *Fanny Hill*. In the past, literary histories have preferred to ignore this book. Many critics denounced it as pornography, with the implication that such literature ought not to be discussed, either for moral or aesthetic reasons.

Recently, however, Oxford University Press and Penguin Books decided to publish *Fanny Hill* in their reputable series of classic English novels. This indicates a reassessment of what has often been termed either a dirty or a trashy book. In fact, *Fanny Hill* is neither. Its author was an impoverished hack writer of Scottish extraction. Cleland had read widely in contemporary literature, including French erotic novels, and attempted something quite unique with *Fanny Hill.*

To begin with, the novel is a clever parody of the moralistic whore biography as exemplified by Defoe's novels and William Hogarth's pictorial series, *The Harlot's Progress* (1732). The better-known whores in English fiction and art before 1748 ended in misery or death, but Fanny rises from poverty to a comfortable middle-class existence as wife and mother. Like Pamela (who is also satirized in style and content), Fanny sees money and status as important aims in her life, though she continuously stresses the importance of love, including emotion and sex. Unlike Pamela, Fanny is not horrified by sex; it is precisely by giving in to temptation, not by resisting it, that she makes good in the end. The plot of the book is very simple, relating Fanny's social rise from a poor and innocent country girl, via several stages as a prostitute and kept woman, to a happily married wife. Cleland attempted a fusion of natural sexuality, acceptable to a middle-class audience, and an aesthetic framework incorporating the current of sentimentalism. This combination of sex and pathetic sentiment is one of the characteristic features of the novel.

Written in the form of an exchange of letters between two whores *Fanny Hill* mocks *Pamela* and sums up more than two centuries of erotic fiction, most of it of French origin though well known in England. While *Fanny Hill* is no doubt a highly erotic book, its periphrastic style is bound to amuse modern readers rather than enflame them. It is also important as an example of libertine fiction, a current in eighteenth-century literature which was more influential than literary histories usually admit: a wave of erotic and licentious books poured into England from France throughout the century, and it was this sort of literature that helped pave the way for the French Revolution through attacks on social and moral order. John Cleland gave expression to this stream of libertine fiction in French and English literature. Thus *Fanny Hill* is a novel that should not be hidden away or ignored for reasons of twentieth-century propriety. It deserves a place beside the works of Richardson, Smollett, and Sterne.

4. Nonfiction

Prose became a serviceable medium for the powerful minds in the age of the Enlightenment. The subjects of study became more numerous, and with the advancement of literacy there was much speculation and fierce questioning. Individual human experience was the focus of attention.

Journalism flowered throughout the century. No fewer than 250 periodicals were published, and from Jonathan Swift to William Godwin there was hardly a writer who did not put pen to paper for a newspaper or journal. Defoe, Fielding, Johnson, Goldsmith, and Smollett were all editors of, or major contributors to, literary periodicals. Offering information, education, and entertainment in a balanced mixture that also accommodated fiction, the journals became important voices in public life and literary criticism. Vastly influential were the periodicals of the essayists, **Joseph Addison** (1672-1719) and **Richard Steele** (1672-1729). Between 1709-1711 Steele published *The Tatler,* in which he wrote under the pseudonym of Isaac Bickerstaff. Addison also contributed to this weekly journal. Together, they published *The Spectator* (1711-12), a moral-literary journal which appeared daily. Other important periodicals were *The Gentleman's Magazine,* published from 1731 onward. It contained gossip, news, literary pieces, and reviews. Journals like *The Monthly Review* (1749-1845) and *The Critical Review* (1756-1817), although basically concerned with London and the literary world, did not hesitate to take sides in politics.

Apart from journalism, biography and letter writing also prospered. **James Boswell's** *The Life of Samuel Johnson* (1791) and **Lord Chesterfield's** *Letters to his Son* (1774) are outstanding examples.

In moral philosophy, the **earl of Shaftesbury's** *Characteristics of Men, Manners, Opinions, Times* (1711) propagated nature and moral sense as important categories. Philosophy gained additional momentum with the works of the sceptical writers. **Bernard de Mandeville** (1670-1733) exposed the difference between private morality and the morality of states in *The Fable of the Bees* (1714). Unlike Chesterfield, he suggested ironically that the more corrupt a state is the more successful it will be. **David Hume,** originally an historian, laid bare the inadequacies of the human mind in his *Treatise of Human Nature* (1738) and his "magnum opus", *An Enquiry Concerning Human Understanding* (1748).

The art of history writing gained substantially from **Edward Gibbon** (1737-94). His *The History of the Decline and Fall of the Roman Empire,* successively published between 1776 - 1788, was to become the classic work in English history.

In the area of political writing it was **Edmund Burke** (1729-97) who made a name for himself with his speeches in Parliament (later published), when he tried to prevent the separation from England of the American colonies, and with his *Reflections on the Revolution in France* (1790), in which he rejected the French Revolution while proving the advantages of the British political system. Literary criticism was dominated by **Dr. Samuel Johnson** (1709-84). He published biographies, such as his *Life of Sarpi* (1738); and *Life of Boerhaave,* a famous doctor, but is mainly remembered for his great works, the *Dictionary of the English Language* (1755), the predecessor of the modern *Oxford English Dictionary;* an edition of Shakespeare; and his *Lives of the English Poets* (1779-81). The *Lives* is a collection of critical introductions to the major English poets, written at the request of some publishers and combining biography and critical appreciation. Dr. Johnson exerted great influence on his contemporaries with the essays he wrote and published in his own journal, *The Rambler* (1750-52). The aim of this series of moral-didactic issues (about 200 in all) was mainly to educate; it was often reprinted. Johnson had taken over as the leading figure in literary criticism after the death of Alexander Pope in 1744. For Johnson, reason and good sense were the basis of all fiction; inspiration was less important. Other critics, such as Edmund Burke, stressed taste as an important aspect. "Taste" and "sensibility" are central terms in Burke's study of aesthetics, *A Philosophical Inquiry into the Origin of our Ideas of the Sublime and Beautiful* (1756). Among the works on literary criticism published in the second half of eighteenth century, the most important are **Edward Young's** *Conjectures on Original Composition* (1759), which stresses genius and originality as opposed to mere imitation; and **Richard Hurd's** seminal *Letters on Chivalry and Romance* (1762), a book which prepared the ground for the developing Gothic taste in literature.

VI. The Nineteenth Century

1. General Background

It would be convenient, but not altogether correct, to call the nineteenth century the age of the middle class. The merchants solidified their newly gained importance in the economic and political fields, and the Reform Bill[1] of 1832, later followed by the Act of 1867, finally guaranteed more genuine representation for the people, an aim **William Cobbett** (1762-1835) had been agitating for in his *Weekly Political Register.*

The second half of the century saw an unprecedented economic growth which seemed to confirm both bourgeois capitalism and Jeremy Bentham's philosophical "utilitarianism."[2] Under Queen Victoria, who gave her name to an entire age, the Empire achieved its largest extension, thus increasing the feeling of contentedness among the middle class. But materialism and pride in progress could not hide contradictory ideas and insecurities. At the beginning of the century, the French revolutionary ideas of "liberty, equality and fraternity" were displaced by the terror that followed the execution of Louis XVI in 1793, and by 1804 Napoleon threatened England's freedom from the Continent. A decade was to pass before the Emperor was deposed and banned to Elba. Thus England's middle class could never feel really secure. The widespread revolutionary movements on the Continent in 1848 were accompanied by the publication of Karl Marx's *Communist Manifesto,* followed in 1867 by *Das Kapital.* The security of the Victorian middle class was further endangered by the rising agnosticism after 1860. **Charles Darwin's** *Origin of Species* (1859) seemed to disprove the book of Genesis. Some representatives of religion and a few artists fought agnosticism and materialism. The Church of England split into a High Church, initiated by the Oxford Movement[3] that was led by John Keble and E.B. Pusey, and a Low Church much influenced by rational and Deist ideas. **Thomas Carlyle** (1795-1881) and **John Ruskin** (1819-1900) opposed the ideological mainstream of their time. Carlyle hated materialism and progress and advocated both social and moral reforms. If Carlyle was concerned with history and politics, Ruskin concentrated on art and beauty. His works praise modern painters and attempt a synthesis of art and faith. Ruskin was also in favour of social reforms and national education and strongly opposed utilitarianism.

In literature, the nineteenth century witnessed three periods: Romanticism (c. 1790-1830), Victorianism (1830-1890), and the Decadence or "fin-de-siècle" of the

---

1. The Reform Bill of 1832 increased parliamentary representation by extending the vote to the rich middle classes and it removed some of the inequalities in the system of representation.
2. See page 45, note 3.
3. A movement of thought and doctrine within the Church of England. It was begun by Keble in 1833 and attempted to revive the High Church traditions of the 17th century. The members of the movement influenced intellectual, religious, and cultural life with their publications, creating an interest in the medieval and 17th-century church that affected Tennyson, Morrison, and the Pre-Raphaelites.

1890s. Prepared by Thomson, Gray, Collins, Blake and Burns, the Romantic movement produced a rich harvest in the first three decades of the century. At first inspired by the ideas behind the French Revolution, the Romantics revolted against the rules and conventions of the eighteenth-century classicists. Intellectual attitudes were to be replaced by a wider outlook, recognizing the claims of passion and emotion. The critical spirit was to give way to imagination, and wit was to yield to humour and pathos. The romantic poets in particular proclaimed the return to nature, both in subject and style. But their humanitarian idealism was bitterly disappointed by the incidents in France after 1792, and poets like Coleridge, Wordsworth, Scott, and Shelley learned more from German culture and literature.

The longer period of Victorian writing, in which middle-class authors entertained middle-class readers with a mixture of optimism, guilt, and doubt, came to an end in the 1890s. It was an age largely dominated by the ideals and ideas of the bourgeois. A strict but sham morality prevailed which demanded that such subjects as sex were to be ignored in popular literature. Significantly, **Thomas Bowdler** (1754-1825) published his expurgated *Family Shakespeare* in 1818, thus creating the term "to bowdlerize". And though some writers revolted against the prudishness, priggishness, and narrow-mindedness of the middle class (Ruskin denounced materialism, Thackery ridiculed snobbery, and Matthew Arnold attacked philistinism) hypocrisy could never be eradicated: the seemingly moral Victorian period saw the rise of pornography in underground literature, and an unprecedented increase in prostitution in London. Queen Victoria embodies the hypocrisy of the age to which she lent her name: her public image was that of a virtuous and morally upright monarch, yet in her private life she had a long-drawn-out affair with her Scottish groom.

The literature produced in the 1890s has been termed "decadent". During this period, art became a substitute for religion, which seemed dead. **Walter Pater** (1839-94) prepared the ground with his demand, "art for art's sake". Beauty and pleasure became aims in themselves, and hedonism a way of life. Oscar Wilde was the outstanding writer of this movement.

2. Poetry

While it is true that the Romantic period proper may be dated from the publication in 1798 of the *Lyrical Ballads* by **William Wordsworth** and **Samuel Taylor Coleridge,** the ideals of eighteenth-century Neoclassicism did not come to an abrupt end. They survived in the fascinating works of **Erasmus Darwin** (1731-1802), Charles Darwin's grandfather, who recorded the botanical system of Linnaeus[1] in his *The Botanic Garden.* This poem is written in heroic couplets and

---

1. Linnaeus (Carl Linné, 1707-78), Swedish naturalist and botanist and the founder of the internationally used system for naming animals and plants. His most important works were *Species Plantarum* (1753) and *Systema Naturae* (1735).

appeared in two parts, part II, "The Loves of the Plants", in 1789, and part I, "The Economy of Vegetation", in 1791. Darwin's description of flowers as "beaux" and "belles" with a love life was soon ridiculed and parodied. Among the poets writing in the tradition of Neoclassicism were **George Crabbe** (1754-1832). **Samuel Rogers** (1763-1855), and the Scotsman **Thomas Campbell** (1777-1844).

The principles of Romantic poetry were formulated by **Wordsworth** (1770-1850) in the preface to the second and third editions of the *Lyrical Ballads* which appeared in 1800 and 1802. Wordsworth opposed the very idea of poetic diction, demanding an utmost simplicity of subject and style. The language of poetry, he insisted, should be the language of ordinary people, and the poet should be inspired by legend, feeling, and imagination. The poet was to be a prophet proclaiming the beauty and splendour of life and nature. A disciple of Rousseau, and also of the Augustans and their immediate successors, Wordsworth taught his contemporaries, who received his ideas rather unfavourably, to look at nature with the eyes of imagination and to recognize in its beauty the presence of an unseen Goodness. As a Pantheist, he was neither Christian nor Deist or rationalist, but rather a believer in the natural universe that signifies God. Wordsworth's theory of poetic language is based on a nature-philosophy that led him to adore country people, rural life, and natural scenery. Though the wish to be simple implies the danger of banality, Wordsworth was able to impress with even very short poems on "everyday" subjects, such as a rainbow:

My Heart Leaps Up

My heart leaps up when I behold
  A rainbow in the sky:
So was it when my life began;
So is it now I am a man;
So be it when I shall grow old,
  Or let me die!
The Child is father of the Man;
And I could wish my days to be
Bound each to each by natural piety.

Wordsworth spent almost all his life in the Lake District[1]. In fact, he became known, together with Coleridge and Southey, as one of the Lake Poets. He spent his youth in the mountains of Cumbria. After studying at Cambridge, he lived for a few months in London before moving to France where he took an active interest in the revolutionary movement. His dreams of brotherhood shattered by the reign of terror after 1792, he returned to the solitude and seclusion of Grasmere in the Lake District. After visiting Germany with Coleridge in 1798, he devoted his life

1. The Lake District is now a National Park in the county of Cumbria in northwest England. Its impressive scenery (lakes, mountains, woods, valleys) has made it a popular holiday area and a celebrated topic for Romantic poets, such as Wordsworth and Coleridge.

entirely to poetry. Wordsworth's best verse is contained in the mainly narrative poems of the *Lyrical Ballads,* the *Poems in Two Volumes* (1807), and *The Prelude,* a long reflective and autobiographical poem in blank verse commenced in 1799 and completed in 1805 but not published until 1850. In 1800 he finished two other long poems in blank verse, *The Excursion* and *The Recluse,* and between 1801–1803 he also wrote two series of sonnets, including "Upon Westminster Bridge":

Composed upon Westminster Bridge, September 3, 1802

Earth has not anything to show more fair:
Dull would he be of soul who could pass by
A sight so touching in its majesty;
This City now doth, like a garment, wear
The beauty of the morning; silent, bare,
Ships, towers, domes, theaters, and temples lie
Open unto the fields, and to the sky;
All bright and glittering in the smokeless air.
Never did sun more beautifully steep
In his first splendor, valley, rock, or hill;
Ne'er saw I, never felt, a calm so deep!
The river glideth at his own sweet will:
Dear God! the very houses seem asleep;
And all that mighty heart is lying still!

His most productive period seems to have been the decade after 1800 when he wrote his great ode "Intimations of Immortality."

Wordsworth's closest friend was **Samuel Taylor Coleridge** (1772–1834). His work, though mainly a genial collection of plans and fragments, embodies the ideas and themes of the Romantic movement by exploring the magical and the mysterious. Like Wordsworth, he sympathized with the Revolution in France and became acquainted with **Robert Southey** in the early 1790s. Together, they planned to put into practice a sort of Communist society, "Pantisocracy", in America. But this plan, like several others of Coleridge's schemes, never took shape.

However, it was the friendship with Wordsworth that was to influence Coleridge's life and work. To their joint publication, the *Lyrical Ballads,* Coleridge contributed poems dealing with the supernatural, such as *The Ancient Mariner,* whereas Wordsworth chose subjects from ordinary life. Coleridge read literature and philosophy at Göttingen, thus absorbing German literature, and in 1798 decided to become a clergyman. But when he met William Hazlitt in 1803 he gave up this career and went to the Lake District. After 1803 he suffered from ill health and became addicted to opium. This impaired his mental faculties and ruined both his career as a poet and critic and his domestic happiness. Coleridge was important to the Romantic movement because, influenced by German writers like Lessing, Schiller and Kant, he taught England to revere Shakespeare as a literary artist, and because he introduced transcendentalism and mysticism of German origin. Coleridge's greatest poems, *The Ancient Mariner, Kubla Khan,* and *Christabel* were composed during the period of his closest association with Wordsworth. Written in the style and metre of the ancient ballads, *The Ancient Mariner* creates a fantastic dream world in the story of an old sailor who kills an albatross and is tormented with the most frightening visions and visitations. *Kubla Khan,* published in 1816, is, according to its subtitle, a "vision in a dream" in which Coleridge came close to verbalized music. The theme of the poem, the fabulous ancient Orient, is one of the major preoccupations of Romantic writing. Here are the first 11 lines of the poem.

Kubla Khan

OR A VISION IN A DREAM. A FRAGMENT

In Xanadu did Kubla Khan
A stately pleasure dome decree:
Where Alph, the sacred river, ran
Through caverns measureless to man
   Down to a sunless sea.
So twice five miles of fertile ground
With walls and towers were girdled round:
And there were gardens bright with sinuous rills,
Where blossomed many an incense-bearing tree;
And here were forests ancient as the hills,
Enfolding sunny spots of greenery.

Christabel (1816), like *Kubla Khan* an unfinished poem, shows flexible metre foreshadowing the later Hopkins and is concerned with the mystery of evil.

The treatment of the unknown and of exoticism is a dominant theme that helped to shape Romanticism. It is apparent in the works of the first generation of Romantic poets, Wordsworth and Coleridge, and also in the poetry of such minor writers as **Robert Southey** (1774-1843) and **Thomas Moore** (1779-1852). Together with Coleridge and Wordsworth, Southey became known as one of the "Lakers". His *Thalaba* deals with the Islamic world while *The Curse of Kehama* (1810) is set in India. Moore's *Lalla Rookh* (1817) is also an Oriental poem made up of a series of tales in verse that are connected by a story in prose.

What distinguishes the first generation of Romantic poets from the second, i.e. from Byron, Shelley, and Keats, is the fact that the former became old and experienced enough to modify the ideas of their youth while the latter died young and immature. **George Gordon, Lord Byron** (1788-1824), for instance, would seem to be the archetypal tragic Romantic poet. Even in his lifetime, he became a legend. He was a boisterous student at Cambridge and he very early inherited the title and estates of Newstead Abbey, near Nottingham. In 1809 he took his seat in the House of Lords and soon set out for a long journey to the Orient (1809-1811). Back in England, he published the first two cantos of *Childe Harold's Pilgrimage* (canto III appeared in 1816, and canto IV in 1818). This poem is a veiled autobiographical description in Spenserian stanzas of the travels and reflections of a young "Romanticist" whose life corresponds in many ways to Byron's own. The two cantos were followed by tales in verse, such as *The Bride of Abydos* (1813), *The Corsair,* written in heroic couplets and published in 1814, and *Lara* (1814), which is set in Turkey

Lord Byron (in Albanian dress)

and Greece. Byron then began to enjoy himself in the role of the handsome cynic with the club-foot, the atheist and debauchee, and the hero who had swum the Hellespont[1]. In 1815 he married a rich heiress only to separate from her a year later. In the same year he left England for good and travelled through Belgium, Germany, and Switzerland. In Geneva, he met Shelley, and then he left for Italy, residing in Venice, Ravenna, Rome, Pisa, and Genoa. After a prolonged love-affair, he decided in 1823 to go to Greece and help that country in its fight for independence. However, before he could join the Greek insurgents attacking Turkish troops, he died of a fever in Missolonghi, at the young age of 36. Byron's most important and convincing poetic works are beyond doubt *Childe Harold's Pilgrimage* and his epic satire *Don Juan.*

Based on a Spanish story dramatised by Tellez and Molière, and on Mozart's *Don Giovanni* (1787), Byron's poem is written in ottava rima, in 16 cantos, and appeared between 1819-24. Like Byron himself, Don Juan is a charming, handsome and unprincipled young man. His love affairs and adventures serve as the connecting thread for the social satire of the poem. In canto I of *Don Juan,* Byron sneered at the ideas of the older Romantic poets:

> Young Juan wandered by the glassy brooks,
>   Thinking unutterable things; he threw
> Himself at length within the leafy nooks
>   Where the wild branch of the cork forest grew;
> There poets find materials for their books,
>   And every now and then we read them through,
> So that their plan and prosody are eligible,
> Unless, like Wordsworth, they prove unintelligible.

Like the Augustan satirists, Byron plays with the reader in his long description of Julia's seduction, which hides as much as it unveils:

> Julia had honor, virtue, truth, and love
>   For Don Alfonso; and she inly swore,

---

1. The Old Greek name for the strait connecting the Aegean and the Marmara seas and separating Europe (Greece) and Asia (Turkey). The strait is also called Dardanelles or Bosporus Straits and is prominent in Greek legend.

By all the vows below to Powers above,
　　She never would disgrace the ring she wore,
Nor leave a wish which wisdom might reprove;
　　And while she pondered this, besides much more,
One hand on Juan's carelessly was thrown,
Quite by mistake - she thought it was her own;

Unconsciously she leaned upon the other,
　　Which played within the tangles of her hair;
And to contend with thoughts she could not smother
　　She seemed by the distraction of her air.
'Twas surely very wrong in Juan's mother
　　To leave together this imprudent pair,
She who for many years had watched her son so -
I'm very certain *mine* would not have done so.

[...]
And Julia sate with Juan, half embraced
　　And half retiring from the glowing arm,
Which trembled like the bosom where 'twas placed;
　　Yet still she must have thought there was no harm,
Or else 'twere easy to withdraw her waist;
　　But then the situation had its charm,
And then - God knows what next - I can't go on;
I'm almost sorry that I e'er begun.

Such poetry was much too daring for Georgian society. The prudery of the Victorian critics withheld these poems from the public. This is also true of Byron's satires *Beppo* (1818), which shows life as a carnival, and *Visions of Judgment* (1822), in which he ridicules Southey.

Like Byron, **Percey Bysshe Shelley** (1792-1822) was of aristocratic origin. The son of a wealthy baronet, he was expelled from the University of Oxford for issuing a pamphlet on *The Necessity of Atheism.* Scorned by his father, he went to London and married the daughter of an innkeeper. In 1814 they separated, and two years later Shelley married William Godwin's daughter. During a journey to Switzerland he met Byron, and together they read and wrote ghost stories. Shelley's wife Mary contributed *Frankenstein,* which, at her husband's request, she developed into a long story. After briefly returning to England, Shelley left England forever in 1818 and travelled in Italy. In 1822 he drowned in a thunderstorm while at sea.

Shelley's longer poems, such as *Queen Mab* (1813), *The Revolt of Islam* (1818), the allegorical tragedy *Prometheus Unbound* (1820), and the lyrical drama *Hellas* (1822) take up the themes of revolt and human suffering. If Byron expressed the diabolical and Faustian aspects that fascinated several Romantic writers, Shelley tried to put into verse the idealism of the Romantic movement. His "Ode to the Westwind" possesses great melodic power in the treatment of his favourite themes of freedom, beauty, and love. Equally famous are his fine short lyrics, such as the sonnet "Ozymandias" which reminds the reader of the vanity of human pride and power.

I met a traveler from an antique land
Who said: Two vast and trunkless legs of stone
Stand in the desert...Near them, on the sand,
Half sunk, a shattered visage lies, whose frown,
And wrinkled lip, and sneer of cold command,
Tell that its sculptor well those passions read
Which yet survive, stamped on these lifeless things,
The hand that mocked them, and the heart that fed:
And on the pedestal these words appear:
"My name is Ozymandias, king of kings:
Look on my works, ye Mighty, and despair!"
Nothing beside remains. Round the decay
Of that colossal wreck, boundless and bare
The lone and level sands stretch far away.

When Shelley's body was washed ashore in the Gulf of Spezia, a volume of Keats's poems was found in one of his pockets. Shelley had written an elegy, "Adonais", when Keats died in 1821. **John Keats** (1795-1821) was born in London as the son of a stable-keeper. At first he wanted to become a doctor, but in 1816 he decided to devote his life to literature. His poems were almost all written in the brief space of the five years before his death and are models of the sensuous aspect of Romanticism. Keats's themes were love and death, and beauty in art and nature, tinged with melancholy and heart-ache. His unfinished *Hyperion,* a sort of Miltonic epic, tells of the dethroning of the old gods and the rise of the new. *Endymion* (1818), his first long poem, deals with the Greek myth of a beautiful youth who was loved and plunged into eternal sleep by the Moon goddess. Beauty, love, and death are also dominant themes in his finest lyrics, the "Ode to a Nightingale", the "Ode on Melancholy", and the "Ode on a Grecian Urn", all written in 1819. The last stanza of the "Ode on a Grecian Urn" records Keats's sadness at the thought of the transient nature of beauty and his wish to adore works of art as the preservers of love and happiness.

O Attic shape! Fair attitude! with brede
    Of marble men and maidens overwrought,
With forest branches and the trodden weed;
    Thou, silent form, dost tease us out of thought
As doth eternity: Cold Pastoral!
    When old age shall this generation waste,
        Thou shalt remain, in midst of other woe
    Than ours, a friend to man, to whom thou say'st,
"Beauty is truth, truth beauty," – that is all
        Ye know on earth, and all ye need to know.

For Keats, the love of beauty became a passion. He found beauty in nature, though without the metaphysical notions of Coleridge and Wordsworth, and in the worlds of Greek myth and medieval romance, which he treated in *La Belle Dame Sans Merci,* a ballad written in 1819. Keats died of tuberculosis in 1821 in Rome, where he had gone, much too late, to improve his health. On the voyage to Italy he wrote one of the most beautiful English sonnets, his last poem, "Bright Star."

Bright star, would I were steadfast as thou art –
   Not in lone splendor hung aloft the night
And watching, with eternal lids apart,
   Like nature's patient, sleepless Eremite,
The moving waters at their priestlike task
   Of pure ablution round earth's human shores,
Or gazing on the new soft fallen mask
   Of snow upon the mountains and the moors –
No – yet still steadfast, still unchangeable,
   Pillowed upon my fair love's ripening breast,
To feel forever its soft fall and swell,
   Awake forever in a sweet unrest,
Still, still to hear her tender-taken breath,
And so live ever – or else swoon to death.

By 1830, Romanticism in poetry was coming to an end. Byron, Keats, and Shelley had died, and Coleridge and Wordsworth were poetically silent. A new poetry came with Tennyson and Browning, though the popular poets in the 1830s were still Byron, Scott, Moore, Thomas Campbell, and John Clare. **Alfred Tennyson** (1809-1892) has been recognized as one of the outstanding Victorian poets. Tennyson was the son of a clergyman and went to Trinity College, Cambridge. By 1830 he had published his first volume of poems, followed by another book of lyrical verse in 1832. Already in these early poems, which are reminiscent of the Romantics because of their supernatural atmosphere, one notices a style marked by its musical flow. Tennyson often expressed a profound melancholy and a sense of personal loss, as in the following poem written in 1834 and published in 1842.

Break, Break, Break

Break, break, break,
   On thy cold gray stones, O Sea!
And I would that my tongue could utter
   The thoughts that arise in me.

O, well for the fisherman's boy,
   That he shouts with his sister at play!
O, well for the sailor lad,
   That he sings in his boat on the bay!

And the stately ships go on
   To their haven under the hill;
But O for the touch of a vanished hand,
   And the sound of a voice that is still!

Break, break, break,
   At the foot of thy crags, O Sea!
But the tender grace of a day that is dead
   Will never come back to me.

Tennyson's dramatic monologues, perhaps best exemplified in "Ulysses" (1842), show him as a masterly technician achieving rhythm and melody even when he used blank verse. At the end of "Ulysses", the protagonist addresses his mariners and suggests another trip to unknown worlds in order to escape old age and the boredom of everyday life.

> The lights begin to twinkle from the rocks;
> The long day wanes; the slow moon climbs; the deep
> Moans round with many voices. Come, my friends,
> 'Tis not too late to seek a newer world.
> Push off, and sitting well in order smite
> The sounding furrows; for my purpose holds
> To sail beyond the sunset, and the baths
> Of all the western stars, until I die.
> It may be that the gulfs will wash us down;
> It may be we shall touch the Happy Isles,
> And see the great Achilles, whom we knew.
> Though much is taken, much abides; and though
> We are not now that strength which in old days
> Moved earth and heaven, that which we are, we are,
> One equal temper of heroic hearts,
> Made weak by time and fate, but strong in will
> To strive, to seek, to find, and not to yield.

The death in 1833 of Tennyson's close friend Arthur Hallam may be one of the reasons why the poetry he published after 1840 assumed a stronger note of melancholy. *In Memoriam,* dedicated to Hallam, appeared in 1850. Begun as an elegy, it is a collection of lyrics in a consistant metre and ends in a passionate defense of poetry and the poet's soul. *Maud* (1855), like the earlier *Locksley Hall* (1842) is a dramatic monologue or "monodrama" representing the story of a disappointed lover who joins the army to go to war. With *Idylls of the King* (1857-72), Tennyson indulged his love of old legends. It is a series of twelve romantic tales in blank verse focusing on King Arthur's Round Table. Tennyson was appointed poet laureate on the death of Wordsworth in 1850, and in 1884 he was raised to the peerage[1] for his contribution to literature. When he died eight years later, he was buried in Westminster Abbey, by the side of **Robert Browning.**

Browning (1812-89) differed in many ways from Tennyson. As a Nonconformist[2], he was denied access to Oxford and Cambridge and spent a brief period at University College, London. Browning soon made the acquaintance of a young lady poet and invalid, Elizabeth Barrett, whom he married in secrecy and against her father's wish in 1846. The pair fled to Italy, and until the death of Elizabeth in 1861 they lived and worked in Pisa and Florence, producing some remarkable poetry. She recorded her love for her husband in a cycle of poems, *Sonnets from the Portuguese* (1845), while Robert wrote some of his best dramatic monologues,

---

1. The British aristocracy comprises hereditary peers (noblemen with inherited titles) and life peers (titles awarded to one person for his or her life). Hereditary peers may sit in the House of Lords.
2. See page 21, note 4.

published as *Men and Women* in 1855. Italy seems to have held a powerful fascination for English poets of the nineteenth century. Like Byron, Shelley, and Keats, Browning made this country his temporary home. He returned to England only after his wife's death, but he went back to Italy and died in Venice. The history, culture, and literature of Italy pervade Browning's poems which mirror his vast and eccentric reading. His language and imagery are much closer to our time than to the Victorian period.

In the first two stanzas of "A Toccata of Galuppi's" (1855) he tried to recall eighteenth-century Venetian music and life in a beautiful rhythm:

Robert Browning, portrait by Dante Gabriel Rossetti, 1855

> O Galuppi, Baldassare, this is very sad to find!
> I can hardly misconceive you; it would prove me deaf and blind;
> But although I take your meaning, 'tis with such a heavy mind!
>
> Here you come with your old music, and here's all the good it brings.
> What, they lived once thus at Venice where the merchants were the kings,
> Where Saint Mark's is, where the Doges used to wed the sea with rings?

The proud Duke in "My Last Duchess" (1842) shows a visitor the picture of his deceased wife and the splendour of his castle while almost giving away his horrible secret. The first 13 lines of this poem illustrate how dexterously Browning could handle the dramatic monologue, a poetic and dramatic form that also dominates in his second collection, *Dramatis Personae* (1864).

My Last Duchess

FERRARA

> That's my last duchess painted on the wall,
> Looking as if she were alive. I call
> That piece a wonder, now: Frà Pandolf's hands
> Worked busily a day, and there she stands.
> Will't please you sit and look at her? I said
> "Frà Pandolf" by design, for never read
> Strangers like you that pictured countenance,
> The depth and passion of its earnest glance,
> But to myself they turned (since none puts by
> The curtain I have drawn for you, but I)
> And seemed as they would ask me, if they durst,
> How such a glance came there; so, not the first
> Are you to turn and ask thus. ...

Browning had been experimenting with drama, and his main poetic achievement, the sophistication and improvement of the monologue, is clearly a result of his deep interest in the psychological aspects of characters in plays. Italy again provided the theme and setting for his last great work, *The Ring and the Book* (1869), which is a long murder story in verse set in Rome.

Victorian religious and philosophical skepticism found expression in the works of **Matthew Arnold** (1822–88) and **Arthur Hugh Clough** (1819–1861), who were very close friends. Clough is today remembered mainly for his hexameter poem "Amours de Voyage" (1858). In his parody of the Ten Commandments, "The Latest Decalogue" (1862), he dealt a blow to his materialistic compatriots:

The Latest Decalogue

Thou shalt have one God only; who
Would be at the expense of two?
No graven images may be
Worshipped, except the currency:
Swear not at all; for for thy curse
Thine enemy is none the worse:
At church on Sunday to attend
Will serve to keep the world thy friend:
Honour thy parents; that is, all
From whom advancement may befall:
Thou shalt not kill; but needst not strive
Officiously to keep alive:
Do not adultery commit;
Advantage rarely comes of it:
Thou shalt not steal; an empty feat,
When it's so lucrative to cheat:
Bear not false witness; let the lie
Have time on its own wings to fly:
Thou shalt not covet; but tradition
Approves all forms of competition.
The sum of all is, thou shalt love,
If any body, God above:
At any rate shall never labour
More than thyself to love thy neighbour.

When Clough died in Florence, **Matthew Arnold** produced a moving elegy, *Thyrsis* (1866) on the death of his friend. Arnold, however, was better as a critic than as a poet. His verse is sombre and pessimistic. Thus the ending of "Dover Beach" (1867) expresses the desperate hope that love may help to overcome man's feeling of forlornness.

Ah, love, let us be true
To one another! for the world, which seems
To lie before us like a land of dreams,
So various, so beautiful, so new,
Hath really neither joy, nor love, nor light,

Nor certitude, nor peace, nor help for pain;
And we are here as on a darkling plain
Swept with confused alarms of struggle and flight,
Where ignorant armies clash by night.

Arnold stopped writing poetry after 1867, dedicating his time to literary criticism.

Before turning to the Pre-Raphaelite Brotherhood (hereafter PRB), one ought to mention the name of **Edward Fitzgerald** (1809-83) who produced one poem with a lasting impression. This is the *Rubaiyat of Omar Khayyam* (1859), a free translation in quatrains of the Persian poet Khayyam. The poem brought to complacent Victorian England a little of the melancholy spirit of the East, preaching not the gospel of labour but idleness and hedonistic skepticism. Fitzgerald was discovered and defended by **Dante Gabriel Rossetti** (1828-1882), the true soul of the PRB, which was founded in 1848. The PRB was a group of artists, critics and poets – William Holman Hunt, John Everett Millais, D. G. Rossetti, William Michael Rossetti, William Morris, A. C. Swinburne et al. – who refused to accept the methods of conventional art and tried to find purity of inspiration and moral qualities through a scrupulous study of nature and the depiction of noble subjects. The name of the group indicates that they considered art from Raphael onwards as degenerate (the name was first used in a picture by Hunt in 1849). The PRB looked for the essential qualities of medieval art and wanted to reproduce nature with painstaking fidelity. At first used only with reference to painting, the term PRB was soon extended to literature, not least because several members of the group were both painters and poets. When Rossetti joined the PRB he had already written a poem, "The Blessed Damozel" (finished in 1846 and published in 1850 in *The Germ,* a magazine propagating the ideas of the PRB). This work, like his paintings, suggests an artificial striving for simplicity and a strange religious atmosphere which does not, however, derive from religious faith. As the first two stanzas show, the form of the poem is reminiscent of the ballad

The Blessed Damozel

The blessed damozel leaned out
    From the gold bar of Heaven;
Her eyes were deeper than the depth
    Of waters stilled at even;
She had three lilies in her hand,
    And the stars in her hair were seven.

Her robe, ungirt from clasp to hem,
    No wrought flowers did adorn,
But a white rose of Mary's gift,
    For service meetly worn;
Her hair that lay along her back
    Was yellow like ripe corn.

Lady Lilith by Dante Gabriel Rossetti, 1864

Wallpaper design by William Morris, 1892

Rossetti's debt to Italian art and literature (he was the son of an Italian poet and refugee) can be seen in his series of sonnets, *The House of Life,* published in 1870 and 1881. His sister, **Christina Georgina Rossetti** (1830–94), also excelled in the sonnet form. Some of her best works are collected in the series *Monna Innominata,* which focuses on unhappy love.

Like D. G. Rossetti, **William Morris** (1834–96) was much concerned with art and poetry. His achievement lies more in the field of spreading art in everyday life. Initially a poet and critic, he became a book illustrator, a designer of furniture, wallpaper and stained glass windows. In 1861 he founded the firm Morris, Faulkner & Co., and in 1870 the publishing house Kelmscott Press. Morris was a passionate Socialist and, later, Communist crusading against the ugliness of industrialism. His verse, inspired by medieval, Greek and Scandinavian subjects, also shows Tennyson's influence, particularly *The Defence of Guinevere* (1858). *The Earthly Paradise* (1868-70) is modelled on Chaucer's *Canterbury Tales,* containing 24 verse tales. After a voyage to Iceland in 1871, Morris took an interest in Germanic legend and, in 1871, published his gigantic epic *Sigurd the Volsung and the Fall of the Nibelungs.*

Algernon Charles Swinburne (1837-1909) met D. G. Rossetti at Oxford and later shared a house with him in Chelsea, London. Swinburne's *Poems and Ballads* of 1866 were violently attacked by the critics and outraged Victorian morality with their sensual treatment of lust and despair. He was much influenced by contemporary French poets, especially by Baudelaire's[1] *Les Fleurs du Mal* (1857). In his attacks on morality and religion, Swinburne displayed a Romantic spirit of revolt. His poems stress sound and rhythm to create an impression of beauty, often at the expense of meaning. Thus his "A Forsaken Garden" (1878), the first stanza of which follows, is distinguished by its rhythmic splendour rather than by its message.

---

1. Charles Baudelaire (1821-67), French poet and forerunner of symbolism. *Les Fleurs du Mal* (1857) is a series of 101 poems, including sonnets, in a variety of metres. In musical language and telling images, they explore isolation, sin, boredom, melancholy, and the power of love as well as the attraction of evil. Some of the poems were banned upon publication as offensive to public morals. His reputation as a critic has steadily increased since his death.

A Forsaken Garden

In a coign of the cliff between lowland and highland,
  At the sea-down's edge between windward and lee,
Walled round with rocks as an inland island,
  The ghost of a garden fronts the sea.
A girdle of brushwood and thorn encloses
  The steep square slope of the blossomless bed
Where the weeds that grew green from the graves of its roses
    Now lie dead.

From Swinburne and the PRB it was only a short step to the art-for-art's sake impressionism of the poets of the 1890s. Again, one notices the close relations between painting and poetry. Ruskin's art theories were being replaced by the ideas of Walter Pater, and of the American painter James A. M. Whistler (1834-1903), who came to England in 1866 and was a friend of Oscar Wilde. The poets of the fin-de-siècle movement cultivated pleasure and made hedonism a way of life. Foreshadowed by the pessimistic poetry of **James Thomson** (1834-82) (see his *The City of Dreadful Night,* 1870-74) decadence arose out of the influence of the English Romantic tradition (Keats, Swinburne) and French symbolism. It found expression in the prose and poetry of **Oscar Wilde** (1854-1900), whose *Poems* appeared in 1881, and **Ernest Dowson** (1867-1900), who both adored the French symbolists Baudelaire and Mallarmé[1]; and in the verse of **Lionel Johnson** (1867-1902), **Arthur Symons** (1865-1945) and **A. E. Housman** (1859-1936). Oscar Wilde's "Impression du Matin" is a good example of impressionistic poetry which scorns logic and tries to describe effects, synaesthetic sensations, and feelings in esoteric symbols and musical rhythms. Wilde's poem was inspired by Whistler's painting of the Thames entitled *Nocturne in Blue and Gold.*

Impression du Matin

The Thames nocturne of blue and gold
  Changed to a harmony in gray;
  A barge with ocher-colored hay
Dropt from the wharf: and chill and cold

The yellow fog came creeping down
  The bridges, till the houses' walls
  Seemed changed to shadows, and St. Paul's
Loomed like a bubble o'er the town.

Then suddenly arose the clang
  Of waking life; the streets were stirred
  With country wagons; and a bird
Flew to the glistening roofs and sang.

---

1. Stéphane Mallarmé (1842-98), French poet and founder of modern European poetry. His later poetry is highly allusive and symbolical (e. g. *Poésies,* 1887, and *Vers et Prose,* 1893) and employs syntactical and metaphoric ambiguities as well as typographical innovations.

> But one pale woman all alone,
>> The daylight kissing her wan hair,
>> Loitered beneath the gas lamp's flare,
> With lips of flame and heart of stone.

The representatives of the fin-de-siècle decadence published their art and literature in such periodicals as *The Yellow Book* (1894-97) and *The Savoy* (1896). Both were illustrated by **Aubrey Beardsley** (1872-98), whose fantastic, mannered style is typical of art nouveau.

Robert Bridges (1844-1930) has often been called the last Victorian poet. He was appointed poet laureate in 1913, and when he published his philosophical poem in Alexandrines, *Testament of Beauty* (1929), he had been writing verse for over fifty years. His best known poems are contained in the *Shorter Poems* (1890 and 1893). In 1918 Bridges published a volume of verse of his closest friend, **Gerard Manley Hopkins** (1844-89), who brought a formal renewal to poetry and is today recognized as the most influential Victorian poet. Hopkins converted to Roman Catholicism and became a Jesuit priest. After his ordination, he burned his early poems, but, urged by his superior, he began writing again in his thirties. He thought deeply about poetry and gave a profound expression to religious experience. His technical audacity and his specialized vocabulary, his condensed language and syntax, and his "sprung rhythm" drew on Anglo-Saxon and Germanic poetry in a free variation of the number of syllables within the unit of a verse. Thus Hopkins can be regarded as the first modern poet. "The Windhover" (1877) exemplifies his poetic theory and his religious experience.

The Windhover

TO CHRIST OUR LORD

> I caught this morning morning's minion, king-
>> dom of daylight's dauphin, dapple-dawn-drawn Falcon, in his riding
>> Of the rolling level underneath him steady air, and striding
> High there, how he rung upon the rein of a wimpling wing
> In his ecstasy! then off, off forth on swing,
>> As a skate's heel sweeps smooth on a bow-bend: the hurl and gliding
>> Rebuffed the big wind. My heart in hiding
> Stirred for a bird, - the achieve of, the mastery of the thing!

> Brute beauty and valour and act, oh, air, pride, plume, here
>> Buckle! AND the fire that breaks from thee then, a billion
> Times told lovelier, more dangerous, O my chevalier!

>> No wonder of it: shéer plód makes plough down sillion
> Shine, and blue-bleak embers, ah my dear,
>> Fall, gall themselves, and gash gold-vermilion.

The so-called "terrible sonnets" of his last years speak of the glory of God in nature while exploring his own self-tormented mind.

A survey of the Victorian period would be incomplete without a brief reference to **Edward Lear** (1812-88) whose nonsense rhymes, collected in *The Book of*

Nonsense (1845), became very popular. Lear revived the limerick, a stanza form used exclusively for light verse. The limerick is always comic, often nonsensical, and sometimes bawdy, and it is still popular today. Here is one of Lear's limericks.

> There was an Old Man of the Dee,
> Who was sadly annoyed by a Flea;
> When he said, "I will scratch it",
> They gave him a hatchet,
> Which grieved that Old Man of the Dee.

3. Drama

After the death of Sheridan in 1816, drama suffered a decline in England. This cannot be put down to one single cause. One reason was the fact that between the Restoration and the Theatre Regulating Act of 1843 the only licensed theatres in London were Covent Garden and Drury Lane, and, from 1766, the Haymarket Theatre. The Act of 1843 removed the monopoly, but there were then few dramatists who were able to provide the old qualities and the subtlety of drama. The new middle-class audience had no true appreciation for drama as an art. As a result, melodrama, partly imported from France, became very popular. Initially, the term meant plays with music, but today it has a pejorative aspect, denoting a play that depends for its effect on highly sensational and exaggerated situations. In the melodrama of the early nineteenth century, villains are as bad as possible and the good are angelic. Other typical elements are conventional moralizing, violence, attempted seduction, and low humour.

Most of the Romantic poets wrote plays, predominantly five-act blank-verse tragedies. These "closet dramas" were meant to be read rather than performed; the better known examples were Shelley's *The Cenci* (1819), whose theme of incest made it impossible for the stage, and Byron's *Manfred* (1817), *Sardanapalus* (1821), and *Werner* (1822). Victorian poets like Browning, Tennyson and Swinburne also wrote dramas, though what they composed was closer to poetry than to the stage.

First attempts to bring the drama to life again can be detected in the work of **Thomas William Robertson** (1829-71). His *David Garrick* (1864), based on one of his novels, and *Caste* (1867), though they still contained pathos, sentimentality and melodramatic elements, prepared the way for the more realistic problem plays treating of social and moral issues. **Henry Arthur Jones** (1851-1929) learned a lot from the French drama and from Henrik Ibsen.[1] He produced *Saints and Sinners*

---

1. Henrik Ibsen (1828-1906), Norwegian dramatist and founder of modern prose drama. In the 1890s, he became established in England as a major playwright. Through Archer's continuing translations, his plays - concerned with social and political themes, with women's rights and the forces of the unconscious - exerted great influence on modern dramatists, who admired Ibsen's discarding of traditional theatrical effects and his use of ordinary characters. (*Peer Gynt,* 1867, *A Doll's House,* 1879, *Hedda Gabler,* 1890, and *The Master Builder,* 1892).

Illustration by Aubrey Beardsley for Wilde's *Salomé*

(1884) and *Judah* (1890), which are improvements when compared to his popular but still melodramatic *The Silver King*. **Sir Arthur Wing Pinero** (1855-1934) was superior to Jones. In *The Second Mrs. Tanqueray* (1893) he introduced the theme of the immoral past. Around 1900, Ibsen's shadow was noticeable everywhere in English drama. It was **William Archer** who popularized and defended the Norwegian's plays in England. Archer translated *A Doll's House (Nora)* and *Ghosts* (1891) into English. Another defender of Ibsen was George Bernard Shaw. Ibsen concentrated on the social and domestic problems of his age, and, in *A Doll's House,* performed in London in 1899, he threw some light on the intricate aspects of a failed marriage. But Ibsen's serious criticism was too strong to be popular in England. Shaw was the only playwright deeply affected by him. In England, realism was usually diluted by humour and sentiment.

Toward the end of the century, the comedy of manners was revived by **Oscar Wilde.** The theatre audience had been prepared for his brilliant comedies by the witty comic operas of **Sir William Gilbert** (1836-1911) and **Sir Arthur S. Sullivan** (1842-1900). Gilbert contributed satire and smart lyrics, and Sullivan produced ravishing music that made such operas as *Patience* (1881) and *The Mikado* (1885) irresistible. Gilbert, who ridiculed Oscar Wilde in *Patience,* shared with him a verbal wit that had been dead on the stage since Sheridan. Wilde gave back to the drama fantasy and irony. When he was jailed in 1895 for homosexual practices, both he and the English theatre suffered. Wilde made his reputation as a playwright not in tragedy (the performance of *Salomé,* 1893, first written in French, was prohibited by the censor) but in the light comedy of manners, such as *Lady Windermere's Fan* (1892), *A Woman of No Importance* (1893), and *An Ideal Husband* (1895). Although bordering on farce, *The Importance of Being Earnest* (1895) is the best of his comedies. Full of wit, epigrams and paradox, the play has a singular verbal charm that tends to obscure the social and satirical themes.

Oscar Wilde

The two London friends John Worthing and Algernon Moncrieff lead double lives. John has invented a brother, "Ernest", and has courted Gwendolen Fairfax under this name, while Algernon travels as "Bunbury" in the country. Confusion and comic situations develop when Algernon pretends to be Ernest in the presence of John's ward Cecily Cardew and gets engaged to her. The misunderstandings increase, as Cecily and Gwendolen believe themselves to be engaged to Ernest Worthing, whom his brother John declares dead. In the dénouement, the two men confess their lies and manage a reconciliation between their fiancées and themselves. There is also a sort of deus ex machina in the discovery of John Worthing's true identity. Since he proves to be Algernon's true brother Ernest, who was thought to have disappeared, he is Gwendolen's social equal and thus acceptable as a man and husband.

The many confusions and impossible situations of the play preclude any serious treatment of social or ideological problems. Even the problem of identity, which is central to this comedy, is dissolved in epigrams and paradox. Wilde is here too much in love with punch lines and verbal irony, and with the possibilities of humour in language, plot and situations, to be able to develop any serious social criticism. The play should be taken as "a trivial comedy for serious people", the sub-title Oscar Wilde gave to this comedy of manners.

Oscar Wilde's comedies always seen to hover a few feet above the ground. In his plays, any attempts to be critical of social conditions and class distinctions in late Victorian England are immediately ironicised by witty remarks, puns and aphorisms. It is obvious that his plays are meant as mere entertainment, and this includes the casual and often superficial treatment of social issues.

4. The Novel

At the beginning of the century two novelists stand out who differ greatly in theme and approach - **Sir Walter Scott** and **Jane Austen. Scott** (1771-1832) was both a poet and a novelist. He acquired fame and wealth with such narrative poems as *The Lady of the Lake* (1810). When he started writing novels, his printers and publishers, with whom he was in partnership, went bankrupt (1826), and Scott had to pay off a huge debt. So he turned himself into a sort of writing-machine, like the Frenchman Balzac,[1] producing book after book while necessarily sacrificing quality to quantity. Scott left behind a great number of romantic historical novels, the best of which were those dealing with Scotland's scenery and history, such as *Waverley* (1814), *Old Mortality* (1816), and *The Heart of Midlothian* (1818). His *Ivanhoe* (1820), which has been made into films and TV series and is concerned with English history, is still being read by younger readers.

What Scott lacked (humour, psychologically convincing characters, and social criticism) **Jane Austen** (1775-1817) was able to provide in novels that have stood the test of time. She parodied the Gothic novel in her *Northanger Abbey* (1798; published in 1818) and then focused on a small corner of her society, the moderately rich country families and the gentry. Characters from this social stratum people her novels: *Sense and Sensibility* (1811), *Pride and Prejudice* (1813), *Mansfield Park* (1814), *Emma* (1816), and *Persuasion* (1818).

In *Mansfield Park*, the main character is Fanny Price. At the age of nine she leaves her own poor family and grows up in the house of the Bertrams, Mrs. Bertram being her aunt. Sir Thomas Bertram is a stern yet good-hearted baronet with two sons, Tom and Edmund, and two daughters, Maria and Julia. Mrs. Bertram, like her sister, the widow Mrs. Norris, is selfish and indolent. Although Fanny is constantly bullied by Mrs. Norris, she gradually becomes an important member of the household and, in the absence of Sir Thomas, maintains the family discipline. She is grieved to see her cousin Edmund fascinated by the wordly-minded Mary Crawford. Mary's brother Henry, an attractive but dissolute young man, falls in love with Fanny and proposes to her. When she rejects him, she incurs the displeasure of Sir Thomas. Matters come to a crisis during Fanny's visit at her own home; Henry elopes with Maria, who has married Mr. Rushworth, and Julia runs away with Mr. Yates, one of her suitors. Finally, Edmund discovers Mary Crawford's shallow character. Turning to Fanny for comfort, he falls in love with and marries her.

Jane Austen was impressed neither by the sentimentalism and moralism of the late eighteenth-century novel nor by the French Revolution and the Napoleonic wars. Writing with great care and craftsmanship, she produced ironic pictures of people and their social relations. Her plots are convincing, and her characters are not types but complex figures with faults and virtues, described in a prose that flows easily and naturally.

Scott's historical novels influenced the work of **Edward Bulwer-Lytton** (1803-73), who is remembered today for his *The Last Days of Pompeii* (1834), which has been filmed. The novels of **Thomas Love Peacock** (1775-1866) however, have little to do with Scott. Peacock was a friend of Shelley's and a poet in his own

---

1. Honoré de Balzac (1799-1850), French novelist, whose *Comédie humaine* (written between 1827-47 and published between 1842-48) is made up of 91 interconnected novels that provide a fictional representation of French society at the end of the eighteenth century and in the first half of the 19th century. Balzac aimed at a critical analysis of social customs and manners and also explored the operation of human passions. He had to write in order to pay his heavy debts. His influence on later writers, such as Henry James, has been immense.

right. He satirized Romanticism in eccentric characters and comical situations, as in *Headlong Hall* (1816), *Nightmare Abbey* (1818), and *Crotchet Castle* (1831). These novels proved important for the later Meredith and Huxley. Peacock's odd characters were merely fanfares to the rich fictional world of Charles Dickens.

Charles Dickens (1812-70) was born near Portsmouth, the second of eight children. His father was a poor clerk in the Navy Pay Office and took his family to London when he lost his job. Although the boy's education was badly neglected, he read with eagerness the novels of Defoe, Fielding, Smollett, Goldsmith, Cervantes, and Le Sage, of which he found copies in the household. When his father was arrested for debt and consigned to Marshalsea Prison, Charles was sent to work at a warehouse, where he had to stick labels on bottles. These days of misery and humiliation left their traces in Dickens's literary work. Having taught himself shorthand, Dickens became a parliamentary reporter in 1831 and worked for the *Morning Chronicle.* Very soon after he began to contribute articles to several magazines, and his first literary success came with *Sketches by Boz* (1834).

For all his faults – his novels suffer from unconvincing plots, sentimentality, and clumsy prose – Dickens is still being read because of his vitality, his gallery of grotesque and humorous characters, and his moral seriousness tempered by humour.

Structurally, his novels are interesting in that most were first serialized in newspapers and magazines. *The Posthumous Papers of the Pickwick Club* (1836-39) is basically a series of grotesque incidents involving humorous types. Plot does not matter in the *Pickwick Papers,* which is held together by the central figure of Mr. Pickwick. With *Oliver Twist,* Dickens's first true novel, pathos and melodrama began to displace humour, and Dickens became more concerned with social criticism.

Oliver Twist grows up as an orphan in the cruel environment of a workhouse. After an unhappy apprenticeship, he runs away to London, where he falls into the hands of a gang of thieves led by Fagin, an old Jew. The members of the gang, the burglar Bill Sikes and his companion Nancy, and a young pickpocket named "the Artful Dodger", make every effort to convert Oliver into a thief. Temporarily rescued by Mr. Brownlow, Oliver is again kidnapped by the gang at the request of an evil person named Monks. Accompanying Bill Sikes on a burgling expedition, Oliver is wounded and comes into the house of Mrs. Maylie and her protégée Rose. There he is kindly treated and brought up. After a while, Nancy reveals to Rose that Monks knows something about Oliver's parentage and that there is some relationship between Oliver and Rose. When the gang get to hear of Nancy's action, she is killed by Bill Sikes. Trying to escape, Bill Sikes accidentally hangs himself, and the rest of the gang are arrested. Fagin is executed, and Monks, who is found and threatened with exposure, confesses that he is Oliver's half-brother and has tried to ruin him in order to retain the whole of his father's property. He also reveals that Rose is the sister of Oliver's unfortunate mother. Finally, Oliver is adopted by Mr. Brownlow while Monks emigrates and dies in prison.

In *Oliver Twist* and some of the subsequent novels, such as *Nicholas Nickleby* (1838-39), *The Old Curiosity Shop* (1840-41), and the autobiographical *David Copperfield* (1849-50), Dickens conducted his readers through a nightmare London of prisons, factories, taverns, lawyers' offices, and thieves' shelters peopled by strange and grotesque figures.

He also tried the genre of the historical novel, focusing on the Gordon Riots[1] of the 1780s in his *Barnaby Rudge* (1840-41), and on London and Paris during the French Revolution in *A Tale of Two Cities* (1859). But as his writing advanced, he became more and more concerned with the evils of crime and poverty. The later novels contain much social criticism and are distinguished by their intricate plots and gloomy atmosphere. *Bleak House* (1852-53) attacks and satirizes the slowness and the inhumanity of the English legal system. *Hard Times* (1854) was written against the utilitarians and industrial conditions, while *Little Dorritt* (1855-57) found its target in the "circumlocution office", i.e. the system of administration. With one of his last novels, *Great Expectations* (1860-61), Dickens resumed the humorous element that distinguishes his early works. This novel marks the peak of his achievement in the handling of plot, comedy, character, and theme, which his last completed novel, *Our Mutual Friend* (1864-65), could not surpass. In *Great Expectations* Dickens reveals his understanding of the mind of a child who is trying to make sense of the world of the adults.

The novel deals with the youth of Philip Pirrip, called Pip, who is brought up by his sister, the wife of the kind and humorous blacksmith Joe Gargery. Introduced to Miss Havisham, a lady who hates men because she was once deserted by her lover, Pip falls in love with the girl Estella, who is brought up by Miss Havisham. When Pip receives money from a mysterious source, he aspires to become a gentleman, goes to London and forgets his benefactor Joe Gargery. Pip learns that his money came from an escaped convict, to whom, as a boy, he had rendered a service. However, his great expectations soon dissolve in London. Penniless, he is informed that Estella has married his enemy, Bentley Drummle, who treats her in a cruel way. Having learned his lesson, Pip eventually returns to Joe Gargery and begins to work hard and honestly. He is finally reunited with Estella who has also been taught a lesson by adversity.

Dickens was at heart a philanthropist and a sentimentalist. He also wrote some charming Christmas stories, such as *A Christmas Carol* (1843). These tales, too, indicate his basic problem as a writer: his melodramatic tendencies and his sentimentalism often work against his purpose as a social critic. Nevertheless, Dickens's fictional world is too rich and fascinating to be ignored. He remains one of the great and original writers of English literature.

The humanitarianism and social criticism which characterized Dickens's fiction were continued by a number of writers who also adopted his melodramatic plots. Among them were **Charles Reade** (1814-84), **Charles Kingsley** (1819-75), **Benjamin Disraeli** (1804-81), **Elizabeth C. Gaskell** (1810-65), and the first writer of detective fiction, **William Wilkie Collins** (1824-89).

If Dickens wrote of low life and drew his material from London's poor inhabitants, **William Makepeace Thackeray** (1811-63) dealt with the rich in a less

---

1. Led by Lord Gordon (1751-93), fanatical Presbyterians caused bloody riots in London in 1780 while demonstrating against new legislation granting more religious freedom to Catholics.

sentimental style. Thackeray was the son of an official of the East India Company[1]. He was educated at Cambridge and became a journalist, starting with humorous articles for the comic weekly *Punch*. Thackeray's realism is ironic and antiromantic and can already be noticed in his early character sketches contained in *The Book of Snobs* (1848). His first novel was a satirical romance, *The Luck of Barry Lyndon* (1844), which, in 1974, served as the script for Stanley Kubrick's beautiful film of the same title. In *Barry Lyndon* an Irish adventurer recounts his wild adventures in the manner of Henry Fielding's *Jonathan Wild*. Thackeray's major novel, *Vanity Fair,* published in monthly instalments, followed in 1847-48. The book has as its theme "snobland", i.e. Thackeray's England. The subtitle is "a novel without a hero", indicating that the plot is less important than the characters.

Vanity Fair traces the careers of two strongly contrasted girls. Amelia Sedley, the sentimental and naive daughter of a merchant, marries a young officer, George Osborne, Osborne's father, however, is against the marriage, since Amelia's father has meanwhile been ruined by speculations. When George is killed in the battle of Waterloo, Amelia is left in poverty, as his father has disinherited him.

Amelia's friend, Becky Sharp, with whom George Osborne has an affair before his death, is the clever and courageous daughter of a poor artist and a French opera-dancer. After several unsuccessful attempts, Becky finally manages to marry into the upper class, though her marriage with Rawdon Crawley remains a secret until Rawdon's father, Sir Pitt, proposes to Becky on the death of his wife. Becky flies to the Continent, where the chief characters are again brought together. Becky continues her intrigues, at first in Paris and then in London, and wins her way into the highest society. But her adultery with Lord Steyne is discovered and she leaves England for France and Germany.

Amelia, too, lives a life of poverty with her parents and is still grieved by the loss of her husband. It is only after Becky has told her of George's infidelity that she decides to marry Captain Dobbin, who has been secretly giving her money over the years. Meanwhile, Becky has succeeded in seducing Amelia's brother, Joseph Sedley, and she exploits him until his death.

Thackeray manages in this novel to provide a broad satire not only on England's upper class but also on Paris, Brussels and Weimar. A quick sequence of episodes and a vast gallery of actors reveal the "vanity" of the high and mighty and their value system, which is based on wealth and property.

In *Pendennis* (1848-50) Thackeray introduces a hero whose career resembles his own, but again the events and the people around Arthur Pendennis are at least as interesting as the protagonist. With *Henry Esmond* (1852) and its sequel, *The Virginians* (1857-59), William Thackeray turned to the historical novel and the England of Queen Anne's day, displaying his love for, and knowledge of, the eighteenth century. Abhorring sentimentalism, Thackeray preferred to use satirical hu-

---

1. The English East India Company (there were also Dutch and French equivalents) received its charter from Elizabeth I in 1600. The company was granted a monopoly of trade in Asia, Africa, and America; it was managed by a governor and 24 directors chosen from its stockholders. Reorganized under Cromwell, the company flourished, and became a dominant power in India in the 18th century. In 1773 the British government established a governor-generalship in India, and in 1813 the company's monopoly was abolished.

mour and some cynicism in his novels. He often wavered between irony and pity and was technically superior to Dickens, though his work lacked the grotesque and strange glamour Charles Dickens was able to create.

Thackeray's realism found an admirer in **Anthony Trollope** (1815-82). A civil servant in the General Post Office, Trollope invented a county called Barsetshire and a town called Barchester, and in several novels described provincial life. Trollope wrote to please his readers, turning out almost 50 novels that show more mechanical skill than inspiration. Today, his six Barsetshire novels are recognized as the most valuable, among them *The Warden* (1855) and *Barchester Towers* (1857).

Some of the best novels of the Victorian period were written by women. In the isolation of a Yorkshire vicarage, three sisters wrote poems and prose fiction: **Anne Brontë** (1820-49) was less talented than her sisters **Charlotte** (1816-55) and **Emily** (1818-48). The novels of the Brontë sisters feature female heroines described from a female point-of-view. In Charlotte's best novel, *Jane Eyre* (1847), a governess falls in love with her master who is married to a madwoman. The book presents passion and a love-story, but also realism, observation and wit. The charm of *Jane Eyre,* which is partly autobiographical, arises from the convincing descriptions of passionate sincerity and the author's courage to explore human life with greater fidelity than was common in her age. With *Wuthering Heights* (1847), Emily Brontë created a passionate world set against the Yorkshire moors. Emily, the most gifted of the three sisters, died of tuberculosis at the age of thirty. Avoiding the melodramatic effects of her sister's *Jane Eyre,* she accomplished in one novel what other writers tried to realize in a lifetime.

Wuthering Heights has as its central figure Heathcliff, a gipsy boy of unknown parentage. He is picked up in Liverpool by Mr. Earnshaw who takes him home and rears him as one of his own children. Heathcliff is constantly bullied by Hindley, Earnshaw's son, especially after his benefactor's death, but he falls in love with Hindley's sister Catherine, a girl as passionate and ferocious as Heathcliff himself. Heathcliff leaves the house when he overhears Catherine say that marrying him would degrade her. After three years he returns a wealthy man and finds Catherine married to the neighbour, Edgar Linton. Catherine dies at the birth of her daughter Cathy, and Heathcliff marries Edgar's sister Isabella, although he does not love her. His vindictive nature shows in his mistreatment of Isabella and Hindley's son Hareton. Heathcliff finally manages to get Hindley completely in his power and lures Cathy to his house, forcing a marriage between her and his own sickly son, his aim being to secure Linton's property. But when his son dies, Cathy and Hareton are attracted to each other and Heathcliff, now worn out, dies after unsuccessfully trying to destroy the houses of Earnshaw and Linton. Hareton and Cathy are left to live a happy life together.

The fact that both Emily and Charlotte Brontë originally published their works under men's names indicates that Victorian society considered novel writing a man's activity. Not surprisingly, **Mary Ann Evans** also chose a male pseudonym, **George Eliot,** when she began writing fiction. Whereas the Brontë sisters showed what human passion and emotions could do, **George Eliot** (1819-80) was more concerned with intellectual and moral problems. When her father died in 1849, she went to London and became sub-editor of the *Westminster Review,* contributing essays and sketches. Equipped with a powerful intellect, she was deeply interested in philosophy and religion. She translated David Friedrich Strauss and Feuerbach before turning to the novel. For several years she lived with George Lewis, the English biographer of Goethe who encouraged her to write prose fiction. As a writer, she was torn between the rational attitude of the intellectual and religious feelings and emotions. Most of her novels are constructed around an idea, sometimes much too obviously. *Adam Bede* (1859) presents a story of seduction with much psychological insight, and *The Mill on the Floss* (1860) is concerned with the simple but honest Maggie Tulliver and her brother Tom. Simple people like linen-weavers also figure in her *Silas Marner* (1861). In her later works Eliot treated social rather than individual problems, producing in *Felix Holt the Radical* (1866) a study of political idealism. Her fictional analysis of provincial life at the beginning of the Victorian period, *Middlemarch* (1871-72), has become one of the major novels of English literature.

The novel takes its title from a provincial town and tells the story of Dorothea Brooke, a girl with a high ideal of life. Rejecting her neighbour, Sir James Chettam, she marries an elderly pedant, Mr. Casaubon, a cleric and scientist engaged in mythological studies. Because of Casaubon's lack of sympathy, the marriage is very unhappy. Suspecting that his wife prefers his young cousin Will Ladislaw, he changes his will and, on his death, Dorothea learns that she forfeits her fortune if she marries Ladislaw. But in the end Dorothea and Ladislaw are brought together.

Eliot develops two sub-plots parallel to this first story. The first describes the unhappy marriage and the career of Tertius Lydgate, a young doctor, and his wife Rosamond Vincy, and the second tells the love-story of Fred Vincy and Mary Garth.

Eliot uses these three couples to analyse the social and individual changes in an English province around 1830. Her characters develop because they are shown as products of their environment. This positivist theory was also shared by **Henry James** and **George Meredith**.

It was the concern with intellectual problems that **Meredith** (1828-1909) had in common with George Eliot. He revolted against Victorian ideas of a woman's status. Meredith has been called the Browning of prose. He also wrote poetry, and his sonnet sequence *Modern Love* (1862) contains some very beautiful poems. His first novel was *The Ordeal of Richard Feverel* (1859).

Richard Feverel, the son of a wealthy baronet, stands in the centre of the novel. Deserted by his wife, the father has his own system in bringing Richard up, which consists of keeping him away from school and supervising him at home. However, during Richard's adolescence, this "system" breaks down, and Richard falls in love with Lucy Desborough, the niece of a neighbouring farmer. When Richard's father objects to their courtship, the couple contract a secret marriage. But the cruel baronet arranges for the young couple to be separated and sends Richard to London where he is seduced by a beautiful woman. Lord Mountfalcon, who is interested in winning Lucy for himself, spreads rumours about Richard who does not dare visiting his wife until he learns that he has become a father and that Lucy and the baronet are reconciled. Returning home to his wife, he is informed about Lord Mountfalcon's schemes, challenges him and is seriously wounded in a duel. Lucy, severely shocked at hearing this news, goes mad and dies.

The central characters in Meredith's novels are all subject to a minute psychological analysis which achieves its purest form in *The Egoist* (1879). This novel preserves the dramatic unities. As a novelist, Meredith provided a key to it in his essay *On the Idea of Comedy*. Meredith has never been as popular as Dickens or Hardy, and the reasons for this lack of public response can be found in his demanding and sometimes obscure style as well as in his psychological approach and exploration of men's actions and motives. A master of language, and also of humour and pathos, Meredith defended the cause of women (several of his novels bear women's names, e.g. *Sandra Belloni*, 1864, and *Rhoda Fleming*, 1865) and tended to didacticism and ironic commentary. He steered a course between Romanticism and realism.

Victorian pessimism entered English fiction in the novels of **George Gissing** (1857-1903), **George Moore** (1852-1933), and **Thomas Hardy** (1840-1928). To some extent, they continued Dickensian social criticism. Gissing began with *Workers in the Dawn* (1880), recounted the life of a prostitute in *The Unclassed* (1884), and described the misery of the proletariat in *Demos* (1886) and *The Nether World* (1889). In *New Grub Street* (1891) and *Born in Exile* (1892), Gissing recorded the fate of impoverished writers like himself who struggled to make a living by publishing whatever they could. Like Gissing, **Moore** wrote very much under the influence of French naturalism as represented by Emile Zola[1] and Guy de Maupassant.[2] His early works are mostly concerned with the tragic destinies of women (see, for instance, *A Mummer's Wife,* 1884; *A Drama in Muslin,* 1886; *Spring Days,* 1888; and *Esther Waters,* 1894).

The novels of **Thomas Hardy** achieved an epic quality, and he was undoubtedly the most remarkable exponent of the current of pessimistic realism. His works are masterpieces of realistic description and psychological penetration. Hardy produced a whole series of books set in his native Dorset, the "Wessex novels", which are dominated by the notion of a relentless fate and an uncompromising determinism. In his novels, men are slaves to the environment, to history, and to their instincts. While *Far from the Madding Crowd* (1874) is still positive in its message, private sadness and the universe of sorrow dominate in *The Return of the Native* (1878) and in *The Mayor of Casterbridge* (1886). Tragic elements come to the fore in *Jude the Obscure* (1895) and *Tess of the D'Urbervilles* (1891) which Roman Polanski made into a film.

---

1. Émile Zola (1840-1902), French novelist and the leading figure in the naturalistic movement. Influenced by contemporary theories of heredity and experimental science, he chronicled the lives of individuals and of families in a series of novels that establish a panorama of mid-19th-century French life in the middle and working classes while analysing vice, misery, and human instincts. His major works are *Thérèse Raquin* (1867) and the twenty novels in the series entitled *Les Rougon-Macquart* (1871-93).
2. Guy de Maupassant (1850-93), French writer of short stories and novels and a member of the naturalistic group around Zola. He published hundreds of stories about country people and simple city dwellers, with a few dealing with other social groups. The best known among his novels are *Bel-Ami* (1885) and *Pierre et Jean* (1888).

In *Tess,* whose sub-title is "A pure woman", Hardy tells the tragic story of the daughter of a poor villager who believes he is the descendant of the ancient family of the D'Urbervilles. Tess is seduced by Alec, who bears the surname D'Urberville, and gives birth to a child. When this child dies in infancy, Tess starts working as a dairymaid on a large farm and becomes engaged to Angel Clare, a clergyman's son. On their wedding-night, Tess confesses her affair with Alec, and Angel abandons her and goes to Brazil. After a period of hardship. Tess again meets Alec. He has now become a preacher and manages to persuade her to become his mistress again. When Angel returns from Brazil, prepared now to forgive Tess, he finds her with Alec. Tess has been trying to contact Angel, appealing for help, and, maddened by Alec's second wrong to her, she kills him so that she can live with her husband. Briefly, they enjoy some happiness while hidden in the New Forest, but Tess is eventually arrested, tried, and hanged.

Even though Hardy's art was sombre, as this novel shows, it was never nihilistic. Later in his life, he turned to poetry and again made the countryside and the people of Dorset the main objects of his writing. His verse is collected in the *Wessex Poems* (1898). As in his novels, he proved a great master in depicting nature. At the end of his literary career stands a "closet drama", *The Dynasts* (1903-08), an epic in blank verse and prose surveys dealing with the Napoleonic Wars as seen by men and immortal ghosts.

There was much social criticism but little satire in the English novel of the nineteenth century. The great exception is **Samuel Butler** (1835-1902), a writer who may have most to say to our own age. Like Meredith and Hardy, he was influenced by the teaching of Darwin and the biological scientists, yet he recognized man's will as an essential force. After a quarrel with his father, Butler emigrated to New Zealand. He later returned to England. New Zealand merely served as the setting for his satirical novels *Erewhon* (1872), which is "nowhere" spelled backwards, and *Erewhon Revisited* (1901), in which he ridiculed England's institutions and values. Butler showed no mercy to Victorian England and its ideas of family life, morality and religion. His masterpiece was *The Way of All Flesh,* published in 1903 after the author's death.

This novel studies the relationship between parents and children. And though Butler had bitter memories of his own childhood, his novel, gloomy as it may be in several passages, is always more than a mere accusation. It sparkles with wit and irony. The author traces the development of the members of the Pontifex family through several generations, finally concentrating on Ernest, the son of the clergyman Theobald Pontifex and his smug wife Christina. During his childhood, Ernest suffers cruelly from the tyranny of his pharisaical father. After being ordained, he has a breakdown and insults a young woman, taking her for a prostitute. As a result, he is sentenced to six months' imprisonment. Ruined upon emerging from prison, he lives with Ellen, a former servant of his family, but soon discovers that she is already married. Finally, a fortune he inherits from an aunt allows him to devote himself to literature.

The novel is an onslaught on everything Victorians held dear. Because of his attacks on the false gods of his contemporaries, Butler, who lived and wrote in comparative obscurity, has become a considerable influence on several modern writers. In his prose fiction as well as in his essays he showed himself one of the most original minds of his time.

Satire was just one means to escape the atmosphere of despondency that reigned toward the end of the century. Romance, adventure, and sensation were others. **Robert Louis Stevenson** (1850-94), who emigrated to Samoa later in his life, was one of the more influential writers of adventure and romance. Also a poet and essayist, he became the pioneer of a new sort of literature with *Treasure Island* (1883) and *Kidnapped* (1886), which are today read mainly by younger readers and have often been filmed. From the novel and tale of adventure, Stevenson moved to historical romances in the style of Scott, and finally to the novelistic treatment of the duality of good and evil in one man in *The Strange Case of Dr Jekyll and Mr Hyde* (1886). This book is one of the prototypes of the modern thriller and is also of psychological interest because it deals with a split personality.

The physician Dr Jekyll discovers a drug that allows him to turn himself into a personality uniting all his evil instincts. Calling this being Mr Hyde, he assumes this personality from time to time in order to give in to his evil impulses. Gradually, the personality of Hyde gains a greater influence and commits a horrible murder. Jekyll now finds that he is frequently transformed into Hyde, even against his own will, and that his drug loses its efficacy in restoring his original personality. When he is about to be arrested, he takes his own life.

Stevenson had a number of followers who developed the various elements of his fiction – adventure, romance, sensation, and horror – in their own ways. **Sir Henry Rider Haggard's** (1856-1925) *King Solomon's Mines* (1885), which is set in Africa, and **Maurice Henry Hewlett's** (1861-1923) *The Forest Lovers* (1898), a medieval romance, have today lost their popularity, whereas *Dracula* (1897), by **Bram Stoker** (1847-1912), continues to hold a special fascination for the reading and TV audience, especially after Roman Polanski's successful and still popular movie *Dance of the Vampires* of 1966.

The novel of adventure found another representative in **Rudyard Kipling** (1865-1936), the great singer of the Empire,[1] who proclaimed in verse and prose the grandeur of all he deemed best in English tradition. Kipling was born in India, and in his novellas *Plain Tales from the Hills* (1888), he described the lives of Englishmen in this country. Time and again, it was the people as well as the scenery and the charms of India that inspired him for his works. Thus his novel *Kim* (1901) relates the adventures of a half-caste orphan, the child of an Irish sergeant in India. Kipling's obvious weakness was his strident imperialism. It permeates all his works, with the notable exception of the famous *Jungle Books* (1894-1895), which served as the script for one of the best animated cartoons ever made. Set in the Indian jungle, with exquisite descriptions of animal life, Kipling's

---

1. Formerly, the British Empire included the United Kingdom and all the colonies. Since the end of the 19th century the Empire has developed into the British Commonwealth of Nations, and, since 1945, the Commonwealth of Nations. This latter term signifies a loose and mainly economic union of independent states under the symbolical rule of the British crown (Great Britain, Canada, and many of the former English colonies in Asia and Africa). There are at present 49 members in the Commonwealth.

Jungle Books tell the story of the child Mowgli who is suckled by a she-wolf and brought up by wild beasts of the jungle.

It is remarkable that in the last decade of the nineteenth century several new literary genres began to develop. The utopian novel reappeared forcefully on the scene with *News from Nowhere* (1890), by **William Morris**, who tried to combine Socialist ideas with a romantic longing for a better past. And **Herbert George Wells** (1866-1946) soon turned utopia into a dreadful dystopia when he described scenes of fear and terror in *The Time Machine* (1895) and *When the Sleeper Wakes* (1899). By contrast, the decadents had no particular political or moral message for their readers. Their ideology consisted in the description of art and in the discussion of aesthetics. Reading the works of **Walter Pater** proclaiming "art for art's sake", and such French sources as Joris Karl Huysmans's vastly influential novel *A Rebours* (1884), the English decadents recorded their hedonism above all in poetry, although Pater's *Marius the Epicurean* (1885) and Oscar Wilde's *The Picture of Dorian Gray* (1890/91) are fine novels exemplifying the artistic and literary ideas of the fin-de-siècle movement.

The subject as well as the style of *The Picture of Dorian Gray* remind one very much of Stevenson's *Dr Jekyll and Mr Hyde.* The beautiful and Faustus-like Dorian Gray wishes to remain eternally young and handsome. And though he leads a life of viciousness and immorality, his wish is granted: while Dorian remains ever-young, his portrait, which he hides away from the public, shows signs of increasing age as well as the scars of murder, seduction, and debauchery. Dorian decides to kill the painter and also intends to destroy his portrait. But when he tries to do so, it is he who dies, disfigured by age and ugliness, and his portrait is restored to its former state of youthful beauty.

Writers toward the end of the century began to realize that their audience consisted of highbrow, middlebrow, and lowbrow readers. Thackeray, Meredith and, to some extent, Hardy, wrote for a highbrow audience, for the intellectuals; Stevenson and Kipling were read by a much wider section of society. Novelists began to be aware of the needs of children, and some, like Dickens, proved that they understood children's minds and psychology. Apart from Dickens, Stevenson, Stoker, and Kipling, another Victorian writer explored the world of fantasy for children, so much so that one gets the impression he would have liked to live in this world rather than in late nineteenth-century England. This was **Lewis Carroll,** pseudonym of **Charles Dodgson** (1832-98), a clergyman and lecturer in mathematics at Oxford. Carroll's *Alice's Adventures in Wonderland* (1865) and *Through the Looking Glass* (1871) although allegedly children's books, are very close to the Dickensian world of grotesque figures and the absurd.

Such literature, at least for those who produced it, was escapism, and it is hardly surprising that, beside the literature for children and the novel of adventure,

The Mad Hatter, an illustration from *Alice's Adventures in Wonderland*

the detective story and crime fiction also appeared on the literary scene. The detective novel developed out of the adventure story, and with writers like **William Wilkie Collins** and especially **Sir Arthur Conan Doyle** (1859-1930) it became an accepted form of fiction. Doyle's Sherlock Holmes, who first appeared in *A Study in Scarlet* (1887), proved to be one of the most famous characters in the English novel. Doyle pits his amateur detective and his friend Dr. Watson against the best detectives of Scotland Yard. Holmes is a perfect gentleman, taking drugs in moderate quantities and exploring the London of the 1880s, with its hansom cabs, gas-lamps, and eerie streets, a lost world that makes the books all the more fascinating for the modern reader. In the twentieth century, Agatha Christie's Hercule Poirot became the successor of the always brilliant and mysterious Sherlock Holmes.

5. Nonfiction

A great deal of significant prose was written by four Romantic essayists who are often grouped together: Charles Lamb, William Hazlitt, Leigh Hunt, and Thomas De Quincey. They all identified with the younger poets. Hunt's influence on, and encouragement of, Keats is as well known as the preference the others had for Wordsworth. **Charles Lamb** (1775-1834) cultivated a style that shows the influence of Robert Burton and Thomas Browne. He encouraged a wider appreciation of Renaissance drama and, in his *Essays of Elia* (1823) and *Last Essays* (1833), described everyday people and events in London in an informal and humorous way which endeared him to generations of English readers. **Leigh Hunt** (1784-1859), when compared to Lamb or Hazlitt, is a less important figure, despite Keats's admiration for him. Some of his essays were published in the periodical *The Examiner* (1808-13), which he launched with his brother John, and others were collected in *Men, Women, Books* (1847). The prose of **William Hazlitt** (1778-1830) is much more vigorous. He started out as a portrait painter, which may explain his colourful and lively style. Reflecting his passionate opinions, his phrases are illuminating and biting. Like Lamb, he encouraged the reading of the Elizabethan playwrights in *The Dramatic Literature of the Age of Elizabeth* (1820). In *The English Poets* (1818) and *The English Comic Writers* (1819), he voices his highly individual ideas on English literature. In 1825 he published *Spirit of the Age*, which deals with his contemporaries and includes some harsh judgments on Wordsworth and Coleridge who, in Hazlitt's opinion, did not fulfil the promises they had made in their earlier works. Hazlitt was one of the first critics to appreciate the landscape art of Turner[1] and revealed much of his own personality in *Liber Amoris* (1823), a record of a love-affair.

---

1. J. M. William Turner (1775-1851), the outstanding English painter of landscapes. His pictures provide an essentially Romantic vision of the beauty and violence of nature. Turner travelled in England, France, Switzerland, and Italy, and he painted in a variety of styles, from topographical watercolours to historical landscapes and, in his late work, almost abstract forms dissolved in brilliant colours. He was often inspired by contemporary poetry, James Thomson being among his favourite poets.

What links the work of Hazlitt with that of the more eccentric **Thomas De Quincey** (1785-1859) is an absolute frankness accompanied by forceful analysis. At Worcester College, Oxford, De Quincey became an opium addict, like Coleridge. With incomparable skill, he recorded his visions and nightmares in *The Confessions of an English Opium Eater* (1822; enlarged in 1856). This biographical book earned him more fame than his critical work, such as his essay "On the Knocking at the Gate in *Macbeth*" and the interesting assessments of the characters of Coleridge, Wordsworth and Southey in *Reminiscences of the English Lake Poets.*

Contrasting with these essayists' work is the prose of **William Cobbett** (1763-1835) who described England's counties with a quick eye for detail in his *Rural Rides* (1830). **Walter Savage Landor** (1775-1864) was both poet and essayist. With his *Imaginary Conversations* (1824-29), he proved that his prose is superior to his verse. In this book, he collected a series of about 150 "talks" between historical personalities on various subjects. After Landor, the essay seems to have declined. **R.L. Stevenson** revived it to some extent in *Memoirs and Portraits* (1887) and *Travels with a Donkey in the Cevennes* (1879), which prove him to be a belated Romantic.

Many essays and a great part of the literary criticism of the nineteenth century first appeared in periodicals. Critics, poets, and novelists waged bloodless yet often vicious battles in such journals as *The Gentleman's Magazine* (1731-1868), the longest-lived of the periodicals with a continuous publication from Pope to Browning. With the appearance of *The Edinburgh Review* in the first decade of the nineteenth century, political journals began to circulate. The editor of this journal, Francis Jeffrey, attacked the Romantic poets. The Tory answer to *The Edinburgh Review* was *The Quarterly Review* (1809), to which Scott contributed. It was followed by *Blackwood's Magazine,* still remembered for its attacks on Keats, and numerous other periodicals.

Almost all the poets and novelists of the nineteenth century published their views on literature. Some writers, however, excelled in literary criticism. In his *Biographia Literaria* (1877), **Coleridge** anticipated the modern philosophical and psychological criticism of literature and the arts. His approach was later taken up by Arnold and Pater. **Thomas Carlyle** (1795-1881), a Scottish Calvinist[1], made a reputation for himself as an historian, literary critic, and novelist. As a translator of German literature (of Goethe's *Wilhelm Meister* and tales by Tieck and Jean Paul) he was exposed to German culture and philosophy. His own *Sartor Resartus* (1833-34) is a sort of "Bildungsroman" recording his philosophical development in the story of Professor Diogenes Teufelsdreckh at the university of Weissnichtwo. Turning to history in *The French Revolution* (1837), Carlyle rejected materialism

---

1. Jean Cauvin (later Calvin, 1509-64) was a French theologian and Protestant reformer. He settled in Geneva and became known for his strict morals and his religious views – Calvinism – which were based on biblical authority and the moral nature of man. Calvin advocated the doctrine of predestination, which some economists and philosophers have seen as the ideological source of capitalism: economic success proves that one has been selected as one of God's saints. Protestant Calvinism proved important for the social and economic development of Western Europe and North America. His principal written work was *Institution de la religion chrétienne* (1536).

and advocated his own moral views of history. Chaos, he argued in *On Heroes and Hero Worship* (1841), could be overcome only by following and obeying outstanding leaders. This doctrine anticipated the German Fascists, though it must be said that Carlyle's aim was a positive one – to lead England from materialism to a more spiritual life.

John Ruskin (1819-1900) did for art what Carlyle tried to do for history. A humanitarian moralist and art critic, Ruskin defended the art of Turner in the five volumes of *Modern Painters* (1843-60) while constructing a theory of aesthetics that, to him, became a substitute for religion. In *The Seven Lamps of Architecture* (1849) and *The Stones of Venice* (1851-53), he attempted to prove the value of Gothic art whose origins he perceived in religious faith. Ruskin exerted great influence at Oxford, where he was Professor of Art. With religious fervour he condemned modern materialism and the Utilitarians, suggesting instead the pursuit of the beautiful. Ruskin's later works are concerned with poverty and ignorance and the need to bring beauty and a sense of purpose into the lives of the workers. His proximity to the ideas of **William Morris** and **Matthew Arnold** is undeniable. Morries tried to put into practice what Ruskin had taught and written. But he was not very successful. Arnold was Professor of Poetry at Oxford and, for several years, Inspector of public schools. He applied Ruskin's moralism to England's culture and literature in *Essays in Criticism* (1865), *Culture and Anarchy* (1867), and *Literature and Dogma* (1873). Arnold demanded of literature a criticism and explanation of life as well as guidelines and solace. Rebuking the philistines of his day, he saw in poetry a moral purpose which the writers refused to provide.

Finally, in the later part of the century, **Walter Pater** (1839-94), who had studied Ruskin, made art an end in itself. Completely opposed to Arnold, Pater expounded his own theory of pure aesthetic experience and pleasure as a satisfactory activity in such works as *On Style in Appreciations* (1889) and *Studies in the History of the Renaissance* (1873). He demonstrated his hedonistic theory in a novel, *Marius the Epicurean* (1885), which portrays the life and intellectual conflicts of a Roman patrician in the dying world of pagan beliefs and during the rise of Christianity.

In addition to Carlyle, Ruskin and Pater, a number of writers contributed to the writing of history, philosophy and the sciences. **Charles Darwin's** (1809-92) *The Origin of Species* (1859) and *The Descent of Man* (1871) possess the qualities of works of art, as far as style is concerned. Darwin's books challenged orthodox religion, and the consequences of his ideas were further explained in the prose of **T. H. Huxley's** (1825-95) *Man's Place in Nature* (1863). The more influential philosophers of the century were **Jeremy Bentham** (1748-1832) and **John Stuart Mill** (1806-73). Their works advocated utilitarian ideologies that helped to develop Victorian materialism. The nineteenth century also produced several historians, but only **Thomas Babington Macaulay** (1800-1859) was outstanding. From the viewpoint of the Protestant liberal Whig he wrote a *History of England* (1848-61), which was unfortunately never finished, tracing the English story from James II to William III in prose that seems to be inspired by the novels of Scott, and also by the philosophy of David Hume and by Gibbon's mastery of form.

VII. The Twentieth Century

1. General Background

Queen Victoria died in 1901, but the period termed Victorian did not suddenly come to an end. Starting with the writers of the 1890s, a time of transition had begun that lasted until about 1914 when the Great War marked both an end and a new beginning in literature. Novelists and poets like Hardy, Kipling, and others, continued to write well into the twentieth century, and the ideas of Victorianism competed with those of the early modernists[1].

A number of political and historical events brought about significant changes in England. The Labour Party was founded in 1893 and immediately became the voice of the working class in its fight for political influence against the established middle and upper classes. In 1923, and again in 1929-31, the Labour Party formed the government. After World War II it even achieved an absolute majority and put into practice a great part of its reform programme.

Social changes were accompanied by the dismantling of the Empire under the successive reigns of George V (1910-36), Edward VIII (1936), George VI (1936-52), and the present Queen, Elizabeth II. The loose union of the Commonwealth[2] replaced the former Empire. In 1913 the Irish Home Rule Bill was passed, though its implementation was deferred until after the war – by which time a bloody rebellion had taken place. The Irish Free State was granted the status of a Dominion[3] in 1922, and became a Republic and left the Commonwealth in 1949. England lost her influence in Egypt and Iraq, and granted independence to India and Pakistan in 1947. The idea and the organization of the Commonwealth made it difficult for Great Britain to join the EEC. Refused entry to the Common Market in 1963, Britain had to wait for another ten years to become a member of the European Community.

The twentieth century has seen two cruel and devastating world wars. The first is still sometimes called the Great War in English, although poets like Sassoon, Owen and the Surrealists[4] tried to show its ugliness. This first mass slaughter showed that scientific progress and industrial power harboured evil and inhuman possibilities. In their art, the Surrealists recorded the nightmares and the psychological and mental impact this war made on sensitive people. The second World War proved, if anything, that man could do worse. Technical ingenuity and fanatic Fascism brought the world to the brink of annihilation. Hitler, and those who followed him, made a mockery of human advancement, and science announced its

---

1. See pp. 119-20. In poetry, the modernists included Ezra Pound and the Imagists, and T. S. Eliot; in prose, the most important innovators were D. H. Lawrence, James Joyce, and Virginia Woolf. In art, modernism comprises such schools as cubism, dadaism, and surrealism.
2. See the note on page 106.
3. One of the self-governing territories of the British Commonwealth.
4. See Glossary of Literary Terms.

A Battery Shelled by Wyndham Lewis, 1918

terrible potential when in 1945 two atom bombs were dropped on Hiroshima and Nagasaki. Forty years after the end of World War II and the end of the Cold War[1] of the 1950s, the human race is still in danger of being annihilated by an atomic holocaust.

Politically, the Russian Revolution of 1917 and Marxism proved influential for Europe, but less so for Britain. The 1980s have seen, in addition to the persisting feelings of anxiety in the area of politics, the return of an economic crisis affecting Europe in general and Britain in particular. The British trade unions seem to be engaged in a last desperate warfare of their own against the Conservative Government of Mrs Thatcher. In this atmosphere, younger people are apparently unwilling to follow traditional political paths. As a consequence, the membership of those movements has increased which concentrate on ecology and peace, but there is also an increase of urban violence as predicted in Burgess's novel *A Clockwork Orange (1962)*.

Twentieth-century philosophy in England has refused to give answers to the basic problems of everyday life, concentrating instead on a discussion of truth and perception. Mathematical and scientific methods of philosophical analysis came to the fore with the works of **A. N. Whitehead** (1861-1947), especially in his *Principia Mathematica* (1910), written in collaboration with **Bertrand Russell** (1872-1970), *Process and Reality* (1929), and *Science and the Modern World* (1925). With his monumental *A Study of History,* published in 10 volumes between 1934 and 1954, **A. J. Toynbee** (1889-1975) contributed to cultural philosophy by continuing Oswald Spengler's line of thinking, though without the latter's pessimism.

Still under the influence of two horrible world wars, the art and literature of the twentieth century have long been concerned with interrogation and experiment. Artists and writers have been looking for something to believe in, a most difficult task after Auschwitz and Hiroshima and in the face of a triumphant materialism that is accompanied by spiritual poverty.

---

1. The period between 1947 and 1962 in which the United States and the Soviet Union fought each other on all political and economic levels while avoiding the direct military confrontation of a war (which would have meant a world catastrophe).

It was not until the 1960s that writers turned away from these burdensome issues. They did so because the reading public, increasingly made up of younger people with little or no experience of the war, demanded a different sort of entertainment. They got it, for instance, in London's pop culture, in which music played a dominant role. One of the most fascinating developments of the last 25 years has been the appearance of a new heterogeneous audience of readers and of listeners and viewers. The newer media – at first radio, then film, and more recently, television – have become powerful competitors for the book. The new reading public is divided into many sections, from highbrow to lowbrow, each market having its own laws and authors; those writers who can cater to all divisions are few and far between. New genres, such as Science Fiction and Crime Literature, which burgeoned in the nineteenth century, have been flourishing. Some critics complain about a decline in the cultural level, arguing that mass literature, like the movie industry and television, suffers from clichés and prejudices and has adopted the tastes of the lowest common denominator. But one should not exaggerate the alleged consequences of these new developments. Good poetry continues to be written. And television, though an overpowering competitor for the book, has provided new markets for script writers and dramatists. Rupert Murdoch, Britain's modern press baron, recently said that Shakespeare, if he wrote today, would work for television, and although one wonders whether the bard of Stratford would have produced anything like *Dallas,* there is no denying the fact that some excellent drama has been written for television, Dennis Potter's *Pennies from Heaven,* recently also made into a film, being just one splendid example.

2. Poetry

Some of the Georgian poets (so called because their verse was represented in the five volumes entitled *Georgian Anthologies,* edited by Edward Marsh between 1912-22) have been severely criticized for their alleged lack of emotions and profundity. Yet this charge is somewhat unjustified, for the poetic works of the Georgians – **Rupert Brooke** (1887-1915), **William H. Davies** (1871-1940), **John Drinkwater** (1882-1937), **John Masefield** (1878-1967), **Walter de la Mare** (1873-1956), **D. H. Lawrence** (1885-1930), **Robert Graves** (1895-1985), **Edmund Blunden** (1896-1974) – cannot be dismined as smooth, gentle lyrics about rural life. Rejecting the work of their predecessors, the Edwardians (i. e. those writing under Edward VII, 1901-10), the Georgians, especially Lawrence, Graves, and Brooke, saw themselves as "modern" and "realistic". Brooke belonged to the avantgarde, despite his romantic view of war and the patriotism of his sonnets. Walter de la Mare explored the world through the eyes of a child (examples can be found in his *Songs of Childhood* 1902, and *Peacock Pie,* 1913) and introduced a fresh exotic imagery in his *The Golden Journey to Samarkand* (1913). He also wrote a novel, *Memoirs of a Midget* (1921), in the form of a diary of a Lilliputian. John Masefield's best works are *Salt Water-Ballads* (1902) and the narrative poems *Dauber* (1913) and *Reynard the Fox* (1919). He was made poet laureate in 1930. Masefield also wrote fiction and became a noted playwright.

Edmund Blunden started out with poems studying country life in Sussex, Suffolk, and Kent, but his experience in the war introduced a note of sorrow and pity into his poetry. What has become known as war poetry, however, is much more bitter and desperate. The patriotic idealism of the beginning of the war soon gave way to aggressive criticism, satire, and attacks on the hero worship current at home. **Siegfried Sassoon** (1886-1967) and **Wilfred Owen** (1893-1918) wrote about the realities of war, the senseless sacrifices and the inhuman misery. Owen was killed a week before the Armistice. His "Dulce et decorum Est" is a bitter comment on Horace's phrase that to die for one's country is sweet and fitting.

> Bent double, like old beggars under sacks,
> Knock-kneed, coughing like hags, we cursed through sludge,
> Till on the haunting flares we turned our backs
> And towards our distant rest began to trudge.
> Men marched asleep. Many had lost their boots
> But limped on, blood-shod. ...

Other poets deeply influenced by the war experience were **Herbert Reed** (1893-1968), who was also a critic and later defended Surrealism (see his *Surrealism* of 1936), and Robert Graves. Also a successful novelist with *I Claudius* and *Claudius the God* (1934), Graves broadened his poetry in the 1940s and 1950s by including mythical and magical elements.

In the early part of the new century, several American writers, disappointed with American Puritanism and materialism, came to Europe in search of history and myth. Some of them, like the novelist **Henry James** (1843-1916) and the poet, playwright, and critic **T. S. Eliot** (1888-1965) eventually became British subjects; others, like **Ezra Pound** (1888-1972) remained Americans in exile. Pound was born in Idaho and came to Europe in 1908. In 1914 he founded the so-called Imagist school of poets that included American, Irish and British poets like **Richard Aldington, "H. D."** (i. e. **Hilda Doolittle**), **Amy Lowell, James Joyce, T. E. Hulme,** and others. After studying Browning and medieval French and Italian poets and translating Chinese poetry, Pound laid down the principles of Imagism in 1913. The school of Imagists rejected Romanticism and advocated the use of free rhythms as well as concreteness and conciseness of language and imagery. Precise images were to guarantee the clarity of poetic expression. Some of the best poetry of this school is contained in the anthology *Some Imagist Poets* edited by Amy Lowell in 1915. Here are two examples of Imagist poetry.

Autumn (T. E. Hulme)

> A touch of cold in the Autumn night –
> I walked abroad,
> And saw the ruddy moon lean over a hedge
> Like a red-faced farmer.
> I did not stop to speak, but nodded,
> And round about were the wistful stars
> With white faces like town children.

In a Station of the Metro (Ezra Pound)

The apparition of these faces in the crowd;
Petals on a wet, black bough.

The Imagists prepared the ground for modern poetry which, in the first half of the century, was dominated by **William Butler Yeats** (1865-1939) and **T[homas] S[tearns] Eliot** (1888-1965). It is significant that neither of these two great poets, critics and dramatists was English. Yeats was an Irishman and the son of a Pre-Raphaelite painter. In his early poems he dealt with Irish legend in the decorative manner of Rossetti and Morris. Ireland's history and mythology fascinated him, and he became an ardent patriot and one of the leading figures in the Irish literary Renaissance. Through the influence of Thomas Huxley and the agnostics, Yeats lost his religious faith. As a consequence, he searched for a mythology that was to combine his interests in literature, history and philosophy. Blake's mysticism, Irish legend and landscape, and Indian philosophy provided the subjects and symbols for his early works, such as *The Wanderings of Oisin* (1889) and the collections *Crossways* (1889) and *The Rose* (1893). His symbolism of the late 1890s, further strengthened by his reading of Walter Pater and French poets, was merely a transitory phase. Deeply moved by the political events in Ireland, he recorded his feelings and thoughts caused by the Easter rebellion[1] in "Easter 1916". The opening of this poem, quoted below, shows that Yeats had found a new kind of rough, terse verse in which both romantic Ireland and his decorative style are forgotten.

Easter 1916

I have met them at close of day
Coming with vivid faces
From counter or desk among gray
Eighteenth-century houses.
I have passed with a nod of the head
Or polite meaningless words,
Or have lingered awhile and said
Polite meaningless words,
And thought before I had done
Of a mocking tale or a gibe
To please a companion
Around the fire at the club,
Being certain that they and I
But lived where motley is worn:
All changed, changed utterly:
A terrible beauty is born.

---

1. An Irish Nationalist uprising began on Easter Monday 1916. Key points were seized and the Irish Republic was proclaimed. But the British took prompt military action and 300 insurgents were killed. The seven signatories of the Proclamation were shot the following month.

Using both poetic diction and simple phrases while avoiding easy rhyme, Yeats now began to forge his own philosophy of life, religion and love. For him, the image and art of ancient Byzantium became symbols of the union of nature, art, and spirit, and thus of the eternal quality of art. In "Sailing to Byzantium", and again in "Byzantium", Yeats discusses the relation between art and life, heart and mind, and the inherent value of works of art.

His most interesting verse of the later period is collected in *The Wild Swans at Coole* (1919), *Michael Robartes and the Dancer* (1921), *The Tower* (1928), and *The Winding Stair* (1933). Yeats's rhetorical power, his symbolism and rhythm, have had a considerable influence on modern poets. To his verse must be added numerous prose works, such as collections of Irish stories, essays, and autobiographical studies. Yeats was also one of the influential playwrights in the renewal of Irish drama.

T. S. Eliot shared with Yeats an interest in drama, literary criticism and poetry. Eliot started a revolution in the poetic taste of his generation. An American by birth, he was educated at Harvard, the Sorbonne, and Oxford, arriving in England in 1915. He entered the Anglican Church and adopted British nationality in 1927. In 1948 he was awarded the Nobel Prize for Literature. Rejecting the aesthetic theory of the later Romantics, Eliot demanded that the poet be objective, taking as examples Dante and such metaphysical poets as John Donne. His poetic career began with *Prufrock and Other Observations* (1917), in which the principal poem, "The Love Song of J. Alfred Prufrock", records the interior monologue of an elderly neurotic bachelor. Irony and satirical descriptions dominate in this poem which contrasts the trivial present with the meaningful past. There are also many scenes from New England's society of Puritans and philistines, described with a new poetical technique that combines colloquial language with metaphors and symbols taken from the European cultural heritage. The poem opens rather casually with an invitation addressed to Prufrock's friend, or, if the poem is read as a dramatic monologue, to the speaker himself. The motto is from Dante's *Inferno*.

T. S. Eliot

The Love Song of J. Alfred Prufrock

S'io credesse che mia risposta fosse
A persona che mai tornasse al mondo,
Questa fiamma staria senza piu scosse.
Ma perciocche giammai di questo fondo
Non torno vivo alcun, s'i'odo il vero,
Senza tema d'infamia ti rispondo.

Let us go then, you and I,
When the evening is spread out against the sky
Like a patient etherized upon a table;
Let us go, through certain half-deserted streets,
The muttering retreats
Of restless nights in one-night cheap hotels
And sawdust restaurants with oyster-shells:
Streets that follow like a tedious argument
Of insidious intent
To lead you to an overwhelming question. ...
Oh, do not ask, "What is it?"
Let us go and make our visit.

In the room the women come and go
Talking of Michelangelo.

It was with *The Waste Land* (1922) that Eliot established his reputation as the new century's leading poet. In contemporary and historical images and scenes this "heap of broken images", as the poem of some 400 lines has been called, presents a microcosm of the twentieth century and the emptiness of life without faith. *The Waste Land* is a rather demanding poem. Even with Eliot's explanatory footnotes it is difficult to understand, for he frequently quotes from the literature of Europe and India and employs various points of view and personae, such as the poet, a woman in a pub, a prostitute, and the Greek seer Tiresias. In addition, the changing styles are reminiscent of many English poets of the past. The verse form Eliot developed for this poem is a kind of free verse derived from the blank verse of the Elizabethan playwrights, which means that it is highly dramatic and capable of much variety.

The many allusions, implications, paradoxes and symbols render this poem highly ambiguous, almost mocking Eliot's own notes (which may, after all, be an ironic comment on the rationalist approach to poetry that seeks to explain the poetic with sources and background). Eliot then wrote *The Hollow Men* (1925), which is closely related to *The Waste Land*; and, after joining the Anglican Church he turned to the discussion of religious and philosophical problems in his *Ariel Poems* (1927). This collection contains "Journey of the Magi", a beautiful Christmas poem for the twentieth century.

The poems assembled in *Ash Wednesday* (1927-30) are meditations on the themes of sinfulness and repentance, showing Eliot on his way to the more religiously oriented poetry of his later period. After 1930 he wrote some plays, including verse drama, and published *Four Quartets* in 1943. The four poems in this

W. H. Auden

book take their titles from places in which Eliot had lived. They reflect his reading of F. H. Bradley's philosophy[1] and of the Catholic mystics while concentrating on man's experience of time and the possibilities of redemption. Technically, it is interesting to note that the four "quartets" return to the form of *The Waste Land* in that each poem consists of five parts which, like the movements of a sonata, introduce and vary several themes. For his own generation, Eliot's poetic revolution proved a major influence.

This is noticeable in the poetry of writers who began publishing in the 1930s: **W. H. Auden** (1907-73), **Stephen Spender** (1909), **Cecil Day Lewis** (1904-72), who was appointed poet laureate in 1968, and **Louis Mac Neice** (1907-63). Of this group Wystan Hugh Auden was the leader and the most versatile poet. Recognizing Hopkins, Yeats and Eliot as great examples to be followed, these poets tried to write verse on social and political problems. Faced with the economic depression of the 1930s, mass unemployment, and the rise of Fascism, these young Oxford students became dedicated Socialists and defended the cause of the Republicans in the Spanish Civil War (1936-39). After World War II, most of the members of the Auden group gave up their Socialist convictions and wrote more traditional verse.

Auden was a homosexual; he emigrated to America in 1939, together with his friend **Christopher Isherwood** (1909-86), with whom he collaborated in writing verse drama. Collected in *Poems* (1930), *The Orators* (1932), and *Look Stranger* (1936), Auden's early poems reflect his belief in Marxism as well as Freud's influence. With his move to the United States, a new phase began, as humanism gradually displaced his Marxist views. A good example is his poem on human suffering, "Musée des Beaux Arts", written in 1940.

---

1. F(rancis) H(erbert) Bradley (1846-1924), writer and philosopher. He drew attention in England to Hegel's philosophy and is remembered for his *Principles of Logic* (1883), *Appearance and Reality* (1893), and an *Essay on Truth and Reality* (1914).

About suffering they were never wrong,
The Old Masters: how well they understood
Its human position; how it takes place
While someone else is eating or opening a window or just walking dully
  along;
How, when the aged are reverently, passionately waiting
For the miraculous birth, there always must be
Children who did not specially want it to happen, skating
On a pond at the edge of the wood.
They never forgot
That even the dreadful martyrdom must run its course
Anyhow in a corner, some untidy spot
Where the dogs go on with their doggy life and the torturer's horse
Scratches its innocent behind on a tree.

As this poem indicates, Auden had adopted Christian ideas by 1940. His main contribution to modern poetry was the introduction of slang and jargon into poetic comments on religious, philosophical and psychological themes of a typically modern kind. Christian themes and ideas of Kierkegaard and Reinhold Niebuhr[1] recur in his American verse, such as *Another Time* (1940), which includes poems on the deaths of Yeats and Freud, *New Year Letter* (1941), published as *The Double Man* in the United States, *The Age of Anxiety* (1948), and *The Shield of Achilles* (1955), containing symbolic poems on landscape. Auden also wrote some humorous poems in *Homage to Clio* (1960), returning to a liberal humanitarianism in his last poems published in *City without Walls* (1967) and *Thank you Fog* (1973).

While it is true that Eliot, Auden and their friends drew the main critical attention, it would be unjust to ignore those poets who chose different ways of expressing themselves. Among them were **Edith Sitwell** (1887-1964) and her brothers **Osbert** and **Sacheverell,** who wrote satires and verse criticizing social customs and manners, Dame Edith's poems are distinguished by their musical quality. **William Empson** (1906-84) is the best known of a group of Cambridge poets. He wrote an important book of literary criticism, *Seven Types of Ambiguity* (1930), and produced poems that are extremely difficult, using analytical argument and imagery drawn from modern physics and mathematics. Surrealism also found a few proponents. The best known of the Surrealist poets, who emerged forcefully after the international exhibitions of paintings in the 1930s, was **David Gascoyne** (born 1916). He translated French poets and published *A Short Survey of Surrealism* (1935). Indebted to Blake, Yeats, and Apollinaire, but also to such artists as Max Ernst and René Magritte, his poetry explores myths and archetypes from a post-

---

1. Søren Aabye Kierkegaard (1813-55), Danish theologian and philosopher. He wrote many books on a wide variety of issues, and is chiefly remembered as an initiator of existentialist philosophy. He argued that freedom is an inescapable condition of life and action and that it fascinates and repels the individual.
Reinhold Niebuhr (1892-1971), American Protestant theologian. He advocated a Christian realism that revolutionized American theological thinking.

Freudian viewpoint. Most remarkable are Gascoyne's *Man's Life is This Meat* (1936), *Hölderlin's Madness* (1938) and the long poem *Night Thoughts* (1956). The English Surrealists continued a formal existence until the late 1940s. One of the younger poets they influenced was **Dylan Thomas**.

Scotland has had two important poets in **Edwin Muir** (1887-1959), who was also a novelist and critic, and **Hugh MacDiarmid** (1892-1978). Muir was indebted to T. S. Eliot, and his contemplative poems are better understood in an international tradition, whereas MacDiarmid made impressive use of Lowland Scots, one of Scotland's major dialects.

Britain's late poet laureate, **Sir John Betjeman** (1906-1984), saw himself as a defender of Victorian architecture on which he wrote several books. He was one of the last popular poets, and his verse, published in *Collected Poems* (1958), the poetic autobiography *Summoned by Bells* (1960), and *High and Low* (1966), found an unusually large audience by twentieth-century standards. Admittedly, Betjeman was not an outstanding poet and definitely inferior to Auden or contemporary poets like Larkin, but he was a good observer, and his simple and traditional forms evoke the beauty of times past. Betjeman could be satirical and compassionate when dealing with human loneliness and death, as in the ballad-like "Death in Leamington". Here are the first two stanzas of this unpretentious poem:

> She died in the upstairs bedroom
> By the light of the evening star
> That shone through the plate glass window
> From over Leamington Spa.
>
> Beside her the lonely crochet
> Lay patiently and unstirred,
> But the fingers that would have worked it
> Were dead as the spoken word.

The dominant voice of the 1940s and early 1950s was that of the Welshman **Dylan Thomas** (1914-53). Thomas read his poems and essays to radio audiences and, just before his death, wrote a play for radio, *Under Milk Wood* (1954), which has often been performed as a "play for voices". At a time when, under Eliot's influence, poetry was in danger of becoming too intellectual, Thomas injected new vigour into English verse. Borrowing from Hopkins, Joyce, Freud, and the Bible, he tried to affirm the unity of life and became a legend in his own day. Thomas's curious images are a mixture of the erotic, procreation, birth, death and religious faith, suggesting a Surrealist influence. Though Thomas did not speak Welsh, his romantic style and his impressive rhythms seem to suggest an influence of Welsh poetic traditions with their metrical complexities. Thomas was deeply aware of his cultural heritage. In "Fern Hill", published in 1946, he celebrates innocent childhood and his own youth as paradise regained.

The final illness of his father in 1951 led him to write a poem in the form of a villanelle, "Do Not Go Gentle into That Good Night", furiously rejecting the idea of death while dealing with the transcience of human life. Here are the first and the last stanzas:

Do not go gentle into that good night,
Old age should burn and rave at close of day;
Rage, rage against the dying of the light.

[...]

And you, my father, there on the sad height,
Curse, bless, me now with your fierce tears, I pray.
Do not go gentle into that good night.
Rage, rage against the dying of the light.

English poetry after Thomas reacted against his romantic and emotionally direct verse. Younger poets called for a rejection of the heroic and the extraordinary, of Socialist utopias and rhetorical flourishes. Instead, they offered poised, intelligent comments in a verse that is formally strict and both rationally and morally coherent. **William Empson's** intellectually demanding poetry had a brief vogue in the early 1950s. In 1956 an anthology entitled *New Lines* was published (echoing *New Country,* the anthology published by the Auden group in 1933). It contained verse by poets who came to be known as "The Movement", among them the novelists **Kingsley Amis** and **John Wain** as well as **Donald Davie** (born 1922), **D. J. Enright** (born 1920), **Thom Gunn** (born 1929), **Geoffrey Hill** (born 1932), **Elizabeth Jennings** (born 1926), **Philip Larkin** (1922-85) and **Charles Tomlinson** (born 1927). There is not enough space here to discuss the work of each of these fine poets who are more different in their approaches and styles than the group name "The Movement" suggests. They have a few points in common: they are almost all agnostics from the lower middle class, and most of them were or are university lecturers.

Philip Larkin worked as a librarian in Hull and brought to his work an admirable touch of provincial settings. Before 1950, he published two novels and then abandoned prose fiction for poetry. His volumes of verse, *The North Ship* (1945), *The Less Deceived* (1955), *The Whitsun Weddings* (1964), and *High Windows* (1974), lack large romantic gestures or defiant modernist assertions. Attracted at first by Yeats, Larkin came to admire Hardy as a poet. His main themes, recorded in mostly melancholy tones, were small human defeats and triumphs, loneliness, and the inexorable passing of time. "Sad Steps" from 1974 is an example of his occasional mood of laconic melancholy and regret.

Groping back to bed after a piss
I part thick curtains, and am startled by
The rapid clouds, the moon's cleanliness.

Four o'clock: wedge-shadowed gardens lie
Under a cavernous, a wind-picked sky.
There's something laughable about this,

The way the moon dashes through clouds that blow
Loosely as cannon-smoke to stand apart
(Stone-coloured light sharpening the roofs below)

High and preposterous and separate –
Lozenge of love! Medallion of art!
O wolves of memory! Immensements! No,

One shivers slightly, looking up there.
The hardness and the brightness and the plain
Far-reaching singleness of that wide stare

Is a reminder of the strength and pain
Of being young; that it can't come again,
But is for others undiminished somewhere.

Thom Gunn, who published his first book of verse, *Fighting Terms,* in 1954, initially treated tough and potentially violent subjects like urban crime. Since the mid-1950s, Gunn has lived in California. As a consequence, he has become more assimilated to American poetry. The poems in *The Sense of Movement* (1957) explore the question of human existence. "On the Move" focuses on the behaviour and the ideas of the motor-cycle "boys":

On motorcycles, up the road, they come:
Small, black, as flies hanging in heat, the Boys,
Until the distance throws them forth, their hum
Bulges to thunder held by calf and thigh.
In goggles, donned impersonality,
In gleaming jackets trophied with the dust,
They strap in doubt – by hiding it, robust –
And almost hear a meaning in their noise.

In Gunn's later verse – *My Sad Captains* (1961), *Touch* (1967), *Moly* (1971), and *Jack Straw's Castle* (1976) – his Hemingway-myth of toughness has undergone a change. Influenced by the American examples of **Marianne Moore** and **W. C. Williams,** Gunn has tried new metrical possibilities, such as syllabic verse, and has experimented with myth.

Geoffrey Hill has published only four books: *For the Unfallen* (1959), *King Log* (1968), *Mercian Hymns* (1971), and *Tenebrae* (1978). He read English at Oxford and, after receiving a B Litt, has taught at Leeds University. Fascinated by the metaphysical poets, Hill has used a considerable variety of forms. In his *Mercian Hymns,* he wrote a sequence of short poems about the past and present of that area of the English Midlands which was once the kingdom of Mercia.

The ideas of the members of "The Movement" did not last beyond the 1960s, and it would be wrong to assume that they ruled the field. Other groups, loosely formed, reacted against the sober and empirical attitudes of "The Movement". They published their poems in *Mavericks* (1957) and *A Group Anthology* (1963). The ideas of Imagism were revived in the poetry magazine *Review,* edited by Ian Hamilton from 1962-74, with contributions by Colin Falck, Michael Fried, and others.

Ted Hughes (born 1930) was initially admired by the poets who contributed to *A Group Anthology.* Born in Yorkshire, Hughes has dwelt in his poetry on the qualities and powers of birds and animals, stressing their strangeness and alien features. The following poem, from *Hawk in the Rain* (1957), introduces "The Jaguar".

> The apes yawn and adore their fleas in the sun.
> The parrots shriek as if they were on fire, or strut
> Like cheap tarts to attract the stroller with the nut.
> Fatigued with indolence, tiger and lion
>
> Lie still as the sun. The boa-constrictor's coil
> Is a fossil. Cage after cage seems empty, or
> Stinks of sleepers from the breathing straw.
> It might be painted on a nursery wall.
>
> But who runs like the rest past these arrives
> At a cage where the crowd stands, stares, mesmerized,
> As a child at a dream, at a jaguar hurrying enraged
> Through prison darkness after the drills of his eyes
>
> On a short fierce fuse. Not in boredom –
> The eye satisfied to be blind in fire,
> By the bang of blood in the brain deaf the ear –
> He spins from the bars, but there's no cage to him
>
> More than to the visionary his cell:
> His stride is wildernesses of freedom:
> The world rolls under the long thrust of his heel.
> Over the cage floor the horizons come.

Hughes has continued his exploration of the life force in animals and plants in *Lupercal* (1960) and *Crow* (1970). Containing Surrealist elements, this last book presents a violent mythical bird, both human and animal, who seems to be the personified principle of evil. Cruel and cynical, Crow resembles a caricature and knows about an imminent destruction of the world, but like *Prometheus on the Crag* (1973) it accepts human pain and suffering. In his work of the last decade, Hughes has moved away from the brutal and mythological elements and returned to the study of rural life and nature in his native Yorkshire (see his *Selected Poems,* 1982).

In 1984 Hughes was appointed poet laureate. This event and the equally publicized and unprecedented nomination of a "Professor of Poetry" at Oxford saw poetry in the news. In fact, since the late 1970s there has been a remarkable revival of public interest in poetry. Kingsley Amis launched a poetry column in the *Daily Mirror,* and publishers started printing more verse and promoting their authors. In the 1980s a few poets have commanded the kind of attention once given to Tennyson: *Station Island* (1984), one of the more recent works of the internationally known Northern Irish poet **Seamus Heaney** (born 1939), sold more than 30,000 copies within a very short time.

Looking at the poetry of the 1970s and 1980s, it seems inadequate to talk of schools. Yet some poets share common themes in their approaches to twentieth-century reality. **Craig Raine** (born 1944) is often said to have started a "school" with his book *A Martian Sends a Postcard Home* (1979). The poem which gives this collection its title, is a classic example of the way younger poets like Raine, **Andrew Motion** (born 1952), **James Fenton** (born 1949), **Tony Harrison** (born 1937) and **Douglas Dunn** (born 1942) are enamoured of the ordinary and how they revitalize our view of everyday life.

Caxtons are mechanical birds with many wings
and some are treasured for their markings –

they cause the eyes to melt
or the body to shriek without pain.

I have never seen one fly, but
sometimes they perch on the hand.

Mist is when the sky is tired of flight
and rests its soft machine on ground:

then the world is dim and bookish
like engravings under tissue paper.

Rain is when the earth is television.
It has the property of making colours darker.

Model T is a room with the lock inside –
a key is turned to free the world

for movement, so quick there is a film
to watch for anything missed.

But time is tied to the wrist
or kept in a box, ticking with impatience.

In homes, a haunted apparatus sleeps,
that snores when you pick it up.

If the ghost cries, they carry it
to their lips and soothe it to sleep

with sounds. And yet, they wake it up
deliberately, by tickling with a finger.

Only the young are allowed to suffer
openly. Adults go to a punishment room

with water but nothing to eat.
They lock the door and suffer the noises

alone. No one is exempt
and everyone's pain has a different smell.

At night, when all the colours die,
they hide in pairs

and read about themselves –
in colour, with their eyelids shut.

The verse of the "fetishistic poets of domestic life" as they have been called (to the names mentioned above should be added those of **John Fuller,** born 1937, and **John Ash**), shows a distrust of ideas, of social and political conceptions, and it celebrates the world of inanimate objects with a great love of detail.

In addition to these English poets, a number of writers in Scotland and Wales, and especially in Northern Ireland, have produced some remarkable verse. In Scotland, **Sidney Goodsir Smith, Robert Garioch** and **Tom Scott** have obviously profited from the dialect lyrics of Hugh MacDiarmid in the 1920s and 1930s. Wales has found in a clergyman, **R. S. Thomas** (born 1913), a gifted poet who has written moving verse about the remote parts of his homeland. And Northern Ireland has seen the rise of **Seamus Heaney** (in addition to the book cited above, see his *Death of a Naturalist,* 1966, and *Field Work,* 1979), **Derek Mahon** (born 1941; see *Poems,* 1979), **Michael Longley** (born 1939), **Tom Paulin** (born 1949), who was born in Leeds but brought up in Belfast, and **Paul Muldoon** (born 1951).

Heaney is beyond doubt the outstanding and the most gifted writer in what could be termed a new Irish poetic Renaissance. Born in County Derry, Ireland, in 1939, he was educated at Queen's University, Belfast. He has held teaching positions at the University of California at Berkeley, and at Harvard University as well as in Dublin. As a poet, Heaney has tried to describe the Irish national problem in works that are deeply moving without taking sides. He has written beautiful verse about the Irish landscape and he has shown his supreme skill as a poetic explorer of the pains and the glories of human love. The following poem is from his *Glanmore Sonnets* (1979), named after Glanmore, in County Wicklow, where he lived for several years. It celebrates erotic love in apposite comparisons, and in allusions to the literary and mythical past (lovers from Shakespeare's *The Merchant of Venice* and lovers from Irish legends are recalled) as well as to the lasting natural beauty of Ireland. In addition, Heaney provides several hints at Eros' cruel companion, Thanatos, and at the religious-mythical dimension of erotic love.

> I dreamt we slept in a moss in Donegal
> On turf banks under blankets, with our faces
> Exposed all night in a wetting drizzle,
> Pallid as the dripping sapling birches.
> Lorenzo and Jessica in a cold climate.
> Diarmuid and Grainne waiting to be found.
> Darkly asperged and censed, we were laid out
> Like breathing effigies on a raised ground.
> And in that dream I dreamt – how like you this? –
> Our first night years ago in that hotel
> When you came with your deliberate kiss
> To raise us towards the lovely and painful
> Covenants of flesh; our separateness;
> The respite in our dewy dreaming faces.

Finally, **Peter Porter** (born 1929), an expatriate Australian, is one of the most intelligent and lively poets now working in England. His witty and allusive lyrics are often cosmopolitan in their outlook and message (see *Fast Forward,* and *Collected Poems,* both published in 1984). Porter shares this approach with **Michael Hulse** (born 1955), one of the younger poets. Hulse has received several literary awards and his poems, collected in *Knowing and Forgetting* (1981) and *Propaganda* (1985), reveal a vision that is emphatically European rather than national.

3. Drama

Early twentieth-century drama pursued the realistic tradition established by Pinero and Jones and by William Archer's translations of **Ibsen's** (1828-1906) plays. A number of playwrights had the courage to shock their audience by introducing themes like hypocrisy, notably hypocrisy about sex and the sexual double standard (which allowed men, but not women, to have sexual relations before marriage), and the rights of women and their role in society. Such social and moral criticism occurs in the plays of **St John Ervine** (1883-1971), an Irish dramatist and critic, **St John Hankin** (1860-1909), **William Stanley Houghton** (1881-1913), **Harley Granville-Barker** (1877-1946), **John E. Vedrenne** (1867-1930), and the novelists and poets **John Masefield** (1878-1967), **John Galsworthy** (1867-1933), and **George Bernard Shaw** (1856-1950). The kind of realistic drama they wrote was initially faced with both public and political hostility. Thus Granville-Barker's *Waste* (1907), which deals with the death through an illegal operation of the mistress of a promising politician, and Shaw's *Mrs. Warren's Profession* (1893), which focuses on prostitution as well as other seemingly shocking subjects, were banned by the Lord Chamberlain, the English censor. The censor's office was not abolished until 1968, by which time important plays by Arthur Miller *(View From the Bridge),* Tennessee Williams *(Cat On a Hot Tin Roof),* Osborne *(A Patriot For Me),* and Bond *(Saved; Early Morning)* had been banned from the English stage.

If problem plays were eventually accepted, it is largely through the achievement of Galsworthy and Shaw. **Galsworthy,** who was a better artist as a novelist, tackled contemporary social problems in his plays. *The Silver Box* (1906) and *Justice* (1910) are on the inhumanity of legal practices and injustice before the law, while *Strife* (1909) is concerned with strikes and capitalism. Galsworthy's later dramas *The Skin Game* (1920) and *Loyalties* (1922) often degenerate into sentimentalism and melodrama. Despite convincing plots, his plays suffer from simple characterization and a didactic tendency that presses home the messages with a heavy emphasis.

The playwright who eclipsed all other dramatists at this time was **George Bernard Shaw.** An Irishman, he came from Dublin to London in 1876 and began his literary career with five unsuccessful novels as well as essays, theatre criticism and reviews. Shaw defended Ibsen against the attacks of the critics in *The Quintessence of Ibsenism* (1891) and decided that his own plays should also be vehicles for ideas. It was with *Widowers' Houses* (1892) and *Mrs. Warren's Profession*

George Bernard
Shaw

(1893) that he began to dominate European theatre. However, the social criticism of what he termed his "plays unpleasant" was not too well received. In *Widowers' Houses,* for instance, he exposed the rich landlords who exploited the inhabitants of London's slums. So Shaw added some comedy and wit to the following dramas, the "plays pleasant," ridiculing the idealization of war in *Arms and the Man* (1894) and showing the true position of modern married women in *Candida* (1895). In 1901 he published his three "plays for Puritans": *The Devil's Disciple* (1897) figures a hero despite himself in the American War of Independence; *Caesar and Cleopatra* (1898; performed in 1906) reduces Caesar to human size while still leaving him his greatness; and *Captain Brassbound's Conversion* (1899), a true comedy, is about a pirate who ends up as a henpecked husband.

Shaw wrote a great many other plays that exposed illusions and false values. Thus *Major Barbara* (1905) shows that even the Salvation Army depends on dirty money. With *Pygmalion* (1913), a play that has seen numerous film and opera versions as *My Fair Lady* (New York, 1956), Shaw wrote a satire on snobbism in which Professor Henry Higgins turns a cockney[1] girl into a lady without considering her feelings. G. B. Shaw's philosophy of a "life force," a power that seeks to raise mankind to a higher and better existence, is derived from Schopenhauer, Samuel Butler and Friedrich Nietzsche's Creative Evolution.[2] Shaw demonstrated it in *Man and Superman* (1903), sub-titled "a comedy and a philosophy", where a woman – not a man – is chasing for the father of her child, a future "superman". *Heartbreak House* (1919) and *Back to Methuselah* (1921) are both very much concerned with the development of culture and and the failure of our civilization as demonstrated by World War I. *Saint Joan* (1923) is an attempt to show the functioning of the "life force" at a particular historical moment: Shaw's Joan of Arc

---

1. A native of the East End of London, or a Londoner with a working-class accent and/or background.
2. The term Creative Evolution covers some of Nietzsche's ideas, such as the need of a Superman, the will to power, and the superiority of life over consciousness.

appears as the first "Protestant" martyr who prefers private judgment to ecclesiastical dogma and opinion.

Shaw used his dramatic skill to publicize all sorts of ideas, so much so that many of his plays seem to be debating platforms. But there can be no doubt that the mixture of nineteenth-century notions of evolution, scientific progress and Socialism in Shaw's plays is entertaining. Shaw was a rationalist whose literary gift prevented him from ever writing a boring scene. What his dramas lack, however, is a human and emotional dimension that would be able to move deeply.

Shaw published his critical views of drama in the prefaces to his plays. To some extent, these critical introductions are the consequences of censorship, for only the performance – not the publication – of some of his plays was intitially banned by the Lord Chamberlain. But Shaw's critical views in print impressed a number of playwrights. Thus the Shavian influence is to be found in the plays of the two Scotsmen **J. M. Barrie** and **James Bridie** as well as in those of **J. B. Priestley** and **Somerset Maugham,** who were both also novelists.

James Matthew Barrie (1860–1937) introduced fantasy with his *Peter Pan* (1904), today mainly read and watched by children, and wrote a number of more sentimental comedies before producing in *The Admirable Crichton* (1902) and *Dear Brutus* (1917) two plays that contain both pathos and irony and are distinguished by their craftsmanship. **James Bridie** (1888–1951) experimented in Shaw's manner with dialogue, staging and plot. In such plays as *A Sleeping Clergyman* (1933), *Mr. Bolfry* (1943), and *Daphne Laureola* (1949), he commented on moral questions of his day while incorporating elements of myth and fantasy. Bridie's plays may lack philosophical depth, but their irony and cleverly constructed plots make them as entertaining as the comedies of Priestley and Maugham.

Somerset Maugham (1874–1965) began with light comedies in the style of Sheridan and Wilde – *Caesar's Wife* and *Home and Beauty* (1919) – and advanced to more sophisticated comedy in *The Circle* (1921) and *Our Betters* (1923), which are concerned with marriage and adultery. In *For Services Rendered* (1932) and *Sheppey* (1933) Maugham examined the place of human charity in a cynical and non-religious age. Somerset Maugham was a homosexual, like **Noël Coward** (1899 – 1973), who wrote very successful but superficial comedies, and **Terence Rattigan** (1911–1977), a representative of the social comedy. The shallowness of their plays may in part derive from the fact that they had to translate their personal experience and viewpoints into heterosexual terms.

J. B. Priestley (1894–1985) began with social dramas that appear more profound than they really are. Continuing with traditional comedies with a touch of his native Yorkshire humour – *Eden End* (1934); *When We Are Married* (1938) – Priestley then experimented in his plays after reading and studying the modern philosophical time theories of J. W. Dunne and Ouspensky.[1] Hence the focus on

---

1. John William Dunne (1875-1949), author of the popular *An Experiment with Time* (1927) and *The Serial Universe* (1934), in which he developed a theory of time that was to explain precognition and dreaming about future events. Ouspensky (1878-1947) was an unorthodox philosopher and a journalist of Russian origin who disseminated the theosophical teaching of G. I. Gurdjieff.

destiny, predestination and notions of time in his *Dangerous Corner* (1932), *Time And the Conways* (1937), and *I Have Been Here Before* (1937). After the war Priestley returned to more traditional ways of constructing his plays with *The Linden Tree* (1947), in which an academic and his wife are confronted at a family reunion with the contrasting philosophies of their adult children, and the successful *An Inspector Calls* (1945), which stresses the need of mutual responsibility. *Take The Fool Away* (1956) is set in an Orwellian world of terror and technology, from which the central character, a clown, finally manages to escape. Though Priestley has failed in several instances to write convincing dialogue, it is evident that he possesses dramatic skill and a lively method of conveying his themes.

The strongest impulses in early modern drama came from Ireland as part of what has been called the Irish Literary Renaissance. This movement was best expressed in poetry and drama and in the marriage of both in poetic drama. The Irish Literary Theatre was established in 1899, mainly through the efforts of **Lady Isabella Augusta Gregory** (1852-1932), who wrote a few one-act comedies, and **William Butler Yeats**. This theatre soon developed into the Irish National Theatre Society, housed in the Abbey Theatre, Dublin, founded in 1904. Yeats brought his poetical gift to the movement, and the new Irish theatre began with his *The Countess Cathleen* (1892), which is the story in blank verse of a woman (the symbol of Ireland) who sells her soul to the devil to save her countrymen. The countess is eventually rewarded for her sacrifice by angels chasing the devil away. Yeats again used blank verse in *The Land of Heart's Desire* (1894) while also drawing on Irish folklore and superstitions. Objecting to realistic drama, Yeats employed his characters as symbols, most obviously in *The Shadowy Waters* (1900) of which there are several versions. This play figures King Forgael who, driven by his longing for love, follows the seabirds until he finds Dectora and his dreams come true. *Deirdre*[1] (1907) and *On Baile's Strand* (1904) also focus on characters from Irish legend and explore tragic dimensions (see also Synge's plays below).

Under the influence of Ezra Pound, who introduced him to the Japanese Nō-theatre, Yeats changed his style during World War I. His *Four Plays For Dancers* (1921) elaborate the tension between the natural world and the metaphysical. As in Nō-drama, there is little plot and scenery, the actors wear masks, and dialogue is limited and abstract. The larger audience failed to respond to such plays, but Yeats was content with his coterie. He refined his symbolical poetic drama in *Purgatory* (1938), which shows the dead doing penance by returning to the places of their misdeeds, and in *The Death of Cuchulain* (1939), a sort of ritual report on the death of an Irish mythical figure. Though Yeats found much opposition from conservative Irish audiences who resented his esoteric philosophy, magic ritual, and symbolism, he did much for drama by rediscovering myth and verse. His pioneering

---

1. An Irish mythical figure reported to have been of extraordinary beauty. The daughter of a harper, Deirdre became the victim of King Conchubar's revenge, when she fell in love with Naoise and ignored the king. Conchubar lured the lovers back to Ulster, when they fled to Scotland; Naoise was slain and Deirdre took her own life.

work, not always convincing, proved vitally important for playwrights in the area of poetic drama.

Apart from Yeats, the Irish Theatre profited from the works of Synge and O'Casey. **John Millington Synge** (1871-1909) died prematurely, yet his six completed plays established him as the greatest of modern Irish dramatists. Synge was discovered by Yeats. After travelling on the Continent, he found in the Aran Islands off the west coast of Ireland the rhythm of a simple, rich and poetic language for drama based on the speech of Irish peasants. With his Gaelicized English Synge created a new idiom that worked exceptionally well in his plays. Two of these are tragedies: *Riders to the Sea* (1904) has a Greek quality in its story of a mother acknowledging the power of fate that will destroy her last son. In *Deirdre of the Sorrows* (1910), which was almost finished when Synge died, the Irish mythological figure has found one of its most convincing dramatic interpretations. In his comedies, Synge dealt with the theme of appearance and reality, but also with such traditional topics as cuckolds and henpecked husbands. *In the Shadow of the Glen* (1903) and *The Tinker's Wedding* (1908) comment on the conflict between the boring security of an honourable life and the passion and joviality in the life of the Irish vagabonds. Finally, Synge's *The Playboy Of The Western World* (1907) is a comedy of bitter and ironic realism, the climax of his achievement. The play caused riots in the Abbey Theatre on its first production.

Christy Mahon, a weak and frightened young man, arrives at a town in Mayo and announces that, having killed his bullying father in a quarrel, he is now a fugitive from justice. Christy is well received and hospitably treated, and his dare-devil image gives him great advantage with the women, especially with the publican's daughter Pegeen who eventually becomes his fiancée. But the admiration of the villagers and several women gives way to angry contempt when Christy's father arrives and it is revealed that he has merely received a crack on the head. Exposed as a liar at the very moment of his triumph, Christy now really tries to batter his father to death with a spade, only to be seized by the villagers who are afraid of being accused of the murder. Finally, Pegeen turns against Christy, the indestructible older Mahon crawls onto the stage, and the father and son leave for home.

Although he wrote only for about 10 years, Synge brought new life to drama with his understanding of human nature, his realistic characters and language, and a pervasive humour governed by an extraordinary poetic imagery.

Sean O'Casey (1880-1964) was the last important representative of the Irish Literary Renaissance. As a child, O'Casey experienced the sordidness of the Dublin slums. Later, he became involved with the Irish Citizen Army.[1] If Yeats wrote from a kind of aristocratic viewpoint, O'Casey's early plays touch the rockbottom of reality. *The Shadow of a Gunman* was produced in the Abbey Theatre at Dublin in 1923 and is concerned with the suffering of the Irish Republicans in their fight for freedom. Though basically tragic, the play is laced with uproarious laughter and elements of the grotesque. Realistic detail and a peculiar mixture of tragic and

---

1. The Irish Citizen Army was a paramilitary organization formed to protect the workers in the general strike of 1913. They joined forces with the Irish Republican Brotherhood (later Irish Republican Army) in the Easter Rebellion of 1916 (see the note on page 115).

comic aspects also distinguish O'Casey's masterpiece, *Juno and the Paycock* (1924).

The play treats of the destiny of a family in the slums of Dublin. Jack Boyle, a drunk and a spendthrift, and his wife, Juno, are told that they have inherited a large sum of money. On this expectation, the family gets heavily into debt, discovering too late that a fault in the will means they will receive nothing. The Boyle's daughter, Mary, is abandoned by her lover, by whom she is pregnant, and the son, Johnny, is shot by the revolutionaries because he has betrayed a friend to the Irish Free-Staters. Juno then leaves her husband Jack and joins Mary to help her.

Juno and the Paycock thus presents a grim story of destruction inflicted both by the outside world and by the inner failings of the characters. Technically, it may be rather a conventional drama, but it offers moving moments of tragedy, melodrama, irony, and a colourful language.

The Plough and the Stars (1926), concerned with the Irish Easter Rebellion of 1916, led to a riot at the Abbey Theatre because the public believed that O'Casey had ridiculed the Irish rebels and their cause. Two years later, the Abbey rejected his pacifist war drama *The Silver Tassie*. O'Casey went to England and began experimenting with the techniques of expressionism. Non-realistic effects, such as symbolism, song, and poetry, can be found in such later plays as *Within The Gates* (1934) and *Red Roses For Me* (1942). O'Casey's last dramas again find their motifs in Ireland. Set in imaginary Irish villages, *Cock-A-Doodle Dandy* (1949), *The Bishop's Bonfire* (1955) and *The Drums of Father Ned* (1958) mock Irish bourgeois hypocrisy and criticize the dominance of the Catholic Church and its clergy.

No Irish dramatist after O'Casey has been able to surpass his dramatic mixture of realism, romance, and symbolism in a prose that is always highly poetic. **Samuel Beckett,** born in Dublin in 1906, must be seen as an international playwright rather than as an Anglo-Irish writer as he has written most of his plays in French and in France. **Brendan Behan** (1923-1964), like O'Casey of lower-class origin, and **Padraic Colum** (1881-1972) are minor dramatists who have written in O'Casey's shadow.

In the 1930s, a few attempts were made in English drama to return to the use of verse. Yeats had broken new ground, and T. S. Eliot, Christopher Fry and W. H. Auden developed verse drama in different directions and with special targets. What they had in common was a small audience, almost a coterie, and today one can say that, apart from Eliot's earlier work, the achievement of poetic drama hardly matched the hopes that were initially expressed.

W. H. Auden, in collaboration with **Christopher Isherwood,** used the stage for left-wing propaganda in works like *The Dance of Death* (1935), *The Dog Beneath the Skin* (1935), *The Ascent of F6* (1936), and *On the Frontier* (1936). Employing verse of a racy and colloquial kind, songs and Expressionist devices, Auden basically repeated the political ideas of his non-dramatic verse. *The Ascent of F6* is the most remarkable of these plays. Its central theme is the problem of power examined in the description of an expedition to the highest mountain in the world (F6) and the conflicts in the mind of the leader of the group. Auden and Isherwood packed into this drama not only Wordsworthian blank verse but also colloquial comments by "ordinary" people and by a radio-studio, popular songs, a chorus, and mime.

T. S. Eliot aimed at making drama a form of art. His verse – from *Prufrock* to *The Waste Land* – has undeniable dramatic qualities. In his *Dialogue on Dramatic Poetry,* published in 1928, he argued that realistic prose drama ignores the fundamental and merely deals with appearances, and that "the human soul, in intense emotions, strives to express itself in verse." With his fragmentary *Sweeney Agonistes* (1932), Eliot first ventured into poetic drama. The world of this play is still very much that of *The Waste Land.* What makes it interesting is the use of chorus, jazz rhythms, and its sense of dread. Sweeney is a symbolic character who also occurs in Eliot's poetry and represents the vulgar but vital force of life. Eliot's first complete play was *The Rock* (1934), a pageant largely written in prose, with one scene and choruses, involving historical and biblical figures as well as political groups of the 1930s. *The Rock* ends with a triumphant affirmation of faith and hope.

Murder in the Cathedral brought Eliot success. It was written in 1934 for the Canterbury Festival of 1935. The character and the fate of Thomas à Becket (1118–1170)[1] had been used in drama before Eliot – as in Tennyson's *Becket* of 1884 – and were again selected, after Eliot, by Jean Anouilh[2] in 1959 and Christopher Fry in 1961 *(Curtmantle).* Eliot's drama consists of two parts and focuses on the last days of the Archbishop, his temptation, and his final martyrdom. An interlude – Becket's Christmas sermon – unites the two parts. Essentially, *Murder in the Cathedral* is a modern mystery play involving the audience. First performed in the Chapter House of Canterbury Cathedral, it remains the most popular of Eliot's plays. With *Murder in the Cathedral* Eliot proved that verse might be suitable for a historical play on a religious subject.

But what he really wanted was a poetic drama in the spirit of our time. This he tried to achieve with *The Family Reunion* (1939), which owes something to the Greek story of Orestes pursued by the Furies. The modern Orestes, Harry, Lord Monchensey, has allegedly killed his wife. His misdeed eventually affects his whole family. The Furies materialize on two occasions, and his aunts and uncles intermittently abandon dialogue to become a chorus. Harry's crime is finally expiated by his son. Though still not a very convincing drama, *The Family Reunion* is a step forward, technically speaking. In this play Eliot found a form of verse so close to prose (he rejected blank verse as being too reminiscent of Shakespeare) that the average listener cannot tell the difference. Eliot used the same verse in *The Cocktail Party* (1949), *The Confidential Clerk* (1954), and *The Elder Statesman* (1959), which he wrote to capture a larger audience. *The Cocktail Party* suffers from a long and tedious exposition. It transposes into the twentieth century Euri-

---

1. See the note on page 13.
2. Jean Anouilh (born 1910), One of the most popular French dramatists in the first half of the 20th century. Notable are his *Le Bal des Voleurs* (1938), *L'Invitation au Château* (1947), and his plays dealing with historical figures, such as *L'Alouette* (1953), on Joan of Arc, and *Becket ou l'honneur de Dieu* (1959), on Thomas à Becket.

pides'[1] *Alcestis,* a tale of guilt and atonement. Superficially, it is a comedy of manners, like *The Confidential Clerk* which treats of the old theme of mistaken identity in the story of a young man resisting others' plans for him and seeking fulfilment in church music. Again inspired by Greek mythology, *The Elder Statesman* is a better play. Lord Calverton, a politician and modern Oedipus, faces the inadequacies and evils of his misspent life. Haunted by ghosts, he repents and, reconciled with his victims and himself, goes out to die under a beech tree. There is no doubt that Eliot's poetic plays are less convincing than his verse and criticism. Nevertheless, his attempts in drama stimulated a few younger playwrights.

Christopher Fry (born 1907) is the most remarkable representative of verse drama, apart from Eliot. Fry began with religious plays, such as *The Firstborn* (1946), in which Moses liberates the captive Israelites, and *Thor, With Angels* (1948), where a Jute warrior is converted to Christianity. Fry's best religious drama is *A Sleep of Prisoners* (1951). This play presents in dramatic scenes the dreams of four English soldiers locked up in a church as prisoners of war. But Fry has shown that he is also able to handle human paradoxes and conflicts more playfully. This he achieved in his comedies. Thus *A Phoenix Too Frequent* (1946) praises the power of love and life in a modern version of Petronius'[2] tale of the widow of Ephesus who wanted to entomb herself with her dead husband but fell in love with a soldier at the grave. The theme of life-preserving love also dominates *The Lady's Not For Burning* (1948). Set in the Middle Ages, it features a desperate soldier bent on suicide and a girl accused of sorcery. Both characters are saved by their love for each other. With this comedy, Fry began his tetralogy of the seasons or "comedies of mood": the first was the "spring" play; *Venus Observed,* the "autumn" drama, followed in 1950; and the "winter comedy", *The Dark Is Light Enough,* in 1954. The series was completed with the "summer" play *A Yard of Sun* (1970), which is set in Italy. Fry was praised for the brilliancy of his imagery and the felicity of his language in free but regularly stressed verse with richly imaginative word-play. And though his plays sometimes lack dramatic depth, they emerge as delightful defenses of faith, hope, and charity, especially when compared to the thinness of the products of the commercial theatre.

The "Renaissance" of British drama in the second half of the century came with the establishment in 1956 of the **English Stage Company,** dedicated to promoting new work, and its presentation in the same year of John Osborne's *Look Back In Anger* at the Royal Court Theatre in Chelsea, London. In East London, John Littlewood's **"Theatre Workshop"** gave help to younger playwrights, such as **Brendan Behan** (1923-64) and **Shelagh Delaney** (born 1939). But it was Osborne's play that caught the imagination of a generation. **John Osborne** (born 1929), like the novelists Alan Sillitoe, John Wain, and John Braine, has made his

---

1. Euripides (480-406 BC), Greek tragedian who exerted influence on Milton, Dryden, Shelley, Browning, and T. S. Eliot. His best known plays (19 have survived) are *Medea, Helena,* and *Alcestis.*
2. Petronius (Petronius Arbiter, died AD 66), Roman writer and the author of the *Satyricon,* a realistic novel about the low life and vices of Nero's time. Only excerpts of the work have been preserved, but modern writers have repeatedly made use of scenes from the book. There is also an excellent film by Fellini, based on the novel.

Richard Burton and Claire Bloom in *Look Back in Anger*

reputation as one of the "angry young men" of the provinces who expressed the disaffection of a sector of the British population that had been previously silent. The "angry young men" resented the English establishment, educated at public schools and "Oxbridge",[1] and the hypocrisy in church and state. Many of Osborne's contemporaries found in Jimmy Porter, the almost hysterical hero of *Look Back In Anger,* an image of their own lives. Of working-class origin, Jimmy has been to a university, but he has discovered no satisfactory profession and rages at the establishment and his middle-class wife Alison. Unable to endure her husband's furious attacks, Alison abandons him. But the ending of the play, not without a touch of sentimentality, leads the couple together again, temporarily reconciled. Since *Look Back In Anger* was dramaturgically still traditional, Osborne looked for new techniques, yet none of his following plays met with the success of his first great drama. Since the 1950s, Osborne has tackled a wide range of subjects, from *The Entertainer* (1957), featuring a shabby and self-deceiving character from the final days of the music hall, and the historical play *Luther* (1960) to the study of a sex-obsessed lawyer in *Inadmissable Evidence* (1964). *A Patriot For Me* (1965) explores recent history in the character of a homosexual Austrian officer on the eve of World War I. It was filmed by Istvan Szabo (*Oberst Redl*). Osborne's *The Hotel In Amsterdam* (1968) and *West Of Suez* (1972) analyze problems of human relations and the nature of English identity. Though John Osborne has retained some of his original anger – expressed again in his recent *A Sense Of Detachment* (1973), which abandons both plot and realism, and *Watch It Come Down* (1976) – his implicit stance now seems to be nostalgically conservative.

In Osborne's works one notices the influence of Bert Brecht, whose Berliner Ensemble visited Britain in 1956, and of **Samuel Beckett**. Their voices can also be clearly heard in the plays of John Arden and Arnold Wesker, who have both tried to express their feelings of protest against social injustice and cultural decay. **John Arden** (born 1930) is difficult to categorize, not because he takes unpopular views but because critics have found it difficult to detect what they term moral

---

1. The term Oxbridge refers to the universities of Oxford and Cambridge, and, by implication, to the intellectual establishment trained in these institutions.

commitment. It is obvious that Arden is indebted to Brecht in theatrical technique and in his view of historical change, but he has consistently refused to take sides in the presentation of problems. Arden's early *Live Like Pigs* (1958) juxtaposes the vitality of anarchic vagabonds with the dreary life of the bourgeois. *Serjeant Musgrave's Dance* (1959) is today recognized as his best drama. It is the story of a deserter from the Victorian army who comes to a British coal town pretending to seek recruits while really looking for victims for an act of reprisal. Musgrave sets violence against violence, but in the end he fails because of the resistance of women and some of his men. *The Workhouse Donkey* (1964) is a frequently funny play about the corruptness of local politics. As in most of his other dramas, Arden wrote large sections in rhyming verse and added songs and dances in the Brechtian manner. One of Arden's favourite themes is the conflict between anarchy and order in society. This is the central theme of *Armstrong's Last Goodnight* (1965), which contains characters of the morality plays and returns to sixteenth-century Scotland. Like Brecht, Arden has constantly tried to deceive the audience's expectations while reminding it of the theatrical situation, but unlike Brecht he offers no underlying political message. Instead, his plays written before 1965 offer gripping character studies and valuable social comment. Arden's latest plays are both political and historical, aiming at a dismantling of some of England's cherished myths. *Left-Handed Liberty* (1965) is about the moral and social problems of the Magna Carta of 1215[1] and shows the barons as rather selfish characters. *The Hero Rises Up* (1968) mocks the hero-worship of Nelson;[2] and *The Ballygombeen Bequest* (1972), set in Belfast, focuses on the problems in Northern Ireland. Since the late 1960s, Arden has written most of his plays in collaboration with his wife **Margaretta D'Arcy,** who is an outspoken Marxist. In 1972 they wrote *The Island of the Mighty* for the BBC (published in 1974), which is a play based on the Arthurian legends. Their latest works are overtly Marxist and propagandistic, and the poetic qualities of the earlier plays are less evident.

Arnold Wesker (born 1932) shares with Arden a "Socialist" view of drama. Like Harold Pinter, Wesker comes from a Jewish family in London's East End. The plays assembled in his *Wesker Trilogy* (*Chicken Soup With Barley,* 1958; *Roots,* 1959; and *I'm Talking About Jerusalem,* 1960) deal with Jewish working-class life, the nature of Socialism, and the cultural poverty of the masses. Wesker has continued to defend passionately both Socialist and humanitarian ideas in *The Kitchen* (1961), *Chips With Everything* (1962), which is an anti-Establishment study of Royal Air Force conscripts, and *Their Very Own and Golden City* (1966). With *The Friends* (1970) Wesker returned to the treatment of problems of the individual, retreating a little from general social themes. *The Old Ones* (1973), for instance, explores the meaning of life from the viewpoint of elderly people, and *The Merchant* (1976), a reworking of Shakespeare's *The Merchant of Venice,* analyses the Jew Shylock much more sympathetically than the original.

1. See page 10, note 2.
2. Horatio Nelson, Duke of Bronte (1758-1805), British admiral. He defeated the French in the Battle of Abukir and became notorious for his love affair with Lady Hamilton. He fell in the Battle of Trafalgar, but the victory of the British fleet over the French and Spanish fleets made Nelson a popular hero.

If Wesker and Arden have tried to establish a new British left-wing theatre, **Edward Bond** (born 1935) has struck a harsher note in radical dramatic diagnoses of cultural deprivation and the dangers of modern society. Bond uses crude realistic detail (in his *Saved,* 1965, for example, a baby is killed) and Surrealist settings, but his message, in which the ugliness of evil often triumphs, is entirely moral. A disciple of Rousseau, Bond believes that man has been corrupted by his environment as well as by his education and the established morals. According to Bond, the artist must not merely seek truth and justice but must also try to put them into social practice. In *Lear* (1972) Bond criticized Shakespeare's hero because he did not initiate political and social change, and in *Bingo* (1973) Shakespeare himself appears as a selfish landowner who ignores the needs of the Stratford tenants. With the exception of the comedy *The Sea* (1973), which attacks the social hierarchy in a small English town, in the early twentieth century, Bond's plays indicate that he has been preoccupied with the relations between the artist and society. He returned to this theme in 1975, when *The Fool* was performed. In this play the Victorian poet John Clare, who became insane in the 1830s, berates the society of his day. Since Bond depicts much cruelty and brutality in his paradigmatic presentation of the artist's role in society, he has been accused of sensationalism. Whatever controversy his plays may arouse, one cannot deny their message of human suffering and compassion.

Among the many young playwrights who came to the fore in the 1960s, some continued to use the theatre as a means in their fight for social and political change. **David Halliwell** (born 1937), **David Hare** (born 1948), and **Heathcote Williams** (born 1941) have experimented with theatrical techniques and have written for the fringe theatre.[1] **Howard Brenton** (born 1942) came to prominence and notoriety with his *Magnificence* (1973), which deals with squatters[2], and his cynical *The Romans in Britain* (1980), a play that draws a parallel between the Roman invasion of Britain and the British presence in Northern Ireland. The violent scenes of bloodshed and homosexual rapes in this drama aroused a good deal of controversy.

Mention should also be made of **Joe Orton** (1933-67), a skilled practitioner of black comedy who made use of scandalous themes. A social nonconformist, Orton lived in permanent conflict with the law. Before he was killed by his bed-fellow, Kenneth Halliwell, he wrote a number of plays that will last, though they are technically conservative. His *Entertaining Mr. Sloane* (1964) is a parody of the comedy of manners and shocked and amused its audience by the contrast between its proper and conventional dialogue and the violence and outrageousness of its action. *Loot* (1966) is a satire on police corruption and the conventions of detective fiction – murder and perversity appear to be almost normal in this play. And *What*

---

1. Theatres of minor (national) importance which often experiment with new techniques and receive little if any financial support from the state. The British fringe theatre is the equivalent of the American off-Broadway and off-off-Broadway theatre.
2. A squatter is a person who takes unauthorized (and illegal) possession of unoccupied flats or houses.

Tom Hulce starred in the film version of Peter Shaffer's *Amadeus*

the Butler Saw (1969) is an extravagant farce in the style of Oscar Wilde and plays with mistaken identities.

Playwrights like **Robert Bolt** (born 1924), **Alan Bennett** (born 1934), **Peter Barnes** (born 1931), **Simon Gray** (born 1936), **Christopher Hampton** (1946), **Peter Nichols** (born 1927), and **Charles Wood** (born 1932) may not have a particular political or class axe to grind, but their plays have shown a new eloquence in British theatre. An outstanding name among the dramatists now writing for the theatre is **Peter Shaffer** (born 1926). His *The Royal Hunt of the Sun* (1964) received considerable attention. It focuses on the Spanish conquest of Peru.

In *Equus* (1973) Shaffer wrote a psychological study in which a psychiatrist, Martin Dysart, is confronted with a 17-year-old, Alan Strang, who has blinded six horses. The play shows the slow unravelling of the motives behind the deed as well as the crisis of the psychiatrist who questions the aim of his therapy. Shaffer's *The Battle of Shrivings,* performed in 1970 and published as *Shrivings* in 1974, shows an elderly pacifist professor in conflict with an anti-liberal poet. *Amadeus* (1979) is Shaffer's Mozart drama portraying the bitterness aroused in the Italian composer Antonio Salieri by the success of his rival Mozart (see also the film directed by Milos Forman).

Since the 1950s a number of dramatists have developed what Martin Esslin has termed the "theatre of the absurd", which is concerned with the metaphysical question of the purpose of human existence. The concept of absurdity derives from the existentialist works of Albert Camus[1] and Jean-Paul Sartre[2]. Existentialist man

---

1. Albert Camus (1913-60), French writer and dramatist. Algeria, where he was born, provides the setting for many of his works. He explored the absurd dimensions of the human condition from a semi-existentialist viewpoint (he was less doctrinal in this respect than Jean-Paul Sartre). His influential novels include *L'Etranger* (1942), *La Peste* (1947), *Le Mythe de Sisyphe* (1942), and *La Chute* (1956). He was awarded the Nobel Prize for literature in 1957.
2. Jean-Paul Sartre (1905-80), French philosopher and writer and the major representative of existentialism in France. After 1945, he had a considerable influence on French and European intellectual life. Throughout his life he involved himself personally in many important issues of freedom and moral responsibility. His many works include philosophical treatises (*L'Etre et le néant,* 1943, *Critique de la raison dialectique,* 1960), novels (*La Nausée,* 1938), and plays (*Les Mouches,* 1943, *Huis clos,* 1945). His autobiography, *Les Mots* (1964), appeared in the same year in which he received the Nobel Prize for literature.

is a lonely creature confronted by a vast emptiness in which his acts seem insignificant. Desperately trying to confirm their human identity, the characters in the drama of the absurd are both stoically hopeless and strangely heroic. Playwrights like **Samuel Beckett** (born 1906), **Eugène Ionesco** (born 1912), a French writer of Romanian origin, **Harold Pinter,** and, to some extent, **James Saunders** and **Tom Stoppard,** have expressed in their plays the basic belief that man's life is essentially without meaning and that human beings are unable to communicate. As a consequence, some of these dramatists have abandoned dramatic form and coherent dialogue: the futility of existence is shown by illogical speeches and, ultimately, by absolute silence.

Samuel Beckett (born 1906) has voiced in his novels and plays the disillusionment of the post-atomic age in which God seems to have failed man by not existing. Beckett grew up in Dublin and studied at the local Trinity College. At the age of 22 he went to Paris, beginning his literary career in the circle of **James Joyce.** After writing some remarkable literary criticism on Proust[1], short stories, poems, and novels, which are indebted to the style of Joyce, Beckett spent the war in Paris and has since settled there. Since 1945, he has written most of his works in French. This fact may help to explain the distance, the precision, and the degree of abstractness his plays achieve. The theatre of the absurd can be said to have begun with his *Waiting For Godot* (1955), which conquered Paris in 1953 and then London and New York.

Waiting For Godot has no particular place, and the two days represented in two acts symbolize the passing of time. The play tells us far less about Godot than about hope and waiting. The two tramps Estragon and Vladimir spend consecutive days on a country road whose sole landmark is a tree which is totally bare in Act I but – as if mocking spring – sprouts four or five leaves in Act II. Indecisive and bickering, the tramps wander from subject to subject in their conversation. In order to avoid boredom and to pass the time they play while waiting for the mysterious and undefined Godot who never arrives. Twice they are visited by the wip-cracking Pozzo and his slave Lucky. These two men, like the two tramps, are dependent on each other: thus in Act II Pozzo enters blind, less leader than led. Vladimir and Estragon wait without hope, yet they dare not give up their waiting.

Waiting For Godot is a play that makes its audience laugh as well as wince. This mixture of comic and tragic elements characterizes almost all the plays in the theatre of the absurd. The tramps are conceived as clowns, and the play incorporates elements of the circus and the music hall, but their clowning is tragically sad as it only masks the vast emptiness and meaninglessness of life which they are much too afraid to admit. What makes *Waiting For Godot* an outstanding drama is its audacious technique, which uses two tramps/clowns and a bare stage to ex-

---

1. Marcel Proust (1871-1922), French novelist and critic and one of the most influential modernists. His sequence of novels entitled *A la recherche du temps perdu* (1913-27) is written in the form of an autobiographical report and deals with characters from the French aristocracy and upper class around the turn of the century. His handling of time and interior monologue, his use of memory as a structural device of plot and writing/thinking, and his view of literary art have had a profound influence on several European and American writers.

plore the meaning of life, as well as its poetic style and tragi-comic tone. It is not as negative a play as some critics suggest, for Beckett has faced the hideous uncertainties of existence with pluck and humour. It was not least for this play that he received the Nobel Prize for Literature in 1969. By this time he had written a few other dramas exploring the helplessness of man in an apparently meaningless universe. *Endgame* (1958) figures Hamm, blind and paralyzed, surrounded by his parents, stuck in dustbins, and a servant who keeps threatening that he will go away. Beckett moved further and further away from conventional theatre in an effort to convey with a minimum of speech and action man's inability to communicate and the tragi-comic ignorance of his own role. *Krapp's Last Tape* (1958) has only one actor, an old man who listens uncomprehendingly to recordings he made as a young man. *Happy Days* (1961) shows the actress Winnie being progressively buried in dirt until only her head remains visible; and in *Play* (1964) the heads of two nameless women and one man speak from urns. With *Breath* (1969), which lasts about thirty seconds, beginning with the cry of a newly born child and ending with the last gasp of an elderly man, and *Not I* (1971), which shows merely the speaking mouth of a woman and the figure of a male listener, Beckett reached a point where theatrical means are radically reduced. This may be a significant step, but there is no denying the fact that it leads to a dead end in theatrical production.

Harold Pinter (born 1930) has tried to find a way out of this dilemma. Although influenced by Beckett and Ionesco, he has his own voice, and it would be misleading to categorize his plays as merely absurd. Pinter, too, has dealt with the problem of human relations, but unlike Beckett he uses traditional techniques and quasi-realistic language that exploits everyday speech in a very remarkable way. Pinter has exposed in his plays the underlying fear, brutality, and human isolation in everyday life. His characters are presented in particular situations and are driven by motives that often remain obscure. *The Room, The Dumb Waiter* (1957), and *The Birthday Party* (1958) are "comedies of menace" in which powerful forces suddenly enter private lives. It was with *The Caretaker* (1960) that Harold Pinter came to prominence.

Aston, a mentally damaged man lately released from an apparently hellish asylum, takes in Davies, a shabby and smelly tramp. Aston's room is in chaotic disorder and full of all sorts of useful and useless things. Since he needs company and, probably, a friend, he has offered to let Davies stay with him. Davies is suspicious and mistrustful, seeing people either as threats or cheats, and his identity remains unclear – he pretends to have lost his papers. Though treated kindly by Aston, who gives him a bed, a key, and money, Davis is not a man to feel genuine gratitude. As the action unfolds, it becomes clear that Aston is not the real owner of the house where he lives: his brother Mick, a self-employed builder with ambitious plans, gradually makes his proprietorship brutally clear by first bullying and then terrorizing Davies. The old tramp finally betrays Aston and tries to become Mick's caretaker. But Mick exposes Davies's treachery and rejects him, and the play ends with Davies again imploring Aston for help.

The search for identity, one of the themes of this play, has continued to fascinate Pinter. Thus *The Collection* (1962) and *The Lover* (1963) show different or alternative lives of one person, which is a topic that also recurs in *The Homecoming* (1964). Pinter's *Tea Party* (1965) is about a seemingly confident but essentially insecure businessman driven mad by the imaginings caused in him by his secretary and the close relationship between his wife and her brother. *Old Times* (1971) and *No Man's Land* (1975) treat of the relations between the present and the past as seen through the minds of the characters, who prove with their differing versions that past experience is unreliable reality. Since the 1970s, Pinter has written adaptations for the cinema and for television, such as *The French Lieutenant's Woman*, based on John Fowles's novel, and *Betrayal* (1978). He also worked as a theatre director. His latest play is *The Hothouse*, which he wrote in 1958, but did not allow to be performed until 1980. It is a grotesque satire on the inhumanity of bureaucracy and is set in a government-run "rest home" whose staff mercilessly exploit the patients. Taking revenge, the latter apparently massacre their torturers.

Apart from **James Saunders** (born 1925) and his successful *Next Time I'll Sing to You* (1969), which is based on the life and death of a hermit, **Tom Stoppard** has also contributed to the English theatre of the absurd. Stoppard was born in Czechoslovakia in 1937, his original name being Straussler, and became a British subject. Stoppard is concerned with the comic and absurd as results of almost ordinary situations and attitudes. His success came with *Rosencrantz and Guildenstern Are Dead* (1967). It is a tragi-comedy in which the two minor characters from Shakespeare's *Hamlet* have moved to the focus of a drama that plays with identities, perception, and human existence. In this play Stoppard has fused several layers of reality and illusion, involving scenes and characters from *Hamlet* and its play within a play – even death is played on several occasions. The same fusion of two levels of reality and fiction occurs in his comedy *The Real Inspector Hound* (1968), which is about two dramatic critics who get drawn into the action of the play they comment on. In *Jumpers* (1972), a professor of moral philosophy defends intuition against contemporary rationalism. Stoppard has used both parody and direct statement to attack what he perceives as the triviality and cynicism of modern philosophy. The playing with consciousness and historical reality was resumed in *Travesties* (1974), in which Stoppard presents a lively debate, involving James Joyce and Lenin, on the justification for art. With his latest dramas, Stoppard has remained faithful to both absurd drama and comedy. *Dirty Linen* (1976) shows MPs investigating immorality in Parliament, and *Night and Day* (1978) is an almost naturalistic play on the freedom of the press set in a fictitious African country. *Professional Foul* (1977) derives fun from the coincidence in Prague of a convention of philosophers and an English football team. *Cahoot's Macbeth* (1979), also set in Prague, figures oppressed actors who can perform only in private houses.

Finally, the plays of **Alan Ayckbourn** (born 1939) have a touch of the absurd, though, seduced by commercial success in London, he has chosen to remain on the border between conventional farce and absurd drama. Ayckbourn's *Absurd Person Singular* (1973), *Bedroom Farce* (1975) and *Sisterly Feelings* (1979) throw an ironic light on class distinctions, sexual and other stresses of English middle-class life, without going too deeply into philosophical questions. But Ayckbourn has shown that he is quite able to transform suburban problems into more universal insecurities.

The influence of television on drama has been considerable over the last 15 years. TV plays have provided a living for numerous artists. Outstanding playwrights like Pinter and Osborne have written for TV, and other very able dramatists have worked mostly for the small screen, among them **Dennis Potter,** whose *Pennies From Heaven* may yet prove to be one of the best theatrical productions for TV in the late 20th century, and **David Mercer** and **John Hopkins.** The scripts of their plays have been published. Thus the future of British drama, whether in print, in theatrical performances or on the screen, looks brighter than some contemporary pessimistic observers would have it.

4. The Novel

Many of the novelists writing between 1890 and World War I spent their formative years in the Victorian age. Such late Victorians as Butler, Hardy, Moore, and the American-born Henry James influenced English prose fiction until well into the 20th century. In his early novels the Irishman **George Moore** (1852-1933) emulated French naturalism, and Zola in particular; but Moore gradually abandoned determinism. Upon his return in 1901 from Paris, where he was educated, he became absorbed in the Irish Literary Renaissance. Moore's *The Lake* (1905) portrays the inner unrest of an Irish priest who abandons his parish and country for the love of a woman and emigrates to America. In the novels that followed Moore reduced dialogue and developed a rich prose that reminds one of both Pater and Proust. Apart from a number of autobiographical narratives, such as *Confessions of a Young Man* (1888), *Hail and Farewell* (1911), and *Avowals* (1919), it is mainly his agnostic novel on Christ, *The Brook Kerith* (1916), and his treatment of the great love story from the 12th century, *Héloïse and Abélard* (1921), that are today remembered.

More, and consciously, at home in the realistic tradition were **Arnold Bennett** and **John Galsworthy.** Bennett (1867-1931) has left behind a great number of works, yet only three of his novels have stood the test of time. Like some of his contemporaries, Bennett owed much to Zola, Balzac and Maupassant[1]. His outstanding novel, *The Old Wives' Tale* (1908), was inspired by Maupassant's *Une Vie* and relates the lives of two sisters, Constance and Sophia Baines, during a time when Victorian traditions were coming to an end. Bennett was best in the description of the area where he was born, the pottery district of Staffordshire. It is this element of "local colour" which also distinguishes the two other works set in Staffordshire, *Anna of the Five Towns* (1902), and the Clayhanger-trilogy, *Clayhanger* (1910), *Hilda Lessways* (1911), and *These Twain* (1916).

---

1. On Balzac see page 98, note 1, on Zola and Maupassant see page 104, notes 1 and 2.

If Bennett was concerned with provincial life in the lower middle class, **John Galsworthy's** (1867-1933) reputation rests on his realistic treatment of the upper middle class in his six novels entitled *The Forsyte Saga, A Modern Comedy* (1929), and *The End of the Chapter* (1935). *The Forsyte Saga,* which consists of *The Man of Property* (1906), *In Chancery* (1920), and *To Let* (1921), presents the reactions of a well-to-do English family to the events challenging their values and ideas, such as World War I and socialism. The hero of *The Man of Property,* Soames Forsyte, embodies the money-seeking class while his wife Irene stands for beauty and resists possession as well as the negative influence of property. Galsworthy was drawn into the fictional world of the Forsyte family, and what starts off as social criticism ends in the silent acceptance of the values and principles initially exposed and condemned. The TV series of the 1960s made the trilogy popular once more, but critics agree that it is of interest more as a cultural-historical record of the end of Victorianism than as a literary work in its own right.

Among the more traditional writers at the beginning of the century **Joseph Conrad** (1857-1924), né **Josef Teodor Konrad Korzeniowski,** is an outstanding figure who brought a new quality into the novel. His Polish origin and his love for the sea – he spent 20 years of his life at sea on French and British merchant ships before settling in England – had an impact on both his vision and his writing. He was less interested in social conditions than in man's capacity to cope with nature and exotic countries. After reading Shakespeare, Keats, Dickens and Henry James, Conrad produced his first novel at the age of 38. He then turned out a book every year, eventually completing 13 novels and 7 volumes of short stories. Conrad became popular with his early novels of the sea and far-away places, such as *Almayer's Folly* (1895) and *An Outcast of the Islands* (1896), which have a common Malayan background and show characters trying to survive in an alien and often hostile environment. He won critical acclaim with his masterful long novella *The Nigger of the Narcissus* (1897), which tells the story of the Negro James Wait on his voyage aboard the ship "Narcissus" from Bombay to England. Many critics agree that *Lord Jim* (1900) is Conrad's finest novel.

Concerned with moral conflict, with sin and evil, **Lord Jim** focuses on an officer in the English merchant marine whose cowardice proves to be fatal. When his ship "Patna", laden with pilgrims on a voyage to Aden, appears to be sinking, Jim instinctively leaps to join other officers taking to a boat. But the ship is saved and towed to a harbour. Whereas Jim's fellow officers escape, he alone has the courage to face the Court of Inquiry, and he is ordered to return his certificate. The story is then continued by another narrator, Marlowe (who is also the teller of the story in *The Heart of Darkness*), who relates Jim's rehabilitation after the "fall" in a remote tropical community. There, Jim saves the natives from the Arabs, thus earning his title 'Tuan' (Lord), but makes a great mistake in letting a notorious criminal escape. This person kills the only son of the tribe's chief, and Jim, in a sort of self-sacrifice, has himself shot by the chief.

Jim is thus a romantic idealist who, faced with difficult situations, takes the wrong decisions and perishes. In *Lord Jim* Conrad used a complicated narrative technique that includes an omniscient narrator, a skeptical commentator (Marlowe), and "factual" reports by Jim himself. In addition, the novel has a dense pattern of symbolism and a sophisticated episodic time scheme.

Conrad treated the subject of evil again in his novella *The Heart of Darkness,* published in 1902 in a collection of tales entitled *Youth.* This story inspired Francis Ford Coppola's memorable movie *Apocalypse Now* (1979). Told by Marlowe, the story describes how Mr. Kurtz, an ivory trader in the Congo, gives in to the strange and evil power of the jungle while recognizing with horror the negative potential of his character.

The most influential sources for Conrad were Robert Louis Stevenson and Henry James. From Stevenson he borrowed the frame of the adventure story, and from his pen-friend James a convincing psychology of characterization. *Nostromo* (1904) impresses one with its rich political and social background in a novel exploring human and social corruption in Costaguana, an imaginary South American republic. In *The Secret Agent* (1907) Conrad dealt with revolution and the London underworld and achieved the suspense of a detective novel, while *Under Western Eyes* (1911) treats of Russian revolutionaries. The influence of James on Conrad is most striking in *Chance* (1914), which has two narrators and explores man's loneliness and the problem of individualism.

For all his occasional sentimentality in handling love scenes and his stylistic overstatement, there can be no doubt that Conrad is an outstanding writer quite capable of exploring moral dilemmas with a complex prose and a brilliance of detail.

The majority of novelists writing between 1890 and 1914 were traditionalists in the sense that they cared less about the form of the novel and more about their message, which was either artistic, as with Conrad who emulated James, or didactic. The most conspicuous representative of the didactic wing was **H. G. Wells** (1866-1946), who saw in literature a means to achieve social equality and scientific advancement. In literature Wells is especially known for his scientific romances combining elements of science fiction and social criticism. Whereas *The Shape of Things to Come* (1933) is a utopian novel in praise of scientific perfection, his better-known *The Time Machine* (1895) is in essence an anti-utopian novel.

The book describes the efforts of the protagonist who, with the help of his time machine, is carried forward some 800,000 years. But instead of an ideal future of comfort and ease, he finds that 19th-century class distinctions have led to the development of two distinct species. There are the Eloi, i.e. the lazy, degenerate and pleasure-seeking descendants of the upper class, and the Morlocks, the former servants who live underground and come out only at night to eat those of the Eloi they can capture. Though the planet Earth is now a garden, horror lurks behind the deceiving facade of human "development". The Time Traveller undertakes a second journey into the future from which he never returns.

In addition to his utopian and dystopian fiction, Wells wrote novels with a political bent. Thus *Kipps* (1905) traces the way to wealth and success of a young man working at a draper's shop, and *The History of Mr. Polly* (1910), which is partly autobiographical, develops the theme of the lower-middle-class man shaking off the shackles of convention and rising to a comfortable middle-class life. Wells's masterpiece is *Tono-Bungay* (1909). The title of the novel refers to a basically useless medicine with which clever salesmen make a fortune while cheating the public.

Although Modernism can be said to have started in the second decade of the century, there were writers who seemed to be undisturbed by the events of World War I and the innovation in fiction as embodied in the works of Lawrence, James Joyce, and Virginia Woolf. **J. B. Priestley,** for instance, served on the Western front and yet his subsequent works seemed untouched by the war. In fact, diversity is a hallmark of Modernism, which saw a vast innovative output but also the continuing productivity of the older and younger realists. This is often ignored when the harbingers of a new era in literature – Joyce, Pound, Eliot, Yeats, Woolf – are discussed. Before turning to the early Modernists in the novel, it is important to have at least a brief look at the traditionalists writing between the two wars.

Unlike Wells, **G. K. Chesterton** (1874-1936), who often collaborated with his friend **Hilaire Belloc** (1870-1953), championed an aggressive Christianity and, after his conversion, Roman Catholicism. Chesterton wrote a great many short stories and is also remembered as a poet (see *Lepanto* and *The Ballad of the White Horse*). His best works are the detective stories featuring Father Brown, collected and published between 1911-27, and the novel *The Man Who was Thursday* (1908), a fantastic tale of anarchists and secret agents with a serious message about the struggle between good and evil and the mystery of suffering.

W. Somerset Maugham (1874-1965) started out in the naturalistic tradition of Gissing with his study of London life, *Liza of Lambeth* (1897), followed by *Of Human Bondage* (1915), a novel with strong autobiographical elements tracing the unsuccessful career of the would-be artist Philip Carey. Maugham qualified as a doctor before he turned to writing. The clinical detachment in his study of human character was undoubtedly reinforced by the fact that he was a homosexual and thus had an outsider's view. With *The Razor's Edge* (1944) he came close to a philosophical novel; yet his wittiest book is *Cakes and Ale* (1930). It relates satirically the story of an eminent novelist with a shady background. The study of French naturalists, and of Maupassant in particular, enabled Maugham to exclude sentimentality from his fiction and to discuss sex with a frankness surpassed only by D. H. Lawrence. Maugham was fascinated by the Orient. China and Malaya provide the settings for *The Trembling of a Leaf* (1921) and *The Painted Veil* (1925) while *The Moon and Sixpence* (1919) is a novelistic treatment of the life of Gauguin[1] in Tahiti.

Among the writers attracted by the East, **T. E. Lawrence** (1888-1935) and **E. M. Forster** (1879-1970) must be mentioned. Lawrence led the Arab revolt against the Turks and became a legendary figure in his own lifetime. He recorded his experiences in *The Seven Pillars of Wisdom* (1926), reissued in 1927 in an abbreviated form as *Revolt in the Desert,* which stands between military chronicle, essay and novel. Forster, a homosexual like Maugham, contributed to the novel proper six works of which only *Howard's End* (1910) and his magnificent *A Passage to India* (1924) are remarkable. The first novel treats of the complex relations be-

---

1. Paul Gauguin (1848-1903), French painter and engraver. Gauguin gave up his career in a bank and his middle-class existence and joined the Impressionist painters. He lived for some time on the Marquesas in the South Sea and died there, leaving works that proved influential for the Expressionists.

Le chien rouge by Gauguin

tween an insensitive English middle-class family and the cultured half-German Schlegel sisters. *A Passage to India* is concerned with the English and the nations in British India trying to achieve a mutual understanding. David Lean made a film based on this novel. Forster had travelled in India, and his novel, with its realism and genuine affection for the Indian people, is an admirable correction to Kipling's romanticism. But *A Passage to India* is more than a novel about the exotic East. What makes it an outstanding work of fiction is its treatment of fundamental human situations and personal relations, of tolerance, love, and of the exposure of conventionalism. Forster was also an able if conservative literary critic (see his *Aspects of the Novel,* 1927).

The three **Powys brothers,** together with **Wyndham Lewis** (1882-1957), **Compton Mackenzie** (1883-1972) and **Hugh Walpole** (1884-1941), belong to the late Victorian tradition of realistic and satirical fiction. **John Cowper Powys** (1872-1963) was a novelist of great imaginative energy. His *A Glastonbury Romance* (1933) is set in Somerset and combines associations of King Arthur's realm with a panorama of the modern world. **Charles Langbridge Morgan** (1894-1958) brought philosophy and mysticism to his fictional exploration of love, art and death in *Portrait in a Mirror* (1929), *The Fountain* (1932) and *Sparkenbroke* (1936). Finally, **Ford Madox Ford** (1873-1939) is a figure between traditionalists and modernists. His work has long been neglected, but there are signs that he is at last being recognized as a great novelist. Ford is remembered for his novels on Katherine Howard[1], such as *The Fifth Queen* (1905), and especially for *The Good*

---

1. Katherine Howard (?1520-42), the fifth wife of King Henry VIII. Accused of immoral conduct in 1541, she admitted to premarital relations. She was beheaded in the Tower of London in 1542.

Plate from *Une Semaine de Bonté* by Max Ernst, 1933

Soldier (1915). The latter has in Dowell an unreliable narrator who proved influential for the technical development of modern fiction. Ford's final work was the tetralogy *Parade's End* (*Some Do Not,* 1924; *No More Parades,* 1925; *A Man Could Stand Up,* 1926; and *Last Post,* 1928). The major character of these penetrating satires of England from 1910 to the late 1920s is a late Victorian, Christopher Tietjens, whose old-fashioned moral standards clash with the values of a new age.

The advancement of Modernism in English prose fiction is not an event that can be related to one single cause. Nor was Modernism confined to literature. In painting, for instance, there was a revolt against representation and impressionism, which brought a reevaluation of design, texture and colours. Painters like **Wassily Kandinsky** (1866-1944) and **Pablo Picasso** (1881-1973) abandoned imitation and description in favour of abstraction while others like **Max Ernst** (1891-1976) and **Salvador Dali** (born 1904), two representatives of surrealism, presented strange forms and symbols in their attempts to lay bare the unconscious. These artists, as well as the innovators in literature – D. H. Lawrence, James Joyce and Virginia Woolf – shocked their audience. The modernists were opposed to the naturalistic tradition represented by Gissing, Moore, and Bennett. What stood behind these innovations in art, music and literature were the rejection of Victorian values by a new generation coming of age in a new century, the social and political upheavals caused by the Great War (many of the Surrealists had either served as soldiers or dealt with shell-shock victims), and the new socialism heralded and symbolized by the Russian Revolution of 1917. For literature, however, the propagation of Sigmund Freud's work between 1910-1940 must be seen as a major factor in the artistic innovation. The increasing discourse on, and indeed obsession with, sex in modern literature owes a great deal to the teachings of Freud who described the libido as an instinctual force at odds with the needs and demands of society. The founding father of psychoanalysis recognized that repression of sexual instincts could lead to neurosis and psychosis, but that repressive sublimation was necessary for the rise of civilization. Civilization, Freud argued, rechanneled sexual energy into art and religion.

For innovators such as Lawrence and Joyce, sex and the unconscious became central issues, and – at least for Joyce and Woolf – so did the question of how they were to be represented in the novel. **D(avid) H(erbert) Lawrence** (1885-1930)

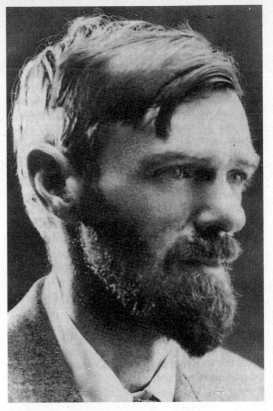

D. H. Lawrence

did not care much for the experiments of his contemporaries Marcel Proust (1871-1922)[1] and James Joyce. The son of a Nottinghamshire coalminer, Lawrence knew the cruelties of working-class life. He owed his education to his mother, a former school teacher who was anxious for her favourite son to rise above his origins. For Lawrence it was not the form of the novel that mattered – he was quite satisfied with the Victorian types he knew – but the ideas about sex and the relations between men and women he tried to express in his works. Disgusted with modern civilization, he rejected the intellect and wanted to go back to the repressed natural instincts and thus restore man's happiness. When his German-born wife Frieda, née von Richthofen, who abandoned her husband and her three children to join Lawrence in 1912, acquainted him with the work of Freud, Lawrence felt reconfirmed. He also wrote tracts on the unconscious (See *Psychoanalysis and the Unconscious,* 1923) and with his novels appealed to readers to have the courage to accept and explore physical love, instinct, and human passion.

His first major novel, *Sons and Lovers* (1913), is a fictionalized autobiographical account of Paul Morel, a miner's son, whose development Lawrence traces with psychological subtlety. Sexual passion is the dominant theme in *The Rainbow* (1915) and *Women in Love* (1920). These novels describe the lives of three generations of a Nottingham family, the Brangwens, and especially Ursula Brangwen's rejection of the deadening mechanization of mind and soul by the mining industry and her love for Rupert Birkin, a school inspector. Lawrence's heroes all look for self-realization and are prepared to make sacrifices. Thus Aaron Sisson leaves his wife and child in *Aaron's Rod* (1922), and Kate Leslie, in *The Plumed Serpent* (1926), abandons Europe and Catholicism to find happiness in the ancient Aztec culture, with its roots in sex, violence, and its exaltation of the dominant male over the passive female. In 1928 Lawrence published *Lady Chatterley's Lover.* Its frank descriptions of the sexual relations of two lovers made it his most notorious book – the unexpurgated version was banned until 1959. Much of the sensation the novel

1. See the note on page 138.

caused can be seen in the unabashed style, including four-letter-words, Lawrence used to express his sexual philosophy of the pleasures of the flesh.

The novel is set in Nottinghamshire. At Wragby, seat of the Chatterleys, Constance Chatterley is frustrated by her husband, Sir Clifford, who returned from the war an impotent and paralysed man. For Lawrence, Sir Clifford's impotence is a symbol of the sterile and moribund upper-class establishment that has ruled the country and defiled the landscape. Sir Clifford's adversary is a miner's son, the gamekeeper Mellors. It is Mellors, the representative of lower-class virility and instinct, who provides Constance with the sexual satisfaction she needs. Constance stays with him, even after getting pregnant.

Lady Chatterley's Lover has elements of realism (Mellors's dialect and his drastic and unbuttoned style), symbolism (forest and game) and mysticism (sexuality). And although the intended realism does not always work and is apt to lead to comic obscenity, there is no denying the fact that Lawrence's prose is unique. He had a rare eye for nature and landscape and he could present human passion and the vitality of life in ways that remain unsurpassed.

Whereas Lawrence tried to uncover the neglected instincts and mysterious areas of feeling we are not aware of, **James Joyce** (1882-1941) focused on both the unconscious and language as used in the novel. Although not the first writer to use what came to be known as "stream of consciousness", Joyce was the most original of the modern novelists. Literary fashion in England in the 1920s, inspired by Continental ideas, demanded that fiction explore the minds of characters rather than social and outer reality. One of the first to find an appropriate narrative technique, "interior monologue", for this sort of expressionism was **Dorothy Richardson** (1873-1957) in her series of ten novels entitled *Pilgrimages* (1915-1938). But it was the Irishman Joyce who proved a master of this method.

Joyce was educated in Catholic schools and at Unversity College, Dublin. And though much of his life was spent on the Continent, he never left Dublin in his mind. His native city, Catholicism, and the social and mental environment they created for youths, distinguish his early impressionistic short stories collected in *Dubliners* (1914). They already contain elements of stylization and of symbolism foreshadowing his later works. In 1916 *A Portrait of the Artist as a Young Man* was published. Like Lawrence's *Sons and Lovers,* this is rooted in autobiographical experience, showing the young Stephen Dedalus (an ironic allusion to the Christian martyr and the Greek mythical figure who built himself wings) revolting against the Catholic Church, Irish patriotism, and Dublin bourgeois society. Stephen's character, his consciousness, his feelings and moods, are here recorded with an unprecedented subtlety. Stephen's development until his decision for "life and art" is shown from within his own mind and involves a number of styles reflecting the thought of infancy, childhood, adolescence, and early manhood. It is in the sensitive adjustment of style to the character's stage of development and mood that Joyce proves a real master of modern fiction.

The great innovative novel of the twentieth century appeared in 1922. With *Ulysses,* a title that immediately establishes the ironical connection with Homer's epic, Joyce created a masterpiece of epic proportions.

In *Ulysses,* Stephen Dedalus appears again as one of the major characters. The novel deals with events, mainly thoughts and reflections caused by actions, on a single day (16 June, 1904) in Dublin. Unlike Homer, Joyce focuses on the mental, not the geographical, wanderings of his characters. Homer's heroes, Odysseus, Telemachus and Penelope, are recast as modern anti-heroes in Dublin; they are Leopold Bloom, an advertisement canvasser, Stephen Dedalus, in search of a spiritual father, and Molly, Bloom's sexually neglected wife. The eighteen episodes of the novel are divided into three books. The first part (3 episodes) introduces Stephen as a suffering artist. The central part of *Ulysses* (12 episodes) is dedicated to Leopold Bloom, a small, mediocre Jew henpecked by his wife. Bloom's past life is shown with the stream-of-consciousness technique; he emerges as a modern tragi-comic hero, Falstaff, Don Quijote and Pickwick rolled into one. Eventually, Stephen and Bloom are brought together. In Dublin's red light district they have a long conversation and afterwards, tired and drunk, they hallucinate and celebrate a black mass. The final episodes (3) record their return home. In Bloom's kitchen they have another conversation which is followed by Molly's final interior monologue, which runs to 40 pages, with no punctuation marks, and expresses her sensuality and the animal force of life.

It took Joyce seven years to write *Ulysses.* It is a very consciously structured book whose prose often sounds like verse. Its form links it satirically with Homer's epic. In addition, Joyce tried to capture everything that is important to men – birth and death, love and sex, faithfulness and adultery, religion, politics, national pride, literature and philosophy. The numerous allusions to literature, religion and classical mythology as well as the abundance of symbols and puns, often well hidden, make it difficult to read this monumental novel without a commentary (See, for instance, Stuart Gilbert, *James Joyce's Ulysses*, London, 1930). *Ulysses* is a supreme novel because it combines stylistic artistry and virtuosity, complicated yet convincing narrative techniques (stream-of-consciousness, realistic description, association, musical patterns such as leitmotiv, and montage as used in films), sophisticated characterization, and earthy humour in a panorama of life and human consciousness. Like Shakespeare, Sterne and Rabelais, Joyce was able to be funny and serious in a work with many layers of meaning.

Nothing in the English novel of the twentieth century can compare to Joyce's work; and Joyce's experiments in *Ulysses* have influenced almost all modern English and American novelists. Joyce tried to surpass himself with *Finnegan's Wake* (1939). This novel attempts to portray all of human history as a dream in the mind of a Dublin inn-keeper called H. C. Earwicker. The unconscious world of dreams is central to this book in which new techniques of verbal ambiguity constantly create complex meanings. This makes the text extremely difficult, even for "Joyceans", but it enriches the tale of Earwicker and his family. The ending of *Finnegan's Wake* picks up a sentence that starts the book and thus suggests Joyce's creed: man and human society change continually, but they do so in a circular fashion, for life is always renewed.

London's and England's literary life received some impulses in the 1920s from the members of the "Bloomsbury Group", a number of writers and intellectuals who championed art, truth, and aesthetics while rejecting the kind of literary realism Bennett and Wells had stood for. One of the key members of this group was **Virginia Woolf** (1882-1941). She is often mentioned together with Joyce, because

Virginia Woolf

like the Irishman she used interior monologue in a stream-of-consciousness technique to depict the inner life of her characters. Instead of traditional plotting, description, and dialogue she aimed at a representation of the fluidity of consciousness. Reality, for Woolf, was thus what goes on in the mind, while experience meant aesthetic experience. Her first novel in this new way of writing was *Jacob's Room* (1922), which gradually creates the hero through impressions given by other characters. The mental reflections and flashbacks that reconstruct the heroine's past in *Mrs. Dalloway* (1925) are the real substance of a novel in which "realistic" events take place within a single summer day. Woolf extended her technique in *To the Lighthouse* (1927). This novel recreates two days separated by a gap of ten years. The first and last parts are concerned only with the inner lives of the members of the Ramsay family while the central part of the book is held in a prose approaching poetry in its power to evoke mood and feeling. But Virginia Woolf was always dangerously close to pretentiousness and some of her passages seem to be over-written. The lighthouse, and the voyage to it, gradually emerge as symbols of human life. Woolf's technique reached an extreme in *The Waves* (1931) where no concession is made to ideas of plot or imposed design. The six characters of this book, three female and three male, do not have realistic conversations; there is merely the interior dialogue of the several consciousnesses reflecting aspects of other personalities. Two other novels by Woolf deserve to be mentioned. In *Orlando* (1928) the hero/heroine lives through four centuries and changes sex on the way. With this book Virginia Woolf celebrated her love for Victoria Sackville-West; the lesbian implications of the novel are obvious. Finally, *Between the Acts* (1941) treats of human life, art, and history, analysing the relations of a couple, Giles and Isabella Oliver, and the central symbol of a village pageant.

Virginia Woolf's characters, like herself, live in isolated worlds distinguished by cultured atmospheres, and they rarely encounter other consciousnesses. To many readers, her books seem too static and in need of human interest. Compared to Joyce, she lacks earthiness, ribaldness and wit. Her main achievement lies in the transforming of the form and substance of the novel, although it must be said that even some of her avant-garde contemporaries criticized her severely.

Samuel Beckett (born 1906) is another innovator in the field of the novel, though he has become much better known as a dramatist. Beckett emigrated to Paris early in his life and became acquainted with his countryman Joyce. Like

Joyce he has been concerned with reality and fictional technique. In 1938 he published *Murphy,* and in 1953, *Watt.* These two novels try to tap "non-literary" verbal sources and play with the traditional ideas of plot and character until, in *Watt,* a surrealistic world full of strange logic and multiple irony is achieved. Beckett's major work is the tetrachy *Molloy* (1955), *Malone Dies* (1956), *The Unnamable* (1958) and *How It Is* (1964), which were all first published in French. Beckett makes use of French to write "without style", and this development in his plays and novels is paralleled by a gradual reduction of plot and characterization through description and an increasing and deliberate confusion of real and imaginary worlds. This is done with irony and humour, elements that are also present in his parable of life in hell, *The Lost Ones* (1971). Given his existentialist and surrealist ideas, Beckett as a novelist is thus rather a lonely and somewhat belated figure in the contemporary novel.

A great many writers born before 1900 were less concerned with the form of the novel. **Wyndham Lewis** was a propagandist of modernism as a painter and writer. He published philosophical and critical works and wrote a fantastic satirical trilogy entitled *Childermass* (1928), *Monstre Gai* and *Malign Fiesta,* both published in 1955. **Joyce Cary** (1888-1957), an Irishman, wrote lively novels about Africa – *An African Witch* (1936) and *Mister Johnson* (1939) – and about the world of the young, as in *A House of Children* (1941). His best novels are *Herself Surprised* (1941), *To Be a Pilgrim* (1942), and *The Horse's Mouth* (1944). They contain picaresque themes, deal with British social history and have a typical modern rogue-hero in Gully Jimson, an unprincipled artist.

The historical novel found two representatives in **Hugh Walpole** (1884-1941), whose *The Herris Chronicle* started in 1930 with *Rogue Herris,* and the late **Robert Graves** (1895-1985), also a distinguished poet, who enjoyed a great success with his *I Claudius* and *Claudius the God,* first published in 1934, in which the Roman emperor Claudius tells his own story and that of Rome.

L. P. Hartley (1895-1972) did not become known before 1947 when the third novel of a trilogy entitled *Eustace and Hilda* appeared. The series is distinguished by sensitive and ironic control of character and plot in the description of a tragic brother-sister relationship. Hartley's *The Go-Between* (1953) is also concerned with the psychology of children. An excellent film version was made of this in 1971, winning him a wide audience for his last novel, *The Harness Room* (1971). Other traditionalists are **P. G. Wodehouse** and **J. B. Priestley. Wodehouse** (1881-1975) wrote a number of humorous novels on idle gentry and their servants and was read by a vast audience. Such characters as Bertie Wooster and his butler Jeeves became as well known in English literature as any, and more than sixty years after the publication of *The Inimitable Jeeves* (1924) and *Carry On Jeeves* (1925) British advertisements still allude to these figures. The Yorkshireman **John Boynton Priestley** (1894-1984) wrote journalistic pieces, plays and a series of successful novels. His *The Good Companions* (1929) resurrected the picaresque novel, and his *Angel Pavement* (1930) drew a realistic picture of lower middle-class life in London. Since then his most important novels have been *Bright Day* (1946), *Festival at Farbridge* (1951) and *Lost Empires* (1965).

George Orwell

Of the satirists born around the turn of the century, **Aldous Huxley, George Orwell** and **Evelyn Waugh** are still being read today. A man of great intellect who wrote superb fiction, **Huxley** (1894-1963) had Matthew Arnold among his ancestors. He attended Eton and Balliol College, Oxford, and began his literary career with satirical and comic studies of the cultural life of the 1920s: *Crome Yellow* (1921), *Antic Hay* (1923), and *Those Barren Leaves* (1925) are all indebted to the dialogue technique of Thomas Love Peacock. *Point Counter Point* (1928) is Huxley's best novel from this period. Technically, this novel aims at a musicalization of fiction by arranging characters in groups that describe and satirize each other in turns (the musical device of counterpoints). Huxley creates a cynical panorama of negative characters and of modern society. He warned against too positive a view of the technological developments in *Brave New World* (1932). This is a dystopian novel about a totalitarian and mechanized world controlled by the gods Marx and Henry Ford, a world in wich culture is suppressed, pleasures are standardized, and hygiene replaces ethics. After this novel Huxley became increasingly interested in pacifism. His *Eyeless in Gaza* (1936), while less valuable as a novel, is a plea for peace and an accusation of fascism. In 1937 Huxley settled in California, and his susequent works are strongly influenced by pacifism, mysticism, and the occult. *Ape and Essence* (1949) is his last anti-utopian novel and a moving and horrible description of the world after an atomic war. *The Island* (1962), his last work, expresses a milder pessimism.

George Orwell (pseudonym of **Eric Blair,** 1903-1950) used fiction as a vehicle for his political views. During his time at Eton and in the service of the Imperial Police in Burma, Orwell became uncomfortably conscious of the disadvantages of the English class system. *Burmese Days* (1934) contains some of his early impressions. He then lived voluntarily in poverty and with the working class. From this experience emerged his autobiographical *Down and Out in London and Paris* (1933). This was followed by a number of novels depicting the desolation of poverty and unemployment in France and England (see *Keep the Aspidistra Flying,* 1936, and *Coming Up for Air,* 1939). Apart from *Burmese Days,* Orwell wrote two outstanding works of fiction in which the political message is balanced by the artistry of the fictional framework. *Animal Farm* (1945) was written after Orwell had fought in Spain and expresses his disillusionment with communism. It is a satirical fable about a revolution that ends in totalitarianism. The animals chase away their oppressor, farmer Jones, and take over the farm. But very soon the pigs, convinced of their own superior qualities, take over, and the dictator Napoleon establishes his reign of terror and gets rid of the democrat Snowball. Orwell's great dystopian novel, much more scary than Huxley's *Brave New World*, is *1984* (1949). It predicts the terrifying triumph of totalitarian rule in Oceania, of which England is merely a small part, when Big Brother and the Thought Police manipulate the masses and run a permanent war.

The hero of *1984* is Winston Smith, an employee in the Ministry of Truth, whose job it is to falsify history by adapting past records to the latest party policy. Smith turns into a rebel, starts a diary, and tries to establish contacts with the working-class population. In the second part of the novel Smith falls in love with the girl Julia, and they both intend to join the resistance by contacting Smith's superior, O'Brien. But O'Brien proves to be a staunch supporter of the Oceanian system, and he has Smith and Julia arrested. The final part shows Smith's forced reintegration into totalitarian society through torture and brainwashing. He betrays Julia and recognizes Big Brother as the central figure in his life.

Orwell's dystopian vision in this novel was certainly inspired by political developments in Germany, Russia, and England. His picture of a state controlling the thoughts and feelings of its people, even their language, was meant as a warning.

Orwell's awareness of class distinctions in Britain influenced a number of younger writers, among them the "angry young men", notably Kingsley Amis and John Wain.

Orwell's contemporary, **Evelyn Waugh** (1903-66), was less pessimistic in his outlook. He preferred entertaining his audience with satirical novels bordering on farce. Like Huxley, he began with ironic criticism of fashionable society in such novels as *Decline and Fall* (1928) and *Vile Bodies* (1930). *Black Mischief* (1932) and *A Handful of Dust* (1934) are set in Africa and South America and also discuss serious and religious issues. Waugh became a Roman Catholic in 1930; this fact and his experience in World War II may have led to a tone of greater seriousness in his subsequent works. His *Brideshead Revisited* (1945; revised in 1960) bears the sub-title, "the sacred and profane memoirs of Captain Charles Ryder". In this last nostalgic view of the English aristocracy Waugh tried to show the working of God's grace and the power of religious values in the portrait of a group of people fatefully held together by sins of the past. Waugh also contributed to the genre of the war novel with his trilogy *The Sword of Honour* (*Men at Arms*, 1952; *Officers and Gentlemen*, 1955; and *Unconditional Surrender*, 1961), which was revised in 1965. These novels tell of the war-time experiences of a Catholic from the upper class who finally surrenders to the will of God.

Several writers born in the first decade of the century have proved influential for contemporary novelists. **Henry Green** (1905-73), with such novels as *Living* (1929), *Party Going* (1939), and *Loving* (1945), was a conscious stylist and a brilliant observer who made an impact on John Updike. **C. P. Snow** (1905-80) has left a great number of novels, most of them written in the traditional Victorian form and concerned with intellectuals of the upper-middle class. His *Strangers and Brothers* (1940-70) is made up of 11 volumes and focuses on the power centres and the social circles of London. Snow also wrote thrillers set in upper-class society, such as *A Coat of Varnish* (1979), but he never achieved the literary excellence of his contemporaries, **Anthony Powell** and **Malcolm Lowry. Powell** was born in 1905. His pre-war novel *Afternoon Men* (1931) satirizes fashionable bohemian life in the 1920s in the manner of Huxley and Waugh. After the war Powell began an ambitious sequence of twelve novels entitled *A Dance to the Music of Time.* Powell is indebted not only to Proust's *À la recherche du temps perdu* (1913-27) and to Laurence Sterne's fiction but also to Dickens. His narrator, Nick Jenkins, faces the problems of life from university days in the 1920s through the Spanish Civil War down to the post-war years. From the first novel, *A Question of Upbringing* (1951), to the last two, *Temporary Kings* (1973) and *Hearing Secret Harmonies* (1975), Powell has recorded the disintegration of modern society, and especially of middle-class life, creating some 200 characters in a series that is symphonically structured and has been widely acclaimed. **Malcolm Lowry** (1909-57) put all his skill and energy into one novel, *Under the Volcano* (1947), of which there is now also an excellent film version. Born in England, Lowry lived for some time in Canada and Mexico while struggling with misfortune and alcoholism. His novel is about the final hours in the tragic life of an alcoholic British consul in Mexico. In addition to the moving study of an alcoholic's state of mind and the suffering of his wife, the novel also contains more universal dimensions. Like Joyce, Lowry managed to achieve artistic complexity in a combination of ambiguous and symbolically charged tragi-comic scenes and realistic narrative that often alludes to myth.

Only a handful of novelists born in the second decade of the century can be said to have added appreciably to the English novel. The novel sequence "à la Powell" found a further representative in **Lawrence Durrell** (born 1912), who is also a poet. His tetralogy, *The Alexandria Quartet* (1957-60), is written in a rich prose style well suited to the atmosphere of the Near East. The four novels provide a study of passion, guilt, intrigue and espionage in Alexandria, the whole presented from different angles. Durrell's "doubledecker" novels *Tunc* (1968) and *Nunquam* (1970), published together in 1974 as *The Revolt of Aphrodite,* make use of all the liberties modern novelists possess and explore the question whether the individual can withstand the forces at work in any given culture. Since 1974, when he published *Monsieur or the Prince of Darkness,* Durrell has been at work on another series of five books, *The Avignon Quintet*, of which *Livia* (1978), *Constance* (1982), *Sebastian* (1983) and *Quinx* (1985) have appeared to date.

Like Powell and Durrell, **Mervyn Peake** (1911-68), an artist and novelist, preferred grouped novels. His reputation rests on a trilogy – *Titus Groan* (1946), *Gormenghast* (1950), and *Titus Alone* (1959) – set in a gigantic castle peopled with grotesque characters. This bizarre world, from which the hero, Titus, tries to escape, is disturbed by young Steerpike who becomes a murderer and destroyer. Peake's nightmare world holds a particular fascination and presents the ridiculous beside the momentous.

After writing a number of short stories, **Angus Wilson** (born 1913) turned to novels and concerned himself with cruelty and horror and the sudden appearance of nightmares in everyday life. Such novels as *Hemlock and After* (1952) and

Anglo-Saxon Attitudes (1956) show Wilson's remarkable wit and gift for minute observation, while *The Middle Age of Mrs. Eliot* (1958) and *Late Call* (1964) prove his ability to portray female characters and minds in a sensitive and persuasive way. These novels seem superior to his long and technically ambitious *No Laughing Matter* (1967) and *As If By Magic* (1973). With *Setting the World on Fire* (1980) he returned to a more tightly constructed form to tell the story of the destinies of two brothers.

By 1945 modernism had largely lost its shaping force in the novel. Lawrence, Joyce and Woolf were all dead. A new impetus came in the early 1950s with the literary works of the "angry young men". One explanation for the rise of this new type of fiction must be seen in the fact that socialism had made it possible for many young men and women from the working class to get a university education but not the desired access to élite circles and professional jobs. This younger generation voiced its criticism of the British establishment by creating comic, aggressive and picaresque anti-heroes who figured in a number of novels. The "angry young men" among the novelists – Kingsley Amis, William Cooper, John Braine, Alan Sillitoe, David Storey, John Wain, and Keith Waterhouse – have always refused to be considered as a movement, but their works have a few features in common. They are mostly set not in London but in the provinces, develop situations in the lower middle class or working class, and have discontented young heroes trying to cross class barriers and to get ahead in life. *Scenes from Provincial Life* (1950), by **William Cooper** (born 1910), is generally credited with having started the line of anti-heroes with Joe Lunn; yet Amis's Jim Dixon in *Lucky Jim* (1954) and Wain's Charles Lumley in *Hurry on Down* (1953) became the archetypes of the neo-picaresque "déclassé" heroes.

John Wain (born 1925) was one of the first "angries". He studied at Oxford and, for several years, taught as a lecturer in English literature. Also a poet indebted to William Empson, Wain achieved his first success with *Hurry on Down* (1953).

Charles Lumley is the anti-hero of this novel. With his lower-middle-class background and his university education, Charles has become very class-conscious and, in an attempt to escape middle-class conventionalism, tries a number of jobs including window-cleaning, drug-running, hospital-portering, and, finally, "gag-writing" for radio. Although Charles resents the establishment, he is not opposed to a lucrative occupation, which he finally gets.

Written with irony as well as moral commitment, Wain's novel stresses the value of the individual while exposing the disadvantages of modern society. *Hurry on Down* suffers from an overdone criticism of middle-class respectability and from its almost sentimental love story. But as a first novel that revived the picaresque tradition of Fielding and Smollett and set the tone for a new way of writing, it must be considered an achievement.

Wain has continued his study of the individual up against society in *The Smaller Sky* (1967) and has experimented with the novel form in *A Winter in the Hills* (1970) and *The Pardoner's Tale* (1978).

Kingsley Amis (born 1922) is also a great admirer of the picaresque novel. Technically and stylistically, he is superior to Wain. His hero in *Luck Jim* (1954) became the idol of middle-class intellectuals in England. With the handling of Jim Dixon, the young university lecturer fighting pretentiousness and phoney dilettantism while trying to make a decent living, Amis showed his talent for farce and slapstick, for exact social observation and verbal sophistication. Since the 1950s Amis has further developed his comic potential and has taken a more conservative position in such novels as *Take a Girl Like You* (1960) and *I Want It Now* (1968). These novels already allude to the themes of death and the supernatural which he studied in detail in *Ending Up* (1974). With *Russian Hide and Seek* (1980) Amis again proved his talent for irony and farce and for social criticism in a melodramatic spy novel. His novel *Stanley and the Women* (1984) is a pseudo-attack on the feminist movement that was probably provoked by the charge, made by several critics, that the sexist heroes of his novels, who are stirred to enthusiasm only by alcohol and female breasts, reflect Amis's own anti-feminism.

In *Room at the Top* (1957), **John Braine** (born 1922) shows the social rise of Joe Lampton, a working-class hero, who gets what he wants at the expense of his lover and his ideals. *Life at the Top* (1962) continues Joe's story, but Braine's subsequent works, such as *Jealous God* (1965), did not fulfil the promises of his first novel. The same can be said of **Alan Sillitoe** (born 1928), who has often been compared to D. H. Lawrence. Sillitoe's Arthur Seaton in the much celebrated novel *Saturday Night and Sunday Morning* (1958) has no intellectual ambitions. For him, drinking and sex make up for the dreariness, the brutality and the injustice of working-class life in the Midlands. Sillitoe's novel presents a good if bitter picture of class warfare in Britain and of the violence and "un-consciousness" generated by a disadvantageous social environment. It has remained his best book and surpasses such sequels as *Key to the Door* (1961).

The provinces were investigated with serious concern in some of the novels of **Keith Waterhouse** (born 1929), such as *Billy Liar* (1959) and **David Storey's** (born 1933) *This Sporting Life* (1960).

The twentieth century has seen some formidable works from the pens of women novelists. Among the "first generation", the novels of **Ivy Compton-Burnett** (1892-1969) and **Elizabeth Bowen** (1899-1969) stand out. **Compton-Burnett** has left some 20 novels dealing with conflicts in upper-class families. In *Brothers and Sisters* (1929), *Elders and Betters* (1944), and *Mother and Son* (1955), tyranny, brutality, murder and malice are revealed behind the facade of Victorian drawing rooms. Indebted to Henry James, Compton-Burnett excluded the post-war scene in her novels, whereas her contemporary, the Irishwoman **Elizabeth Bowen**, dealt with new developments in the new century. She, too, had learned from James, and also from Virginia Woolf. Bowen put into practice her knowledge of recent discoveries in psychology in such novels as *The House in Paris* (1935), *The Death of the Heart* (1938), *A World of Love* (1955), and *The Little Girls* (1964), all subtle studies of emotional life and the tragi-comic aspects of events in the worlds of sensitive women.

Younger women novelists have recognized the literary importance of these two writers. Among these, **Barbara Pym** (1913-80) **Olivia Manning** (1917-80), and **Elizabeth Taylor** (1912-75) were all able and gifted writers. Remarkable works are Pym's *Quartet in Autumn* (1978) and Manning's *Balkan Trilogy* (1960-65). From the group of women born in the second decade of the century, three have gained an international reputation. **Iris Murdoch** (born 1919), in such novels as *Under the Net* (1954) and *The Bell* (1958), studied the philosophical problems of freedom and responsibility. As a professional philosopher she flirted with structuralism in *A Severed Head* (1961), a novel which revives the mystery of the Gothic novel and features characters caught up in bizarre sexual entanglements. These themes have also dominated such works as *Bruno's Dream* (1969), *The Black Prince* (1973), *The Sacred and Profane Love Machine* (1974), *The Sea, the Sea* (1978), and *Nuns and Soldiers* (1980).

The work of **Muriel Spark** (born 1918), a Catholic convert, is as prolific but has a wider scope. The fictional worlds of her novels can be seen as microcosms of reality described with detached irony. Her best works are *Memento Mori* (1959), a study of old people faced with the prospect of death, *The Prime of Miss Jean Brodie* (1962), which shows a charismatic and progressive Scots schoolmistress waging pedagogic war with the authorities in the 1930s, and the technically more traditional *The Mandelbaum Gate* (1965), set in Jerusalem. Critics have judged her more recent fiction – *The Hothouse by the East River* (1973), *The Takeover* (1976), *Territorial Rights* (1979), and *Loitering With Intent* (1981) – less convincing.

Doris Lessing (born 1919) was born in Southern Rhodesia, now Zimbabwe, and went to England in 1949 with a strong dislike of racism and the experience of a broken marriage. In *The Grass Is Singing* (1950) she looks back on her early life in Africa. Her sequence of five novels called *Children of Violence* (1952-69) chronicles the attempts of Martha Quest to find sexual fulfilment and political satisfaction in Africa and England. *The Golden Notebook* of 1962 is an experimental novel assessing reality and fiction by interweaving various themes and levels of narrative with notebook entries. More recently, Doris Lessing has turned to fantasy, writing "inner-space fiction" such as *Briefing for a Descent into Hell* (1971) and a "cosmic chronicle" entitled *Canopus in Argos Archives* which consists of *Shikasta* (1979), *The Marriages Between Zones Three, Four and Five* (1980), *The Sirian Experiments* (1981), *The Making of the Representative for Planet 8* (1982), and *Documents Relating to the Sentimental Agents in the Volyen Empire* (1983), which are all fictional studies of man's social and scientific future.

Between 1960-1980 several young women writers have come to the fore. **Margaret Drabble** (born 1939) has dealt with pregnancy and motherhood from an educated feminist viewpoint in *The Millstone* (1965) and has focused almost exclusively on London's academics in *The Needle's Eye* (1972) and *The Middle Ground* (1980). Like Drabble, the Irish novelist **Edna O'Brien** (born 1932) has been a spokeswoman for feminism. In such novels as *The Country Girls* (1960), *Girl With Green Eyes* (1962), and *Girls in Their Married Bliss* (1968), she has dealt with women's sexual needs and rebellious discontent. Another Irishwoman, **Jennifer Johnston** (born 1930), has portrayed Ireland and the Anglo-Irish gentry with compassion and humour in *The Gates* (1973) and *How Many Miles to Babylon?*

Margaret Drabble

Graham Greene

(1974). Mention must also be made of **Susan Hill** (born 1942) and her fine historical novel on World War I, *Strange Meeting* (1971); of **Fay Weldon** (born 1935) and her amusing treatment of the battle of the sexes in *Female Friends* (1975) and *Little Sisters* (1978); of **Beryl Bainbridge** (born 1934), who has written tragi-comic novels on self-delusion (e.g. *Sweet William*, 1975); and of **Penelope Mortimer's** (born 1918) frank treatment of the female experience in *The Pumpkin Eater* (1962) and *Long Distance* (1974).

Three men – Graham Greene, William Golding, and Anthony Burgess – each with a special approach and a distinct style, have made the exploration of good and evil in modern man and society the subject of their prose fiction. **Graham Greene** (born 1904), like Waugh a converted Roman Catholic, has turned from moral inquiry to the treatment of political and ethical issues. He has divided his work into "entertainments" and "novels". But even the "entertainments", which combine adventure and detective fiction, are concerned with moral problems. Examples are *A Gun For Sale* (1936), *The Confidential Agent* (1939), *The Ministry of Fear* (1943), *The Third Man* (1950), originally a film script, and *The Human Factor* (1978). Greene's best works of fiction appeared between 1938-1951. *Brighton Rock* (1938) is poised between thriller and serious novel. It is a study of a Catholic teenage delinquent, Pinkie, who commits multiple murder and, finally, suicide. Sinners also figure in the other "Catholic" novels from this period – *The Power and the Glory* (1940), *The Heart of the Matter* (1948), and *The End of the Affair* (1951). The hero of *The*

Power and the Glory is a "whisky priest" suffering from cruel treatment by the police in Mexico, while the protagonist of *The Heart of the Matter* is persecuted by his own conscience. Greene's experience of the Cold War and of the McCarthy era, and his changing political views, are reflected in *The Quiet American* (1955) and *Our Man in Havana* (1958). Such later novels as *The Comedians* (1966), which is set in Haiti, and *The Honorary Consul* (1973), set in Argentina, show an emerging humanism and the influence of Teilhard de Chardin[1] as Greene deals with fear, persecution, sex, atheism and faith in a world apparently abandoned by a mysterious God. Greene's growing concern with political and humanitarian problems is most obvious in the books he has published since 1980. *Doctor Fisher of Geneva* (1980) is a black comedy on the greed of the rich; *J'Accuse,* published in French and English in 1982, put Greene under considerable criticism because he sided – too rashly as it proved – with a girl involved in the world of organized crime in Nice. Also published in 1982 was *Monsignor Quixote*. It is a modern parody of Cervantes's seventeenth-century classic, with Don Quixote and Sancho Panza replaced by a priest and a Communist mayor. Their travels and adventures in Spain are merely the backdrop for conversations and discussions exploring politics, ethics, faith, and the modern world.

Ever since he published his *Lord of the Flies* in 1954, **William Golding** (born 1911) has been preoccupied with the nature of evil, original sin and civilization from a distinct Catholic viewpoint.

Lord of the Flies is a simple and exciting story of a group of English schoolboys left to themselves on a desert island in an atomic war. Based on R. M. Ballantyne's 19th-century story *The Coral Island, Lord of the Flies* reverses the pattern of the children's adventure story as the boys gradually regress to savagery and find that evil is located in themselves and not in nature or "wild savages".

Ralph, the archetype of the good in man, is deprived of his leadership by the brutal Jack who establishes a rule of terror and reverts to a primitive cultural level. Jack's regime has no need for intellectuals or prophets, and so the representatives of these groups – Piggy and Simon – are killed. Ironically, Ralph is finally saved by a British man-of-war that takes the boys into a world where an even more savage fight is going on.

In his fiction, Golding has worked with symbols, archetypes, and myths in a continued effort to comment on the fall of man. *The Inheritors* (1955) turns evolution upside down, with the result that "homo sapiens" appears as the destroyer of innocent life and the pious state of mind of Neanderthal man. *Pincher Martin* (1956) presents the consciousness and imagination of a shipwrecked sailor clinging to a rock in the sea and refusing to accept death. In *Free Fall* (1959) an artist looks back on his life and the events that led to the loss of his soul, and in *The Spire* (1965) the forces of heaven and hell are shown at work in a complex study of

---

1. Pierre Teilhard de Chardin (1881-1955) French Jesuit priest and author of a series of works published after his death. His *Le Phénomène humain* (1955) establishes a system of cosmic evolution in which every physical being has an inner consciousness. Man's appearance marks the emergence of self-consciousness and of a new dimension in evolution.

Dean Jocelyn who is obsessed with building the spire of Salisbury Cathedral. After the publication of *The Pyramid* (1967), set in a rural environment, Golding took a long pause that was interrupted only by a collection of short stories in 1971. He returned to the novel with *Darkness Visible* (1979). This treats of the upbringing of the orphan Matty in a post-war world that is evil and unwilling to listen to Matty's prophecies. The prophet is eventually killed in a bombing. Golding's more recent novels, *Rites of Passage* (1980) and *The Paper Men* (1984), pursue with much irony his favourite themes of the corruption of modern man. There can be no doubt that Golding's artistic talents are limited. Fiction, for him, is a mere vehicle allowing him to express his view of the human condition. More often than not, this means that Golding turns into a moralist with a didactic message. He analyses his protagonists with a psychology that is far too simple, while the structural patterns of his fiction – fable, allegory and myth – seem too neat and schematic. If Golding received the Nobel Prize in 1983 it was no doubt because of his persistent moral vision, which remains his strong point, although it hampers the artistry of his fiction.

Anthony Burgess (1917) is a better fictional craftsman than Golding, although he has found less favour with the critics. The sheer volume of his fiction has been held against him. But Burgess argues that he must write to earn a living and seems to be unperturbed. Together with several works of less interest, he has produced a number of outstanding novels that rank among the best of twentieth-century English fiction. As a novelist, Burgess has tried to remain on the border separating "serious" from "popular" literature. Shakespeare and Joyce are the writers that have influenced him most; this is evident in his love of puns and his general verbal virtuosity as well as in his comic use of fable and allegory. Unlike Golding, Burgess, who is a lapsed Catholic, is less moralistic and vastly more entertaining in dealing with the issues of good and evil and man's freedom of choice. Burgess's vision, tempered by humour and irony, seems to suggest that evil is a powerful force and often a condition for good, while man must be given the choice between the two to be really free. After a witty and melancholy account of the end of British rule in the Far East in his *Malayan Trilogy* (1956-1959), success came with what is often regarded as his most famous work, *A Clockwork Orange* (1962), a novel Burgess himself does not rank among his best. Stanley Kubrick made the novel into a much discussed film in 1971. Burgess's book is an anti-utopian novel whose moral theme of human freedom is beautifully balanced by literary artistry. A comparison with Golding's *Lord of the Flies,* which is on the same subject, reveals Burgess's superiority.

A Clockwork Orange shows a future England terrorized by gang warfare. The narrator, Alex, is the leader of a group of teenage delinquents who commit theft, rape, and murder for the sheer pleasure they take in violence. But Alex, though he loves violence, is not entirely painted in black. His love of music (Beethoven) and his special "nad-sat" slang render him not altogether negative for the reader. Captured by the police, Alex is subjected to brainwashing and develops a disgust for violence and classical music. Emotionally and ethically, he has thus become a neutral creature, a living machine or "clockwork orange", that is exploited by the state and reckless politicians. After a failed attempt at suicide, Alex is

Study after Velasquez's Portrait of Pope Innocent X by Francis Bacon, 1953

restored to his former self, but, in a chapter left out in the American edition and in the film script, eventually loses his taste for violence.

This novel indicates Burgess's great potential as a writer. An important ethical issue, man's freedom of choice (much debated after Skinner's behaviourist theories[1] had been published in the 1950s), is here treated in a subtle narrative framework and in an allusive language that creates irony and multiple meanings and is highly entertaining. The threat to the human freedom of choice has become one of Burgess's central themes. It is present in the novels on the comic middle-aged poet Enderby, who can compose only on the toilet seat (*Inside Mr. Enderby,* 1963, *Enderby Outside,* 1968, *The Clockwork Testament,* 1976, and recently, *Enderby's Dark Lady,* 1984), as well as in the spy thriller *Tremor of Intent* (1966) in which the spy becomes a Catholic priest. Burgess has also written fictional biographies of Shakespeare (*Nothing Like the Sun,* 1964) and of Napoleon (*Napoleon Symphony,* 1974). He has a vast knowledge of music, has composed several operas and symphonies and parodied Wagner's *Ring der Nibelungen* in *The Worm in the Ring* (1961). In 1980 he published his most ambitious novel, *Earthly Powers,* a panorama of the 20th century presented by an old pessimistic and homosexual writer of popular fiction. Rich in characters, both real and invented, and linguistic skill, this is one of the best works of fiction written since the 1960s. As Kenneth Toomey relates his life and entanglements with his former friend, the poet and sectarian Godfrey Manning who leads his followers into death, and with the later pope Carlo Campanati, Burgess develops his theme of the forces of good and evil at work in man's nature and in society. Toomey's story ends with himself and his beloved sister Hortense retired to the provincial cosiness of Sussex; but in the course of the novel one becomes aware of Burgess's distrust of moral institutions created by man. The book is a great pleasure to read and must be justly termed an outstanding novel. Burgess's *The End of the World News* (1982), a pun

---

1. B(urrhus) F(rederic) Skinner (born 1904), American psychologist and teacher. Through experiments with animals he developed a theory of learning that is based on conditioning (behaviourism). His books include *Walden Two* (1948, rev. in 1969), and *The Technology of Teaching* (1968). Skinner's theories were popular and much discussed in the 1960s and '70s, although practical teaching, at least in Europe, has not profited much from his theory. See also p. 222.

on a BBC radio program, is an ingenious science fiction novel uniting the dying Sigmund Freud, a Broadway musical on the subject of Trotsky in New York, and the last throes of the planet Earth in A. D. 2000. *The Kingdom of the Wicked* (1985) is Burgess's satire on the early Christians.

In comparison with Burgess, **John Fowles** (born 1926) seems a lesser writer because his literary effects are too laboured and because his experiments with fictional forms do not always produce the desired effects. In a number of his novels, Fowles has worked with literary allusions and the philosophy of existentialism[1], from the tragic study of a psychopath who imprisons his lover in *The Collector* (1958) to *The Magus* (1966, revised in 1977), an "educational" novel inspired by Ann Radcliffe's *The Mysteries of Udolpho* (1794), and the best-seller *The French Lieutenant's Woman* (1969). The latter is a nineteenth-century love story with three endings, Victorian and modern ones, in which the Victorian idiom is parallelled by a twentieth-century perspective. Harold Pinter reworked the novel into a script that served as the basis for a celebrated film. The post-modern preoccupation with the problem of telling a story is quite central in *The French Lieutenant's Woman*, and Fowles has dealt with it repeatedly. Thus *Daniel Martin* (1977) shows experiments with the point of view and with time; and *Mantissa* (1982) consists of extended erotic fantasy.

As the case of John Fowles proves, some novelists have responded with self-questioning and parody to the doubts about the viability of the novel form and to the appearance of strong competition from documentary prose and the non-verbal media. But the contemporary English novel is very much alive, and a great number of writers testify to it.

Paul Scott (1920-1978) served in India during the war and left a beautiful and penetrating record of the final years of British rule in that country with his four novels *The Raj Quartet*, of which *The Jewel in the Crown* (1966) was selected for a TV series. **William Trevor** (born 1928) has focused on cranky misfits in *The Old Boys* (1964), *Mrs. Eckdorf in O'Neill's Hotel* (1969), and *Other People's Worlds* (1980). **Malcolm Bradbury** (born 1932) and **David Lodge** (born 1935) have produced satires of university life. Bradbury became known with *Eating People Is Wrong* (1960) and *Stepping Westward* (1965), concerned with British and American academics, and especially with his satire of the "revolutionary" late 1960s, *The History Man* (1975), which was recently made into an excellent TV drama series. David Lodge made fun of the academic jetsetters in *Changing Places* (1975) and *Small World* (1984).

Still younger writers include **D. M. Thomas** (born 1935; *The White Hotel*, 1981), **Melvyn Bragg** (born 1939), who made his native Cumbria the subject and

---

1. The name given to a group of loosely associated doctrines expressed in the works of Camus, Sartre, Heidegger, and Jaspers. These writers emphasize the unique in human experience; they place man at the centre of their idea of the world; and they distrust general laws and principles allegedly controlling human nature. Existentialists give priority to honesty in moral issues and would defend any decision as justified if it is made in perfect sincerity. The appeal of their writings can be attributed to their impressive insights that have greatly extended the area of human self-knowledge. See also the notes on page 137.

setting of such novels as *For Want of a Nail* (1965) and *Kingdom Come* (1980), **A. N. Wilson** (born 1950; *The Healing Art,* 1980), and **William Boyd** (born 1952). Boyd's *An Ice-Cream War* (1982) tells the story of the English presence in East Africa during World War I. **Martin Amis** (born 1949) has made a successful entry into the world of novelists with two ironic studies of sex and class in modern Britain and America, *Success* (1978) and *Money* (1984). In addition to the English novelists, a few names from Ireland and Scotland have come to the fore. Irish writers include **Edna O'Brien**, discussed above, and **John McGahern** (born 1934); and Scots writers of importance beyond their country are **Alasdair Gray** (born 1934; *Lanark,* 1981, and *Janine 1982,* publ. in 1984), and **Ian McEwan** (born 1948; *The Cement Garden,* 1978).

Finally, several Commonwealth writers should not be excluded from a history of English literature, not least because they are much read in Britain and because some of them have been living in England for many years. Southern Africa and South Africa have produced a substantial body of protest literature. To the work of Doris Lessing may be added the achievement of **Nadine Gordimer** (born 1923), **Dan Jacobson** (born 1929), and **J. M. Coetzee** (born 1940). Indian novelists cherished in Britain are **R. K. Narayan** (born 1907; *The Painter of Signs,* 1977) and **Salman Rushdie** (born 1947; *Midnight's Children,* 1981), who, like the West Indian **V. S. Naipaul** (born 1932), has been living in England for some time. Naipaul has written a superb novel about his native Trinidad, *A House for Mr Biswas* (1961), several more overtly political works and a sensitive study of Africa, *A Bend in the River* (1979).

5. The Short Story

In practice and theory the Americans **Washington Irving** and **Edgar Allan Poe** may have done much for the development of the short story in the nineteenth century, but they did not invent it. With its roots in the fairy tale, the French "conte" and "fabliau", and the Italian and Spanish "novella" – early prototypes can be found in Boccaccio's *Decameron* (1349-53), Chaucer's *Canterbury Tales* (1478), the anonymous *Les Cent Nouvelles Nouvelles* (1486), the *Heptameron* (1558-59), Cervantes's *Novelas Ejemplares* (1613), and La Fontaine's *Contes et Nouvelles* (1666-96) – the short story has become in the twentieth century one of the most popular genres of prose fiction.

The writers at the beginning of the century treated it as a minor novelistic form, producing naturalistic and realistic tales with detailed description, fascinating plots, and moral commentary. Apart from the stories of **H. G. Wells** and **Arnold Bennett,** typical examples are the character studies by **Thomas Hardy,** *Life's Little Ironies* (1894) and *A Changed Man* (1913), **Hugh Walpole's** more humorous stories concerned with provincial life, and the tales of exotic adventure, loneliness, and threat from the pens of **Rudyard Kipling, William Somerset Maugham,** and **Joseph Conrad.**

Both Conrad and Maugham, each from their specific angles, dealt with the problems primitive instincts create for isolated Europeans in the jungles of Africa and the Far East. In Conrad's "An Outpost of Progress", a story from his *Tales of Unrest* (1898), two ordinary white men, Carlier and Kayerts, gradually revert to the level of savages while serving as superintendents at a trading station in central Africa. The wilderness surrounding them is mirrored by the wilderness they discover in their own hearts: Kayerts kills his companion and then hangs himself. In this story, Conrad's nihilistic message is underlined by symbolism that is at times too obvious to be convincing in the literary context. The use of symbols links Conrad with Maugham. In "The Force of Circumstance", from *The Casuarina Tree* (1926), Maugham presents the tragic story of Doris, who follows her English husband, Guy, into the jungle of Malaya where Guy has grown up. Doris finds out that her husband had been living with a Malayan woman and had had children by her. When she decides to leave Guy and to return to England, it is not so much because of her deception but because of Guy's transgression of the racial limits: Guy takes back his Malayan family, and Maugham presents this as a sort of punishment.

Whereas Conrad's story suggests that, under stress and in isolation, man's primitive instincts always prove stronger than his European civilized manners, Maugham's stance borders on imperialistic racism: Guy must be punished, according to Maugham's underlying ideology, for taking a black concubine, not for his concubinage.

Modernism in the genre of the short story began with the impressionistic forms and techniques with which the writers of the fin-de-siècle experimented, especially those authors who contributed to the journals *The Yellow Book* and *The Savoy*. The

short story as developed by **James Joyce** and **Katherine Mansfield** tends to focus on basic situations and isolated human problems. It restricts itself to types, rather than launching into full characterization, and makes use of allusions, multiple meaning, and symbolism while assessing issues of modern life without providing definite answers. Thus Joyce's fifteen stories in *Dubliners* (1914) treat with much psychological insight of children, youths, and adults caught in the religious, social, and marital conventions of Dublin. Most of the characters are unable even to recognize their desperate situations; and only a few, such as the narrators in the first three stories ("The Sisters", "An

Design for *The Savoy* by Beardsley, 1896

Encounter", "Araby"), change their mental state by undergoing the typical Joycean experience of "epiphany". This "recognition of oneself" is expertly handled in the final story, "The Dead", in which the protagonist, Gabriel Conroy, gradually becomes aware of the illusions governing his life and marriage. In a long exposition, which mainly serves to characterize the intellectual decline and the growing paralysis of Dublin society, Joyce sketches a representative group of Dubliners. They gather at the annual reception of Conroy's aunts and discuss mainly the past and the dead. Later, in their hotel room, Gabriel and his wife Gretta undergo the typical Joycean "epiphany" as Gretta confesses that, during her youth in the west of Ireland, she loved a young man who died because he did not want to live without her. Gabriel realizes that his wife has never truly loved him – the dead rule over the living. Unlike Conrad, Joyce never employs too much symbolism. "The Dead" impresses because it is both realistic and symbolic and sums up the major themes of *Dubliners.* For the reader, all these are stories of self-recognition and revelation which Joyce presents with a sophisticated technique of changing points of view, casual openings, and open endings.

Whereas Joyce demonstrated his particular idea of revelation and recognition (epiphany) in his stories, **Katherine Mansfield** (1888-1923) attempted to catch the essential in seemingly ordinary moments of everyday life. Born in New Zealand, she came to Europe at the age of 14, suffering from a disease of the lungs. Her constant illness may have contributed to the development of a particular vision that is both ironic and wistful. Like Joyce, she was influenced by Chekhov. Her stories illustrate significant moments of beauty, pain, and fear in the lives of women and girls. The best of her short fiction, written in a poetic and symbolic prose, is collected in *Bliss* (1920), *The Garden Party* (1922), *The Dove's Nest* (1923), and *Something Childish* (1924).

Nearly all novelists, with varying success, have tried to exploit the technical possibilities of the short story, from **Virginia Woolf** and **E. M. Forster** (*The Celestial Omnibus,* 1911, and *The Eternal Moment,* 1928) to **Elizabeth Bowen** (*The Demon Lover,* 1945, and *Collected Stories,* 1980), and **Graham Greene** (*Collected Stories,* 1972). One of the great names often neglected by literary histories is **Saki,** the pseudonym of **Hector Hugh Munro** (1870-1916). He was born in Burma and later worked as a writer in London. His first volume of short stories, *Reginald* (1904) proved successful and was followed by *Reginald in Russia* (1910), *The Chronicles of Clovis* (1911), and other collections as well as two novels. A selection of his best stories was edited and published by J. W. Lambert as *The Bodley Head Saki* in 1963. Saki's stories show a deep interest in animals that often act as agents of revenge upon men. The stories are presented in a satirical, macabre, and supernatural framework.

As in his novels, **D. H. Lawrence** wrote in his short stories of men dominated by Eros, for example in "Love Among the Haystacks", "The Fox", and "The Horse-dealer's Daughter", which are all written in a traditional narrative technique. Lawrence also wrote stories of recognition. Thus "Second Best" deals with the development of a girl in love, Frances, comparing her with a more naive character, Anne.

H. E. Bates (1905-74) in his *Country Tales* (1974) proved an able writer in the tradition of Joyce and Chekhov, and **Aldous Huxley** also showed his satiric talent in many of his stories collected and published in 1956. Among the post-war authors, outstanding writers of short stories include the novelists **Evelyn Waugh** and **Angus Wilson** (see Wilson's *The Wrong Set,* 1949, and *Such Darling Dodos,* 1950), as well as **V. S. Pritchett** (born 1900; *Collected Stories,* 1982) and **Roald Dahl** (born 1916) who are mainly short story writers. Pritchett's short fiction is distinguished by its wide social range, its detailed observation of human oddity, and sympathetic irony.

The Celtic fringe in Ireland and Scotland has also excelled in the short prose narrative. Apart from James Joyce, Irish writers of great skill are **Samuel Beckett,** whose reductive handling of language and fiction reveals itself in the early *More Pricks than Kicks* (1934), and the singers of Ireland's beauty and magic, **Liam O'Flaherty** (1877-1984; *Two Lovely Beasts,* 1948) and **Sean O'Faolain** (born 1900; *Teresa,* 1947, and *Collected Stories,* 1981). **Frank O'Connor** (1903-66), whose real name was Michael O'Donovan, wrote stories that combine the moving and the comic and appeal to a large reading audience. Some of his stories deal with the problem of Irish identity. Thus "Guests of the Nation" (1931) tells of IRA men guarding two English prisoners. They all become friends, but eventually the Irish are ordered to shoot their hostages. Scottish writers of note include the novelist **Muriel Spark,** who spent several years in Central Africa and made it the setting of her collection *The Go-Away Bird* (1958), **Naomi Mitchinson** (born 1897), **Ian Hamilton Finlay** (born 1925), who is also a poet and artist, and **Eric Linklater** (1899-1974).

6. Children's Literature, Science Fiction, and Fantasy

Children have become an important reading public, and a much contested economic market for publishers. In order to understand British culture and literature it is essential to realize that some books for children, and their authors, have become part and parcel of the cultural heritage and are considered as influential as *Alice in Wonderland.* Thus **Beatrix Potter's** (1866-1943) *The Tale of Peter Rabbit* (1902) started off a series of stories, many of them beautifully illustrated, in which animals are dressed up and talk like late Victorian people. The case of Beatrix Potter also proves that children's literature, especially at the beginning of the century, could be decidedly conservative and strongly bourgeois. Potter's occasionally naughty Peter Rabbit was joined in 1908 by the animals in **Kenneth Grahame's** (1859-1932) *The Wind in the Willows,* in which Rat, Mole, and Badger have to deal with the irresponsible Toad of Toad Hall. In the 1920s, **A. A. Milne's** (1882-1956) books were the rage of the day. Milne equipped his animals with human characteristics. His Pooh Bear is still as popular today as it was when the book *Winnie-the-Pooh* first came out in 1926. It was followed by *The House at Pooh Corner* (1928).

Science Fiction (SF) is one of the most popular genres in contemporary literature.

Illustration from *The Tale of Peter Rabbit* by Beatrix Potter

Swift's *Gulliver's Travels* (1726) and Mary Shelley's *Frankenstein* (1818) are precursors of this type of fiction, although the Frenchman **Jules Verne** (1828-1905) and **H. G. Wells** must be credited with the introduction of the major themes: voyages to other planets, invasions from outer space, biological changes and atomic catastrophes, and time travel. The literary quality of SF is extremely variable, ranging from cartoons in sensational magazines to the respectable novels of the Pole **Stanislaw Lem** and some of **Anthony Burgess's** fiction. While it is true that SF can be stereotyped and schematic, several authors have produced works of literary merit. In addition to a number of works by Burgess and the later novels of Doris Lessing, there is the fiction of **Brian Aldiss** (born 1925, *Enemies of the System,* 1978), **Arthur C. Clarke** (born 1917), whose *2001: a Space Odyssey* (1968) Stanley Kubrick made into an equally excellent film, **C. S. Lewis** (1898-1963; *Out of the Silent Planet,* 1938), **Michael Moorcock** (born 1939; *The English Assassin,* 1972), and **John Brunner** (born 1934), who has described a horrible, totally computerized America in *The Shockwave Rider* (1976). Clarke and Moorcock have done much to invest the genre with literary aspects and so has **J. G. Ballard** (born 1930, see *High Rise,* 1975). Aldiss and Kingsley Amis (see Amis's, *New Maps of Hell,* 1961) have both written important critical studies of SF.

Related to SF is Tolkien's alternative world of fantasy and myth. From 1945-59 **J. R. R. Tolkien** (1892-1973) worked as professor of English language and literature at Merton College, Oxford. He became internationally known for two books that combine elements of the fairy tale, the epic, the saga, and myths in a fantastic imaginary world peopled with strange beings that have their own languages, history, culture, and mythology. *The Hobbit* (1937), the story of the reluctant dwarf-adventurer Bilbo Baggins, and its longer sequel, the trigoly *The Lord of the Rings* (1954-55), have sold several million copies. With their magic and closed world of elves and dwarfs, dragons and wicked rulers, beautiful landscapes and strange adventures, the novels continue to fascinate readers all over the world. In his books, Tolkien made no overt allusions to politics and the social order of the twentieth century. He has been attacked as an "escapist" and as a writer who seems to be in favour of a male sexist order. Against this accusation can be held Tolkien's powerful statement about the force and influence of evil, and his books' epic qualities and fantastic atmosphere that make up for his occasional glorification of traditional values and his rejection of everything modern. Tolkien has found a successor, though of inferior talent, in the American **Stephen Donaldson** (born 1947).

7. Crime Fiction

Crime fiction is a general term for a variety of prose fiction covering mystery, the detective novel, and the spy novel. Tales of crime, terror and mystery, whether factual reports or fictional narratives, have been popular for several centuries. In the late seventeenth and throughout the eighteenth century, the chaplains of Newgate Prison in London published with great success reports on the careers of English criminals entitled *The Newgate Calendar;* it was soon imitated and surpassed by rival publications. **Defoe,** in his *Moll Flanders* (1722) and *Roxana* (1724), drew on this crime literature as did **Fielding** in *Jonathan Wild* (1743). Another source for crime fiction is the Romantic tale of terror as produced by **Horace Walpole, Ann Radcliffe, William Godwin,** and **Matthew Lewis** and the novels of the Irishman **J. S. Le Fanu** (1814-73), *Uncle Silas* (1864) and *Checkmate* (1871).

The modern detective novel is greatly indebted to the autobiography of **Eugène François Vidocq** (1775-1857), a former criminal who became a police spy and, in 1811, chief of the Paris "Sûreté". Vidocq published his memoirs from 1828 on, and these accounts of his sensational exploits in hunting down criminals singlehandedly were immediately translated into English and became a source of inspiration for writers such as Edgar Allan Poe, Conan Doyle, Chesterton, Dorothy Sayers, and Agatha Christie. These authors created incredibly clever detectives who, like Vidocq, are often more efficient than the police.

Drawing on Vidocq's memoirs as well as on Poe's Dupin and Wilkie Collins's novel *The Moonstone* (1868), **Arthur Conan Doyle** (1859-1930) created the first modern detective. Few characters in fiction have been so widely accepted, sometimes as if they were living celebrities, as the eccentric and often anti-social Sherlock Holmes and his friend and chronicler Dr Watson. Sherlock Holmes made his first appearance in *A Study in Scarlet* (1888). This was followed by the very popular detective stories *Adventures of Sherlock Holmes* (1891-92). When Doyle had Holmes killed in a fatal struggle with the arch-enemy, Professor Moriarty, in *The Memoirs of Sherlock Holmes* (1893), there was a public outcry, and Doyle reluctantly revived his detective in *The Hound of the Baskervilles* (1901-2), *The Valley of Fear* (1915) and numerous short stories.

Embodying the characteristics of his most notable predecessors – intellectual brilliance, an excellent social and cultural background, and "scientific" knowledge – Holmes was admired by Doyle's international reading public and became the ancestor of several detective heroes in English fiction. Thus **Dr R. Austin Freeman** (1862-1943) invented a scientist, Dr Thorndyke, who was modelled on Sherlock Holmes and, in such novels as *John Thorndyke's Cases* (1909) and *The Singing Bone* (1912), specialized in chemical analysis. **G[ilbert] K[eith] Chesterton** (1874-1936) gave Holmes's intuition and psychological flair to his Father Brown, a little Catholic priest whose skill lies in his understanding of human nature (see *The Innocence of Father Brown,* 1911, *The Wisdom of Father Brown,* 1914, and *The Scandal of Father Brown,* 1935). Similarly, **Alfred Edward Woodly Mason** (1865-1948) drew on Doyle's hero for his French Inspector Hanaud in *At the Villa*

Rose (1910), *The House of the Arrow* (1924), and *The Prisoner of Opal* (1929); and so did **Agatha Christie** (1890-1976) for her little Belgian detective Poirot, and **Dorothy Sayers** for her aristocratic Lord Peter Wimsey. In crime fiction women are strongly represented. **Agathie Christie** was one of the most prolific writers among them. She introduced her Hercule Poirot in *The Mysterious Affair at Styles* (1920) and wrote at least one best-seller a year. Perhaps the best-known of the Poirot novels are *The Murder of Roger Ackroyd* (1926), with its surprise ending, and *Dead Man's Folly* (1956). Christie also made a remarkable addition to women detectives in her small and gentle Miss Marple, whose most entertaining cases are recorded in *A Murder Is Announced* (1950) and *The 4.50 from Paddington* (1957). **Dorothy L. Sayers** (1893-1957) first presented her hero, Lord Peter Wimsey, in *Whose Body* (1923) and displayed his skill in a long series of novels and short stories. Her best works are *Strong Poison* (1930), *Murder Must Advertise* (1933), and *The Nine Tailors* (1934).

Other popular women writers of detective fiction are **P. D. James** (born 1920, *Innocent Blood,* 1980, and *The Skull Beneath the Skin,* 1982) and the American **Patricia Highsmith** (born 1921), who has lived in Europe for many years. Their works lack the traditional superman-detective and thus indicate the change that took place in the genre after 1930. The hero of some of Miss Highsmith's novels, the amoral and leisure-loving amateur villain Tom Ripley, seems to be the typical modern substitute for the former detective. Ripley is an ex-criminal, now married and leading a comfortable life with his French wife in Paris; but when necessary he can slip into his second skin and kill. Patricia Highsmith's novels, such as *Ripley Underground* (1971) and *Ripley's Game* (1974) – she has also written novels in which Ripley does not appear – are stylishly written and have a distinctive black humour. They are far superior to the hastily written works of the very productive **Edgar Wallace** (1875-1932). **Leslie Charteris** presented another modern rogue-hero with Simon Templer ("The Saint") whose career began with *Enter the Saint* (1930) and has continued ever since. A number of writers have aimed at crime fiction that is supposed to be more highbrow and literary. **Anthony Berkeley Cox** (born 1893) assumed the pseudonym **Francis Iles** and produced several excellent studies of criminal psychology in *Malice Aforethought* (1931) and *Before the Fact* (1932). Similarly **Nicolas Blake** (i. e. the poet **Cecil Day Lewis**) developed sophisticated characters and displayed a masterful handling of suspense in *A Question of Proof* (1935), which introduces his detective Nigel Strangeways, *The Best Must Die* (1938), *Malice in Wonderland* (1940), and *The Whisper in the Gloom* (1954). Younger authors like **Julian Symons** and **John Bingham** have tried new forms in which the police are largely non-existent (see Symons's *The Narrowing Circle,* 1954, and *The Colour of Murder,* 1957; and Bingham's *My Name is Michael Sibley,* 1952).

Especially after World War II, the detective novel began to face strong competition from crime fiction concerned with espionage. Early examples of the spy novel are **John Buchan's** (1875-1940) "Richard Hannay novels" *The Thirty-Nine Steps* (1915), *Greenmantle* (1916), and *Mr. Standfast* (1912), with the detective replaced by an intelligence officer and enemy spies substituted for criminals, and *The Riddle* *of the Sands* (1903) by **Erskine Childers** (1870-1922), in which two Englishmen on a sailing tour discover German plans for an invasion of England. A similar type of popular fiction were the tales starring "Bulldog Drummond" (an early James Bond), written by **Sapper** (**H. C. McNeile,** 1888-1937), which appeared between 1920 and 1937 (see, for instance, *Bulldog Drummond,* 1920, and *The Black Gang,* 1922), and the more than 110 novels published between 1903 and 1946 by **Edward Phillips Oppenheim** (1866-1946), who manipulated with ingenuity and occasional humour a set of stereotypes and clichés in an improbable world of diplomatic salons, expensive hotels, and mysterious intrigue.

The realistic spy novel began with two works that appeared in 1928 and were written by insiders who had served in intelligence: **Somerset Maugham's** *Ashenden* and **Compton Mackenzie's** *Extremes Meet.* They are both concerned with espionage in World War I and convincing novels in their own right. Mackenzie's *The Three Couriers,* on the same theme, followed in 1929. Important spy novels of literary value written in the 1930s and '40s are **Graham Greene's** *A Gun for Sale* (1936), in which the murderer Craven appears as a perverted type of the English secret agent, *The Confidential Agent* (1939), which owes more than its title to Joseph Conrad's *The Secret Agent* (1907), and *The Ministry of Fear* (1943). In recent years, Greene has written two more novels, *Our Man in Havana* (1958) and *The Human Factor* (1978), which are concerned with duplicity and treachery and qualify as literature and crime fiction. **Michael Innes** (i.e. **J. I. M. Stewart,** born 1906) and **Margery Allingham** (1905-66) both wrote for a highbrow audience and combined detective fiction with the spy novel.

In the genre of the spy novel proper, several writers have achieved international popularity. Since the 1930s **Eric Ambler** (born 1909) has produced a series of thrillers on espionage that are distinguished by their realism, such as *The Dark Frontier* (1936), *Epitaph for a Spy* (1938), *The Light of Day* (1962), and *The Intercom Conspiracy* (1970). **Len Deighton** (born 1929) has continued this realism and has applied his knowledge of military history in *The Ipcress File* (1962), *Horse Under Water* (1963), *Billion-Dollar Brain* (1966), and his last spy novel, *An Expensive Place to Die* (1967). Realism, with a touch of Greene's moral concern, also dominates the work of **John Le Carré** (**David Cornwell,** born 1931) who has written on the seedy world of ugly violence in which it is difficult to find one's moral bearings. Successfully combining elements of the thriller and the psychological novel, Le Carré has created in George Smiley a figure that is pained by scruples and appeals to the modern reader. His best novels are *The Spy Who Came in from the Cold* (1963), *The Looking-Glass War* (1965), *A Small Town in Germany* (1968), *Tinker, Tailor, Soldier, Spy* (1974), and *The Honorouble School Boy* (1977), all concerned with espionage and mostly pitting Smiley against the Russian intelligence officer Karla and his helpmates in England. *The Little Drummer Girl* (1983) deals with the Israeli-Palestine conflict. **Frederick Forsyth** (born 1938) is a younger writer who has carried to an extreme the factual realism of Ambler and Deighton in *The Day of the Jackal* (1971), in which the minute details and preparations for a plan to murder General de Gaulle are recorded, and *The Odessa File* (1972). **Anthony Price** (born 1928) has linked modern espionage with aspects of historical research in novels addressed to the highbrow market (*October Men,* 1973, *Our Man in Camelot,* 1975, *Soldier No More,* 1981). Half-way between this more realistic fiction and the escapist spy novel lie the novels of **William Haggard** (*Slow Burner,* 1958, *The Antagonists,* 1964). Since the 1960s, when the first film versions made **Ian Fleming's** (1908-1964) super-hero James Bond internationally known, Fleming's books, such as *Live and Let Die* (1954), *Goldfinger* (1959), and *You Only Live Twice* (1964), though technically no improvement on the novels of earlier decades, have seen a steady success. James Bond, secret agent 007 and counter-spy, is a latter-day Sherlock Holmes, Bulldog Drummond and Richard Hannay rolled into one, with a touch of the lonely heroes of Hammett and Chandler and an active sex life that proved an innovation to the spy novel. Like Superman, James Bond appeals to the myths of success, wealth and power in a time without ideals.

8. Nonfiction

The field of literary criticism has seen the rise and the end of several movements as well as the work of a few outstanding critics who are not easily categorized. Eminent Shakespeare critics include **A. C. Bradley** (1851-1935), **E. K. Chambers** (1866-1954), **J. Dover Wilson** (1881-1969), and **G. Wilson Knight** (born 1897). They each stand for a particular approach to Shakespeare's plays, which they explained in their critical studies and annotated editions. Literary criticism received new impulses from the Imagist **T. E. Hulme,** who was opposed to the art and philosophy of Romanticism and demanded precise and concise language and imagery, and from **I. A. Richards** (1893-1979), the central figure of the New Criticism in England and America. Richards looked for new standards of criticism that were to be based on the close analysis of language, as he explained in *Principles of Literary Criticism* (1924) and *The Philosophy of Rhetoric* (1936). In his *Practical Criticism* (1929) he focused especially on semantic ambiguity and structure. One of the poets and critics inspired by Richards was **William Empson** (1906-84), who developed a semantic and psychoanalytic approach to poetry (see his *Seven Types of Ambiguity,* 1930). A moral and ethical dimension of literary criticism was formulated by **F.R. Leavis** (1895-1978) and his circle, opening the way for Hopkins and Eliot. The influence of psychology and of Jung's theories[1] on literature is recognizable in Virginia Woolf's *The Common Reader* (1925 and 1932) and in Maud Bodkin's *Archetypal Patterns in Poetry* (sec. ed. 1948).

---

1. Carl Gustav Jung (1875-1961), Swiss psychiatrist and, from 1907 to 1913, a collaborator with Freud. Jung then founded his own school of "analytical psychology". He introduced into psychology such terms as "collective unconscious", "extrovert" and "introvert", and "archetype." His concept of psychological types has been adopted in experimental psychology. His central idea is that mental illness mirrors a disunity of the personality. He has influenced many artists and writers.

Historiography has profited from the work of politicians, among them **Sir Winston Churchill** (1874-1965; see the 6 vols. of his *The Second World War,* 1948-54), and academics such as **G. M. Trevelyan** (1876-1962; see his *History of England,* 1926, and *English Social History,* 1942), **A. J. Toynbee** (1889-1975; see the 11 volumes of *A Study of History,* 1934-59), and **H. Butterfield** (born 1900; see *The Whig Interpretation of History,* 1931). Many poets and writers have profited from **James Frazer's** (1854-1941) *The Golden Bough,* which was published in 12 volumes between 1890 and 1915 and provides a thorough study, with a new approach, of primitive societies. Frazer's work prepared the way for the critical view of modern rational cultures.

The most gifted writer in early twentieth-century biography was **Lytton Strachey** (1880-1932). His *Eminent Victorians* (1918) applies a brilliant and often ironic style to the genre of the biographical essay. He also attacked Victorianism and revealed the hypocrisy behind the public facade, thus ushering in a new wave of writing. Strachey's imitators and successors perfected the analytical and psychological approach. The last decades have seen some excellent works combining high scholarly standards with imagination and verbal skill. They include the biographies of Keats (1968) and Hardy (2 vols., 1975 and 1978) by **Robert Gittings** (born 1911), **Richard Ellmann's** (born 1918) much-praised and monumental study, *James Joyce* (1959; rev. ed. 1982), **Michael Holroyd's** (born 1935) biography in 2 volumes of Lytton Strachey (1967-68), and the confessional *Portrait of a Marriage* (1973), **Nigel Nicolson's** personal exploration of the life of his mother, the poet and novelist Victoria Mary Sackville-West.

Finally, the essay has seen a new flowering with the introduction of decidedly partisan viewpoints - Christian, Socialist, psychological, feminist, and ethnic. **Hilaire Belloc** (1870-1953) wrote his essays (e. g. *Heretics,* 1905) with an implicit and often explicit Christian belief. **William Ralph Inge** (1860-1954) criticized his country from the perspective of an active Christian, though he was more interested in the power of mysticism (see his *Outspoken Essays,* 1919 and 1922, and *The Platonic Tradition,* 1926). Unlike Belloc and Inge, **H. G. Wells** and **George Bernard Shaw** saw the salvation of mankind in socialism and said so in their didactic essays. A more stylish writer was **Henry Havelock Ellis** (1859-1939), best known for his *Studies in the Psychology of Sex* (1897-1928), who toned down his message sufficiently for the sake of rhetoric. The old literary tradition was continued by **Max Beerbohm** (1872-1956), who was also a gifted caricaturist. His elegant and witty essays have been collected in *Yet Again* (1909) and *And Even Now* (1920).

American Literature

I. The Colonial Period

1. General Background

American literature consists not only of literature written in English; properly speaking, it embraces a whole range of cultural and linguistic traditions. Since the rise of the American ethnic movements in the 1960s, literary historians have taken more notice of this fact. And although this survey also focuses on literature written in English in the colonies and the territory that became the USA, one should not forget that from the very beginning there have been several cultures in North America; either native ones like those of the Indians or imported ones like those from Africa, France, Spain, and Britain.

The discovery and settlement of what later became the United States occurred almost by accident. **Christopher Columbus** (1451-1506) was not looking for America, but for the Indies, when he arrived in the Caribbean in 1492 and discovered the Bahamas, Cuba and Haiti. The name "America" is derived from Columbus's compatriot and successor, the Italian explorer **Amerigo Vespucci**. In 1497 Vespucci reached the American mainland, before Columbus and **John Cabot,** another Italian, who served the English king Henry VII. When the English began to settle in the New World in the late sixteenth century, they did not treat the

native Americans, the Indians, as cruelly as the Spanish conquistadors before them. Nevertheless, they took the Indians' land, ignored their cultures and religions, and, as far as possible, tried to christianize and Europeanize them. Today, only the names of regions, states, cities, and rivers on the East Coast testify to the existence of Indian nations long extinct (Massachusetts, Narragansett and Potomac, for instance). Early attempts at settling, by **Sir Humphrey Gilbert** in Newfoundland in 1583 and by **Sir Walter Raleigh** in North Carolina in 1585, failed. So did some ventures in what is now

Engraving of Captain John Smith

Virginia, before **Captain John Smith** established the first permanent settlement at Jamestown in 1607. It was with John Smith's reports about this enterprise that American literature started.

The American sense of mission – religious, moral and political – and the myth of America as "God's own country" and the "New Jerusalem" began with the arrival of the Pilgrims and Puritans in the early seventeenth century. In 1620, some 100 Pilgrims[1], a group of Protestant Separatists from Britain who had emigrated to Holland and found a leader in **William Bradford** (1590-1657), reached America in the "Mayflower" and settled in Plymouth, Massachusetts. They were followed in 1630 by the Puritans[2], who, organized as the Massachusetts Bay Company and with their first governor **John Winthrop** (1588-1649), arrived in the "Arbella" and founded the Massachusetts Bay Colony, their "City upon the Hill"[3], in what is now Boston. There was soon disagreement over church policy, and this led to the founding of further colonies (the Connecticut valley was settled by **Thomas Hooker** and his group, and Rhode Island by **Roger Williams**). Puritanism became the dominant force in the northern colonies, whereas the South was more secular from the very beginning. A greater religious tolerance and more cultural variety developed in the Middle Colonies: **William Penn** (1644-1718) and his Quakers[4] founded Pennsylvania (1681), New Jersey, and Delaware; and Maryland was settled in 1634 by a group of English Catholics.

By 1700, some 250,000 people lived on the East Coast, where four distinct regions had come into being: New England, economically prospering and theocratically governed; the Middle Colonies, with New York and Philadelphia as centres of economic and cultural life; the South (Virginia and Maryland), characterized by aristocratic social structures and the slavery plantations; and the newly settled colonies in the Carolinas and Georgia, which later adapted to the social fabric of the "old" South.

---

1. The persons who came to Massachusetts on the Mayflower in 1620 and, by extension, all the early settlers of Plymouth Colony. The Pilgrims, unlike the Puritans in the Massachusetts Bay Colony, were Separatists who had split from the Established Church of England, organizing independent congregations. The Pilgrims first emigrated from Scrooby, England, to Amsterdam (1608) and then to Leiden. Those who came to New England included William Bradford, William Brewster, and Edward Winslow.

2. In England, the Puritans demanded a thorough reformation of the Church under Elizabeth I. At first, they wanted only to eliminate certain (Catholic) ceremonial rituals but believed in a state church. The Puritans who went to America came mainly from the middle class. They believed in the theology of Calvin (predestination) and preferred congregationalism as a form of church organization.

3. The idea derives from Christ's sermon on the mount (cf. Matthew 5.14: "Ye are the light of the world. A city that is set on a hill cannot be hid.").

4. A religious group also called The Society of Friends that was founded in England by George Fox (1624-91). The Quakers avoid rigid doctrines and set forms of worship and have no trained leaders. Until the Toleration Act (1689), they were persecuted in England because they refused to support the Anglican Church. The first Quakers came to America in the 1650s, and in Massachusetts they were also persecuted by the Puritans because of their opposition to theocracy. After the founding of Pennsylvania, they became widely known for their humanitarianism. They were the first to oppose the slavery of Africans and to deal kindly with the Indians. Today, the Society of Friends consists of various groups in America, with a total membership of over 130,000.

It would be wrong to assume that most of the colonists went to the New World in search of religious and political freedom. To be sure, the clergymen and many political leaders praised America as the New Eden. The American jeremiad is one form of theological prose that arose out of the need of the colonists to justify their mission, to give a meaning to their lives in the wilderness, and to overcome the bitter truth that America soon resembled the Old World in many respects. Jamestown and the Massachusetts Bay settlements were important economic ventures, and those in search of religious freedom and political liberty were soon outnumbered by those who wanted to make money or who were forced to come to America: indentured servants[1], slaves, criminals, and the desperately poor. This silent majority left very few literary records, but they had a great influence on the development of the country, not least in the practical undermining of the established official myths of equality and opportunity.

The major ideologies at work in early American literature were the Calvinistic Puritanism of New England, which controlled the work of writers as diverse as Cotton Mather and Anne Bradstreet and lasted well into the eighteenth century, and the more worldly mercantilism of the South. Toleration of diversity in religious and political organizations, as practised in the Middle Colonies, became increasingly important in the eighteenth century. Towards the mid-eighteenth century, the influence of the Enlightenment made itself felt in America, with **Benjamin Franklin** as a major spokesman, teaching Americans to be reasonable, human, and frugal. As Puritanism lost its influence, the Great Awakening[2], prepared in America by the preaching of the Methodists (**John** and **Charles Wesley** and **George Whitefield**), found in **Jonathan Edwards** a proponent of religious emotionalism who exhorted his listeners to search their own hearts. Both religious revivalism and Enlightenment thought championed individualism, which was to become a central idea and motif in American literature and culture.

Considering the harsh frontier conditions in the seventeenth century and the Puritan dominance in New England which discouraged imaginative literature, the Puritan colonies produced a surprising quantity of literature.

2. Poetry

In New England, poetry had to be either religious or pragmatic to be acceptable. It had to serve a purpose, and in most cases this meant praising God and his works and warning men not to forget the worship of their creator. The essence of such

---

1. Until the 19th century, English apprentices had to sign an agreement which usually bound them to their masters for several years. Until the end of the period of training, the master was legally responsible for the servant, and the servant had to obey his master's orders. The agreement, the indenture as it was called, controlled the personal life of the servant to an often excessive degree. There were a few minor rebellions by servants in London.
2. A series of religious revivals beginning with Jonathan Edwards's evangelicalism c. 1734. The movement had its centre in New England but then extended throughout the colonies (1740–50).

poetry was of course its message rather than any refinement of form. It was published in popular almanacs and funeral elegies. The best examples of verse made subservient to didactic and moral purposes are the two books that were meant to spread the Puritan ideology – the *Bay Psalm Book* in the "meeting house" (the Puritan church), and the *New England Primer* in schools.

Edited by such eminent clergymen as, among others, **Richard Mather** and **John Eliot**, the *Bay Psalm Book* (1640) was the first book to be printed in the British colonies and it saw many editions between 1640 and 1752. The rhymed psalms in this collection were sung, and the singers probably did not mind the odd syntax and the rhythmic irregularities of the doggerel verse. Here is an example, David's psalm "The Lord is my shepherd."

> The Lord to me a shepherd is,
>   want therefore shall not I.
> He in the folds of tender grass,
>   doth cause me down to lie:
> To waters calm me gently leads
>   Restore my soul doth he:
> he doth in paths of righteousness:
>   for his name's sake lead me.
> Yea though in valley of death's shade
>   I walk, none ill I'll fear:
> because thou art with me, thy rod,
>   and staff my comfort are.
> For me a table thou hast spread,
>   in presence of my foes:
> thou dost anoint my head with oil:
>   my cup it overflows.
> Goodness & mercy surely shall
>   all my days follow me:
> and in the Lord's house I shall dwell
>   so long as days shall be.

Similarly, the school and conduct book, the *New England Primer,* edited between 1683-1690 by **Benjamin Harris** (by the nineteenth century it had sold close to 6 million copies), hammered Calvinist principles in simple forms into the heads of large sections of the population while teaching them the alphabet and the prayers:

In *Adam's* fall
We sinned all.

Heaven to find,
The *Bible* mind.

The idle *Fool*
Is whipt at school.

As runs the *Glass,*
Our life doth pass.

In Adam's Fall
We finned all.

A Dog will bite
A Thief at Night.

My book and *Heart*
Shall never part.

Job feels the rod
Yet blesses God.

The idle Fool
Is whipt at School

The most prominent representatives of Puritan religious poetry were **Michael Wigglesworth** and **Edward Taylor**. **Wigglesworth** (1631-1705) came to Massachusetts as a child. He studied at Harvard (founded in 1636) and became a minister in Malden, Massachusetts. His *Day of Doom* (1662) is, according to its subtitle, "a poetical description of the great and last judgment", and as such a jeremiad[1] in verse. It was widely read in the Puritan colonies. The first stanza of this gloomy ballad describes the false security of the world before Christ's Second Coming:

> Still was the night, serene and bright,
>   when all men sleeping lay;
> Calm was the season, and carnal reason
>   thought so 't would last for aye.
> Soul, take thine ease, let sorrow cease,
>   much good thou hast in store:
> This was their song, their cups among,
>   the evening before.

Surpassing Wigglesworth in form and style, **Edward Taylor** (c. 1644-1729), another Harvard-trained clergyman, is today recognized as the most eminent of the Puritan sacred poets. Like the works of Bradford and Winthrop, Taylor's poems were discovered much later and first published in 1939. His verse is in the direct line of the English devotional metaphysical poets (among them Herbert, Donne and Crashaw) and analyses problems of life and faith in a rich and concrete language, comprehensive imagery, and conceits that are based on the colonial experience and are thus early examples of truly American verse. His best poems are to be found in a series called *Preparatory Meditations,* written for his own pleasure after preparation for sermons he delivered at monthly communion. Like Donne, Taylor created surprising new meanings by blending incongruous images. His technique is masterfully displayed in the short poem "Huswifery", which develops metaphors of spinning until the climax brings the central image, a garment made by God through man, combining the ideas of work, piety, religion and God's grace:

> Make me, O Lord, Thy spining wheel complete.
>   Thy Holy Word my distaff make for me.
> Make mine affections Thy swift flyers neat
>   And make my soul Thy holy spool to be.
>   My conversation make to be Thy reel
>   And reel the yarn thereon spun of Thy wheel. [...]

---

1. See p. 182.

Then clothe therewith mine understanding, will,
Affections, judgment, conscience, memory,
My words, and actions, that their shine may fill
My ways with glory and Thee glorify.
Then mine apparel shall display before Ye
That I am clothed in holy robes for glory.

In Puritan secular poetry, the work of **Anne Bradstreet** (c. 1612-1672) is remarkable, especially the shorter pieces in which she deals with everyday life in the colonial situation with a simple narrative efficiency and religious conviction. Together with her father, **Thomas Dudley,** and her husband **Simon,** she went to New England in 1630 in the "Arbella". In England, she had received a good education which included studying the works of the metaphysical poets and of Sidney and Spenser. As the mother of eight children and wife to a man who became governor of Massachusetts, she still found time for writing verse. Her first book of poetry, *The Tenth Muse Lately Sprung up in America,* was published in London in 1650 without her consent and contains in its prologue a covert defense of women's right to compose poetry. But it is in the posthumously printed *Poems* (1678) that one finds her most convincing verse recording personal experiences, rather than discussions of faith and religion, such as "Upon the Burning of Our House" and the poems on her deceased grandchildren. "To My Dear and Loving Husband" is one of the several love poems she wrote to Simon Bradstreet, expressing a rather un-Puritan concern with life and love in this world.

If ever two were one, then surely we.
If ever man were lov'd by wife, then thee;
If ever wife was happy in a man,
Compare with me ye women if you can.
I prize thy love more than whole Mines of gold,
Or all the riches that the East doth hold.
My love is such that Rivers cannot quench,
Nor ought but love from thee, give recompense.
Thy love is such I can no way repay,
The heavens reward thee manifold, I pray.
Then while we live, in love let so persever,
That when we live no more, we may live ever.

John Berryman wrote a moving biographical poem on New England's first woman poet in his *Homage to Mistress Bradstreet.*

Outside New England, the mundane spirit found expression in the poetry of **Ebenezer Cook** and **William Byrd II.** Not much is known about **Cook** (c. 1672-1732). He was probably a malcontent Englishman in Maryland recording his failure to succeed as a tobacco merchant because of the frauds of the colonists. A realistic satire in the tradition of Butler's *Hudibras,* Cook's, *The Sot-Weed Factor* (1708; revised in 1731) – which means "the tobacco merchant" – makes fun of the rough frontier conditions and lacks any sort of religious background. America, to Cook, is not the New Jerusalem, but the country of banishment where the sons and daughters of Cain try to make a living. In the following passage, a local farmer is described in a manner reminiscent of Butler and Rabelais:

Then out our Landlord pulls his Pouch,
As greasy as the Leather Couch
On which he sat, and straight began
To load with Weed his Indian Gun,
[...]
The Reverend Sir, walks to a Chest,
Of all his Furniture the best,
[...]
Which seldom felt the Weight of Broom:
From thence he lugs a Keg of Rum,
And nodding to me, thus began:
I find, says he, you don't much care
For this our Indian Country Fare;
But let me tell you, Friend of mine,
You may be glad of it in Time,
Though now your stomach is so fine

John Barth made this mock-heroic and polemical description of early America the basis of his prose satire *The Sot-Weed Factor* (1960), playing with the form of the historical novel as well as with the popular idea of American history.

The Virginia gentleman **William Byrd of Westover** (1674-1744) loved literature as much as the ladies and the good life and has left us a number of valuable chronicles of colonial life. No Puritan could have written such a poem as Byrd's "Upon a Fart", which was found among his papers and literary exercises and is written in the scatological[1] tradition in which Jonathan Swift also distinguished himself.

Westover Plantation, Charles City County, Virginia, c. 1730

---

1. Scatological literature is concerned with excrement, usually in a comical or satirical context. This tradition was popular throughout the Middle Ages and well into the eighteenth century. Many s. and humorous poems or songs were publicly recited and sung. The tradition came to a stop in the Victorian period. In modern America, such literature would be considered obscene: there is a large and euphemistic vocabulary in American English that indicates a strong dislike of scatological words or subjects.

3. Drama

As the Puritan authorities were opposed to music and drama as mere entertainment, the theatre found no favourable atmosphere in New England. However, in the Middle Colonies and in the South plays were performed. In Virginia, we know of an early play, *Ye Bear and ye Cub,* through a court case. European acting companies like the Hallams travelled in Virginia, New York and South Carolina, staging mainly English plays but probably also the American **Thomas Godfrey's** (1736–63) romantic blankverse tragedy *The Prince of Parthia,* written in 1759 and published in 1765. But drama did not really find a foothold in America until the late eighteenth century.

4. Prose

Utilitarian forms of prose – reports of discovery, histories, diaries, sermons, and theological treatises – dominated in the colonial period. American literature is often said to have begun with the several reports and histories of **Captain John Smith** (c. 1580–1631), a former adventurer and soldier who became governor of Virginia and helped the Jamestown settlers to survive. His *A True Relation of Such Occurrences and Accidents as Have Happened in Virginia* (1608) is a report to the Virginia Company in London while *A Description of New England* (1616), which the "Mayflower" settlers used as a source of information, as well as *Advertisements for the Unexperienced Planters of New-England* (1631), are propaganda pieces for future settlers describing America as a land of plenty and of great opportunities. Smith's *General History of Virginia, New England, and the Summer Isles* (1624) is the most fascinating of his works, apart from *The True Travels, Adventures and Observations* (1630), and probably contains a few passages that are invented. Even the myth-making Pocahontas story in this book may be pure fiction: it tells how Smith was saved from being killed by the daughter of an Indian chief. This girl, Pocahontas, later married an Englishman, John Rolfe, and died in England. The episode gained symbolic value and was treated in American plays, poetry and fiction during the following centuries. Other important reports of travel and discovery in the colonies are **George Alsop's** *A Character of the*

Engraving of Pocahontas from Captain John Smith's *The General History of Virginia*

Province of Maryland (1666), **John Josselyn's** *New England's Rarities Discovered* (1672), and **William Byrd's** witty and entertaining records, *History of the Dividing Line* (1728) and *A Journey to the Land of Eden* (1733), in which he comments on the life-style of colonists in Virginia and North Carolina. Byrd's work, like that of other eminent colonial writers, was published posthumously, and in some cases only in the 20th century. There is a rich stock of historical prose that has survived from the colonial period. The story of the Pilgrims was taken down by **William Bradford** (1590-1657) in his *History of Plymouth Plantation,* written between 1620-51 and published in 1856, while **John Winthrop,** one of the governors of Massachusetts, made a history out of his journal (1630-49), later published as *The History of New England* (1825/26). **Edward Johnson's** *Wonder-working Providence of Sion's Saviour in New England* (1654) is a sort of Calvinist history of the New England colonies. An example of the genre of Puritan "providences", it is written with great pathos and foreshadows the cultural-theological history of Puritan New England and of its congregations and ministers, Cotton Mather's huge *Magnalia Christi Americana* (1702). **Cotton Mather** (1633-1728) was New England's most prolific theologian of the third generation. He wrote more than 400 sermons, theological and scientific treatises. His *Magnalia* is a long collection of histories of the various congregations and includes reports about the Indian wars, sermons, vitae of ministers and governors, records of witch trials, and "wonderful providences." A more satirical account from New England is **Thomas Morton's** *New English Canaan* (1637). Morton was a kind of early anarchist and separatist who founded an "irreligious" settlement at Merry Mount (now Quincy, Massachusetts) and was finally forced by the Pilgrims to leave. In his book he makes fun of Winthrop and Bradford. If Morton pleaded for tolerance, **Nathaniel Ward** defended Puritan religious intolerance in *The Simple Cobler of Aggawam in America* (1647). The Quaker's point of view has entered the pages of **William Penn's** *A Brief Account of the Province of Pennsylvania* (1682), and a lighter and wittier tone is discernible in **Robert Beverley's** (c. 1672-1722) *The History and Present State of Virginia* (1705), written from a royalist's angle.

Puritan practical literature included *A Key into the Language of America* (1643), by the separatist **Roger Williams** (1603-83) who founded Providence Plantation, and the countless treatises in medicine and the natural sciences from the pen of New England's prodigy, Cotton Mather. However, Puritan literature is especially known for two genres, the diary and the sermon. Many Puritan diaries have survived, but none is as lively and in-

Portrait of Cotton Mather by Peter Pelham, 1727

teresting as that of Judge **Samuel Sewall** (1652-1730), who provided a sober record of New England life that even includes details about his meals. **Cotton Mather's** journal is much more self-conscious, as Mather was permanently concerned with his soul and with the impression he was to leave. Two other types of colonial diaries are the Quaker **John Woolman's** (1720-72) *Journal* (1774), an honest record of his love for God and man, and **William Byrd's** *Secret Diary,* covering the years 1709-1712, in which he reports freely and openly about his most intimate experiences in London and Virginia. A rather spectacular journal is *A Narrative of the Captivity and Restauration of Mrs. Mary Rowlandson* (1682), which is the first Indian captivity report by a woman who was in the hands of the Narragansett Indians for almost twelve weeks. Such reports soon became a literary genre and were published until the late nineteenth century.

The American Puritans created an unsurpassed sermon literature, and within this tradition a particular sermon form, **the jeremiad,** which has had a lasting influence on American political rhetoric and ideology. The outstanding preachers whose sermons were published in America and England were **John Cotton** (1584-1652), who reached Massachusetts in 1633; **Thomas Hooker** (1586-1647), **Roger Williams** (1584-1652), banished from Massachusetts in 1635; and the "Mather dynasty," i. e. **Richard Mather** (1596-1669), **Increase Mather** (1639-1723), and Increase's, eldest son, **Cotton Mather. Jonathan Edwards** (1703-58), was one of the last in this line of outstanding preachers, and his most famous sermon, "Sinners in the Hands of an Angry God" (1741), is both a jeremiad and an emotional sermon typical of the Great Awakening. The Puritan jeremiad was developed in the early 1640s and was in its full bloom by the 1660s. It made use of a rhetoric, "the plain style", and a view of Americans and America that can still be noticed today in the speeches of American presidents. The jeremiad was devised by the clergymen to remind a sinning people of their duty toward God (like the Israelitis, they believed in a covenant with God) and as a psychological help to overcome the cruel reality of life on the frontier. In their jeremiads, the preachers continued to tell Americans that, though there were many sinners in the land, America was a special country, chosen by God for His people and set apart from the rest of the world; and since this was so, it was the duty of God's people to spread His glory. Thus the Puritan jeremiad can be seen as a major source of American rhetoric and of America's understanding of herself. The notion that America was to give an example, politically and morally, to the rest of the world has survived the era of self-doubt of the Vietnam War.

II. From the Revolution to 1800

1. General Background

Even in the age of Revolution and Enlightenment, America never lost her interest in religion. For although Puritanism was on the wane after 1700, the Quakers were among those who dominated America's cultural and economic life in the eighteenth century. Toward the mid-eighteenth century, the Great Awakening became one of the first waves of religious-emotional revivalism that have characterized American religious practice down to Billy Graham and Jerry Falwell.[1] Most of the American leaders during the Enlightenment were not atheists but deists[2] who wanted to serve God by doing a good job on earth, trusting in the power of reason and the natural rights of man.

In an age of Revolution, literature was greatly influenced by political texts. In many cases these texts are of more interest than the fiction and the didactic verse they provoked. The American Revolution was a consequence of British greed and the American wish for more freedom and less taxation. Although the American colonies were not represented in the British parliament, they were forced to pay increasingly repressive taxes, as determined by the Sugar Act (1764), the Stamp Act (1765), and the Townshend Acts that charged duty on imported glass, paint, lead, paper, and tea. Resistance, first in print, led to the Boston "massacre" in 1770, when five protesters were killed by British troops. In 1773 Americans attacked British merchant ships in what became known as the Boston Tea Party. Thereafter, several states organized joint resistance, and by 1774 the First Continental Congress met in Philadelphia and denounced "taxation without representation." In the War of Independence, which began rather haphazardly in 1775, George Washington was appointed by Congress to lead the Continental Army. He faced a succession of military failures and had difficulty recruiting sufficient numbers of soldiers from a divided population. But as the popular demand for independence grew, so did military success. On July 4, 1776, Congress approved the *Declaration of Independence,* one of the most important political texts of the Enlightenment. Aided by France from 1778 on, the Americans finally defeated Lord Cornwallis's army at Yorktown in 1781. By the Treaty of Paris in 1783 Britain recognized the independence of the United States of America. By 1789 the USA had a constitution. Confidence was great and history to be made by a new country that finally saw the optimism of the founding fathers reconfirmed. As far as American litera-

---

1. Billy Graham (William Franklin Graham, born 1918), American evangelist and Baptist preacher. A forceful and eloquent preacher, he has toured the United States and Europe, attracting audiences totalling millions and winning thousands of converts. He has published several books and has done numerous radio and TV programs.
Like the fundamentalist Jerry Falwell, Billy Graham maintains the traditional, often literal, interpretations of the Bible, which the fundamentalists consider the ultimate and inerrant authority.
2. See page 45, note 4.

ture from this period is concerned, it is very much rooted in political events. Many writers were politicians themselves, siding with the Royalists and Loyalists or with the Independents.

2. Poetry

Starting in the 1760s, a great number of poems dealt with the issue of independence. Mostly didactic or satirical, these works appeared in newspapers and almanacs and provide an impression of how the "big question" was treated in popular culture. As so often in revolutionary periods, satire flourished, especially among a group of poets known as the Connecticut Wits (also called Hartford Wits, Yale Poets, or Connecticut Choir). The members of this group (John Trumbull, Timothy Dwight, Joel Barlow, Lemuel Hopkins, Richard Alsop and others) wanted to achieve America's literary independence and focused on native history and society. Most of the Connecticut Wits were conservative intellectuals in favour of Federalism and opposed to Jeffersonian Republicanism.[1] As they never really went beyond the poetic patterns established by the English Augustans, their attempts to create a new American poetry failed. Only three, Trumbull, Dwight, and Barlow, wrote poetry that is worth remembering.

John Trumbull (1750-1831) taught at Yale University and wrote a satire in verse and prose against the follies of university life and theological instruction entitled *The Progress of Dullness* (1773). It is largely indebted to Addison, Swift, Pope, and the comedy of manners. Trumbull is best remembered for his burlesque satire *M'Fingal* (1782), which is written in the manner of *Hudibras* and mocks the English Tories supporting the Crown in America. **Timothy Dwight** (1752-1817) was the grandchild of Jonathan Edwards and also taught at Yale, serving as its president from 1795-1817. Both an excellent rhetorician and a passionate patriot, Dwight described Washington's victory in *The Conquest of Canaan* (1785), an allegorical epic in 11 books written in the manner of Pope and as nationalistic as **Joel Barlow's** (1754-1812) Miltonic *The Vision of Columbus* (1787; later published as *The Columbiad,* 1807), which is Barlow's attempt at a "national" epic in heroic couplets and in eight books. The Wits were at their best when they brought local colour into their verse. It is this native element that makes Barlow's *The Hasty Pudding* (1796) one of the few outstanding poems from this period. Written in France, where Barlow tried to find supporters of the American Revolution, the poem on a native American dish (made from Indian corn and water) is a mock epic celebrating American simplicity over the sophisticated decadence of aristocratic Europe. Here is an excerpt.

---

1. Thomas Jefferson (1743-1826) found himself in opposition to Alexander Hamilton (1755-1804), who favoured a strong centralized government and urged the encouragement of manufacturing. Jefferson feared that Hamilton's program would lead to the establishment of a monarchy, and he therefore championed individual liberties, the rights of the states, and an agrarian system.

Dear Hasty Pudding, what unpromised joy
Expands my heart, to meet thee in Savoy!
Doomed o'er the world through devious paths to roam,
Each clime my country, and each house my home,
My soul is soothed, my cares have found an end,
I greet my long lost, unforgotten friend.
For thee through Paris, that corrupted town,
How long in vain I wandered up and down,
Where shameless Bacchus, with his drenching hoard,
Cold from his cave usurps the morning board.
London is lost in smoke and steeped in tea;
No Yankee there can lisp the name of thee;
The uncouth word, a libel on the town,
Would call a proclamation from the crown.

Another patriotic writer of satiric verse was **Francis Hopkinson** (1737-91), a lawyer from Philadelphia who signed the *Declaration of Independence* and satirized the English in *The Battle of the Kegs* (1778), a ballad celebrating American military ingenuity on the Delaware River.

However, the poet most often associated with the Revolutionary period is **Philip Freneau** (1752-1832). He studied at Princeton and wrote patriotic verse at an early age. As a prisoner of war he was badly treated by the British in 1780 and developed a lifelong hatred of England. Freneau worked in Philadelphia and also owned a ship with which he sailed the Atlantic and the Caribbean. After 1790, he edited newspapers (*The National Gazette*, 1791-93) and returned to his plantation, Mount Pleasant, in 1799. Because of financial difficulties, he had to return to shipping between 1803-1807. He died in a blizzard, impoverished and almost forgotten. Freneau tried almost all contemporary forms of poetry: political satire, elegies, didactic verse, and poems describing nature and his travels. His patriotism and his political views were always in competition with his undeniable lyrical gifts. He poured his American pride into *The Rising Glory of America,* written together with Brackenridge as the Commencement[1] poem for 1771 at Princeton, and voiced his dislike of the English in the heroic couplets of *The British Prison-Ship* (1781), which is based on his own experience. In his later life Freneau refused to eat food, or wear clothing, of British origin, but he could not resist imitating English poetic diction, as in the Gothic allegoric-philosophical elegy *The House of Night* (1775), a poem that stands clearly in the tradition of Young and foreshadows Poe. As a poet, Freneau was most convincing when he described nature, the sea, and his countrymen and the Indians. His imaginative poems, such as "The Beauties of Santa Cruz" (1776), "The Wild Honey Suckle" (1786), and "On a Honey Bee" (1809), mark him as a Romantic writer. As the first American poet to write on the Indians, he made a strong impression on Walter Scott and Thomas Campbell. Freneau's "The Indian Student", for instance, reports about one of the "children of the forest" who studies at Harvard but then leaves civilized Boston to return to his tribe. The poem ex-

---

1. The day, and the ceremonies in connection with this event, when degrees are conferred in American schools and universities.

presses an Indian's disappointment with the white man's world. Indian culture, though poetically romanticized, is also the focus of his "The Dying Indian" (1784) and "The Indian Burying Ground" (1788), of which the beginning follows.

> In spite of all the learned have said,
> I still my old opinion keep;
> The posture, that we give the dead,
> Points out the soul's eternal sleep.
>
> Not so the ancients of these lands –
> The Indian, when from life released,
> Again is seated with his friends,
> And shares again the joyous feast.
>
> His imaged birds, and painted bowl,
> And venison, for a journey dressed,
> Bespeak the nature of the soul,
> Activity, that knows no rest.
>
> His bow, for action ready bent,
> And arrows, with a head of stone,
> Can only mean that life is spent,
> And not the old ideas gone.
>
> Thou, stranger, that shalt come this way,
> No fraud upon the dead commit –
> Observe the swelling turf, and say
> They do not lie, but here they sit.

Black literature did not develop before the nineteenth century, and black poetry came even later than prose. But the case of **Phillis Wheatley** (c. 1753-84), an educated slave in a Boston household who achieved literary attention with her *Poems* (1773) in England and America before ending in poverty, illustrates a phase of black identity in the New World. Although Wheatley's poems are essentially "white", employing the forms and themes of traditional English poetry, they remain historically important as documents of a period when the racial question was almost totally ignored. In the following poem, she celebrates America and "civilization"; her twentieth-century successors were to do the opposite, seeing their influential roots in Africa.

On Being Brought from Africa to America

> 'Twas mercy brought me from my pagan land,
> Taught my benighted soul to understand
> That there's a God, that there's a Savior too:
> Once I redemption neither sought nor knew.
> Some view our sable race with scornful eye,
> "Their color is a diabolic dye."
> Remember, Christians, Negroes, black as Cain,
> May be refined, and join the angelic train.

3. Drama

Drama, as far as it existed in America in the later part of the eighteenth century was dominated by growing patriotism. The most typical example is *The Contrast* (1787), a light social comedy by the lawyer **Royall Tyler** (1757-1826). While on a visit to New York City, Tyler attended a performance of Sheridan's *The School for Scandal.* Within a few weeks he wrote *The Contrast,* which was consciously modelled on Sheridan's successful comedy and which was the first play by an American to be produced by a professional American troupe. After its successful staging in New York, it was published in 1790. It is indicative of the reigning spirit in New England, however, that the comedy had to be disguised as a "moral lecture in five parts" when it was given in Boston. Tyler's comedy contrasts homespun and honest American dignity with the foreign and ridiculous foppery of the British. It has a conventional plot of intrigue, love and misunderstandings and is mainly remembered for the upright American hero, Colonel Manly, and the subplot, concerned with Manly's servant Jonathan, the first example of the classic stage Yankee who denies he is a servant and wants to be seen as a "true blue son of liberty".

4. Prose Fiction

In the age of Revolution, there was little room for the novel. Existing needs were easily satisfied by the European market. Between 1760-1800 such works as *The Vicar of Wakefield* (1766), *Robinson Crusoe* (1719), *Tristram Shandy* (1759-67), and *Clarissa* (1748-49) were best-sellers in America. American novels of literary value were few and far between, although the commercialization of literature and the rise of journalism were soon to contribute to the birth of the short story. Richardson's fiction inspired a number of American writers to produce sentimental romance, laced with a bit of eroticism, such as **William H. Brown's** (1765-93) *The Power of Sympathy* (1789), **Susanna Rowson's** (c. 1762-1824) *Charlotte Temple* (1791), and **Hannah Foster's** (1759-1840) *The Coquette* (1797), an epistolary novel dealing with seduction which, by 1800, had sold 50,000 copies.

More substantial novels were written by Brackenridge and Brown. *Modern Chivalry* is a satirical picaresque novel in the manner of *Don Quixote,* published in installments from 1792-1815 by the Scottish-born Federalist **Henry Hugh Brackenridge** (1748-1816).

The heroes are Captain Farrago and his Irish servant Teague O'Regan. They travel through the forests of Pennsylvania, and Teague is eventually tarred and feathered and sent to France, where his adventures continue. Brackenridge fleshes out his story with commentary on, and criticism of, American politics in the new republic in which he perceived a degeneration of liberty into licence. Brackenridge's satirical style refers to Butler, Swift and Fielding.

With his four novels written between 1798-1801 **Charles Brockden Brown** (1771-1810) became the pioneer for several genres of fiction and prepared the way for Cooper, Poe and Hawthorne. In *Wieland, or, The Transformation* (1798) as well as in *Edgar Huntley* (1799), both epistolary novels, he dealt with aberrant psychology and strange adventures in American settings. *Ormond* (1799) is a typical Gothic novel, and *Arthur Mervyn* (1799) is a story of initiation in a complicated romance of intrigue and terror. There are some realistic passages where Brown describes the consequences of yellow fever in Philadelphia. Influenced by Godwin, Rousseau and Voltaire, Brown explored philosophical and moral problems while focusing on the mysterious world of man's psychology and soul.

5. Nonfiction

The intellectual leaders of the Revolutionary period, men such as **Thomas Paine, John Dickinson,** and **Thomas Jefferson,** sought to put into political practice such ideas as liberty, equality, natural rights, and the pursuit of happiness. It was **Thomas Paine** (1737-1809) who provided the ideology for the Revolution. An Englishman, he went to Philadelphia in 1774, summoned by Franklin, and defended the cause of the colonies both in America and Europe. Paine's *Common Sense* (1776) was a severe criticism of the English monarchy and a call to Americans to separate from Britain. It became a huge success, was read before the troops, and fanned the American intellectual fire. Paine was accused of treason in England because of his defence of the French Revolution in *The Rights of Man* (1791/2) and had to flee to France, where he became a French citizen. After a brief period of imprisonment during the French reign of terror (1793-94), he returned to America in 1802, spending the remainder of his life in poverty and illness and despised by his countrymen because of his radical thinking. Paine was a master of style and political propaganda. With *The Age of Reason* (1794/5) he wrote a deistic treatise attacking traditional religion and arguing for religious freedom and tolerance in the light of reason and morality.

John Dickinson (1732-1808) also prepared the way for the Revolution with his denunciation of colonial taxes in the pamphlets entitled *Letters from a Farmer in Pennsylvania to the Inhabitants of the British Colonies* (1768).

COMMON SENSE;

ADDRESSED TO THE

INHABITANTS

OF

AMERICA,

On the following interesting

SUBJECTS.

I. Of the Origin and Design of Government in general, with concise Remarks on the English Constitution.

II. Of Monarchy and Hereditary Succession.

III. Thoughts on the present State of American Affairs.

IV. Of the present Ability of America, with some miscellaneous Reflections.

Man knows no Master save creating HEAVEN,
Or those whom choice and common good ordain.
THOMSON.

PHILADELPHIA;
Printed, and Sold, by R. BELL, in Third-Street.
MDCCLXXVI.

Thomas Jefferson by Rembrandt Peale, 1805

Once the Revolution had started, four men provided the ideas that were needed for a new constitution: **John Adams** (1735-1826), **Alexander Hamilton** (1757-1804), **James Madison** (1751-1836), and **Thomas Jefferson** (1743-1826). They developed their ideas in speeches, political essays, pamphlets, and treatises. Adams was the leader of the conservatives and argued against Paine's *Common Sense* in *Thoughts on Government* (1776). Hamilton and Madison defended the new constitution in the 85 essays contained in *The Federalist* (1787/8). However, the central figure was undoubtedly the Virginian **Thomas Jefferson.** He was educated at the College of William and Mary and became a lawyer and a renowned diplomat. His only book, *Notes on the State of Virginia* (1782; published in 1787), proves his wide-ranging interest in science, history, architecture and other subjects. Jefferson served as Secretary of State under Washington and became the third President of the United States (1800-1809). His draft of the Declaration of Independence, revised by Adams and Franklin, shows the power of his rhetoric; its clear and simple diction has not lost anything of its power:

> When, in the course of human events, it becomes necessary for one people to dissolve the political bands which have connected them with another, and to assume among the powers of the earth the separate and equal station to which the laws of nature and of nature's God entitle them, a decent respect to the opinions of mankind requires that they should declare the causes which impel them to the separation.
>
> We hold these truths to be self-evident, that all men are created equal, that they are endowed by their Creator with certain unalienable rights; that among these are life, liberty, and the pursuit of happiness; that to secure these rights, governments are instituted among men, deriving their just powers from the consent of the governed; that whenever any form of government becomes destructive of these ends, it is the right of the people to alter or to abolish it, and to institute new government, laying its foundation on such principles, and organizing its powers in such form, as to them shall seem most likely to effect their safety and happiness ...

Of course **Benjamin Franklin** (1706-1790) also belongs to the group of intellectuals who served the American cause at home and abroad. Franklin was an active and busy man: an inventor and diplomat, a political agitator and founding father of the Constitution, a journalist and man of letters. He founded numerous American institutions (societies, hospitals, libraries, universities) and wrote on the nature of earthquakes, air and sea currents, heat and electricity; he invented a stove, bifocal spectacles, and the lightning rod, among other things, and became a member of the Royal Society in London (1756). Franklin served his country in many functions and positions, one of them being Minister to France (1776), and he helped to bring about the Treaty of Paris in 1783. When he died, he was one of the best-known and certainly one of the most beloved public figures in America. This is a remarkable story of success for the tenth son in a family of 15 children. Franklin's father was a Boston tallow chandler and soap-maker. Young Ben was apprenticed at age 12 to his half-brother James, a printer. But he soon ran away, working in print shops in Philadelphia and London, England, while educating himself and working hard. He made his literary debut with sniping satires on local affairs published in the *New England Courant* and signed "Silence Dogood". By 1729, Franklin had his own print shop in Philadelphia and edited the *Pennsylvania Gazette* (1729-66). Between 1733-58 he wrote and published the most famous of American almanacs, *Poor Richard's Almanack,* issued in three editions (for New England, the Middle Colonies, and the South) and a phenomenal success. The almanacs presented humorous and wise characters (Richard and Bridget Saunders, for instance) and offered the readers fables, essays, maxims for living, and information about the weather, science, and philosophy. Many of the contributions Franklin wrote were collected and published as *Father Abraham's Speech* in the almanac for 1758.

Franklin's literary gifts are evident in his satires, *An Edict by the King of Prussia* (1773), exposing the British exploitation of the colonies, the moral tale *The Speech of Miss Polly Baker* (1747), which attacks Puritan double morality, and the humorous *Advice to a Young Man on Choosing a Mistress* (1745), in which the young man is told that older women are a better choice for marriage as they "are so grateful". In France Franklin also printed a number of "bagatelles" (short satires), such as *The Ephemera* (1778), addressed to his good friend Madame Brillon, and *The Dialogue between Franklin and the Gout* (1780), proving him a true writer of the Enlightenment. At the age of 65, Franklin began writing his *Autobiography* for his son William. It covers his earlier years, up to 1758, and was not published in its full text until 1868. Tracing his way as a self-made man, Franklin pointed out that frugality and hard work were the means to success. Franklin's *Autobiography* thus shows him to be a writer under the influence of both Puritanism and the Enlightenment. As a Yankee Puritan who had learnt from Cotton Mather's sermons, he also agreed with Rousseau and Voltaire and used the language of Defoe and Addison for his moral propaganda. The *Autobiography* reveals a pragmatic, lucid and enthusiastic mind whose "do-good" complex has influenced large sections of American society.

The new republic was described and praised in the prose of several writers. Some commented on the possibilities of a developing country, and others on the natural scenery of America. In his twelve essays that make up the *Letters from an American Farmer* (1782), **Michel-Guillaume Jean de Crèvecœur** (1735-1813) ignores the harsh reality of the wilderness and stresses the pastoral and idyllic aspects of American life. As a farmer in New York, de Crèvecoeur undertook extensive journeys before returning to France in 1790. Writing in the established genre of the "farmer's letters", he created in Europe a romantic picture of America in the spirit of Rousseau and provided beautiful and detailed descriptions of American natural scenery, some realistic scenes of war, and a few attacks on slavery. De Crèvecoeur had a very positive view of America, praising it as the haven for all persecuted people and thus helping to create the image of a free country that welcomes immigrants from all corners of the globe.

Natural science – or natural philosophy, as it was then called – found a first representative in **William Bartram** (1739–1823), the son of **John Bartram** (1699–1777), botanist and creator of the Botanic Garden at Philadelphia. Like Linnaeus[1] in Europe, William Bartram was interested in the ordering and registering of plants and animals. The "flower hunter", as the Indians called him, became professor of botany at the University of Pennsylvania and wrote one of the most interesting books for the fields of natural science and geography: *Travels Through North and South Carolina, Georgia, East and West Florida* (1791) became a major source of inspiration for, among others, Coleridge, Wordsworth and Southey. In a poetic prose imbued with pastoral pathos, Bartram provided descriptions of landscapes, flowers and animals – but also of the Indians whom he considered, in the spirit of his age, as noble savages.

---

1. See the note on page 80.

III. The Nineteenth Century

1. General Background

Under the first four presidents – George Washington (1789-1797), John Adams (1797-1801), Thomas Jefferson (1801-1809), and James Madison (1809-1817) – the confidence of the new nation increased while the idea of the union and the United States as an entity was boosted by the War with Great Britain (1812-15). The war brought advantages to neither side but saw the birth of the American national anthem: **Francis Scott Key's** "The Star-Spangled Banner". American self-confidence was strengthened by the purchase of the Louisiana territory from France in 1803, and of Florida from Spain in 1819, as well as the Monroe Doctrine of 1823, which stated that no further colonies were to be founded in America and that no interference theatening American independence would be tolerated. In 1845 the United States annexed Texas, obtained the Oregon Country by treaty with Britain in 1846, acquired vast territories, including California, from Mexico in 1848, and in 1867 Alaska was bought from Russia. The annexation of Hawaii took place in 1898. In that year, which also marked the end of the Spanish-American War, Puerto Rico and the Philippines were ceded to the United States by the Treaty of Paris. The acquisition of territories came to an end in 1917, when the U.S. bought the Virgin Islands from Denmark. After Andrew Jackson had been elected president in 1828, the frontier (i. e. the edge of settled and civilized territory) rapidly moved westward. The Jacksonian years favoured the common man and sanctioned expansionist politics and economics. For blacks and Indians the nineteenth century proved to be crucial: for blacks it brought freedom after the Civil War (1861-65), and for the Indians it brought the end of the freedom they had known for centuries.

The submission of the Indians, as the history books call it, is one of the darkest chapters in American history. Overrun by prospectors, such as the Forty-Niners of the California gold rush in 1849, hemmed in by farmers, harassed by the US Army – and often harassing in retaliation – one Indian tribe after another had to cede its land and surrender to be huddled into reservations, i. e. desert land and barren regions where the Indians starved and grew desperate before resigning themselves to their fate. As white men and women moved westward and southward, this became the fate of, among others, the Creeks and Seminoles in Georgia, Alabama and Florida; of the Navajos in the West, "subdued" by Kit Carson in 1863/4; of the Apaches in the Southwest, who surrendered under their chief Geronimo in 1886, and of the Great Plains Indians, such as the Sioux (or Dakota) who, led by their chiefs Crazy Horse and Sitting Bull, annihilated the vainglorious General Custer and his army in the Battle of the Little Big Horn (1876) before being "quelled" in 1891. A few Indian chiefs, such as the Shawnee Tecumseh (1768?-1813) and the Teton-Dakota Sitting Bull (1831?-1890; his Indian name was Tatanka Yotanka), tried unsuccessfully to unite the Indian tribes. On 29 December

Sitting Bull, American Indian Leader

1890 over 200 Sioux men, women, and children were massacred at Wounded Knee. This marked the Indians' last stand. By 1890 the "physical" frontier, too, had reached its end, as there was no free land left. The frontier, already mythologized by such figures as Billy the Kid (New Mexico), Wild Bill Hickock (Kansas), and Daniel Boone (Kentucky), became a metaphor.

The Civil War divided the United States over the slavery question. The plantation economy of the South could flourish only with black labour controlled by a white planter aristocracy. In the face of human suffering, the abolitionists from the North refused to consider economic issues. The consequence was the rupture of American society as the South's eleven Confederate States, led by "President" Jefferson Davis, waged a long and costly war with President Abraham Lincoln's 23 states of the North. Initially, the Confederacy gained the upper hand under General Robert E. Lee. But after 1862 and Lincoln's Emancipation Proclamation of 1863 that freed all slaves in the South, the Confederacy fought the North and human freedom and finally surrendered to General Ulysses S. Grant in 1865. Human values triumphed, and the plantation system came to an end, creating massive economic problems for blacks and impoverished whites. Segregation, as still practised in South Africa, continued well into the twentieth century.

After the Civil War, the industrial power of the North helped America to achieve enormous economic progress. Industrialists and bankers, joined by inventors, cata-

The Plantation,
anonymous
painting, c. 1825

pulted the USA to the top of all Western nations: Andrew Carnegie achieved in steel what Cornelius Vanderbilt did in railroads and shipping, J. Pierpont Morgan in banking and John D. Rockefeller in oil. The transcontinental railway, the Union Pacific, was completed in 1869. Although the money market crashed twice, in 1873 and 1893, the inventions of Remington (typewriter), Bell (telephone), and Edison (phonograph) heralded a new age.

The literature of the nineteenth century is dominated, topically, by the issue of slavery and by the frontier (the Indians, the new territories), and, intellectually, by the ideas of democracy, ethical subjectivism, and the impulses of religion and the Enlightenment, which emerged in Transcendentalism. After mid-century, the "American literary renaissance" turned back, to an analysis of the Puritan past, and forward, creating the modern psychological and symbolic novel. As capitalism triumphed in American society, realism and naturalism – in the fiction of William Dean Howells and Stephen Crane – analysed the darker sides of economic advancement.

2. Poetry

Traces of European Romanticism, i. e. the preference for feeling and imagination and the importance of individualism and patriotism, can be found in the work of several American poets before the Civil War. **William Cullen Bryant** (1794–1878) was the first American poet to gain international reputation. He was born in Massachusetts and worked as a lawyer and journalist. At first an admirer of Pope, he soon abandoned the heroic couplet and became interested in the verse of Gray, Young, Cowper, Thomson, and Wordsworth. Death and transience of the natural world are the themes of his elegy "Thanatopsis" (1817), written in blank verse. In his nature poems he used American surroundings to lyrical effect: "The Yellow Violet" and "To a Waterfowl", both composed in 1815, are charming poems, and "The Prairies" (1834) celebrates the vastness and beauty of American scenery in

View of the Catskills: Early Autumn by Thomas Cole, 1837

the same romantic way as the Hudson River school of painters, above all Thomas Cole (1801-48), with whom Bryant explored the Catskill Mountains near New York.

> These are the Gardens of the Desert, these
> The unshorn fields, boundless and beautiful.
> And fresh as the young earth, ere man had sinned –
> The prairies. I behold them for the first,
> And my heart swells, while the dilated sight
> Takes in the encircling vastness. Lo! they stretch
> In airy undulations, far away,
> As if the ocean, in his gentlest swell,
> Stood still, with all his rounded billows fixed,
> And motionless for ever – Motionless? –
> No – they are all unchained again. The clouds
> Sweep over with their shadows, and beneath
> The surface rolls and fluctuates to the eye;
> Dark hollows seem to glide along and chase
> The sunny ridges. Breezes of the South!

The great lyric poet of the pre-Civil War period was **Edgar Allan Poe** (1809-49). Born in Boston, Massachusetts, he became an orphan at an early age and was sent to school in England by his foster-father John Allan, a Richmond merchant. Poe studied at the University of Virginia and tried a military career, but he was dismissed from the military academy of West Point. Although he always felt a Virginian, he later returned to Boston and began a brief and brilliant literary career that was overshadowed by his inclination for alcohol. In 1836 he married his thirteen-year-old cousin. When she died in 1847, Poe never recovered from the blow.

Ironically, Poe's stories are superior to his verse – and this fact would seem to contradict his own theory. But he was the first American man of letters who made literature his job. In additon to his poetry and literary theory, he practically invented and popularized the tale of terror and the modern detective story. Emerson and English-speaking poets of the time dismissed Poe as "the jingle man", objecting to his excessive use of alliteration and musicality. Yet his verse exerted a powerful influence on the French symbolists (Baudelaire,

Edgar Allan Poe

Rimbaud, Mallarmé)[1] and was appreciated by Browning, Tennyson and Yeats.

Poe laid down the principles for his own poetry and for what he thought poetry should be in such lectures as "The Poetic Principle" (1848/9; published in 1850) and his essay "The Philosophy of Composition" (1846), which influenced later poetic movements. Good verse, according to Poe, has to be brief (a thesis which foreshadows the Imagists), devoid of didacticism (which anticipates the "art for art's sake" movement of the late nineteenth century), and has to treat of transient beauty, best expressed in the death of a beautiful woman as seen by her lover (the union of Eros and Thanatos). A convincing poem, he argued, must have a planned effect, which is achieved by the rational composition of sound, rhythm and meaning. As his various poems show, Poe was often more interested in poetic forms and effects than in content, and his themes never change very much: love and death, preferably involving a child-woman, and art. His theory suggests a rational and theoretical approach to writing verse, but it does not fully explain the charm of his verbal music and lyrical gift. "The Raven" is a variation on his favourite topic. In this poem the bird finally becomes a symbol of death. The first stanza shows Poe's subtle use of rhythm varied by syncopation:

> Once upon a midnight dreary, while I pondered, weak and weary,
> Over many a quaint and curious volume of forgotten lore,
> While I nodded, nearly napping, suddenly there came a tapping,
> As of some one gently rapping, rapping at my chamber door.
> "'Tis some visitor," I muttered, "tapping at my chamber door –
> Only this, and nothing more."

Similarly, sound is put to impressive use in the first stanza of "Ulalume: A Ballad" (1847), which Mallarmé liked very much. The final stanza of "Annabel Lee" (1849) demonstrates Poe's Romantic inclination for the Gothic and the abnormal in a picture of a lover beside the corpse of his bride:

> For the moon never beams, without bringing me dreams
>   Of the beautiful ANNABEL LEE;
> And the stars never rise, but I feel the bright eyes
>   Of the beautiful ANNABEL LEE:
> And so, all the night tide, I lie down by the side
> Of my darling – my darling – my life and my bride,
>   In her sepulchre there by the sea –
>   In her tomb by the sounding sea.

---

1. On Baudelaire and Mallarmé see notes on pages 92 and 93. Arthur Rimbaud (1854-91) was a revolutionary figure in 19th-century literature. He wrote verse very early, completing his most famous poem ("Le bateau ivre") at the age of 17: it inquires into unknown realities and became an important text for the following generations of writers. He then tried to turn himself into a visionary, describing the unsuccessful attempt in *Les Illuminations,* and concluded his life as a tramp and vagabond in Europe and Africa.

Some of Poe's poems, like some of his stories, create a melancholy, sad, and bizarre landscape – "Poeland" as it has been called – in which night is stronger than day and horror becomes familiar. Examples are "Dream-land" (1844) and "The City in the Sea" (1831).

Although Emerson, Henry James and T. S. Eliot considered Poe's verse either too childish or too superficial, many other writers and poets have expressed delight in his lyrics, praising him as a pioneering aesthetician, a literary technician, and a psychological investigator.

What many of Poe's contemporaries objected to was his idea that poetry should not serve a moral purpose. Defenders of moral poetry were Bryant and the Boston "Brahmins" – Whittier, Longfellow, and Lowell – whom Poe attacked on many occasions. The term "Brahmin" was coined by the critic and poet **Oliver Wendell Holmes** (1809-94) to designate the cultural aristocracy of New England who promoted literary consciousness and ethical commitment. **John Greenleaf Whittier** (1807-92) came from a Quaker family and was a farmer (he is often compared to **Robert Burns,** the Scottish poet). His early verse is inspired by his support of the anti-slavery cause. After the Civil War, he focused on history, nature, the people of New England, and religion. Examples of his late Romantic poetry can be found in *Anti-Slavery Poems* (1852), *Home Ballads* (1860), and the nostalgic "Snow-Bound: A Winter Idyll" (1866), in which he looks back at his youth.

Henry Wadsworth Longfellow (1807-82) was the dominating figure among the "Brahmins". He was also the most popular poet of his time. Born in Portland, Maine, he studied in Europe and became professor of modern languages at Harvard. Longfellow was fascinated with the German Romantic writers and, after 1854, he dedicated all his time to literature in a circle of friends. With the exception of a few short poems, his verse suffers from an overdose of moral sentiment and lacks depth, passion, and originality, yet he was a gifted technician with a polished style and used a variety of poetic forms and distinctive metres. His major themes are derived from European history and literature. Sometimes these are transposed to the New World, as in *Evangeline* (1847), a verse epic in hexameters that was inspired by Goethe's *Hermann und Dorothea* and tells the story of the French Canadians driven out of Nova Scotia by the English in 1755. Longfellow had tremendous success with his first two volumes of poetry, *Voices of the Night* (1839; see the excellent "Hymn to the Night") and *Ballads and Other Poems* (1842). His reputation grew steadily with *The Song of Hiawatha* (1855) and *The Courtship of Miles Standish* (1858). The latter is a humorous verse novella on the love story of one of his ancestors, John Alden, and his wife to-be, Priscilla. In *Hiawatha* Longfellow created the romanticized American Indian hero who civilizes his people and leaves with the setting sun, the symbol of a dying culture, before the white man and Christian religion appear on the scene. The narrative poem is written in unrhymed trochaic tetrameter, and owes some of its substance to the Finnish epic *Kalevala.* It proved so popular that several scenes were engraved by Currier and Ives and the whole poem was set to music. Some of Longfellow's best short lyrical poems are contained in *Ultima Thule* (1880; see the sonnets in this collection) and *In the Harbor* (1882; see "Sundown" and "The City and the Sea").

The third "Brahmin", **James Russell Lowell** (1819–91), was born at Cambridge, Mass., and educated at Harvard. He succeeded Longfellow as professor of
modern languages. Also a renowned essayist and critic, Lowell was the first editor
of the *Atlantic Monthly,* an influential magazine established in 1857, and served as
a diplomat in Spain and England. Like Longfellow, Lowell was opposed to slavery
and tried to acquaint the American public with the European cultural heritage. As a
poet, he began with odes, sonnets, and verse parables such as *The Vision of Sir
Launfal* (1848). Lowell was best as a humourist and political satirist, and he demonstrated his gifts in *A Fable for Critics* (1848), which makes fun of contemporary
men of letters, and his major work, *The Biglow Papers.* Containing prose and
verse, this political satire is written in a racy Yankee[1] dialect. It was published in
two series, in 1848 and 1867, discussing such political issues as the Mexican War
and the Civil War in the persona of the New England farmer Hosea Biglow.

The South saw the brief flourishing of some patriotic poets, such as **Henry
Timrod** (1828–67), **Paul Hamilton Hayne** (1830–86) and **William John Gray-
son** (1788–1863), who all defended the Southern cause in the Civil War in odes
and war poems. But none of them can be considered as important as **Sidney
Lanier** (1842–81), a native of Macon, Georgia, and of Huguenot parentage. He was
a soldier in the Confederate army, contracted tuberculosis and, after 1866, tried
several professions including that of musician in a Baltimore orchestra. Before he
died from his fatal disease, he lectured on literature and literary theory and wrote a
novel on the Civil War, *Tiger-Lilies* (1867). Lanier was fascinated by the relations
between music and poetry. Like Poe, he made much use of melody and sound in
his verse and experimented with form. He demonstrated his musical theory of
poetry, laid down in *The Science of English Verse* (1880), in a series of poems, such
as *Symphony* (1875) and *The Marshes of Glynn* (1878). The latter is certainly his

---

1. A native or inhabitant of New England. During the Civil War, the term referred to the Union
soldiers and the inhabitants of the Northern states. Outside the USA, it is now used as a pejorative
nickname for any native of the United States.

most famous poem. In its final part, the speaker decides to remain close to God, whose presence he has felt in the marshes, and compares himself to the marsh-hen:

> As the marsh-hen secretly builds on the watery sod,
> Behold I will build me a nest on the greatness of God;
> I will fly in the gratness of God as the marsh-hen flies
> In the freedom that fills all the space 'twixt the marsh and the skies;
> By so many roots as the marsh-grass sends in the sod
> I will heartily lay me a-hold on the greatness of God;
> Oh, like to the greatness of God is the greatness within
> The range of the marshes, the liberal marshes of Glynn.

The major Transcendentalists – Emerson, Thoreau, Alcott, and Fuller – also wrote poetry, but they could express their ideas better in the essay and related forms of prose. Their poetry, and that of Emerson in particular, tends to be a mere vehicle for ideas and is thus heavily meditative, intellectual and moralistic. The two poets of the Transcendentalist movement, **Jones Very** (1813-80) and **Christopher Pearse Cranch** (1813-90), a Unitarian minister, were concerned with religious issues, writing in traditional forms and in the spirit of the English metaphysical poets.

Only two poets broke with poetic conventions in the second half of the nineteenth century, **Walt Whitman** and **Emily Dickinson**. Both revolutionized and Americanized American poetry. They proved profoundly influential and continue to be read and studied. **Walt(er) Whitman** (1819-92) was born on Long Island, New York, the son of a carpenter. Whitman grew up in Brooklyn and had an erratic life, working as printer, journalist, building contractor and teacher. Self-educated, he read without system or plan: the Bible, Homer, Shakespeare, Dante, the *Nibelungenlied,* Greek poetry, and the English and German Romanticists. After 1840 he edited newspapers in New York and New Orleans and served as a nurse in army hospitals in Washington during the Civil War. Whitman took an active part in politics and advocated democratic ideals. His great poetic masterpiece is *Leaves of Grass.* It was first published in 12 parts in 1855 and was continually augmented until the "Death-bed edition" came out in 1892. *Leaves of Grass* reflects many of Whitman's personal experiences as well as his reading. What makes it remarkable poetry is its rejection of conventionality both in form

Walt Whitman

and content. Whitman refused to borrow verse from European and other foreign sources, discarded rhyme almost entirely, and took considerable liberties with metre. The result, a kind of rhythmic prose ordered by caesura and alliteration and rich in images and allusions, was revolutionary for the age and heralded a new style.

The various editions of *Leaves of Grass* indicate Whitman's development and preoccupations. Thus the 1860 edition reflects his political involvement with the democratic cause and his view of the sexual force of nature (see "Chants Democratic" and "Children of Adam"); the edition of 1867 contains the poems dealing with the Civil War (published in 1865 under the title *Drum-Taps*) and mourning the death of President Lincoln, such as "When Lilacs Last in the Dooryard Bloom'd", a powerful elegy whose opening stanzas provide an impression of Whitman's poetic skill.

> I
>
> When lilacs last in the dooryard bloom'd,
> And the great star early droop'd in the western sky in the night,
> I mourn'd, and yet shall mourn with ever-returning spring.
>
> Ever-returning spring, trinity sure to me you bring,
> Lilac blooming perennial and drooping star in the west,
> And thought of him I love.
>
> 2
>
> O powerful western fallen star!
> O shades of night – O moody, tearful night!
> O great star disappear'd – O the black murk that hides the star!
> O cruel hands that hold me powerless – O helpless soul of me!
> O harsh surrounding cloud that will not free my soul.

In "Passage to India", incorporated into *Leaves of Grass* in 1876, Whitman celebrates the completion of the Suez Canal and of the American transcontinental railway. Among his contemporaries, only Emerson recognized Whitman's stature as a poet. *Leaves of Grass* is in essence one song about America, about her nature, vitality, dynamism, and variety, and about American democracy, which guarantees freedom to the individual. Thus he sings of man, woman and America in the central poem "Song of Myself", which is made up of 52 sections and brims with optimism:

> Smile O voluptuous cool-breath'd earth!
> Earth of the slumbering and liquid trees!
> Earth of departed sunset – earth of the mountains misty-topt!
> Earth of the vitreous pour of the full moon just tinged with blue!
> Earth of shine and dark mottling the tide of the river!
> Earth of the limpid gray of clouds brighter and clearer for my sake!
> Far-swooping elbow'd earth – rich apple-blossom'd earth!
> Smile, for your lover comes.

What Gerard Manley Hopkins did for English poetry, **Emily Dickinson** (1830–86) achieved for American verse. Together with Whitman, she is today recognized as one of America's most important poets, a forerunner of modernism far ahead of her time. Like Hopkins, she was unknown as a poet during her lifetime. Publication of her almost 1,800 short poems began in the 1890s, and it was only in 1955 that a full critical text of her work was made available in a three-volume edition edited by Thomas H. Johnson.

Emily Dickinson was born in Amherst, Mass., and spent almost all her life there in seclusion, apart from a year at a seminary for girls and a few visits to Washington, Philadelphia and Boston. She corresponded with a few people, among them the clergyman Charles Wadsworth, whom she probably loved passionately, and T. W. Higginson, who discussed her poems with her. After 1862 she spent almost all her time in her house in Amherst, concentrating on the inner life of her imagination and her immediate surroundings, the flowers and birds in her garden and the objects in her home. The experience of nature and of seasons ("Apparently with no surprise", "The Day came slow") often led her to the contemplation of death, the central theme of many of her poems. "Because I could not stop for Death" shows that her poetry is indebted, in spirit, to Calvinism and the metaphysical poets, and, in form, to the ballad and the church hymn.

> Because I could not stop for Death –
> He kindly stopped for me –
> The Carriage held but just Ourselves –
> And Immortality.
>
> We slowly drove – He knew no haste
> And I had put away
> My labor and my leisure too,
> For His Civility –
>
> We passed the School, where Children strove
> At Recess – in the Ring –
> We passed the Fields of Gazing Grain –
> We passed the Setting Sun –
>
> Or rather – He passed Us –
> The Dews drew quivering and chill –
> For only Gossamer, my Gown –
> My Tippet – only Tulle –
>
> We paused before a House that seemed
> A Swelling of the Ground –
> The Roof was scarcely visible –
> The Cornice – in the Ground –
>
> Since then – 'tis Centuries – and yet
> Feels shorter than the Day
> I first surmised the Horses' Heads
> Were toward Eternity –

Dickinson's economical use of metre, her preference for assonance and ellipsis, creating both verbal and syntactical ambiguity, and her special way of separating verses by dashes make her poetry essentially modern. She gave expression to a wide range of moods, from the reflection of her own withdrawal from society in

"The soul selects her own society" to the intensity of her imagination and passion in "Wild Nights".

> Wild Nights - Wild Nights!
> Were I with thee
> Wild Nights should be
> Our luxury!
>
> Futile - the Winds -
> To a Heart in port -
> Done with the Compass -
> Done with the Chart!
>
> Rowing in Eden -
> Ah, the Sea!
> Might I but moor - Tonight -
> In Thee!

The poem demonstrates her daring use of seemingly conflicting metaphors (erotic nights, the romantic image of the boat, heavenly paradise) and a style that deliberately refuses to be smooth. Yet the effect, the juxtaposition of Eros and religion, is as convincing as that of the best of metaphysical poetry.

Thus Whitman, the verbose and optimistic singer in free verse of America's beauty and democracy, and Emily Dickinson, the more reserved and pensive explorer of erotic and religious passion and of death and human despair, became America's first significant poets with an international influence.

At a time when they were barred from education and concerned with human freedom, blacks did not write poetry. If they could write, they chose prose, like Frederick Douglass, to voice their complaints. Like the blacks, the Indians had an oral tradition with marked poetic features. Written records, such as the *Walam Olum (Painted Record)* of the Delaware Indians are extremely rare. The speeches of several Indian chiefs (for example, those of Geronimo and Chief Joseph) convey an impression of the Indians' poetic language.

3. Drama

Although by the early nineteenth century, drama was flourishing in New York and Philadelphia, American playwrights were few and far between. In New England, and outside the bigger cities, the Puritan objection to the theatre could still be felt, and the Revolution as well as the frontier conditions did not favour theatrical productions. Where drama was possible, European plays dominated. As there was no copyright[1] law until 1891, numerous English, French and German comedies

---

1. This is the exclusive right to the publication, production, or sale of the rights to a literary, dramatic, musical, or artistic work. It is granted by law for a definite period of years to an author or a company. US copyright protects a work during the lifetime of its author and for 50 years after the author's death.

and melodramas were adapted and performed in America. When Americans finally did write dramatic texts, they catered to an audience interested in sensation and sentimentality. The early commercialization of the theatres led to "show business" and was a further obstacle in the way of a serious and meaningful drama.

Significantly, America's first professional playwright, **William Dunlap** (1766-1839), adapted European plays for American audiences in New York (*The Stranger,* 1798, after Kotzebue; *The Italian Father,* 1799, after Dekker) and wrote a *History of the American Theatre* (1832). **James Nelson Barker** (1784-1858) adapted plays in Philadelphia: Scott's verse romance *Marmion* (1812), and *How to Try a Lover* (1817), based on a French picaresque novel. However, Barker made a first step toward American themes with his *Superstition* (1824), which is about the Salem witchcraft trials[1] in seventeenth-century New England. The story of Pocahontas and Captain Smith, in its romanticized form, was very popular until the end of the century. Theatrical versions include Barker's *The Indian Princess* (1808) and *Pocahontas* (1830), by the Virginian **George Washington Parker Curtis.**

The American city, in this case Philadelphia, was romanticized in **Robert Montgomery Bird's (1806-54)** *The City Looking Glass* (1828). Many of the plays written in the early decades of the century are today forgotten, e. g. **John Howard Payne's** *Clari* (1823) and the plays by **Nathaniel Parker Willis** and **George Henry Boker.**

Toward mid-century, melodrama began to displace historical tragedies and romantic comedies. **Dion Boucicault** (1820-90) enjoyed great success with his adaptations of French plays and dramatizations of Dickens's novels as well as with *Rip Van Winkle* and his own drama, *The Octoroon* (1859), a tragedy on seduction and racism. Equally popular were *Shenandoah* (1888), by **Bronson Howard** (1842-1908), which develops a love story set in the Civil War; the comedies and farces of **Clyde Fitch** (1865-1909), such as *Beau Brummel* (1890); and the melodramatic plays, laced with local colour, of **Augustus Thomas** (1857-1934), **James A. Herne** (1839-1901; see *Margaret Fleming* 1890, and *Shore Acres,* 1892), and **David Belasco** (1853-1931), who was co-author of *Madame Butterfly* (1900), set to music by Puccini. Best-sellers like *Uncle Tom's Cabin* also enjoyed great theatrical success. It was not before the early twentieth century that American play-

---

Until well into the 19th century, in the absence of copyright, authors could not prevent publishers from exploiting them by reprinting published works.

1. Witchcraft, if proved according to the laws then in practice, was punishable by death in England and America until well into the eighteenth century. Around 1692, an epidemic disease resembling epilepsy spread in Salem, Massachusetts. Encouraged by sermons from Cotton Mather, many people began to believe that evil spirits in the form of witches haunted the area. In the spring and summer of 1692, the delusion was highest: 19 people were hanged, one was pressed to death, 55 were tortured into confessions of guilt, and 150 were imprisoned. When the Puritan establishment, including the governor's wife and relatives of Cotton Mather, became the object of suspicion, the delusion was over. Judge Samuel Sewall was among those who did public penance for the wrong verdicts.

The events have often been treated in American literature; Arthur Miller's *The Crucible* (1953) is one example from the 20th century.

wrights, under the influence of Ibsen, Strindberg, and Chekhov[1], turned away from sensational and sentimental melodrama to develop a distinctly American theatre.

4. Prose Fiction

4.1 The Novel

Much impressed by the historical novels of Sir Walter Scott, **James Fenimore Cooper** (1789-1851) turned for his romantic fiction to the recent American past, to the life of the American frontiersmen, to the Red Indians, and the prairies and forests. A native of New Jersey, Cooper grew up in a frontier community in the state of New York. He studied at Yale, served in the American Navy and, in 1817, became a farmer. During a long stay in Europe (1826-33) he acquainted himself with European customs and politics and read the German Romantic writers. Back in America, he became an ardent social critic and attacked Jacksonian society. But the public preferred his fiction concerned with the frontier, which, as one often tends to ignore, amounts to less than a third of his novels.

Cooper's *The Spy* (1821), combining adventure and romance, is a melodramatic historical novel about the Revolution, while *The Pilot* (1823) is one of the better known of his sea stories: both works owe a lot to Scott's style and technique. It was with his *Leather-Stocking* series that Cooper achieved world-wide success. With Natty Bumppo (also called Leather-Stocking, Deerslayer, Pathfinder and Hawkeye), Cooper created a romantic mythological frontiersman. The order in which Cooper wrote his five Leather-Stocking novels does not correspond to the chronology of his hero's life. Thus *The Deerslayer* (published last of the series in 1841) is set in the French and Indian Wars and shows a youthful Natty Bumppo. Natty is portrayed as an experienced hunter and trapper in *The Last of the Mohicans* (1826), prefers the wilderness to marriage in *The Pathfinder* (1840), experiences with mixed feelings the advance of civilization into Indian territory in *The Pioneers* (1823), and, aged almost 90, lives his last adventure on the Western plains in *The Prairie* (1827). For all his weaknesses in style and characterization (stereo-

---

1. On Ibsen see the note on page 95. Johan August Strindberg (1849-1912) was a Swedish playwright and writer. His plays are concerned with the issues of religion, social class, marriage, and sexuality; they combine an aggressive naturalism with a sense of the pathological. His tense, symbolic dramas (*Miss Julie*, 1888, *The Dance of Death*, 1901) usually portray some aspect of human suffering and influenced the plays of O'Neill and the writers of the theatre of the absurd.

Anton Chekhov (or Tchekhov, 1860-1904) was a Russian dramatist and short story writer. He wrote several light one-act comedies but is best remembered for his late plays which blend naturalism and symbolism in detailed portraits of the upper class (*The Seagull*, 1895, *Uncle Vanya*, 1900, *Three Sisters*, 1901, *The Cherry Orchard*, 1904). Checkhov has had an immense influence on English and American literature.

The Life of a Hunter: A Tight Fix, from a lithograph by Currier & Ives

types of good and bad persons, including Indians, abound), Cooper provided much suspense, a marvellous portrait of the American landscape, and a study of the conflict between the values of civilization and the wilderness clashing at the frontier. Cooper's novels admittedly suffer from too much idealization of nature and people and virtually exclude women. Cooper, like Hawthorne, Melville and Mark Twain, was largely unable to create convincing female characters. Nevertheless, he stands at the beginning of a truly American tradition of the novel that made use of native settings, problems, and characters.

What **F. O. Matthiessen** (1902-50) termed the "American literary renaissance" came after Cooper, toward the middle of the century, when within five years Hawthorne, Melville, Thoreau and Whitman published such important works as *The Scarlet Letter* (1850), *Moby-Dick* (1851), *Walden* (1854), and *Leaves of Grass* (1855). **Nathaniel Hawthorne** (1804-64) considered himself a psychological novelist. While Cooper focused romantically on the frontier, Hawthorne was concerned with both the influence and the waning of Puritanism in New England. To some extent, he was inspired by the ideas of the Transcendentalists, but he disliked Thoreau's moral naiveté and was fully aware of the implications of evil and sin, which he treated in his short stories and symbolic novels. A New Englander by birth, he worked as a journalist and customs officer in Salem, Massachusetts, and, in 1841, lived for a few months on "Brook Farm" with the Transcendentalists. Hawthorne got to know Melville and served as American consul in Liverpool (1853-57) before spending two years in Italy and returning to Concord, Massachusetts. Guilt, remorse, isolation, repentance and despair are the themes in his major novels. He termed them romances, "somewhere between the real world and fairy land, where the actual and the imaginary may meet". With his first novel, *Fanshawe* (1828), he was himself dissatisfied. *The Scarlet Letter* (1850) was his first novelistic treatment of Puritanism and the issue of guilt.

Set in seventeenth-century Boston, *The Scarlet Letter* is concerned with the heroic suffering and eventual triumph of Hester Prynne over Puritan society. Because Hester committed

205

adultery with Arthur Dimmesdale in the absence of her husband, Roger Chillingworth (the child Pearl is the living proof of this sin), she is forced by the Puritan community to wear the red letter "A" (for adultery) as a token of her guilt. Hawthorne analyses the mental suffering and the moral conflicts of the three major characters. Chillingworth returns to find his wife in the stocks, refusing to name her lover, and he decides to conceal his identity. In his search for Hester's paramour he becomes a morally degraded monomaniac. The preacher Dimmesdale struggles for years with his conscience. He finally makes a public confession and dies in Hester's arms. Hester, the heroine, does penance for her sin by helping other unfortunates in the Puritan community, but she refuses to live according to the rigid Puritan standards. She even returns voluntarily from her exile in Europe, decides to continue wearing the letter "A" and finds her peace of mind by living according to her own conscience.

The study of sin and evil is also central to *The House of the Seven Gables* (1851), which is concerned with the consequence of a curse pronounced on the author's great-grandfather, a judge in the Salem witchcraft trials, and to *The Blithedale Romance* (1852), which contains episodes from Hawthorne's time spent at "Brook Farm", the idealist community of the Transcendentalists. With *The Marble Faun* (1860), Hawthorne chose a European setting, Rome, but the characters remain essentially Puritan as the psychological drama of the consequences of a crime unfolds. Another theme of this novel, which foreshadows Henry James, is the meeting of European and American ideas and ideals.

Hawthorne shared with **Herman Melville** (1819–1891) a preference for psychological exploration and symbolism as well as his fascination with evil. But Melville had a more tragic vision of life. Although he ridiculed Emerson and the Transcendentalists, he shared some common ground with them, such as the philosophical view of the individual and the tendency to symbolize the soul and see nature as an allegory of human experience. Melville's outstanding work, *Moby-Dick,* had to wait until the twentieth century to be recognized as one of the significant novels in American literature. Melville was born in New York, the son of a

wealthy businessman. He lost his father at the age of 12. Because of his father's bankruptcy, the young Herman's education was cut short, and in 1839 he shipped to Liverpool as a cabin boy. He was much impressed by life at sea, but returned to upstate New York for a brief period to teach school. In 1841 he embarked on the whaler Acushnet for the South Seas. At the Marquesas, he left his ship and lived for a month on those beautiful islands, escaping from the hostile natives on an Australian

Herman Melville

trading ship that took him to Tahiti. Before returning to Boston in 1844, he also visited Hawaii.

This education at sea, as it were, formed the basis for his best fiction. Combining personal experience with imagination and information from books he had read, he wrote a number of novels that, although mere preludes to *Moby-Dick,* made him famous. Thus *Typee* (1846) and *Mardi* (1849) are set in the Marquesas, while *Omoo* (1847) depicts the island life on Tahiti; *Redburn* (1849) makes use of his knowledge of shipping and of Liverpool, and *White-Jacket* (1850) is also partly autobiographical in its realistic description of the occasionally brutal life aboard a man-of-war.

The success of these novels won Melville a large readership and entrance to the literary circles of Boston and New York. In 1849, two years after his marriage, he made a voyage to England and France and then settled on the Massachusetts farm that was to be his home for the next thirteen years. He became a good friend of his neighbour, Hawthorne, to whom he dedicated his *Moby-Dick* (1851). Few of Melville's contemporaries understood the literary value of *Moby-Dick.* Like Hawthorne's *The Scarlet Letter,* it is both a realistic and a symbolic novel. Contained within the realistic account of whaling and adventures at sea is the symbolic description of man's desperate struggle with his fate and his quest for knowledge.

The story is told by Ishmael, a youth who becomes friendly with Queequeg, a Polynesian prince. Together they sign on the Pequod, a whaling ship. The ship's captain, Ahab, has an ivory leg and proves to be a monomaniac: after a few days at sea he reveals that his only aim is to capture the cunning white whale Moby-Dick that tore away his leg in a former encounter. Before the white whale is finally sighted, the Pequod is nearly carried around the world, a few whales are captured, and many accidents and incidents are described. In an almost apocalyptic final fight that lasts for three days, the whale is harpooned but drags Ahab down into the deep after sinking the ship. Ishmael, the only survivor, is saved by another whaler.

In *Moby-Dick* the sea, with its fierce force and dangerous beauty, is of prime importance. Melville describes it in lyrical passages giving it epic grandeur. The plot of the voyage is interwoven with discussions of the nature of the whale and of the whaling industry. Moby-Dick becomes the central ambiguous symbol: the Biblical Leviathan and, for Ahab, the incarnation of evil. Ishmael sees Ahab's chase

Boat Destroyed by a Whale, from a nineteenth-century engraving

of the whale as a demonic self-destruction; to him, the whale is not merely dangerous and destructive but also a creature of God and of fascinating beauty. In a truly epic but unobtrusive manner, Melville tries to present an encyclopedic view of life and the world on board a ship whose crew is made up of whalers from many nations. The various elements of the novel – essays, speeches, sermons, parables and anecdotes – are not always successfully integrated, but the overall effect of *Moby-Dick* is one of deeply moving and symbolic fiction.

Melville was bitterly disappointed by the lack of public appreciation of *Moby-Dick*. As his next novel, *Pierre: or, the Ambiguities* (1852), a satirical and symbolic attack on the bourgeois world, was equally unsuccessful, he had to resort to short fiction to make a living. His beautiful and haunting short stories were published in 1856 as *The Piazza Tales*. After another voyage to Europe and the publication of an historical novel, *Israel Potter* (1855), and another satire on society, *The Confidence-Man: His Masquerade* (1857; this work remained unfinished), Melville moved to New York and wrote short stories, poetry and personal journals. After finishing "Billy Budd" (1891), he died in New York, almost totally ignored by the literary world and the public.

Uncle Tom's Cabin, or Life Among the Lowly (1852), by the New England writer **Harriet Beecher Stowe** (1811–96) is a novel that also belongs to the American renaissance, although literary historians have disregarded the book for almost a century because of its overt pathos and sentimentality and its lack of subtle characterization. However, a few critical studies during the last ten years have pointed out that Mrs. Stowe's novel, for all its melodrama and didactic antislavery stance, has more than historical value (it sold 300,000 copies in the first year and had a powerful influence in America and abroad): it deserves to be studied for its archetypal characters indebted to Puritan typology and because it is one of the first successful novels by a woman in an age when men dominated the literary scene.

Uncle Tom's Cabin describes the dark side of slave life in the South in a story about an old slave sold by his impoverished "good" master to a slave trader and, finally, to a degenerate planter. This man, Simon Legree, is not a Southerner but a Yankee from Vermont. The drunken Legree is impressed by Tom's courage and religious fortitude. But when Tom refuses to disclose the hiding place of two escaped slaves, Legree has him flogged to death.

An advertisement for *Uncle Tom's Cabin*

Mrs. Stowe is fairer to the South than is often realized. Her humanitarian attitude often leads her to create melodramatic scenes. Thus, toward the end of the book, Tom's former "good" master arrives to see him die and vows to devote his life to the cause of abolition. But it is the intense pathos of the novel which helped it to become one of the most influential books in American history. Feminists have argued that, given the woman's place and treatment in nineteenth-century society, Mrs. Stowe could not write differently and that her sentimental style is the product of the way nineteenth-century women were conditioned to see the world.

As the new American nation pushed further west and south, literature tried to capture the rapidly changing conditions on the various frontiers. "Local colour" became a term for fiction, particularly short stories, dealing both realistically and romantically with specific areas of the United States and the people that lived there. For the novel, this meant either realistic and humorous, and later more serious, studies of frontier life or historical romances. The local-colour school produced a great many outstanding authors. In the South, there were writers like **George Washington Cable** (1844-1925), who described Creole[1] life in Louisiana in his novel *The Grandissimes* (1880); **Kate Chopin** (1851-1904), who married a Creole in Louisiana and dealt with her marriage and adultery in *The Awakening* (1899), a novel many found shocking at the time; the Virginian **Thomas Nelson Page** (1853-1922), who made his home state the setting of his novel *Red Rock* (1898), while **Joel Chandler Harris** (1848-1908) set his fiction in Georgia. **Harriet Beecher Stowe** set most of her stories in New England, and New England also provides the background for **Sarah Orne Jewett's** (1849-1909) novel on Maine, *The Country of the Pointed Firs* (1896).

The local-colour movement has been associated especially with the Middle West and the West. Here, the names of the Eggleston brothers, of Bret Harte and Mark Twain are most prominent. The backwoods of Indiana are the backdrop for **Edward Eggleston's** (1837-1902) *The Hoosier Schoolmaster* (1871) and the tales of his brother **George** (1839-1911).

Before turning to Mark Twain, the historical novel deserves a brief glance. It was an offshoot of the local-colour movement and, to some extent, a reaction against the rising realism of the late nineteenth century. Cooper and Sir Walter Scott had written exemplary novels, and they found a few successors. To the genre belong **Sidney Lanier's** Civil War novel *Tiger-Lilies* (1867), **Silas Weir Mitchell's** (1829-1914) novel on the Revolutionary War, *Hugh Wynne, Free Quaker* (1897), and the less known historical fiction of **Maurice Thompson** (1844-1901) from Indiana, **Winston Churchill** (1871-1947) from St. Louis, and the Brooklyn-born **Paul Leicester Ford** (1865-1902). Not concerned with America, but also historical novels, are the major works of the cosmopolitan **Francis Marion Crawford** (1854-1909) and the spectacular *Ben-Hur: A Tale of the Christ* (1880) by the Indiana lawyer and diplomat **Lewis Wallace** (1827-1905). *Ben-Hur* was dramatized and made into two Hollywood film epics in 1926 and 1959.

---

1. Creoles are the descendants of the original French settlers in Louisiana.

It is in the early work of **Mark Twain** that several currents, including local colour, met: realistic-humorous description, convincing dialogue based on regional dialects, and an element of satire mellowed by boisterous comedy. Mark Twain's real name was **Samuel Langhorne Clemens** (1839-1910). He grew up in Hannibal, Missouri, a small town on the Mississippi that was to provide him with incidents and characters for many of his works, as did the great river itself, which he got to know intimately as a river pilot (1857-60). In the Civil War, Twain served for a brief period in the Confederate Army before going to Nevada as a prospector. In 1862 he turned to journalism, beginning with humorous sketches and stories of the frontier. Twain also went on lecture tours and worked as a newspaper correspondent in Hawaii (1866) and in Europe (1867). *The Innocents Abroad* (1869), based on his voyage to Europe, Egypt and Palestine, was his first book. It established his reputation as a humorous writer. The book is a satirical description of overrated and outmoded aspects of the Old World as provided by a self-confident if naive American traveller. A new phase in Mark Twain's life began in 1870, when he married Olivia Langdon, the daughter of a tycoon, and moved with his wife to New England where he became acquainted with William Dean Howells. Mark Twain was unable to handle money. Fascinated by new technology, he speculated on a number of gadgets, including an impractical typesetting machine that returned no profit, and incurred heavy debts when his publishing company (of which he owned a part) went bankrupt in 1894. But he was able to repay his creditors in full by going on a world lecture tour and by publishing further books. Despite this success, he became increasingly depressed, especially after the deaths

of his wife and their two daughters. His bitterness and pessimism found expression in his late works, such as *The Mysterious Stranger* (1916).

One would not do justice to Mark Twain by calling him a satirical humorist, for there are many sides to his work that are often obscured by the popularity of *Tom Sawyer* and *Huckleberry Finn.* Thus it is easily overlooked that in 1873 Twain published *The Gilded Age,* written in collaboration with **Charles D. Warner,** which denounced materialism and political corruption. He also wrote a fictional biography of Joan of Arc (1896), which is marred by a strong sentimental streak and appeared under yet another pseudonym, a satirical report on his trip

Mark Twain

through Germany and Switzerland, entitled *A Tramp Abroad* (1880), and a jibe at contemporary attempts to revive historical fiction with his burlesque, *A Connecticut Yankee in King Arthur's Court* (1889), in which the ingenious Yankee mechanic Hank Morgan teaches King Arthur and his knights, among other things, how to ride a bicycle instead of a horse. But Hank's nineteenth-century technology engenders death and destruction instead of advancement, thus introducing a final pessimistic note. With *The Prince and the Pauper* (1882), a book for children, he satirized social events in Tudor England, and in *Roughing It* (1872) he recollected with much humour his experiences in Nevada and Hawaii.

Mark Twain was at his best when he wrote about the people on the Mississippi. The first 14 chapters of *Life on the Mississippi* appeared in the *Atlantic Monthly* in 1873 and were then enlarged and published as a book in 1883. It shows the rich and eventful world, the comic and tragic experiences, that Mark Twain had enjoyed so much in his youth in Hannibal, Missouri. The Mississippi again figures prominently in two picaresque novels, *The Adventures of Tom Sawyer* (1876), and its superb sequel, *Adventures of Huckleberry Finn* (1884). Tom Sawyer's adventures in the river town of St. Petersburg, Mo., with his friends Joe Harper and Huck Finn, as they discover a murder, play hookey, and hide on a river island, are merely the prologue to *Huckleberry Finn*. Ernest Hemingway saw this novel as the beginning of truly American fiction.

Huckleberry Finn has often been read as a children's story. Its episodic manner can easily hide the implicit complexities of American life. Ironically enough, the book was temporarily banned from some American school libraries because of its alleged use of "racist" vocabulary. (The censors who object to the use of "nigger" ignore that America has a past one should not deny). In this novel of initiation, Mark Twain managed to unite realism and romantic illusion.

Huck Finn is a most unusual narrator. As an uneducated river rat and abandoned child under the protection of the Widow Douglas, he uses his Missouri dialect for his entertaining report about his adventures during a trip on a raft down the Mississippi. Huck's first sentence, brimming with lexical and grammatical mistakes, directly addresses the readers as if they were listeners. Although linguistically unreliable (an essential element of realism), Huck proves a fascinating narrator, as he describes the adventures with his friend, the runaway slave Jim, on their way down the great river. A large part of the novel's satire and humour derives from Huck's seemingly naive comments on aspects of civilized life, on bourgeois families and people he meets. Afraid that Tom Sawyer's aunt will take him under her socializing wings, Huck concludes at the happy ending of the novel, "I reckon I got to light out for the Territory ahead of the rest, because Aunt Sally she's going to adopt me and sivilize me and I can't stand it. I been there before".

As Huck and Jim drift along on their symbolic voyage, which can be read as an initiation into the world, Mark Twain unveils the false morality and conventionality of adult and bourgeois life. At each contact that Huck and Jim make with the world, this world tries to corrupt and deprave them. The American dream is reduced to an illusion ironically upheld by Huck's final words. Against the corrupt image of civilization are set the idyll of the raft and a Rousseau-like though partly world-wise hero. The realistic style and characters in this novel paved the way for the works of Hemingway, Faulkner and Salinger, to name just three novelists who profited from Twain's most influential book.

A Midnight Race on the Mississippi, from a lithograph by Currier & Ives

Inherent in the local-colour movement was an element of realism that is most obvious in the social criticism of Mark Twain's *The Gilded Age* of 1873. As capitalism, "big business", and a fast developing technology began to dominate American public life and politics, literature took up the issues involved in this process in realistic or naturalistic attempts to show how this affected individual lives. Literary influences from Europe, such as Zola's fiction[1], also helped to develop the realistic school in American writing. **William Dean Howells** (1837-1920) was a prominent representative of this movement. Self-educated and antagonistic to the prevailing romantic spirit in American literature, this critic, journalist and novelist called for a truthful portrayal of average characters and everyday life. He put his theory into practice in a large number of short stories and novels. Of his novels, *A Modern Instance* (1882) is the one he cherished most. It deals with a woman's marriage to and divorce from a ruthless Boston journalist. *The Rise of Silas Lapham* (1885) is the story of a "nouveau riche" who, coming from modest origins in Vermont, tries to rub shoulders with Boston's upper social circles, the "Brahmins". The hero eventually recognizes the value of moral standards and abandons his aspirations. Containing strong elements of social criticism, the novel is a masterpiece of realistic description and humour. Big city politics and the conflict between late nineteenth-century capitalism and socialism are portrayed in *A Hazard of New Fortunes* (1890). Basil March, its hero, also figures in other novels by Howells. Like Mark Twain and Henry James, Howells sometimes confronted American simplic-

---

1. See page 104, note 1.

ity with European sophistication, as in *Indian Summer* (1886), which is concerned with an Indiana publisher in Florence, Italy. Unlike the later naturalists, Howells avoided tragic aspects and maintained an optimistic critical attitude that was partly influenced by Tolstoy's[1] Christian socialism. As the editor of *Atlantic Monthly,* Howells promoted the work of his friends Henry James and Mark Twain and of some younger writers who came to be known as naturalists: Hamlin Garland, Stephen Crane, and Frank Norris.

Naturalism grew out of realism as the works of Karl Marx, Charles Darwin's theory of evolution and Hippolyte Taine's (1828-93) studies of environment and "milieu" began to make themselves felt. The American naturalists learned from the fiction of Flaubert, Zola, Tolstoy, and Turgenev.[2] Showing man as a product of his environment and his social situation, naturalistic fiction ignores freedom of will while focusing on the disadvantages of human nature and society. Traditional American optimism opposed the crude determinism of the naturalists, and some writers like **Crane** (whose *Maggie,* 1893, did not sell at all) never became as popular as their European contemporaries. **Hamlin Garland** (1860-1940) dealt with the harshness of life in the Middle West in his short stories (*Main-Travelled Roads,* 1891) and suggested social reforms with his novels. *A Spoil of Office* (1892) attacked political corruption, and *The Captain of the Gray-Horse Troop* (1902) describes the injustice done to the Indians.

Stephen Crane (1871-1900), the son of a Methodist preacher, and **Frank Norris** (1870-1902), whose father was a rich jeweller in Chicago, were both greatly influenced by French naturalism. Crane had an eventful life as a war reporter and ruined his health. Slandered because of his political views and his fiction, he became disappointed with America and settled in Sussex, England, in 1898. He died of tuberculosis in Badenweiler, Germany. Also a master of the realistic short story, Crane has gone down in literary history for two novels. *Maggie* (1893) displays the unpleasant realities of New York slum life in the story of a girl, Maggie Johnson, who struggles and strives hopelessly in a factory and works as a prostitute before committing suicide. Crane had trouble finding a publisher for this novel. He was more successful with *The Red Badge of Courage* (1895). This is a brilliant psychological study of human behaviour during war and successfully de-

---

1. Count Lev Nikolaevich Tolstoy (1828-1910), Russian prose writer. In the West, he is remembered for his *War and Peace* (1863-69), an epic novel about the Napoleonic invasion of Russia and the lives of three aristocratic families, and *Anna Karenina* (1873-77), which is about the tragic passion of a married woman for a young officer. Tolstoy had extreme moral views that included non-resistance to evil, the rejection of property and any kind of secular or religious authority (except God), and a deep love of humanity.

2. Gustave Flaubert (1821-80), French novelist and master of realism. He has gone down in literary history for his authenticity of detail, impersonal narrative method, and a precise and harmonious style. His major novels include *Madame Bovary* (1857), about the adultery and suicide of a doctor's wife in Normandy, *Salammbô* (1862), and *L'Education sentimentale* (1869).

Ivan S. Turgenev (1818-83), Russian novelist and playwright. Turgenev spent much of his life outside Russia and was acquainted with many writers in Europe. His major and influential works are the collection of stories about Russian farmers entitled *A Hunter's Notes* (1847-51), and his play, *A Month in the Country* (1850).

mythifies hero worship and the glories of war. The novel could be termed a psychological analysis of fear: Crane tells the story of Henry Fleming who, after going through a period of cowardice and fright, finally achieves his own kind of courage and understanding of man's importance. Crane's prose gives the impression of being factual and sober; yet his concise style also provides moments of impressionism as the battlefield becomes a symbol of the cruel world the individual has to face.

War of a different kind, the struggle for power between the ranchers and the railroad ("the octopus") in California, is the subject of Frank Norris's *The Octopus* (1901). Norris was a theorist of naturalism and demanded the inclusion of the unusual and the horrible in fiction. For Norris, the big cities harboured evil, and he demonstrated it repeatedly in his short stories and novels by describing the misery of the slums. Thus, in *The Octopus,* descriptions of the huge wheat fields and the farms alternate with scenes of violence and poverty in the cities. Of the originally planned three volumes of *The Epic of the Wheat,* Norris finished only *The Octopus* and a sequel, *The Pit* (1903). His earlier *McTeague* (1899), an experimental novel, records the gradual degeneration of a San Francisco dentist whose animal instincts prove too powerful to be controlled.

The realistic and naturalistic tradition as represented by Crane and Norris, but also in the more romantic novels of **Jack London** (1876-1916; see *The Call of the Wild,* 1903; and *White Fang,* 1906), was further developed in the twentieth century by Dreiser, Anderson, Dos Passos, Hemingway, and Faulkner.

Equally influential for the modern American novel was the psychological realism that marks the fiction of **Henry James** (1843-1916). Born in New York, he came from a rich family of intellectuals. Together with his brother, the philosopher and theorist of pragmatism **William James** (1842-1910), Henry was educated in England, France, Switzerland, and at Harvard. Financially independent, James could dedicate his life to literature and became concerned with the technique of

Henry James

fiction. He largely ignored the world of the working class and the social conflicts and miseries of his time. As an avid reader of George Eliot, Flaubert and Turgenev, Henry James experimented with the form of the novel but did not consider American authors. He was attracted to the elegance and the aristocratic traditions of the Old World. From the late 1860s on he lived mostly in Europe. In 1915, in protest against America's hesitation to come to Britain's aid in the war, he became a British subject. Like T. S. Eliot and Ezra Pound, James stood between the Old and the New World. In fact, one of the central themes of his fiction, especially in his "Atlantic" novels, is the analysis of Americans in European society in ambiguous scenes presenting innocence and experience, purity and corruption. Thus *The American* (1877) contrasts American sincerity with European falsity, and in *Daisy Miller* (1879) an American girl, unaware of European manners, shocks Rome's society with her natural and unperturbed behaviour. James also tried American settings, as in *The Europeans* (1878) and *Washington Square* (1881), but returned to his favourite situation, the American in Europe, with *The Portrait of a Lady* (1881).

The heroine of this novel, Isabel Archer, arrives in Europe and is strongly impressed by the culture and the traditions of England and Italy. Her love of independence and her unconventional behaviour assures her the attention and admiration of her European friends. Isabel marries a Europeanized American, but is disappointed to find out that her husband is merely interested in her money.

As in many of James's novels, the plot is not as important as the psychological art with which the author explores emotions and feelings. The "story" unfolds in the actions and reactions of the hero and heroine as reflected in his and her consciousness. The author is not, like Fielding, the one who knows and controls all, but merely shows the reader a consciousness, as in *What Maisie Knew* (1897), or several consciousnesses, as in such later works as *The Ambassadors* (1902). James's technique allows him to reveal ideas and emotions as well as the reflection of other characters' thoughts and actions. He thus prepared the ground for the psychological novel and the stream-of-consciousness technique.

Henry James put his impressionistic method to masterful use in his later works: *The Wings of the Dove* (1902) and *The Golden Bowl* (1904). The latter is a good example of James's special kind of fiction in which content is often less important than form and art. It analyses life in the morally corrupt world of four people, symbolized by a golden bowl with an invisible crack. The hidden crack refers to the "false art" of the characters who, for the sake of maintaining the illusion of happiness and trust in each other, are willing to ignore adultery. Instead of traditional narrative techniques, James used allusions and reflections of various consciousnesses. Brief impressions eventually establish in the reader's mind a picture of what is going on.

James was also a prolific and gifted short story writer. In addition to some 100 stories, he wrote 20 novels, numerous critical essays, reviews, and portraits of writers and artists.

Realism dominated the closing decades of the century. But some writers, such as Lew Wallace, preferred established traditional or escapist modes of fiction. **Edward**

Bellamy's (1850-98) utopian *Looking Backward* (1880) suggested state capitalism and serious social reforms. The American myth of success through hard work and frugality of the Benjamin Franklin type was kept up by numerous best-selling novels for adolescents from the pen of **Horatio Alger** (1834-1899), such as *Ragged Dick* (1867), *Luck and Pluck* (1869), and *Tattered Tom* (1871). Finally, the cowboy novel arose from frontier literature, a sentimental late romantic genre celebrating lonesome heroes who avoid women and prefer to fight for law and order. The best-known writer in this field was **Owen Wister** (1860-1938). He had studied at Harvard and often went hunting in Wyoming. Wister's melodramatic *The Virginian: A Horseman of the Plains* (1902) became the prototype for a wave of cowboy novels in the twentieth century. One of the most prolific authors of this genre was the former dentist **Zane Grey** (1875-1939; see, for instance, *Riders of the Purple Sage,* 1912).

4.2 The Short Story

As a new form of fiction, the American short story was shaped by magazines, almanacs and literary periodicals. An important step forward was made by **Washington Irving** (1783-1859) in his literary sketches, essays, and tales published in *The Sketch Book of Geoffrey Crayon, Gent.* (1819/20). An admirer of the European Romantics and of the English essayists (Addison), Irving spent many years in Europe. *The Sketch Book* made him famous. The picture of Europe that emerges from the sketches in this collection is coloured by sentiment, but Irving was a good humorist and successfully melded European myths and American settings in such ever popular stories as "Rip Van Winkle" and "The Legend of Sleepy Hollow". In "Rip Van Winkle" a Dutch-American falls asleep in the woods as a subject of King George III and awakes 20 years later as an American citizen in a new republic.

What Irving began in theme and character, Poe completed in form and theory. **Edgar Allan Poe** initiated the tale of horror and the detective story. In 1848, while writing a critical evaluation of Hawthorne's tales, Poe developed his own theory of the short story. The principal points in this theory are brevity and unity of effect. Poe wrote more than 70 stories, many of them collected in *Tales of the Grotesque and Arabesque* (1840) and *Tales* (1845). Roughly, they fall into two categories: those of "Gothic horror" set in a nightmare world of evil and death (see, for instance, "Ligeia", "The Fall of the House of Usher", "The Pit and the Pendulum" and "The Imp of the Perverse"), and those of "ratiocination", which set the standards for the modern detective story (see "The Murders in the Rue Morgue", "The Mystery of Marie Rogêt", and "The Purloined Letter"). Poe's horror stories are symbolical and often have several levels of meaning. Landscapes, rooms and characters contain "an undercurrent of meaning" that leads into the border area of consciousness, hallucination, and insanity.

While Poe treated of fear and horror in his short fiction, **Hawthorne** showed the corrupting force of guilt and pride in his *Twice-Told Tales* (1837), *Mosses from* an *Old Manse* (1846), and *The Snow Image* (1851). Thus "Young Goodman Brown" deals with temptation and the loss of faith in Puritan Salem, Massachusetts. In "Endicott and the Red Cross" Hawthorne wrote of the American fight for independence, and in "The May-Pole of Merry Mount", a symbolical tale of sensual pleasure and Puritan ascetism, he found a more humorous tone.

Herman Melville, like Hawthorne, considered evil as a powerful force in human life. His stories are collected in *The Piazza Tales* (1856) and present his themes in a concentrated form. Most important are "Benito Cereno", the ambiguous story of a mutiny of slaves on a ship bound for America, "Bartleby the Scrivener", which deals with self-isolation in a Kafka-like[1] manner, and "The Encantadas", sketches of the Galapagos Islands and some people living there. "Billy Budd", a longer story, was published in 1924. It is about a young and innocent sailor who kills an evil companion and is sentenced to death. The judge, the ship's captain, is haunted by the question whether Billy was really guilty.

The "local colour movement" developed a kind of short story containing both romantic and grotesque as well as humorous elements in colourful frontier settings peopled with such low-life characters as gold-diggers, whores, and thieves. Apart from **Mark Twain's** humorous and burlesque tales, anecdotes, and sketches of the West, collected in *The Celebrated Jumping Frog of Calaveras County* (1867), the stories of **Bret Harte** (1836-1902) proved of great influence. Between 1854-1871 Harte worked as a journalist in California and acquired literary fame with his stories about the wild and romantic life in the West. In such stories as "The Outcasts of Poker Flat", "Tennessee's Partner", and "Brown of Calaveras", collected in *The Luck of Roaring Camp* (1870) and *Tales of the Argonauts* (1875) – his later work is less successful – he provides realistic and humorous impressions of wild scenery and rough people with hearts of gold. Harte tried to preserve Poe's economy in words and style, but his romantic view of the frontier often came close to sentimentality.

One of Bret Harte's early imitators was **Ambrose Bierce** (1842-1914). In the tradition of Poe, Bierce created the sensational type of the short story that grips its reader and has a surprising or shocking ending. Ambrose Bierce was the son of an Ohio farmer and had to educate himself. Many of his better stories – *Tales of Soldiers and Civilians* (1891; revised and published in 1898 as *The Midst of Life*), *Can Such Things Be?* (1893) – are concerned with death and the horrors of the Civil War, in which Bierce had served as a soldier. His much anthologized "An Occurrence at Owl Creek Bridge" (1891) exemplifies his technique of suspense and shock in the story of a Confederate soldier and saboteur sentenced to death by hanging by the Union army. In the brief moments between life and death, as his body

---

1. Franz Kafka (1883-1924), German-speaking Jewish novelist and a very influential writer among the modernists. Kafka is the author of three novels (*Der Prozeß*, 1925, *Das Schloß*, 1926, and *Amerika*, 1927) and numerous short stories (e. g. "Die Verwandlung", 1915, and "Das Urteil", 1913). Kafka describes lonely and threatened individuals in an enigmatic world. The term "Kafkaesque" is used to describe literature that employs similar narrative techniques and creates the same uneasy response as Kafka's fiction.

drops down on the rope and strangles him, the condemned man creates for himself (and for the reader) the illusion of an escape and a reunion with his family. In such stories as "A Horseman in the Sky" and "Chicamauga", Bierce dealt with the terror of the Civil War in a way that recalls Poe's "Gothic" and has the additional attraction of psychological analysis, although Bierce's love of the sensational was apt to lead him into melodrama.

The surprise ending remained very popular among writers and readers. The realists made use of it - **Stephen Crane** in his Western stories "The Blue Hotel" and "The Bride Comes to Yellow Sky" - as did Hemingway in the twentieth century. Crane's "The Open Boat", contained in the collection of the same name published in 1898, again varied the short story. Stressing fact and true experience, Crane attempted a kind of factual fiction that creates the impression of journalistic precision in the "report" about the thoughts and emotions of four men escaping in a small dinghy after the sinking of a steamer. Only three of the men survive, while the one who helped most to save them drowns in the waves. Crane's sober diction and his exploration of archetypal situations clearly foreshadows Hemingway.

Henry James's psychological realism has also had a number of modern successors. Many of his stories assess the conflict between moral issues and social conventions (e. g. "The Beast in the Jungle", and "The Real Thing"). In *The Turn of the Screw* (1898) he probed the nature of evil in the framework of a ghost story reminiscent of Poe.

Many writers of this period had no literary aims and simply wanted to entertain the public. To these belongs **Joel Chandler Harris** (1848-1908), a Georgian whose knowledge of Black folklore formed the basis of his stories about "Uncle Remus", a Black slave who tells the legends and fairy tales of his people to the young son of his white family (*Uncle Remus*, 1881, and *Nights With Uncle Remus*, 1883).

Beginning with Poe, the short story also found a number of theorists: Hawthorne, Melville, Crane and Henry James all wrote about what a short story should be. Some of the theorists were university professors and critics. Thus **Brander Matthews** (1852-1929) prescribed a catalogue of "necessary elements". But fortunately the writers did not care about such traditionalists and purists, and the result has been the richness, both in form and content, of the short story in the twentieth century.

5. Nonfiction

Several nineteenth-century writers of fiction also produced historical works. Washington Irving's biography of George Washington is one example. The historians proper included the New Englanders, **W. H. Prescott** (1796-1859), **John L. Motley** (1814-77), and **Francis Parkman** (1823-93). They all wrote outstanding histories of European countries, while Parkman was the only one with a deep interest in the American colonial period and the West. The early national period was treated by **George Bancroft** (1800–91) and by **Henry Adams** (1838–1918), the century's most prominent historian. Adams studied at Göttingen and Harvard, where he taught history for a few years before travelling the world. He returned to America only a few times. Adams wrote a brilliant *History of the United States* in nine volumes (1884–89), covering the period from Jefferson to Madison, and analysed the cultural unity of the Middle Ages in *Mont Saint-Michel and Chartres* (1904). In his autobiographical and critical view of American history, *The Education of Henry Adams* (1907), he deplored the emptiness and the superficiality of modern cultures when compared with those of the Middle Ages.

The essay and literary criticism profited from the rise of Transcendentalism. Directed against religious orthodoxy as well as against materialism and pragmatism, Transcendentalism achieved intellectual and spiritual independence for America after the country had gained political independence. It was mainly represented by **Ralph Waldo Emerson** and **Henry David Thoreau,** who formed a "symposium" or "Hedge Club" in 1836 that included **W. E. Channing, Thomas Parker, Margaret Fuller, Hawthorne,** and a few others. Transcendentalism as a term is derived from Kant's use of it in his *Critique of Pure Reason.* Apart from Kant, Coleridge and German idealistic philosophy (Fichte and Schleiermacher) proved important for the movement. In essence, Transcendentalism combined German idealism with the Puritan American heritage. It held that each individual soul is identical with the soul of the world, that God is present in man, and that man is the source of moral law. Underlining the value of the individual and of self-reliance, the Transcendentalists argued that God could be seen intuitively in nature. The idealist spirit of the members expressed itself in a series of practical economical enterprises, the best known being Brook Farm, near Boston, which Hawthorne covered in his *The Blithedale Romance* (1852).

Ralph Waldo Emerson (1803–82) was the leader of the Transcendentalist Club. He came from Concord, Mass., went to Harvard, and became a clergyman and professor, but later resigned from the ministry. While on a visit to Europe, he became friendly with Coleridge, Wordsworth and Carlyle. Emerson expressed his philosophy in a number of lectures that make up his books *Essays* (1841), *Nature, Addresses, and Lectures* (1849) and *The Conduct of Life* (1860). His famous Harvard address of 1837, "The American Scholar", has been called the intellectual American declaration of independence. Emerson laid the foundation for the Transcendentalist movement with "Nature" (1836) and "The Over-Soul" (1841), works that make man the centre of philosophical speculation and argue that the soul of man and God

Ralph Waldo Emerson

meet in nature. These works and his *Representative Men* (1850) show that Emerson was best as an essayist. They contain his moral and philosophical views and demonstrate his belief that history reflects God's grace.

Henry David Thoreau (1817-62) also studied at Harvard. He lived for a few years in Emerson's house and published essays for *The Dial* (1840-44), one of the journals of the Transcendentalists. Thoreau put Emerson's ideas into practice and rebelled against bourgeois-capitalist values, demanding the unimpeded development of the individual. In a hut near Walden Pond, between 1845-47, he led an introspective life in utmost simplicity. *Walden, or Life in the Woods* (1854) was the delightful literary record of this experiment. It describes beautiful natural scenes and reflects on the advantages of a solitary life. Thoreau was both an idealist influenced by Rousseau and a social reformer. Once jailed for refusing to pay taxes, he advised his readers to disobey bad laws in his essay "On the Duty of Civil Disobedience" (1849). Also based on his journal records is his marvellous description of *A Week on the Concord and Merrimack Rivers* (1849). Like *Walden,* this is mostly concerned with nature and philosophical observations.

Oliver Wendell Holmes (1809-94) and **James Russell Lowell** (1819-91) were two New England essayists who are also known for their literary criticism. Holmes contributed satirical essays to *Atlantic Monthly.* These were later collected in several volumes, the most interesting being *The Autocrat of the Breakfast-Table* (1858) and *The Poet at the Breakfast-Table* (1872). Lowell was the most eminent critic among the Transcendentalists. His essays give evidence of his excellent knowledge of the classics and of a sound taste in the field of literature.

Travel literature was written by **Washington Irving** (1783-1859), who described his adventurous journey to the Western frontier in *A Tour on the Prairies* (1835), and by **Bayard Taylor** (1825-78), **George William Curtis** (1824-92) and **Charles Warren Stoddard** (1843-1909). **John James Audubon** (1785-1851) published his pictures of wildlife in *The Birds of America* (1827-38). The best known example from social criticism is **Henry George's** (1839-97) *Progress and Poverty.* One of the most fascinating autobiographies of the century, and an early example of black literature, is the *Narrative of the Life of Frederick Douglass* (1845, revised in 1892) in which the former slave and later politican **Douglass** (1817-95) tells about his escape from Maryland to Massachusetts and about his liberation through education. Although this remained his most famous book, Douglass wrote two further autobiographies, *My Bondage and My Freedom* (1855), and *Life and Times of Frederick Douglass* (1881).

An important work in the field of lexicography was **Noah Webster's** (1758-1843) *American Dictionary of the English Language.* It was first published in 1828, and included a large number of Americanisms not before listed in dictionaries.

IV. The Twentieth Century

1. General Background

Within a few decades after the turn of the century, the United States became the strongest military and economic power in the world. Although there were some social reforms under the presidencies of the Republican Theodore Roosevelt (1901-09) and the Democrat Woodrow Wilson (1913-21), big business and capitalism triumphed again under the Republican presidents Warren G. Harding (1921-23) and Calvin Coolidge (1923-29), not least because behaviourism and John Dewey's philosophical pragmatism created a favourable cultural climate for industrial expansion. American democratic and moral idealism, which was still high when the US declared war against Germany and Austria-Hungary in 1917, gave way to a new isolationism in the 1920s.

As many disillusioned American writers went abroad, the great American economic dream came to a sudden halt with the collapse of the stock market in 1929 which announced a worldwide economic crisis. The years of the prohibition of the sale of alcoholic beverages (1920-1933) were a profitable time for bootleggers[1] and gangsters: Al Capone made headlines and money in Chicago. In 1932 unemployment was at 23 percent. The crisis brought the Democratic Party back to power, and Franklin D. Roosevelt's (1933-45) radical "New Deal"[2] initiated social reforms and a number of laws and programmes in order to fight the depression.

When, after the bombing of Pearl Harbor in 1941, the USA entered WW II, the country's population had risen from 62 million in 1890 to almost 140 million inhabitants. Again, America fought for a good cause and, in saving Western democratic and humanitarian ideals, proved the superiority of American optimism and values. With the end of the war came an economic boom, but also America's involvement and leading position in international politics. After the Korean War (1950-53) and the inauguration in 1953 of President Dwight D. Eisenhower (1953-61), the USA faced internal political and racial problems. The atmosphere of the "Cold War" led to a hunt for Marxists and Communists in America, and between 1953 and 1955 this hunt was orchestrated by Senator Joseph McCarthy. When the Supreme Court ordered the end of racial segregation in public schools in 1954, there began a rapid spread of black protest against continued discrimination in the South. In 1955 Rosa Parks of Montgomery, Alabama, made history by refusing to give up her seat on a bus to a white man. As school integration was being enforced, disturbances occurred at Little Rock, Arkansas. Black protest ranged from

---

1. Slang term for the persons who distribute liquor illegally.
2. President Roosevelt's administrative program, started in the early 1930s, to correct economic and social abuses. The New Deal brought some advantages for workers in the area of social security, and for other socially disadvantaged groups. But in 1937 another recession dealt it a heavy blow.

non-violent demonstrations, often led by the Reverend Martin Luther King (one of the leaders of the Civil Rights March on Washington in 1963, where he gave his famous, "I have a dream" speech), to the extremist Black Muslim movement that rose as the country witnessed widespread race riots in the big cities between 1965 and 67.

The 1960s were overshadowed by a number of assassinations. Malcolm X, a leader of the Black Muslims, was shot dead in 1965, two years after President John F. Kennedy had died at Dallas, Texas, in an assassination that remains mysterious. His brother, Robert Kennedy, and Martin Luther King were both killed in 1968.

International political problems arose with American involvement in Vietnam (1964-1975), which divided the nation, and a domestic political crisis with the Watergate affair (1972-74), which forced President Nixon (1968-74) to resign from office – the first American President to do so. He was succeeded by Gerald Ford (1974-77), Jimmy Carter (1977-81), and Ronald Reagan (1981-1989), who survived an attempt to assassinate him in 1981.

The American Indians organized themselves in the AIM (American Indian Movement) and went to court claiming damages from the US government for the land and rights they had ceded in the past. In 1979 the Sioux Indians were awarded $ 17,000,000 plus $ 105,000,000 interest as compensation for the Black Hills of South Dakota that had been confiscated in 1877. In 1985 a similar decision gave some compensation to the Narragansett Indians. Ironically, some of the barren territory allotted to the Indians by the US government has proved extremely rich in mineral resources.

American confidence seemed bright and promising after President Kennedy's successful handling of the Cuban missile crisis (1961-63), the first US manned space expedition in 1961, and the moon landing in 1968. But this confidence waned rapidly with the revelations about the Vietnam War, the shameful retreat in 1975, and the Iran hostage crisis (1980-81). In the 1980s, as America faced international resistance against her economic and political influence, a new and defiant patriotism arose. It began with the Bicentennial in 1976, swept Ronald Reagan to power, and found a first peak in the Olympic Games of 1984.

As far as the intellectual background is concerned, a few influential books and movements need to be mentioned. Senator McCarthy's witch hunt for alleged Communists in the early 1950s prevented an open and fundamental criticism of American society. Socialism became associated with Soviet Russia and liberation movements in the Third World came to be regarded as as "international Communism". Although this atmosphere changed in the 1960s, large sections of American society still consider Socialism as either subversive or "un-American". Important books – which often created "schools" – include **David Riesman's** sociological analysis of the isolated and conformist American in *The Lonely Crowd* (1950), **C. Wright Mills's** study of the irresponsible and selfish elites in *The Power Elite* (1956), **B. F. Skinner's** behaviorist assertion that happiness and freedom can be conditioned in *Walden Two* (1948) and *Beyond Freedom and Dignity* (1971), and the books that started the "sex revolution", such as those of Sigmund Freud and the German exiles Wilhelm Reich, Erich Fromm, and Herbert Marcuse, and the analyses of sexual behavior made by Alfred Kinsey (1948, 1953) and Masters/ Johnson (1966).

There is a strong fundamentalist religious current in America that can be traced all the way back to the Pilgrims and the Puritans. In the 1970s and 1980s, fundamentalist religious movements have thrived. Billy Graham and Jerry Falwell are two internationally known fundamentalist preachers with a large following. Numerous rich churches exist in America, and many people, including some unscrupulous businessmen, have earned millions of dollars with religion. Worse than the financial exploitation of religious enthusiasm is the dangerous fanaticism of sectarians like the notorious Reverend Jones, who took his people to South America and arranged a mass murder in the jungle. But such catastrophes and the less dramatic expulsion in 1985 of the "Baghwan" from Oregon will hardly stop American religious fervour.

2. Poetry

In 1912 a number of poetry anthologies and magazines appeared of which Harriet Monroe's *Poetry: A Magazine of Verse,* published in Chicago, proved the most influential over the next decades. Monroe's journal opened its pages to the Imagists, printed the works of the pre-modernists Whitman, Dickinson and Hopkins, and became the major voice of the "Chicago school" represented by Sandburg, Lindsay, and Masters.

Imagism owes its name to **Ezra Pound.** As a poetic movement it flourished between 1909 and 1917 and was international. In England, it included T. E. Hulme, F. S. Flint, Richard Aldington, and D. H. Lawrence; in America the Imagists were represented by **"H. D."** (i.e. **Hilda Doolittle,** 1886-1961), **John Gould Fletcher** (1886-1950), and **Amy Lowell** (1874-1925). Opposed to the romantic conception of poetry and inspired by Greek and Roman classics as well as by Chinese, Japanese and French poets, the Imagists looked for new forms of expression that were to include common speech and new rhythms instead of poetic language and traditional metre. Free verse and concise metaphors and images became the favourite forms and modes of expression. Ezra Pound defined "image" as "that which presents an intellectual and emotional complex in an instant of time."

Most of the American Imagists either became permanent expatriates or lived abroad for long periods of time. Like Pound and "H. D.", **Amy Lowell** spent many years in Europe and founded an eccentric literary circle in London. After Pound's interest in Imagism waned in 1914, Lowell became the leader of the American group. In 1915 she published the anthology *Some Imagist Poets.* Her poetry as well as that of her expatriate friend John Gould Fletcher is surpassed by the evocative verse of **"H. D.",** who moved to Europe in 1911. For some years she was married to Richard Aldington and, under the influence of Pound and **Gertrude Stein,** became one of the most ardent representatives of Imagism. Her *Hymen* (1921) and *Helioctera* (1924) indicate the influence of Greek poetic topics and forms and are among the best of Imagist poetry. The early verse of **Conrad Aiken** (1889-1974) and **William Carlos Williams** is also indebted to Imagism. Aiken's *Nocturne of Remembered Spring* (1917) shows his play with sound and musical language. He later came under the influence of Freudian psychology, which is most obvious in his *Selected Poems* of 1961. Although Gertrude Stein is better known for her prose, many of her love poems and other verse were written in the Imagist tradition.

However, of all the expatriates who wrote Imagist poetry, **Ezra Pound** (1885-1972) is the outstanding figure. He is one of the most influential poets of the early modern period. Pound was born in a provincial town in Idaho and grew up in Pennsylvania. Disappointed with American life and culture, he soon went to Europe and took a deep interest in the old literatures of the Provence and of Italy. Pound lived in Italy and, from 1909-1920, in London, working as translator, literary critic, poet and editor of journals. He discovered and promoted such writers as T. S. Eliot, James Joyce, Hart Crane and Ernest Hemingway while living in Paris (1920-24) and again in Italy (1940-45). Opposed to capitalism and Jews, he supported the Fascist movement and saw in Mussolini a follower of Thomas Jefferson. Because of his pro-Fascist and anti-American radio broadcasts during the war, he was arrested and charged with treason in 1945. Until 1958 he was in a mental institution in America and then returned to live in Italy.

For his own verse Pound used the poetic forms and ideas of a number of predecessors. His poetry ranges from the early collection *Personae* (1909), in which he used voices and masks in the style of Browning and Pre-Raphaelite lyrics, to the free poetic adaptation *Umbra* (1920), the superb autobiographical satire in verse, *Hugh Selwyn Mauberley* (1920), and his life's work, *The Cantos.* "The Bathtub" (1913) is an ironic Imagist poem imitating the Japanese "haiku" form.

> As a bathtub lined with white porcelain,
> When the hot water gives out or goes tepid,
> So is the slow cooling of our chivalrous passion,
> O my much praised but-not-altogether – satisfactory lady.

With *Hugh Selwyn Mauberley* Pound made a severe attack on what he considered the corrupt culture of his time and of England in particular. The anti-hero and mediocre poet Mauberley, Pound's persona, is thus introduced in the first stanza:

> For three years, out of key with his time,
> He strove to resuscitate the dead art
> Of poetry; to maintain "the sublime"
> In the old sense. Wrong from the start –
> No, hardly, but seeing he had been born
> In a half savage country, out of date;
> Bent resolutely on wringing lilies from the acorn; ...

This is already a rather demanding poem that explores the tensions between art and life, between aestheticism and the catastrophe of World War I, while alluding to such predecessors as Browning, Ronsard[1] and Greek poets in a style marked by ellipsis, literary quotations, ironically used clichés, and the contrast between the great historic past and the superficial present. Pound began with the writing of the *Cantos* as early as 1917, and this work kept him busy until his death. In concept this huge series of poems is similar to Whitman's *Leaves of Grass* and Joyce's *Finnegan's Wake,* presenting a synopsis of human history as well as a diagnosis of modern civilization in a highly ambiguous verse that is characterized by numerous allusions to the cultural history of the East and West. The unifying centre of this "long poem", which refers to Dante[2], Homer[3] and twentieth-century politics with equal ease, is the "stream of poetic consciousness". Pound contrasts the corruption of Western civilization with the order and harmony of Chinese philosophy and the "universal man" of the Renaissance. Foremost among the corruptions and, in Pound's view, a source of many modern evils, is "usura" or "usury" (i.e. lending money at high interest).

> With usura hath no man a house of good stone
> each block cut smooth and well fitting
> that design might cover their face,
> with usura
> [...]
> with usura, sin against nature,
> is thy bread ever more of stale rags
> is thy bread dry as paper,
> with no mountain wheat, no strong flour

What Pound attempted with *The Cantos* is a poetic vision of the cultural history of the Orient and Occident in a sort of "guided tour" through the history of world literature that includes unresolved philosophical and political problems, formal experiments and parody. Ezra Pound did not achieve a final and complete poetic form, but *The Cantos* continue to impress readers with their numerous masterful lyrical passages, such as the moving sequence of the *Pisan Cantos* (Nos. 74-84), written after his internment in Italy, and such outstanding sections as Nos. 1. 2, 13, 17, as well as his treatment of America in "Jefferson. Nuevo Mundo".

In 1913 the New York Armory Show introduced the American public to mod-

---

1. Pierre de Ronsard (1524-85), French poet and leader of a group of writers who popularized the sonnet and Italian verse in France. His love poetry exercised considerable influence on the English poets of the 16th century.
2. Dante Alighieri (1265-1321), influential Italian poet and writer. He celebrated his love for a girl called Beatrice in his *Vita nuova* and in his masterpiece, the *Divina Commedia,* a long poem he finished just before his death and which comprises the *Inferno,* the *Purgatorio,* and the *Paradiso.* The whole poem is a work of moral edification, full of symbolism and allusions to philosophy, natural science, and history. Dante has influenced English and American writers from Chaucer to T. S. Eliot, and also inspired many artists, such as Salvador Dali.
3. The supposed author of two influential early Greek epics, *The Iliad* and *The Odyssey*, which have inspired writers in the West from the 14th century on. Nothing reliable is known about Homer who may have lived in the eighth century B. C.

ernist European painters and cubism[1]. It caused an uproar. At the same time American poets began to express themselves in new modes. **Vachel Lindsay's** (1879-1931) *General William Booth Enters into Heaven* (1913) combined elements of folk music and musical instruments with poetic language in verses that were meant to be recited before, and shared with, an audience. Accompanied by Salvation Army music and often presented to literary circles by the poet himself, this "apocalyptic" rhythmic poem was followed by *The Congo: A Study of the Negro Race* (1914) which makes use of jazz rhythms and verbal imitations of sound. This work was more successful than Lindsay's later attempts to create an "American hieroglyphic poetry".

Like Lindsay, **Edgar Lee Masters** (1868-1950) came from Illinois. He later worked in Chicago and New York. In his *Spoon River Anthology* of 1915 he exposed in free verse the hypocrisy and the lies of provincial life in a small Illinois town. Held in the form of poetic and confessional self-portraits of characters from a small town, Masters's roughly 250 epitaphs attempt in verse what Sherwood Anderson tried in *Winesburg Ohio* and Sinclair Lewis in *Main Street.*

"Doc Hill" is a typical example. In this poem a former doctor confesses to a wasted life, a ruined marriage, and a secret lover.

> Doc Hill
>
> I went up and down the streets
> Here and there by day and night,
> Through all hours of the night caring for the poor who were sick.
> Do you know why?
> My wife hated me, my son went to the dogs.
> And I turned to the poeple and poured out my love to them.
> Sweet it was to see the crowds about the lawns on the day of my funeral.
> And hear them murmur their love and sorrow.
> But oh, dear God, my soul trembled, scarcely able
> To hold to the railing of the new life
> When I saw Em Stanton behind the oak tree
> At the grave,
> Hiding herself, and her grief!

Free verse was also the favourite poetic form of **Carl Sandburg** (1878-1967) who held many jobs and was a dedicated socialist in Illinois. Sandburg was initially influenced by Imagism (see his poem "Fog"), but his later work reflects his democratic patriotism as well as his love of folklore (*The American Songbag,* 1927) and nature in the Whitman tradition. He described the wild and crude modern city in *Chicago Poems* (1916) and the man-consuming industrial age in *Smoke and Steel* (1920). His personal and political interest in the socially disadvantaged – the old, the poor, and the misfits – is most obvious in the panoramic verses of *The People, Yes*

---

1. An early modernist movement in art, developed by Pablo Picasso and Georges Braque (1882-1963), in which forms are broken down into simple geometric shapes that present several views of a single object. The first Cubist pictures were shown in 1907.

Brooklyn Bridge
from a lithograph
by Currier & Ives

(1936), a poetic description, including folklore and stories, of America, of her spirit and the future of her people.

Another "national epic" of America was published by **Hart Crane** (1899-1932) in 1930, the long poem *The Bridge*. Crane came from Ohio and began to write poetry under the influence of Pound and Eliot and the French symbolists, which is most obvious in his early *The White Buildings*. The changing metres of *The Bridge* try to capture American history from Columbus to Pocahontas and Rip Van Winkle, and from Whitman to the new technical achievement, Brooklyn Bridge, which became a symbol of modern American life.

New England had two early poets in **Edward Arlington Robinson** (1869-1935) and in the outstanding **Robert Frost**. A native of Maine, **Robinson** led a life of poverty until he was discovered and promoted by President Roosevelt in 1902. Robinson was a master of traditional forms, such as the ballad, the sonnet, and blank verse, and later received three Pulitzer Prizes. *The Man Against the Sky* (1916) is among his best works, a sort of modern credo professing an agnostic-stoical view of life. Robinson's *Merlin* (1917), *Lancelot* (1920) and *Tristram* (1927) are dramatic verse epics retelling the legend of King Arthur for the twentieth-century reader while his later poetry, such as *King Jasper* (1935), displays a complex symbolism and an awareness of man's tragic situation in a world suffering from social and moral dilemmas.

Robert Lee Frost (1875-1963) became the singer of New England's charms, but he was much more than a "regional poet". He was born in California but made New Hampshire his home after spending some time in various jobs and in England. Between 1916 and 1938 he taught English literature at Amherst College and won the Pulitzer Prize on four occasions. Frost's popularity arose from the fact that he welded traditional verse forms with distinctly American speech and rhythms. "Desert Places", written in 1936, puts him in the bucolic tradition of nature poetry but also indicates the metaphysical dimensions of his poems that show New England's beauty while exploring loneliness, old age and death.

227

Desert Places

Snow falling and night falling fast, oh, fast
In a field I looked into going past,
And the ground almost covered smooth in snow,
But a few weeds and stubble showing last.

The woods arround it have it – it is theirs.
All animals are smothered in their lairs.
I am too absent-spirited to count;
The loneliness includes me unawares.

And lonely as it is that loneliness
Will be more lonely ere it will be less –
A blanker whiteness of benighted snow
With no expression, nothing to express.

They cannot scare me with their empty spaces
Between stars – on stars where no human race is.
I have it in me so much nearer home
To scare myself with my own desert places.

A Further Range (1936), *A Witness Tree* (1942), and *In the Clearing* (1962) all contain attractive lyrical-metaphysical verse showing Frost's indebtedness to the Transcendentalists and to Emily Dickinson. His seemingly simple verse is based on exact observation and thoughtful interpretation in consciously traditional forms carrying a personal vision.

The South found a number of poets and literary critics who published their verse in *The Fugitive* (1922-25) and who were among the first proponents of what came to be known as New Criticism (see p. 289). Opposed to industrialization, the major members of the group – **John Crowe Ransom** (1888-1974), **Allen Tate** (1899-1979), and **Robert Penn Warren** (born 1905) – met in Nashville, Tennessee, and recalled the literary and historical past of the South in a poetry that favours polished classical forms. **Ransom** was one of their leaders. An outstanding literary critic (see his *The New Criticism,* 1941) and the founder of the distinguished journal *The Kenyon Review,* he treated with much irony of mortality, imagination, reality, passion and morality in such collections as *Chills and Fever* (1924) and *Two Gentlemen in Bonds* (1927), contrasting the glorious Southern cultural heritage with the boring present. **Allen Tate** popularized T. S. Eliot in the South and, as editor of *The Sewanee Review,* made this journal internationally known. His poetry lacks the melody and rhythm of Ransom's verse and has a more intellectual bent. One of his best known works is the "Ode to the Confederate Dead" (1926), which analyses the emotional distance of the modern Southerner from his own past. The still active and versatile **Robert Penn Warren** is an internationally recognized man of letters best known for his influential textbooks of practical criticism, his literary essays and his novels. Like Tate, he began with an intellectual and allusive poetry in the manner of the metaphysical poets, such as

Eleven Poems on the Same Theme (1942). After 1940 he took to a more philosophical exploration of cultural and historical problems, his outstanding work being the long narrative poem *Brother to Dragons* (1953; revised in 1979) which deals with the murder of a black slave by Thomas Jefferson's nephews and reflects Warren's growing concern with the problem of evil. This theme has occupied him in his more recent poetry, *Being Here* (1980) and *Rumor Verified* (1981). Finally, **Stephen Vincent Benét** (1898-1943), although not a Southerner, dealt with the Civil War in his epic verse narrative *John Brown's Body*, which was published in 1928 and was awarded a Pulitzer Prize.

If the major poets from the Midwest, New England and the South were traditional formalists in many respects, Ezra Pound's enormous influence is more strongly felt in the experimental verse of the expatriate T. S. Eliot's *The Waste Land* and in that of Eliot's contemporaries in America: Wallace Stevens, Robinson Jeffers, William Carlos Williams, e. e. cummings, Marianne Moore, Archibald MacLeish, Edna St. Vincent Millay, and Elinor Wylie. **Wallace Stevens** (1879-1955) was a great individualist and did not become known as a poet before his first collection, *Harmonium,* appeared in 1923 (expanded version in 1931), although Harriet Moore had published some of his verse as early as 1915. Stevens studied at Harvard and the New York University Law School and worked for an insurance company. His early poetry stood under the French symbolist influence and the "poésie pure" which stressed precise expression and musical language. Stevens's view of the imagination as "the one reality in the imagined world" is well rendered in his "Anecdote of the Jar".

> I placed a jar in Tennessee,
> And round it was, upon a hill.
> It made the slovenly wilderness
> Surround that hill.
> The wilderness rose up to it,
> And sprawled around, no longer wild.
> The jar was round upon the ground
> And tall and of a port in air.
> It took dominion everywhere.
> The jar was gray and bare.
> It did not give of bird or bush,
> Like nothing else in Tennessee.

For Stevens fantasy dominates the chaos of reality, and he demonstrated his personal view in such collections as *The Man With the Blue Guitar* (1937), whose title alludes to Picasso, *The Auroras of Autumn* (1950), and his *Collected Poems* (1954). Stevens tried to explain his idea of poetry in a collection of essays entitled *The Necessary Angels* (1951).

Robinson Jeffers (1887-1962) did not share Stevens's aesthetic preference for sophisticated verse and ambiguous metaphor. He spent his childhood in Europe and later settled at Carmel in California where he lived a life of seclusion. Inspired by the books of Spengler, Nietzsche, Freud and Jung[7], he developed a pessimistic view of man and life. In his short lyrics he provided beautiful impressions of the California coast and the wild animals he loved (see *Tamar,* 1924). His nihilism preferred wild nature to humanity: in "November Surf" (1929) he looked forward to a future when nature can again assert itself:

> Some lucky day each November great waves awake and are drawn
> Like smoking mountains bright from the west
> And come and cover the cliff with white violent cleanness: then suddenly
> The old granite forgets half a year's filth:
> The orange-peel, eggshells, papers, pieces of clothing, the clots
> Of dung in corners of the rock, and used
> Sheaths that make light love safe in the evenings: all the droppings of the summer
> Idlers washed off in a winter ecstasy:
> I think this cumbered continent envies its cliff then ... But all seasons
> The earth, in her childlike prophetic sleep,
> Keeps dreaming of the bath of a storm that prepares up the long coast
> Of the future to scour more than her sea-lines:
> The cities gone down, the people fewer and the hawks more numerous
> The rivers mouth to source pure; when the two-footed
> Mammal, being someways one of the nobler animals, regains
> The dignity of room, the value of rareness.

The free rhythms of Jeffers's verse tales are reminiscent of Whitman in form, though not in spirit, for Jeffers tells stories of murder, incest, and sexual perversion, in which the characters have symbolic value and refer to classical myths, as in *Roan Stallion* (1925), *The Woman at Point Sur* (1927), and *Give Your Heart to the Hawks, and Other Poems* (1933). His negative outlook is balanced by the ecstatic beauty of his descriptions of California in which are set his metaphorical tales of perversion that make use of Greco-Roman, Biblical and Indian mythologies. Jeffers's poetic version of *Medea* (1946) became a great theatrical success.

A much less dramatic and sensational poetry is that of **William Carlos Williams** (1883-1963), a doctor by profession who spent his life in Rutherford, New Jersey. Although he learnt much from Pound and Eliot in style, he did not turn to

---

1. Oswald Spengler (1880-1936), historical philosopher and author of *Der Untergang des Abendlandes* (1918-22), a history of Western culture and philosophy that was written under the influence of Nietzsche and Darwin.
Friedrich Wilhelm Nietzsche (1844-1900), German philosopher and poet. N. rejected Christian morality and affirmed the idea of the Superman (his main works are *Also sprach Zarathustra,* 1883-92; and the posthumously published *Der Wille zur Macht*).
Sigmund Freud (1856-1939), the founder of psychoanalysis, which has had an enormous effect on both literature and literary theory. Freud practised for many years in Vienna, before he was driven out, as a Jew, by the Nazis. He died in London. He made fundamental discoveries in the development of the sexual instinct in children, in the workings of the unconscious and of repression, and in the study of dreams.
Jung: See page 171, note 1.

the European cultural heritage for his themes. Williams was a poet interested in American speech and everyday life. The sober and precise wording of his early Imagist and impressionistic poems (*The Tempers,* 1913, and *Sour Grapes,* 1921) avoid both poetic diction and metaphysical statements and present details of urban scenes. "The Young Housewife" (1917) provides such a brief impression that is realistic and sensuous.

> At ten A. M. the young housewife
> moves about in negligee behind
> the wooden walls of her husband's house.
> I pass solitary in my car.
>
> Then again she comes to the curb
> to call the ice-man, fish-man, and stands
> shy, uncorseted, tucking in
> stray ends of hair, and I compare her
> to a fallen leaf.
>
> The noiseless wheels of my car
> rush with a crackling sound over
> dried leaves as I bow and pass smiling.

This kind of poetry, but also his verse exploring paintings in the manner of W. H. Auden, such as *Pictures from Breughel* (1962), have had a great influence on younger poets, notably Ginsberg, Olson and Creeley. Like Pound and Crane, Williams tried his hand at the "long poem". The five books entitled *Paterson* (1946-58; an incomplete Book VI was published in 1963) are made up of fragments of Williams's life and environment and present a panoramic view of the history of humanity as reflected in the city of Paterson, New Jersey, and "Dr. Paterson", Williams's mythic persona. Written in free verse, the work contains prose passages from historical documents, literary texts, and even personal letters by Ginsberg and Pound, all of them reinforcing the themes of the poem. Although *Paterson* is uneven in many parts and oscillates between the satire of small-town life and a larger critique of life, the central mythic figure "Paterson" creates a certain unity in a disparate poem. Here is the opening of Book II, a scene called "Sunday in the Park".

> Outside
>   outside myself
>   there is a world,
> he rumbled, subject to my incursions
> —a world
>   (to me) at rest,
>   which I approach
> concretely—
>
>   The scene's the Park
>   upon the rock,
>   female to the city

–upon whose body Paterson instructs his thoughts
(concretely)
                    –late spring,
          a Sunday afternoon!

–and goes by the footpath to the cliff (counting:
the proof)
                    himself among the others,
–treads there the same stones
on which their feet slip as they climb,
paced by their dogs!

laughing, calling to each other–

                    Wait for me!

. . the ugly legs of the young girls,
pistons too powerful for delicacy! .
the men's arms, red, used to heat and cold,
to toss quartered beeves and .

                    Yah! Yah! Yah! Yah!

More than any of his contemporaries, **E(dward) E(stlin) Cummings** (1894-1962)
indulged in formal experiments – he preferred his own name to be spelled e. e.
cummings. A painter, novelist and poet, he studied at Harvard and served as a
volunteer in the French medical corps during World War I. When he was erron-
eously imprisoned in a French concentration camp, he recorded his experience in
the autobiographical prose of *The Enormous Room* (1922). During the 1920s cummings lived in Paris, where he met Gertrude Stein and Ezra Pound, and then
returned to America and lived in Greenwich Village, New York. Attracted by dadaism[1], cummings made daring experiments with poetic form. Unlike Vachel Lindsay and other contemporaries who preferred their poems to be read aloud and
stressed sound, cummings paid more attention to the visual form, playing with
capitalization or lack of it, punctuation, line breaks and hyphenation. He used common speech and elements of popular culture and often wrote poems without beginnings or endings to express the flow of life. It was the spontaneity of expression
that counted for cummings. His main themes were the defence of the individual
against society and the deflation of pathos and false feelings as in the following
poem, which makes ironic use of the American national anthem and patriotic
poems.

---

1. A nihilistic movement in art and literature that lasted from 1916 until the mid-1920s, with Zurich,
New York, and Paris as centres. Dadaists deliberately denied sense and order. The members included
Tristan Tzara (the founder) and Man Ray.

"next to of course god america i

> "next to of course god america i
> love you land of the pilgrims' and so forth oh
> say can you see by the dawn's early my
> country 'tis of centuries come and go
> and are no more what of it we should worry
> in every language even deafanddumb
> thy sons acclaim your glorious name by gorry
> by jingo by gee by gosh by gum
> why talk of beauty what could be more beaut-
> iful than these heroic happy dead
> who rushed like lions to the roaring slaughter
> they did not stop to think they died instead
> then shall the voice of liberty be mute?"
> He spoke.   And drank rapidly a glass of water

Cummings was also capable of short epigrammatic statements summing up the human situation, and he could write love poems, both of the tender and serious and of the burlesque kind. Cummings's idiosyncratic manner is reflected in the very titles of some of his poetry collections: *And* (1925); *Vi Va* (1931); *No Thanks* (1935); and *1 × 1* (1944). Larger collections of his verse are *Poems: 1923-54* (1954) and *95 Poems* (1958).

The verse of **Archibald MacLeish** (1892-1982) indicates the various poetic currents of the early 20th century. MacLeish's career as a poet fell into three stages. The first is characterized by his status as an expatriate in Europe (1923-28) and the influence of Pound, Eliot, and the French symbolists. Such works as *Tower of Ivory* (1917), *The Pot of Earth* (1925), and *The Hamlet of A. MacLeish* (1928) voice the hopeless thoughts of an individual cast into the chaotic postwar world. Upon his return to the United States, then suffering from the economic depression, MacLeish became more aware of social problems and his cultural heritage which became central themes in *New Found Land* (1930), *Frescoes of Mr. Rockefeller's City* (1933), and especially in *Public Speech* (1936) and *America Was Promises* (1938) where he demands in verse that something be done to save democracy. Another poetic statement of his patriotism is *Colloquy for the States* (1943). MacLeish also wrote radio plays and verse epics on related issues. In his more recent poems he dealt with biblical themes, such as Job's trials in the verse drama *J. B.* (1958), and poetic adaptations of classical myths and of events from American history.

Among the women who wrote experimental verse in the wake of Imagism and the poetry of Pound and Eliot, mention must be made of Marianne Moore, Edna St. Vincent Millay, and Elinor Wylie. *The Collected Poems* of **Marianne Moore** (1887-1972) were published in 1951 and received the Pulitzer Prize. She was a friend of Yeats and Pound and contributed to such avant-garde journals as *The Dial* and *Poetry*. Moore favoured capricious metaphors, subtle puns and irony, and had a preference for exotic animals. Her poems often contrast trivial everyday things with abstract terms. The poetry of **Edna St. Vincent Millay** (1892-1950) impresses with its lyricism and technical virtuosity, especially in the handling of the

Elizabethan sonnet (*Weaver and Other Poems*, 1923; *Fatal Interview*, 1931). Millay's themes – disappointed love and mourning – are essentially romantic but are presented in a modern and surprisingly variable diction. **Elinor Wylie**, née Hoyt (1885-1928), who was also a novelist, adored the English metaphysical poets and Shelley. Most impressive are her passionate and self-analysing sonnets in *Angels and Earthly Creatures* (1928) which surpass the dream-like lyricism of her earlier verse in *Nets to Catch the Wind* (1921) and *Black Armour* (1923).

American poetry published after 1945 is as rich in names as it is in schools and movements. Several poets who wrote before the war and continued their careers well into the 1960s and '70s – Aiken, cummings, Frost, MacLeish, Ransom, Tate, Warren – have come to be known as the first generation of "academic poets", because their verse has been concerned with literary precedents, subtle technical effects and ironic allusions. They were followed by a second generation of "formalists" that include **Theodore Roethke** (1908-63), **Randall Jarrell** (1914-65), **Karl Shapiro** (born 1913), **Richard Wilbur** (born 1921), **Daniel Hoffman** (born 1923), **James Merrill** (born 1926), **Anthony Hecht** (born 1923), and such woman authors as the feminist **Adrienne Rich** (born 1929) and the New Englander **Maxine Kumin** (born 1925). **Roethke** was a professor of English at the University of Washington. His poetry shows the influence of such literary predecessors as Whitman, Dickinson and Eliot; but his father's profession – gardening – proved equally important. The organic life of the greenhouse became a central symbol in Roethke's poems, which explore the lost unity of life (*The Lost Son and Other Poems,* 1948). Roethke's quest led him more and more into metaphysical areas, and such works as *Praise to the End* (1951) and *The Far Field* (1964) record voyages into his own soul to find his place in God's creation. **Jarrell**, a Tennessean, and **Shapiro**, a native of New Jersey, both took part in World War II and are best remembered for their war poetry. Jarrell's matter-of-fact style is highly symbolical. He has shown his sympathy for the suffering in the dramatic verse tales collected in *Little Friend, Little Friend* (1945) and in the poems of *The Seven-League Crutches* (1951). Shapiro's verse is more intellectual and distinguished by a precise style and simple form. His *V-Letter and Other Poems* (1944), written on the Pacific front, won him the Pulitzer Prize. **Richard Wilbur** has remained faithful to the elegant traditional forms in *The Beautiful Changes* (1947) and *Ceremony* (1950). The poems in *Things of This World* (1956) display an equal interest in physical objects and abstract beauty. While many of Wilbur's contemporaries engaged in 'political' poetry in the late 1960s, he continued to write detached and witty poems (*Walking to Sleep,* 1969). **Daniel Hoffman** is the distinguished author of several books of poetry and the editor of the *Harvard Guide to Contemporary American Writing* (1979). His carefully measured verse places the search for the meaning of life in the context of ritual and myth (*An Armada of Thirty Wales,* 1954, and *The City of Satisfactions,* 1963). Hoffman's recent poetry, collected in *Broken Laws* (1970) and *Brotherly Love* (1980), a sequence of poems on William Penn and Philadelphia, provides evidence of his technical virtuosity and his unobtrusive humanitarianism. **James Merrill**, like Wilbur, writes poetry with a polished surface and in traditional forms. In such works as *First Poems* (1951) and the trilogy *Book of*

Ephraim (in *Divine Comedies,* 1976), *Mirabell: Books of Number* (1978), and *Scripts for the Pageant* (1980), which invite comparison with Pound's *Cantos* and other long poems, he has preferred the couplet, the quatrain and the sonnet sequence. **Anthony Hecht's** formalist commitment consists in an elevated diction, sophisticated metrical arrangements and literary allusions best demonstrated in *A Summoning of Stones* (1954). Hecht is quite obviously indebted to Wallace Stevens, Matthew Arnold, Eliot, Ransom and Tate. His *The Venetian Vespers* (1979) voices a stronger pessimism and anarchic emotions. **Adrienne Rich** has advanced from the formalism of *The Diamond Cutters* (1955) to the more personal and feminist stance of *Snapshots of a Daugher-in-Law* (1963). A great deal of aesthetic form has gone into her feminist poetry, especially *The Will to Change* (1971) and *Diving into the Wreck* (1973), though her latest verse (*A Wild Patience Has Taken Me This Far,* 1982) moves beyond feminist anger toward a more convincing integration of moral and aesthetic elements. Finally, **Maxine Kumin** has preserved the mature technical competence of her early *Halfway* (1961) and has become more concerned with the environment and the people in the places where she has lived (Europe and New Hampshire). *Up Country* (1972) and *The Retrieval System* (1978) ask questions about life, nature, human beings and homey things in a modest style.

In opposition to the intellectual and allegedly "academic" art of the formalists, a few movements beginning in the late 1950s demanded more spontaneity in the creation of poetry. One of the most influential writers was **Charles Olson** (1910-70). After teaching at Harvard, he was rector of the experimental Black Mountain College in North Carolina between 1951-56. Olson brought together a group of avant-garde artists who came to be known as the Black Mountain School. Olson himself is better known as a theorist than as a poet and explained his view of poetry in the essay *Projective Verse* (1950). According to Olson's poetics, which developed some thoughts of Pound and William Carlos Williams, a poem is "a high-energy construct" that must discharge energy at all points and in which "the perception must immediately ... lead to a further perception". In this process the spontaneous rhythm of the poet controls and orchestrates the "kinetic field" of the poem. This meant a dismissal of abstraction and intellectual aspects in favour of a sort of neo-Romantic primitivism.

Olson's "projective" or "open" verse was varied by a number of poets at his college – **Robert Creeley** (born 1926), **Robert Duncan** (born 1919) and others such as **Denise Levertov** (born 1923) who contributed to the journals *Black Mountain Review* and *Origin.* Thus **Creeley's** poems are brief, laconic and often epigrammatic statements in free-verse improvisations that deal with the problems of erotic and marital love. His best work is contained in *For Love* (1962), while *Words* (1965) and *Pieces* (1968) are less successful and suffer from the extreme reduction in technical means. Unlike Creeley, **Duncan** has written highly allusive poems that stand in a mystical-visionary tradition. Duncan wants to develop the fantastic dimension of the unconscious in order to intensify reality. His *Poems 1953-56* (1958) were followed by two long sequences, his major work, entitled *The Opening of the Field* (1960) and *Passages* (1966). *Bending the Bow* (1968) continues this line of writing which owes much to Pound and Olson. **Denise Levertov** has shown in such collections as *Here and Now* (1957), *The Jacob's Ladder* (1961), and *O Taste and See* (1964) that she shares Duncan's interest in mysticism and Creeley's tendency to record passing phases of awareness. But she transcends the Black Mountain School with her strong preference for ordinary events in daily life. Her "The Willows of Massachusetts" (1966) indicates her intense perception mellowed by mystery.

> Animal willows of November
> in pelt of gold enduring when all else
> has let go all ornament
> and stands naked in the cold.
> Cold shine of sun on swamp water
> cold caress of slant beam on bough,
> gray light on brown bark.
> Willows – last to relinquish a leaf,
> curious, patient, lion-headed, tense
> with energy, watching
> the serene cold through a curtain
> of tarnished strands.

Her social protest and opposition to the Vietnam War found expression in less convincing and occasionally sententious poems (*To Stay Alive*, 1971), but her perception has widened in such recent books as *The Freeing of the Dust* (1975), *Life in the Forest* (1978) and *Candles in Babylon* (1982).

In 1956 **Allen Ginsberg** (born 1926) attracted attention with his sensational *Howl*. It was followed in 1958 by **Lawrence Ferlinghetti's** (born 1919) *A Coney Island of the Mind*. Both authors were central figures among the San Franciscans or Beats. The Beat movement, whose members became known for their prose

and poetry, used some ideas of Olson's in protesting against the commercial "American way of life" and the establishment. The poet **Kenneth Rexroth** (1905-82) initially welcomed and promoted some younger anti-formalist poets in California, but they soon outgrew his patronage and formed a loosely connected group of writers. Apart from Ginsberg and Ferlinghetti, the best known poets of the Beat movement were **Gregory Corso** (born 1930), **Gary Snyder** (born 1930) and **James Broughton** (born 1913) The term "beat" alludes to several ideas of these poets: it implies "beaten", i.e. de-

Allen Ginsberg

jected and lost, but also rhythm. The poetry of this "lost generation" of World War II contains accusations of, and satires on, postwar America as well as new ways and forms of expression. A dynamic free verse inspired by jazz blended several themes, such as leftist politics, Oriental mysticism and the worship of sex. Ginsberg listened back to Blake and Whitman, but also to Hebrew poetry, when he wrote his long flowing lines that impress with their quality of sound. His *Howl* became the Bible of Beat poetry. The poem is an outcry against, and a diagnosis of, modern America. The opening of *Howl* provides an idea of Ginsberg's style that draws on Hebrew prophecy and an oral tradition suggesting declamation. But Ginsberg also employs the jargon of the mass media, the slang of the "beatniks", and surrealist images.

> I saw the best minds of my generation destroyed by madness, starving hysteri-
> cal naked,
> dragging themselves through the negro streets at dawn looking for an angry
> fix,
> angelheaded hipsters burning for the ancient heavenly connection to the starry
> dynamo in the machinery of night,
> who poverty and tatters and hollow-eyed and high sat up smoking in the super-
> natural darkness of cold-water flats floating across the tops of cities contem-
> plating jazz,
> who bared their brains to Heaven under the El and saw Mohammedan angels
> staggering on tenement roofs illuminated, ...

Ginsberg thus brought an apocalyptic and prophetic dimension, and a more orally oriented style, to an American poetry that had been a written and scholarly art. In *Kaddish* (1961), a sort of free-verse elegy, Ginsberg commemorated the life and death of his mother. He then moved on to the cultural criticism of modern life and the exploration of mysticism and hallucinations in *Planet News* (1963), *The Fall of America: Poems of These States* (1972), and *Mind Breaths* (1977). *Plutonium Ode* contains his poems written between 1977–80.

Ferlinghetti, whose City Lights Press made possible the publication of avant-garde Beat poetry, and **Corso** wrote in a similar style and with the same critical-satirical attitude toward the America of the 1960s. Ferlinghetti's major collection, mentioned above, and *Starting From San Francisco* (1961) contain images suggested by paintings and were influenced by jazz rhythms. This musical influence also shaped the more violent and aggressive verse of Corso's *Gasoline* (1958), *Bomb* (1958), *The Happy Birthday of Death* (1960), and *Elegiac Feelings American* (1970), which all pit a prophet-poet against a despicable America of industrialists, technocrats, and warmongers.

The underlying confessional pessimism and the satirical tone of the Beat poets are elements they share with other postwar movements in poetry – with the "Deep Imagists", the New York Poets, and especially with the "Confessionalists".

The group of poets known as "Deep Imagists" cluster around the journals of **Robert Bly** (born 1926) and **Robert Kelly** (born 1935). Apart from these two poets, **James Wright** (born 1927), and **James Dickey** (born 1923), also a novelist, have been associated with this movement. What they look for are archetypes of the unconscious, "deep images", that rise from the poet's uncommon, powerful feelings and create a lost order for the reader. Examples of this kind of verse are Bly's poems in *The Light Around the Body* (1967) and *Sleepers Joining Hands* (1973).

The New York Poets are the most radically antiformalist. The nucleus of the group – **Frank O'Hara** (1926-66), **John Ashbery** (born 1927), **Kenneth Koch** (born 1925) – was influenced by European and New York painters and by contemporary French free verse. They reject logical and coherent presentation. Line, syntax, and stanza are less important than immediacy, open forms, and unconnected images, making this kind of poetry difficult to read. One of the more accessible collections is Ashbery's prize-winning *Self-Portrait in a Convex Mirror* (1975).

With the publication in 1959 of *Life Studies* **Robert Lowell** (1917-77) introduced a new type of "confessional" verse that influenced a number of poets. They include the brilliant **John Berryman** (1914-72), **W. D. Snodgrass** (born 1926; *Heart's Needle*, 1959, and *After Experience*, 1968), **Anne Sexton** (1928-74; *Bedlam and Part Way Back*, 1960; *All My Pretty Ones*, 1962; *Live or Die*, 1966), and **Sylvia Plath** (1932-63) who was the wife of Ted Hughes and focused on mental disorder and death (*Ariel*, 1965, *Crossing the Water*, 1971, and *Winter Trees*, 1972). She took her life in 1963. Also opposed to formalism, these poets revealed painful truths about themselves, partly as a therapy for real or imagined psychoses and partly because they felt that the age called for a new clinical analysis of the self. Their improvised stanzaic forms and odd syntax and metrics suggest the influence of Pound, the Black Mountainists, the Beats, and William Carlos Williams's *Paterson*. Lowell and Berryman rank among the best postwar poets in America. **Lowell** came from an old New England family and studied in Louisiana and at Harvard. He converted to Roman Catholicism in 1940 and was a conscientious objector. His early poetry – *Lord Weary's Castle* (1946) and *The Mills of the Kavanaughs* (1951) – shows his reading of John Crowe Ransom and Allen Tate. It is still rather traditional verse that attacks the atheism and materialism of the age. Lowell then produced poetry closer to the rhythm of speech as he wrote the autobiographical *Life Studies* (1959) which records his mixed feelings about his New England childhood, his relations with his parents, the failure of his first marriage, and his alcoholism and treatment in a psychiatric ward. *For the Union Dead* (1964), of which a part is quoted below, continues his psychological exploration of time past and present: in this case a bronze relief commemorating the deaths of black soldiers in the Civil War serves as a starting point.

> Parking spaces luxuriate like civic
> sandpiles in the heart of Boston.
> A girdle of orange. Puritan-pumpkin colored girders
> braces the tingling Statehouse,
>
> shaking over the excavations, as it faces Colonel Shaw
> and his bell-cheeked Negro infantry
> on St. Gaudens' shaking Civil War relief,
> propped by a plank splint against the garage's earthquake.

Two months after marching through Boston,
half the regiment was dead;
at the dedication,
William James could almost hear the bronze Negroes breathe.

After 1970 Lowell reduced his subjectivism and found a more sober rhetoric. In *History* (1973) he published a series of revised "public" poems tracing life from the beginning of the world to the present, while his more private and confessional poems appeared in *For Lizzie and Harriet* and *The Dolphin* (1973), a collection of sonnets on his third marriage. Lowell's last book, *Day by Day* (1977), is very much in the confessional tradition. It records his experiences in England and at Harvard and new marital difficulties, the whole interspersed with a few poems about his childhood. Lowell was the dominant and most honoured poet of his generation.

Like Lowell, **Berryman** can be considered as a "confessional" poet who dealt in his verse with identity crises, sexual problems, and religious issues. The son of John Smith, a banker who committed suicide, Berryman adopted the name of his stepfather. His childhood was restless. He was brought up a strict Catholic but fell away from the Church. In his later life he taught at various universities, including Harvard and Princeton, and, after an unsuccessful attempt to return to the Catholic Church, he killed himself by jumping from a bridge in Minneapolis. Berryman is remembered for two outstanding works. The first is *Homage to Mistress Bradstreet,* published in 1953 in *Partisan Review,* and as a book in 1956, in which he merges his own consciousness with that of the Puritan poet and reflects on their kinship. Some of the 57 stanzas of the poem are highly erotic as Anne Bradstreet confesses about her personal erotic feelings and experiences and as Berryman imagines her as his mistress. Berryman's major works, however, are his *77 Dream Songs* (1964), *His Toy, His Dream, His Rest* (1968), and *Henry's Fate* (1977). *Dream Songs* is a series of almost 400 18-line poems concerned with the persona Henry that allows Berryman to hide behind masks and to borrow identities. Although he always denied that the work is autobiographical, insisting that *Dream Songs* is "essentially about an imaginary character (not the poet, not me) named Henry", the mask is at times all too obvious. As Berryman admitted, the work is indebted to Stephen Crane and Whitman's *Song of Myself.* The speaker in the various poems, Henry (or "Mr. Bones") assumes a number of roles including that of a white American who affects being a black man. The identities merge with Berryman's own, and the effect is that of psychic vaudeville and, despite Henry's grief, entertaining and self-mocking comedy. In No. 14 of *Dream Songs* Henry starts speaking as a "white" American, then changes into a black speaker and, finally, Berryman joins in, too, as the poem ends in a surrealistic image.

Life, friends, is boring. We must not say so.
After all, the sky flashes, the great sea yearns,
we ourselves flash and yearn,
and moreover my mother told me as a boy
(repeatingly) "Ever to confess you're bored
means you have no

Inner Resources." I conclude now I have no
inner resources, because I am heavy bored.
Peoples bore me,
literature bores me, especially great literature,
Henry bores me, with his plights & gripes
as bad as achilles,

who loves people and valiant art, which bores me.
And the tranquil hills, & gin, look like a drag
and somehow a dog
has taken itself & its tail considerably away
into mountains or sea or sky, leaving
behind: me, wag.

These poems are beyond doubt among the best verse of the postwar era and are far superior to the works Berryman wrote shortly before his death, such as *Love & Fame* (1970) and the posthumously published *Delusions, Etc.* (1972) which reflect his reactivated Catholicism and foreshadow his suicide.

The terms "school" or "movement", which please literary historians more than poets, cannot hide the fact that there are differences and varying approaches among the authors discussed above. But the common ground they share would seem to permit such groupings as in this chapter, not least because they can thus be distinguished from the great number of "independents" now at work in America. For the sake of justice, the names of the most accomplished independent poets must at least be mentioned here. They include **Galway Kinnell** (born 1927), **William Stafford** (born 1914), **A. R. Ammons** (born 1926), **Michael Benedikt** (born 1935), **W. S. Mervin** (born 1927), **Gary Snyder** (born 1930), **Ann Stanford** (born 1916), and, among the younger generation, **Dave Smith** (born 1942), **Louise Glück** (born 1943), **Douglas Crase** (born 1944), and **Larry Levis** (born 1946).

But the white man's and woman's voices are not the only ones in American poetry. Black poetry has blossomed since the Harlem Renaissance brought to prominence the verse of **Countee Cullen** (1903-46; see his *On These I Stand,* 1947), and **Langston Hughes** (1902-67). Both authors wrote poems about black life in conventional poetic forms, but Hughes also experimented with free verse, jazz and blues rhythms. His large body of poetry, from *The Weary Blues* (1926) to *Montage of a Dream Deferred* (1951) and *The Panther and the Lash* (1967), contains verse of two modes: there are lyrics about the way it feels to be black in America, and there are poems of racial protest. Here is an early example whose refrain is an ironic echo of a Southern minstrel song that was popular after the Civil War.

Song for a Dark Girl

Way Down South in Dixie
  (Break the heart of me)
They hung my black young lover
  To a cross roads tree.

Way Down South in Dixie
  (Bruised body high in air)
I asked the white Lord Jesus
  What was the use of prayer.
Way Down South in Dixie
  (Break the heart of me)
Love is a naked shadow
  On a gnarled and naked tree.

Younger black poets have abandoned traditional "white" forms of poetry and prefer a mixture of the styles and techniques of Langston Hughes and **Sterling A. Brown** (born 1901), of free verse and the Beat generation. The Black Power movement of the 1960s helped create a poetry of ethnic pride in which form and technique are less important than the message, which is often politically aggressive. Writers like **Le Roi Jones** (born 1934), who calls himself **Imamu Amiri Baraka,** and **Don L. Lee** (born 1942), now **Haki R. Mahubuti,** shed their "white" American names to underline their Afro-Arab origins and to assert their black identity. Apart from these two, the most distinguished black poets are **Gwendolyn Brooks** (born 1917), **Nikki Giovanni** (born 1943), the late **Robert Hayden** (1913-80), **Mari Evans** (born 1923), **Sonia Sanchez** (born 1934), and **Lucille Clifton** (born 1936).

As this brief list shows, many of the younger poets are women. The women's verse, too, is conditioned by rage and disappointment. **Brooks** is a case in point. Her early poetry (*Annie Allen,* 1949; *The Bean Eaters,* 1960) depicts the ordinary aspects of black life in compassionate portraits of impoverished ghetto-dwellers. But her verse changed radically when she met black activists in 1967. In the poems of *Riot* (1969), *Family Pictures* (1970) and *Beckonings* (1975) she speaks mainly to, and for, black people, replacing the former traditional forms with jagged phrases of anger and defiance that are explicitly political. In this she resembles the

militancy of both Amiri Baraka and Nikki Giovanni. **Baraka** came from the slums of Newark, New Jersey. He received a master's degree in German from Columbia University and considers the Beat poets, Pound, Williams, and Charles Olson the most influential sources for his own verse. Frustrated with his attempts to help create an integrated American society, he left his white wife and turned into a black militant for whom poetry – like prose and drama – is a means to destroy America as it is. His outrage found a first expres-

Le Roi Jones – Imamu Amiri Baraka

sion in *The Dead Lecturer* (1964). The subsequent books, *Black Art* (1966), *Black Magic* (1969), *It's Nation Time* (1970), and *Hard Facts* (1975), advocate his revolutionary ideas in verse that owes much to the oral tradition. **Nikki Giovanni's** poems, published in *Black Feeling, Black Talk* (1968) and *Cotton Candy on a Rainy Day* (1978) are richer in human feeling. She shares Baraka's militancy but makes better personal statements, especially when she discusses black individuals like Aretha Franklin and Angela Davis. Unlike his contemporaries, **Robert Hayden** despised ethnocentric poetry. His best work is contained in *Selected Poems* (1966) and *Ayle of Ascent* (1975). Based on the black experience, his verse makes use of verbal and poetic devices rather than socio-political commentary.

The best work of the black poets is illuminating and fresh and has its strongest sources not in political or sociological attitudes but in personal experience and Black speech – the street and city 'jive' – in the oral tradition and in music.

The American Indians have found in **N. Scott Momaday** (born 1934) a poet and novelist who has chosen the white man's language for his charming poems published in *Angel of Geese* (1974) and *The Gourd Dancer* (1976). Momaday is a Kiowa Indian and has been a university professor for many years (he also taught at German universities). His poetry recalls the geography, the myths, and the speech patterns of his native tribe in a style that is both unpretentious and powerful. Other writers of great skill are **Leslie M. Silko** (born 1948; see *Laguna Woman,* 1974) and **James Welch** (born 1940), who is half Blackfoot and half Gros Ventre. In *Riding the Earthboy 40* (1976) he has recorded the modern literate Indian's feelings when confronted with American nature, as in "There Is a Right Way":

The justice of the prairie hawk
moved me; his wings tipped
the wind just right and the mouse
was any mouse. I came away,
broken from my standing spot,
dizzy with the sense of a world
trying to be right, and the mouse
a part of a wind that stirs the plains.

In the Days of Plentiful by Quincy Tahoma, 1946

3. Drama

The most gifted American playwright around 1900 was the Chicago university professor **William Vaughn Moody** (1869–1910). His *The Great Divide* (1906), originally produced as *A Sabine Woman,* was written in the wake of realism. It is concerned with the relations between Ruth Jordan, a modern representative of inherited Puritan traditions and inhibitions, and Stephen Ghent, the free individualist of the Western frontier.

Change in the commercially oriented American theatre came with the impulses from new dramatic workshops at several universities. The leading and influential figures in these workshops were **Brander Matthews** (1852–1929) at Columbia, who held the first professorship in theatre; **William Lyon Phelps** (1865–1943) at Yale, and **George Pierce Baker** (1866–1935), who taught at Harvard and Yale and whose students included the dramatist Eugene O'Neill and the novelist Thomas Wolfe. Inspired by the activities at the universities, a number of drama groups sprang up all over the country. Experimenting with style and production, they introduced new themes and proved highly important for modern American theatre. The more influential groups included the Neighborhood Playhouse, founded in Greenwich Village, New York, in 1915, the Washington Square Players (1915), later called Theatre Guild, and the Massachusetts Provincetown Players. It was this last group, started in 1916, that began to perform O'Neill's early one-act plays. In the 1920s, the Theatre Guild of New York and the Provincetown Players dominated the dramatic scene. They concentrated on experimental drama and developed a variety of genres, such as expressionist, realistic, poetic and social-political plays. Playwrights who distinguished themselves in poetic drama included the poet **Edna St. Vincent Millay**. (*Aria da Capo,* 1919, and *Two Slatterns and a King,* 1921, written for the Provincetown Players), and especially **Maxwell Anderson** (1880–1959) and **Archibald MacLeish** (1892–1982). **Anderson** worked with the New York Group Theatre, run by Lee Strasberg, beginning with such realistic plays as the moving anti-war drama *What Price Glory?* (1924, written in collaboration with Laurence Stallings). Anderson's *Night Over Taos* (1932) is a verse drama about a nineteenth-century family in New Mexico, while *Winterset* (1935) is his most impressive attempt in this genre. Based on the much publicized Sacco-Vanzetti case[1], it is a symbolic verse tragedy exploring the issues of guilt and revenge. After a series of less successful verse dramas on historical and biblical themes, Anderson again dealt with a moral issue, evil in the character of a child, in his last play, *The Bad Seed* (1955).

---

1. In 1921, Nicola Sacco and Bartolomeo Vanzetti were charged with killing a paymaster and his guard in a robbery of a Massachusetts shoe company's payroll. Although both produced witnesses to prove that they were not involved in the crime, the prejudice against them (they were draft dodgers, anarchists, and agitators) prevailed and they were executed in 1927. Much of the evidence against them was later proved to have been fabricated by the prosecution. Many books, including numerous works of literature, have been written about the two men and their fate.

The Passion of Sacco and Vanzetti by Ben
Shahn, 1931-32

MacLeish began with plays concerned with social issues, e.g. *Panic* (1935). With *J. B.* (1958) he produced his best verse drama. Set in a circus tent, it is a modern treatment of the trials of the biblical figure Job. But verse drama never really became popular, although outstanding poets like **Wallace Stevens** *(Carlos Among the Candles,* 1917) and **Robert Lowell** wrote in the genre.

A different kind of drama that was especially promoted by New York's Theatre Group was concerned with social and political issues. Typical examples are **Clifford Odets's** (1906-63) propagandist *Waiting for Lefty* (1935), about a taxi drivers' strike, and *Awake and Sing* (1935), which deals with the American economic crisis of the 1930s as experienced by a Jewish family in New York. Less Marxist in their message were **Elmer Rice** (1892-1967) and **John Howard Lawson** (1895-1977). Rice experimented with naturalist elements in his didactic plays of social criticism. *The Adding Machine* (1923) attacks the monotony of working life in the machine age, and *Street Scene* (1930) links crime with the social conditions in the slums. Lawson's most important plays are the expressionistic *Processional* (1925), which he termed a "jazz symphony of American life", and *The International* (1928), a dramatic treatment of a future world revolution achieved by workers.

Other playwrights, while also concerned with human problems, put special American scenes and themes in the foreground. **Paul Green** (1894-1981) grew up in close contact with blacks on his parents' farm in North Carolina. For the Carolina Playmakers at the University of North Carolina he wrote a number of one-act plays and longer dramas about blacks and poor whites, some of them in black dialect, such as *In Abraham's Bosom* (1927) and *The Field God* (1927). Southern moral corruption, avarice, and neurosis are the themes of **Lillian Hellman's** (1905-84) melodramatic plays, *The Little Foxes* (1939) and *Another Part of the Forest* (1946). With *Watch on the Rhine* (1940) and *The Searching Wind* (1944) she tried to alert liberal Americans to the dangers of fascism. More successful with the theatre-going public was **William Inge** (1913-73), a Kansas-born dramatist whose

244

plays about ordinary people from the Midwest were made into films (*Come Back, Little Sheba,* 1950; *Picnic,* 1953; *Bus Stop,* 1955; and his best achievement, *The Dark at the Top of the Stairs,* 1957).

Rather than dramatizing social injustice, **Thornton Wilder** (1897–1975) turned to the heart and home of America. His experimental *Our Town* (1938) became internationally known.

It is an idyllic and sentimental play on the life of an average family in Grover's Corners, New Hampshire. Wilder had this play performed on an almost empty stage. Other novelties include the use of pantomime and the participation of a "stage manager" who introduces the scenes. The three acts, "Daily Life", "Love and Marriage", and "Death", focus on the behaviour of an average family in basic human situations. If the play has a message, it lies in the young wife's (Emily) experience upon returning to life for a day: people are too concerned with themselves to see what is really important in life in this world.

Wilder's *The Skin of Our Teeth* (1942) is set in a country destroyed by war and introduces an apocalyptic note. Representing mankind, the members of the Antrobus family survive all catastrophes in this play because they are God's children.

Playwrights such as Anderson, Rice, Hellmann, Odets, and Wilder continued to produce plays after 1945 and thus belong to two periods of the American theatre. But it was **Eugene O'Neill** (1888–1953) who became the dominant playwright during his life and continues to exert influence through his innovative work. O'Neill was of Irish descent. When he joined the Provincetown Players in 1916, he had already had an eventful life: educated in several Catholic schools, he was suspended from Princeton University for bad behaviour; he married and divorced; he went to sea and worked as a reporter in London before spending a year in a tuberculosis sanatorium. There, he found time to read widely. Among other authors, he studied Marx, Nietzsche, Ibsen, Strindberg, Jack London, Joseph Conrad, and the Greek tragedians, and he wrote his first one-act plays. He became acquainted with the new drama groups at Harvard, in New York and Massachusetts, producing his plays for several stages. By 1936 he had his first success on Broadway[1] and won a Nobel Prize. O'Neill was twice divorced but enjoyed a happy third marriage. But after 1931 he suffered a physical breakdown, writing his last works while suffering from Parkinson's disease. O'Neill modernized the American theatre with his introduction of new techniques: Ibsen's realism, the psychology of Freud and Jung, colloquial speech, masks as used in Greek and Roman theatre, music, and symbolism. Rejecting Benjamin Franklin's American ideology of optimism, O'Neill was a convinced determinist and assessed human existence and the meaning of life.

In some twenty early one-act plays he experimented with naturalism and symbolism. Thus *Fog* (1914) and *Thirst* (1916) feature shipwrecked people, in a boat and on a raft, representing mankind, while *The Moon of the Caribbees* (1918),

---

1. A long street in Manhattan. Its theatrical district around 42nd Street (Times Square) became the centre of the commerical theatre in the 20th century. The term is also used for the commercial theatre in general.

Eugene O'Neill

another "sea play", beautifully captures the atmosphere of a wild tropical night and an orgy of alcohol and sex involving sailors and black girls. Between 1917-1924 O'Neill produced a number of works that made theatrical history. *Beyond the Horizon* (1920) was his first successful play on Broadway and won him a Pulitzer Prize. It is a naturalistic study of a woman torn between two men. Tracing the gradual ruin of three people, O'Neill tried to cast doubt on the American idea of "the pursuit of happiness". *Anna Christie* (1921) is less sombre. It evokes realistic scenes of life at sea and of prostitution in the story of captain Christopherson and his daughter, Anna, a prostitute. During this period O'Neill also wrote plays with strong expressionistic elements. *The Emperor Jones* (1920), for instance, presents eight scenes in which the Negro Jones, the "emperor" of a West Indian island, talks in self-revealing monologues about his present and past life in America and Africa, while being hunted by his own rebellious men. They find Jones and kill him. The expressionistic means of the beating drum accompanies and underlines the desperate aspects of Jones's flight and increasing fear. *The Hairy Ape* (1922) exemplifies O'Neill's deterministic view of life. The symbolic plot of the play is concerned with Yank, a strong but unintelligent ship's stoker, who must recognize that technological progress perverts human strength. When Yank realizes that society ignores and rejects him, he tries to take revenge by setting free a gorilla in a zoo, and the beast brutally crushes him. With *All God's Chillun Got Wings* (1924) O'Neill returned to a more naturalistic approach. It treats of the tragic marriage of a black man to a white woman and makes use of symbolic scenery and a chorus. Also naturalistic is *Desire Under the Elms* (1924), a tragedy of human and sexual passion on a New England farm. In this play the trees are symbols of both protection and threat. O'Neill also alludes in this tragedy to classical Greek drama and theatrical archetypes. Greek drama, both formally and thematically, had an undeniable influence on O'Neill's plays. Thus he experimented with the Greek device of masks. They are employed symbolically in his adaptation of Coleridge's long poem *The Ancient Mariner* (1924), and in the plays attacking modern American materialism, such as *The Great God Brown* (1926), where the masks are symbols of falsity. In *Marco's Millions* (1928) Marco Polo takes on features of an American businessman, and the verse drama *Lazarus Laughed* (1927) presents Elizabethan pageants and masked choruses. O'Neill's most daring formal experiment is *Strange Interlude*

(1928). It uses the stream-of-consciousness technique in an effort to combine both epic and dramatic forms in a new theatrical technique.

The year 1931 saw the performance of the first of O'Neill's three outstanding tragedies, *Mourning Becomes Electra*. It is a trilogy that adapts the Greek *Oresteia*[1] to the American Civil War while employing Freud's ideas of neurosis and anticipating French existentialism.

Set in a small New England town and concerned with the Mannon family, the tragedy focuses on the consequences of past guilt and a malignant fate. The three parts (I. The Homecoming; II. The Hunted; III. The Haunted) show how the Mannons are haunted by the sins of their ancestors. In part I, Colonel Mannon (Agamemnon) returns from the war to find out that his wife Christine (Klytemnestra) loves Captain Brant, an illegitimate member of the family. Christine kills her husband. Her daughter Lavinia (Electra) vows to revenge the murder. In part II, Orin (Orestes) returns home and is informed about the tragic events by his sister Lavinia. Orin kills Brant and drives his mother to suicide. The final part deals with Orin's suicide and Lavinia's decision to mourn for the rest of her life in order to do penance for the sins of her family. All the characters in this tragedy are motivated by passions and complexes. Modern psychology turns Greek mythology into human and American problems and thus makes this one of the most convincing expressionistic plays.

Before he produced his next great tragedy, O'Neill wrote a pleasant New England folk comedy, *Ah Wilderness!* (1933). *The Iceman Cometh* was finished in 1940 but not performed before 1946. Indebted to Ibsen and Gorky[2] and based on O'Neill's personal experiences, this tragedy is a moving treatment of the illusions of human life.

Set in the realistic atmosphere of a New York bar, the play presents a number of failed and disillusioned characters who drown their problems in alcohol. The salesman Hickey always entertained the group in the past during his visits. He now returns and tells his friends to face the truth, thus bringing despair to the group. Hickey confesses to the murder of his wife. Relieved of his psychological burden, he is taken away by the police while his drunken companions return to their illusions.

Another tragedy, with stronger autobiographical features, is *Long Day's Journey into Night*. It was finished in 1941 and performed in 1956. The play is essentially a psychological study of a disintegrating family in which the reckless father makes it impossible for his wife to create a home for their two sons. The dialogue, characterized by attacks and accusations, reveals the past and the hopeless present, as the mother becomes an addict and the sons turn into cynics. In the 1940s, O'Neill wrote several other pessimistic plays about human despair: *A Moon for the Misbe-*

---

1. Trilogy of plays by Aeschylus, describing the return of Agamemnon to Argos after the Trojan war; his murder by his wife Clytemnestra; the vengeance of Agamemnon's children, Orestes and Electra; the pursuit of Orestes by the Furies; and Orestes' trial and eventual release by the gods.

2. Maxim Gorky (1868-1936), Russian writer and dramatist. He was self-educated, read widely, and became a supporter of the Communist Russian government. His best-known works are, among his novels, *The Mother*, 1906-07, and *Childhood* (1913); among his plays, *Philistines* and *The Lower Depths* (both 1902).

gotten (1943; performed in 1957), *Hughie* (performed in 1958) and the two posthumously published plays, *A Touch of the Poet* (1957) and *More Stately Mansions,* (produced in 1967). O'Neill's most convincing plays are the short pieces written at the beginning of his career and the two tragedies, *The Iceman Cometh* and *Long Day's Journey into Night.* With his technical experiments and his preference for the marginal and the pathological in human life, O'Neill exerted a profound influence on American theatrical conventions. Not all of O'Neill's experiments with verse drama, interior monologue, and chorus can be termed successful in their effect. But in his powerful "sea plays" he did for American drama what Melville did for the novel. O'Neill's masterful explorations of man's attitudes towards religion and mythology have a poetic force that has helped them to stand the test of time and literary judgment.

It would be totally misleading to equate American theatre with the great names championed by literary criticism. Broadway, that magic street on the island of Manhattan in the city of New York, has become a label for popular and successful plays. It was in the commercial theatres on Broadway that such popular comedies as *Abie's Irish Rose,* by **Anne Nicholls,** were put on and, in many cases, ran for years: Nicholls's play had 2,500 performances. By 1950, the kind of commercial theatre that is associated with Broadway had a stranglehold on the drama market. Success depended on the fact whether a play "made it" on Broadway. To be sure, the commercial theatres also welcomed the works of outstanding post-war playwrights like Tennessee Williams and Arthur Miller. However, as commercially oriented ventures, the Broadway theatres generally preferred lighter theatricals, such as farce and the vastly popular musical comedies. Farce featured types, rather than complicated characters, and frenetic action. The heyday of farce was the 1920s and 1930s, when the plays of **Samuel Nathaniel Behrman** (1893-1973), **George Kaufman** (1889-1961), **George Abbott** (born 1887), **Samuel Spewack** (born 1899), and **Moss Hart** (1904-61) were in vogue. Apart from Nicholls's comedy, the plays most cherished by theatre audiences were **Clarence Day's** *Life with Father* (1939), Spewack's *Boy Meets Girl* (1935) and Kesselring's *Arsenic and Old Lace* (1941). Post-war farcical comedies have come from the pens of **Garson Kanin** (born 1912), **Samuel Taylor,** the novelist **Saul Bellow** (*Under the Weather,* 1966), and the currently popular **Neil Simon** (*The Last of the Red Hot Lovers,* 1969). Many of Simon's comedies, and some by playwrights connected with the off-Broadway and off-off-Broadway theatres, have been filmed or served as scripts for Hollywood movies.

Broadway theatres continue to be especially known for their productions of musicals and folk-operas. An early example of the folk-opera is *Porgy and Bess* (1935), based on DuBose Heyward's novel and play, with music by George Gershwin[1]. Starting with *Oklahoma* (1943), by Rodgers and Hammerstein, the 1940s

---

1. George Gershwin (1898-1937), American song writer and composer, best known for his musical comedies (*Show Girl,* 1929), his piano concerto with jazz orchestra *Rhapsody in Blue* (1924), and the orchestral poem *An American in Paris* (1928). The folk-opera *Porgy and Bess* is his most ambitious composition.

and '50s saw one successful musical after another: Cole Porter's *Kiss Me Kate* (1948; an adaptation of Shakespeare's *The Taming of the Shrew*), *South Pacific* (1949), *Gentlemen Prefer Blondes* (1949), Lerner and Lowe's *My Fair Lady* (1956), an adaptation of Shaw's *Pygmalion*, and Leonard Bernstein's *West Side Story* (1957), which transposes the story of Romeo and Juliet to the context of ethnic gang fights in the slums of New York. These were followed by *The Sound of Music* (1959) and *Fiddler on the Roof* (1964). More recent contributions that originally came from off-Broadway theatres include musicals by the innovative composer Stephen Sondheim, such as *A Little Night Music* (1973) and *Pacific Overtures*, the outstanding works by Fred Ebb and John Kander (*Cabaret*, 1966, and *Chicago*, 1975), and such spectacular shows as the all-black *Bubbling Brown Sugar* (1975).

Among the new playwrights who dazzled Broadway in the late 1940s were **Tennessee Williams** (1911-83) and **Arthur Miller** (born 1915). Thomas Lanier Williams expressed his deep love of the South by adopting "Tennessee" as a first name in 1939. He grew up in Mississippi and worked in New Orleans and St. Louis. As a homosexual, he developed a critical outsider's view of society. He studied the works of Freud and Jung, and the novels of D. H. Lawrence. Williams considered Eros a magic and powerful force. His heroes and heroines are almost all neurotics, suffering from some sort of sexual complex that renders them incapable of dealing with reality. Tennessee Williams advocated what he termed "plastic theatre", i. e. poetic-symbolic plays containing non-realistic elements (light effects, musical leitmotifs, and symbols) in addition to their psychological realism. His first Broadway success came in 1945 with *The Glass Menagerie*.

The title of this play refers symbolically to the non-realistic world of the fragile heroine, Laura Wingfield. Like her collection of glass animals, Laura, a crippled, romantic girl, leads a life of seclusion and illusion with her mother Amanda and her brother Tom. All the characters in this play suffer from complexes and hang on to particular illusions: the mother constantly recalls her youth as a Southern belle, the brother dreams of escaping from his family, and Laura's "gentleman caller" Jim is dominated by his all-American fiancée. Disappointed and left alone by Jim, Laura retreats further into her private world of illusions. The psychologically realistic characters, the tense atmosphere, and the poetic symbols (the horn of Laura's glass unicorn breaks when she tries to dance with Jim and they bump into the table) demonstrate William's personal dramatic lyricism.

Tennessee Williams

Another fragile woman in need of illusions, but also of men, is the heroine in *A Streetcar Named Desire.* It was produced in 1947 and won Williams a Pulitzer Prize.

This tragedy is set in the slums of New Orleans. It traces the gradual psychological disintegration of the neurotic Blanche DuBois, whose telling name is an ironic cover for her true nature. Morally and financially at the end of her tether, Blanche arrives at the squalid home of her sister Stella. In order to keep up appearances and to avoid facing the tragedy of her failed life, Blanche plays the Southern gentlewoman and recalls the good old days she spent with her sister on their parents' plantation. The play reveals that Blanche had been married but had taunted her homosexual husband until he committed suicide. Trying to compensate her empty life with sexual experiences, she was dismissed from her teaching job because of an affair with a young student. In the small and dirty home of her younger sister, Blanche's affected refinement is contrasted with the animal maleness and the brutality of Stella's husband, Stanley Kowalski. When Stanley's friend Mitch falls in love with Blanche, Stanely tells him the truth about her sordid past and eventually rapes his sister-in-law in a fit of violent lust. Returning from the hospital with a newly born baby, Stella refuses to believe Blanche's story and has her committed to a mental institution. Technically, this is one of his best plays, combining as it does a realistic New Orleans atmosphere with symbolic action and characterization.

In many of Williams's plays, women fail because their need for love and human tenderness is not fulfilled; instead, they are offered sex, as in *Summer and Smoke* (1948), or illusions, as in *The Rose Tattoo* (1950).

Apart from sexual problems, Williams also focused on such themes as the survival of the outsider and the quest for the meaning of life. After the "dream play" *Camino Real* (1953), in which a former boxer encounters a great number of personages from history and literature, Williams wrote *Cat on a Hot Tin Roof* (1955). The issue of sex is again central to this play dealing with a family conflict on a Mississippi plantation.

Again, a woman is cast as the major character: Maggie, the "cat" and wife of the alcoholic ex-football player Brick. But unlike Williams's other heroines, Laura and Blanche, Maggie is neither weak nor unrealistic. Faced with scheming and false relatives who are out to inherit the plantation from vulgar and ruthless Big Daddy Pollitt, Maggie remains honest in her struggle to cure her husband and to convince Bid Daddy that Brick and herself are worthy inheritors.

The family tensions come to a head on Big Daddy's sixty-fifth birthday. Maggie tells her husband that she slept with his closest friend Skipper because both needed the warmth Brick's ideally pure relationship could not provide, and that she drove Skipper to suicide by making him face his latent homosexuality. Big Daddy makes Brick see that his flight into alcoholism stems from the disgust with himself for not having helped Skipper; and Brick, in revenge, tells his father that he (Big Daddy) is dying of cancer. Brick's brother Gooper and his wife Mae fail to secure the plantation from Big Daddy's wife, and Maggie, determined to make Big Daddy happy and to inherit the land, announces that she and Brick are expecting a baby.

In a series of plays Williams then continued to explore his basic themes: loneliness, frustration, lust, perversion, violence, and destruction. But none of these reached the artistic skill of his earlier work (*Suddenly Last Summer,* 1958; *Sweet*

Bird of Youth, 1959; *The Night of the Iguana*, 1962). His more recent plays rework his familiar themes but lack the balance of the great plays and suffer from pathos and overdone aberrational psychology (see, for instance, *Red Devil Battery*, 1975; *Vieux Carré*, 1977; *A Lovely Sunday for Crève Coeur*, 1978; and *Clothes for a Summer Hotel*, 1980). With his three outstanding plays, however, Williams proved one of the two most impressive American playwrights of the post-war decades.

In the same year in which Williams caused a sensation with his *Streetcar*, **Arthur Miller** became known with the production of *All My Sons* (1947). Miller has written plays that are, in his own words, "an expression of profound social needs". Of Jewish descent, Miller was born in New York. During the Great Depression his father lost almost all his property, and Arthur Miller had to work as a truck driver and waiter before earning a B A at the University of Michigan in 1938. He took part in World War II and has lived on the East Coast and in Hollywood, where he made headlines as the last husband of Marilyn Monroe. Miller's *All My Sons* shows the influence of Ibsen and O'Neill. It is the tragic story of an airplane manufacturer and war profiteer whose defective products cause the deaths of many young men and cause his son to commit suicide.

With *Death of a Salesman* (1949) Miller attempted a fusion of realism and symbolism in an expressionistic tragedy that does not follow chronological sequence but moves between the past and the present.

The hero of the play, Willy Loman, is a travelling salesman. Looking back at his past, he realizes that he has ruined his life and disappointed his sons and his wife. Miller shows this process in a series of flashbacks and representations of Willy's consciousness that are related to the technique of the modern novel. Dismissed by his boss, Willy deliberately kills himself in a car accident to provide his family with the life insurance money. His son Biff realizes that his father's dream of success is based on a myth. Essentially, Miller's play is a condemnation of the American dream of economic success. As *Death of a Salesman* shows, this dream is often realized at a horrible personal sacrifice.

Arthur Miller's approach as a "social dramatist" is most obvious in *The Crucible* (1953). It draws a parallel between the witchcraft trials in seventeenth-century Salem, Mass., and the political excess of Senator McCarthy's witch hunt for communists in the 1950s. Since this play, Arthur Miller's socialist sympathy has gradually developed into a profound questioning of social morality. His moral concern is as obvious in *A View From the Bridge* (1955), a tragedy of workers and illegal immigrants in the New York docks, as it is in *After the Fall* (1964), an autobiographical scenic report in which Miller also alludes to his marriage with Marilyn Monroe, who committed suicide in 1962. Similarly, *Incident at Vichy* (1964) is concerned with individual responsibility. It features human types in the story of several Frenchmen arrested by the Nazis in 1942. Arthur Miller's latest plays indicate his post-Freudian preoccupation with the problem of original sin. in *The Price* (1968) two brothers analyse guilt and responsibility while judging their past, and in *The Creation of the World and Other Business* (1972) Cain rejects both God and the devil but cannot get rid of evil. *The Archbishop's Ceiling* (1977) returns to the themes of his early plays in its concern with intellectual and personal freedom and the issue of political and moral guilt; and *The American Clock* (1979) studies an American family in the Depression. His recent plays suffer from too much didactic doctrine. Unlike his early works, they illustrate the playwright's didactic intentions too obviously instead of presenting convincing characters with realistic motivations.

American drama received a new impetus in the mid-1950s from the playwrights that came from what has been termed the off-Broadway movement. While Broadway was more and more concerned with pre-tested works and ceased to exist as an initiator of new plays, exciting new drama came from the playwrights who wrote for the experimental theatres in Greenwich Village, New York. As can be expected, they soon moved on to theatrical success on Broadway. These dramatists include Arnold Weinstein, Jack Richardson, William Hanley, Murray Schisgal, and three playwrights who were to become internationally known: **Edward Albee** (born 1928), **Jack Gelber** (born 1932), and **Arthur Kopit** (born 1937).

Albee has been influenced by Tennessee Williams, European experimental plays, and the theatre of the absurd. His one-act play, *The Zoo Story,* was first produced in Berlin in 1959. It demonstrates Albee's method of mingling realism with fantasy in order to question conformity and to express the tragedy of alienation. *The Zoo Story* presents a young homosexual who is disgusted with the world and manages to trick an ordinary New York citizen into killing him. After completing several less impressive short works, Albee wrote his masterpiece, *Who's Afraid of Virginia Woolf?* (1962).

This is a realistic play about a social evening in the lives of two college professors and their wives. In a psychologically painful "showdown", recalling Strindberg's concern with the struggle between the sexes, George and Martha torture and abuse each other verbally until they finally achieve a kind of catharsis: They abandon the illusion that they have a son, an idea that sustained their marriage. Implicitly also attacking the American dream[1], Albee leads his characters from hate and guilt and disappointment to the destruction of illusion and the acceptance of reality.

Tiny Alice (1965) is a symbolic drama Albee termed a "mystery play". It has as its protagonist the richest woman in the world who corrupts a Catholic lay brother and eventually arranges to have him killed. Edward Albee's subsequent works (*A Delicate Balance,* 1966; *All Over,* 1971; and *The Lady of Dubuque,* 1980) reflect his continuing preoccupation with reality and illusion in the European absurd tradition, with a remarkable streak of pessimism.

At the time of its first production in 1959 **Jack Gelber's** *The Connection* caused a grat stir. It is an anti-illusionist play, with jazz music, showing the lives of drug addicts as though they were real. The audience is included in the plot, as the actors beg money for their drugs and improvise on stage. But Gelber's next plays (*The Apple,* 1961; *Square in the Eye,* 1965; *The Cuban Thing,* 1968; *Sleep,* 1972; and

---

1. This term has no clear definition or denotation. It refers to the Declaration of Independence and the rights of man mentioned there, such as "life, liberty, and the pursuit of happiness." This happiness implies the freedom of the individual to do what he/she likes best, and includes the possibility of financial success.

Jack Gelber's New Play: Rehearsal, 1976) did not live up to the great expectations he built up with his first success.

Arthur Kopit made headlines with *Indians* (1969). The play demythologizes Buffalo Bill[1] and denounces U. S. politics, from the wars against the Indians until Vietnam, as cruel and inhuman. Kopit has satirized the American mother cult in *Oh Dad, Poor Dad, Mama's Hung You in the Closet and I'm Feelin' So Sad* (1962), which also makes fun of Tennessee Williams's *The Rose Tattoo* as well as of absurd drama.

In the early 1960s a new movement set in that reacted against the commercialization of off-Broadway theatres. New experimental theatres were established, such as Caffe Cino, La Mama Experimental Theater Club, and Theater Genesis. Together with some regional theatres outside New York, they became known as off-off-Broadway. Playwrights who have worked in this movement are **Jean Claude Van Itallie** (born 1936), **Israel Horowitz** (born 1939), **Jules Feiffer** (born 1929), **Terence McNally** (born 1939), **Ronald Ribman** (born 1932), the internationally known **David Rabe** (born 1940), **Sam Shepard** (born 1943), **Robert Wilson** (born 1941) and **David Mamet** (born 1947). Like their off-Broadway contemporaries, these authors have written about the ambiguous connection between American myth and reality. Examples are Shepard's *Cowboys* (1964), *Operation Sidewinder* (1970), and *Seduced* (1979); Mamet's *Sexual Perversity in Chicago* (1974) and *The Water-Engine* (1977); and Rabe's anti-Vietnam plays, such as *The Basic Training of Pavlo Hummel* (1971) and *Streamers* (1976). Wilson's performances, often very long, stress non-verbal channels of communication and present collages of moving pictures. Since the 1970s, he has commanded great international interest (see, for instance, *Einstein on the Beach,* 1976).

Black American playwrights have been specifically concerned with the role of blacks in American society. In the 1930s **Langston Hughes** wrote a series of plays that focused on life in black communities and avoided strident social criticism. A change came with **Lorraine Hansberry's** (1930-65) *A Raisin in the Sun* (1959). This was produced on Broadway and portrays the generational conflict in a black family in a Chicago ghetto. In her second play, *The Sign in Sidney Brustein's Window* (1964), Hansberry changed her approach. Set in Greenwich Village, this work has a Jewish hero and only one black character and views the problems of blacks within the larger framework of American society.

With the Civil Rights struggle of the 1960s, a socially committed and propagandist black theatre emerged. Older authors who wrote in this spirit include **Alice Childress** (born 1920) and the novelist **James Baldwin** (1924-87). Baldwin moved from the dramatization of black religiosity in *The Amen Corner* (1964) to the propagandist *Blues for Mr. Charlie* (1964), which deals with social and sexual issues in the race conflict between blacks and whites. Baldwin's black hero in this

---

1. Nickname of William F. Cody (1846-1917), a frontier scout who served in the Civil War and in the battles against the Sioux. He acted in Western melodramas and, in 1883, started his famous "Wild West" show which, together with the dime novels about his adventures, is partially responsible for his popular reputation.

play opened the way for the militant drama of **Le Roi Jones** and **Ed Bullins** (born 1935). Under his new African name, Amiri Baraka, Jones used the dramatic form as a political weapon (*Dutchman*, 1964; *The Slave*, 1966; *Slave Ship*, 1967). His *The Motion of History* (1976) puts his Marxist-Maoist views into the words of black protagonists. Ed Bullins has been associated with the the militant New Lafayette Theater in Harlem, founded in the 1960s. Like Jones, Bullins has written for blacks, suggesting militant resistance to the white American political system in such plays as *The Gentleman Caller* (1969), *Four Dynamite Plays* (1971), and *The Taking of Miss Janie* (1975). In the 1980s, however, the black militant theatre began to lose its impetus and its audience. Playwrights producing works for the subsidized Negro Ensemble Company in New York have tried to reach a wider American audience. Among these writers, **Douglas Turner Ward** (born 1930) and **Adrienne Kennedy** (born 1931; see her *Funnyhouse of a Negro*, 1964; and *A Beast's Story*, 1969) represent the Black theatre which has its roots in American realism and avant-garde expressionism. Younger black playwrights who have attracted critical attention are **Philip Hayes Dean** (born 1933; *The Sty of the Blind Pig*, 1971) and **Charles Fuller** (born 1939; *The Brownsville Raid*, 1976; *A Soldier's Play,* 1981). Both authors have written on American history from a decidedly black point of view.

Television has had a powerful influence on American drama. Unlike their British colleagues, American playwrights have not been able to develop their styles and techniques artistically by working for TV and writing film scripts. American TV drama and the soap operas tend to appeal to the lowest common denominator of response. Most TV productions in drama come from the Hollywood studios and are subject to financial pressures that produce high audience ratings but very little dramatic work with an inherent artistic value, although it is worth studying these productions for the highly influential stereotypes and the political ideology they disperse. The influence of the superficial style of Hollywood drama is noticeable in the plays of **Neil Simon, Paddy Chayefsky** (1923-81), and **Frank Gilroy** (born 1926), who were experienced TV veterans before turning to the theatre.

Money makes the world go round. And as Hollywood can often offer more than other locations in America, it has attracted many talents, including European playwrights. Hollywood has produced numerous dramatic TV genres: sit-coms (i. e. situation comedies) such as *Archie Bunker* and *Steptoe and Son;* police and crime series such as *Kojak,* and Western series like *Bonanza.* Meanwhile, they have been either exported to, or imitated in, Europe and other continents. The best-known recent examples of American TV culture are *Dallas* and *Dynasty,* which provoked one of the French TV channels to produce a similar series in France. Such series are certainly of interest in a broader cultural context as vehicles of particular American ideologies. As such they have been studied by literary and university critics. But they lack the subtleties of dramatic art. There is a certain irony in the fact that TV is one of the two most influential media in the United States but that it is extremely difficult for serious and convincing drama to emerge from the TV studios. The emphasis on commercial interests seems to be detrimental to good TV drama.

4. Prose Fiction

4.1 The Novel

The criticism of American society begun by Howells, Crane and Norris continued with the naturalistic novels of Theodore Dreiser, the realistic novels of social protest by Upton Sinclair and the "muckrakers", and the attacks on self-satisfied middle-class life by Sinclair Lewis and Sherwood Anderson.

Theodore Dreiser (1871-1945) was the twelfth child of a poor Catholic German family that emigrated to Terre Haute, Indiana. Largely self-educated, Dreiser became a journalist and an admirer of the philosophical determinism as exemplified in the fiction of Zola and Balzac. As the publishers of his first two books did not like his pessimistic view of American life and his ridiculing of the Horatio Alger myth, it took several years for his works to gain critical attention. *Sister Carrie* (1900) describes the gradual moral corruption of the country girl Caroline Meeber. Before finding a place in the theatre, Caroline becomes the mistress of several men in Chicago and New York. Her last keeper finally marries her. But when financial difficulties arise, she leaves him and he finally commits suicide. Caroline pursues her theatrical career, but fails to attain happiness. Dreiser's impersonal viewpoint, his realistic treatment of sexual relations, and his social determinism provide explanations for the failure of his characters, which was much criticized at the time. But he pursued his themes with *Jennie Gerhardt* (1911), which chronicles the history of another fallen girl, and the trilogy *The Fiancier* (1912), *The Titan* (1914), and *The Stoic* (1947). These three novels cover the rise and fall of a brutal and egoistic "financier" in a plot that is suffocated by too many facts and details.

Dreiser's outstanding novel is *An American Tragedy* (1925). It balances determinism with an emotional identification with the tragic hero.

The novel is based on a sensational murder case and shows the development and moral crisis of a young man obsessed with the ideas of material success and social prestige. When the hero plans to kill his former mistress, who is now pregnant and thus an obstacle in his way to the top, she accidentally drowns. The young man, Clyde Griffith, is arrested, tried and condemned to death. In a long section on Griffith's imprisonment, Dreiser criticizes what he sees as an inhuman legal system and the society that had created it. Basically products of their milieu, Dreiser's characters are driven by their hunger for money and power and remain lonely and unsatisfied figures.

Dreiser's social protest in fiction was accompanied by the humanitarian idealism of the "muckrakers", a term coined by President Theodore Roosevelt (1858-1919) to designate what he considered noxious critics of corruption in politics and business. The leading "muckrakers" - **David Graham Phillips** (1867-1911), **Robert Herrick** (1868-1938), and **Lincoln Steffens** (1866-1936) - published their criticism in their own journals and several newspapers. In prose fiction, the movement was represented by such novels as Phillips's *Susan Lennox: Her Fall and Rise* (1917) and the works of **Upton Sinclair** (1878-1968). Sinclair's *The Jungle* (1906) is a melodramatic description and a condemnation of the working conditions in the Chicago stockyards. With the earnings from the book he founded a cooperative

American Gothic by Grant Wood, 1930

colony and unsuccessfully ran for public office. Sinclair wrote more than 100 works, ranging from social studies to plays, short stories and novels, among them the eleven novels of the Lanny Budd series.

Sherwood Anderson and Sinclair Lewis aimed their criticism at the banality and hypocrisy of middle-class life. A temporary member of Upton Sinclair's "Helicon Home Colony", **Sinclair Lewis** (1885-1951) was a journalist and novelist who travelled widely in the USA and in Europe. He refused to accept a Pulitzer Prize in 1926 and was awarded a Nobel Prize in literature in 1930, the first American to receive this honour. Lewis died in Rome. He was a fierce satirist and ridiculed such American values as optimism and the adoration of financial success. Lewis's first major novel, *Main Street* (1920), contrasts the intolerant and self-satisfied citizens of provincial Gopher Prairie, Minnesota, with cultured big-city characters in a satire of middlebrow and middle-class life in a typical small town of the Middle West. With *Babbitt* (1922) Lewis created the prototype of the superficial and benevolent businessman who prefers to adapt to society instead of following his own inclinations. While Babbitt's entrapment in his pitiful environment still causes sympathy, Lewis was less understanding and more aggressive in his fictional attack on religious hypocrisy in *Elmer Gantry* (1927), and on materialism in *Arrowsmith* (1925). Although excellent social satires, these works lack convincing characters and are at times overplotted.

Sherwood Anderson (1876-1941) was less satirical than Lewis and wrote sympathetic and psychologically interesting studies of small-town people. His sketches in *Winesburg, Ohio* (1919) recall **Edgar Lee Masters's** *Spoon River Anthology* of 1915. Sherwood Anderson was impressed by the works of Freud and D. H. Lawrence. The 23 stories of his *Winsburg, Ohio* describe characters that are puzzled and frustrated. These psychological portraits are written in a simple and intense style and are held together by the consciousness of an observer/reporter, George Willard, thus creating a work that stands half-way between novel and short story. In fact, Anderson's reputation rests on his short stories, but he also wrote a remarkable novel, *Dark Laughter* (1925), which contrasts unrepressed blacks with spiritually sterile whites.

After 1920, realism in American fiction continued along the line taken, on the one hand, by Dreiser, Sinclair and Lewis, and, on the other hand, in the experiments of the American expatriates in Europe, the "lost generation", as Gertrude Stein called herself, Hemingway, and her literary circle in Paris that, at one time or another, included such writers as Cummings, Dos Passos, and Fitzgerald.

The hardship and the human suffering of the Depression of the early 1930s is reflected in the fiction of John Steinbeck and such neo-naturalists as James T. Farrell, John O'Hara and Nelson Algren. Of the several novels of the Californian **John Steinbeck** (1902-68), some are humorous picaresque studies of Mexican-Californian characters (*Tortilla Flat*, 1935; *Cannery Row*, 1945). These works owe much of their style to the local colour movement. Many of Steinbeck's novels have little literary value. Outstanding are his naturalistic works emphasizing heredity and environment in the assessment of poor human "underdogs". Thus *Of Mice and Men* (1937), held mostly in dialogue, is the tragic story of the dreams and adventures of two itinerant Californian farm labourers, while *The Grapes of Wrath* (1939) traces the suffering of the Joad family in the Depression as they migrate from the Oklahoma dust bowl to California. Far from being the promised land, the West proves a great disappointment, and the Joads are left with nothing but their hopes and dreams. The book was made into a film by John Ford in 1940. *East of Eden* (1952) is Steinbeck's treatment of heredity and the power of evil. The actor James Dean made the film, and the novel, a great popular success.

The proletarian naturalistic fiction of **James T. Farrell** (1904-79) is decidedly more pessimistic. Farrell's *Studs Lonigan* trilogy (1932-35) charts the negative influence of environment in the tragic life of an Irish Catholic in the Chicago slums. Comparable works are **John O'Hara's** (1905-1970) bitter satire about a country-club society in *Appointment in Samarra* (1934) and **Nelson Algren's** (1909-81) realistic fictional account of a Texas boy's criminal career in *Somebody in Boots* (1935). O'Hara and Algren wrote more realistic novels after 1945. The best-known works are Algren's fascinating panorama of the Chicago underworld in *The Man With the Golden Arm* (1949), and of a similar setting in New Orleans during the Depression in *A Walk on the Wild Side* (1956).

Because of her pervasive influence on the "lost generation", **Gertrude Stein** (1874-1946) occupies an important place in American literature. As the heart and soul of a group of European and American artists and avant-garde writers in Paris (Picasso, Matisse, Braque, Apollinaire, and Cocteau[1] were some Europeans she knew), she sought to combine the psychology of her teacher William James with

---

1. Pablo Ruiz y Picasso (1881-1973), Spanish painter, who settled in Paris in 1901 and, together with Braque, developed Cubism in 1907. He produced many paintings and etchings and was also a brilliant draughtsman.

Henri Matisse (1869-1954), the principal painter in the group of French artists called "Les Fauves" (wild beasts) because of the violent colours they used.

Georges Braque (1882-1963), French painter and the classical representative of Cubism. He specialized in still life.

Guillaume Apollinaire (1880-1918). French poet and critic and a prominent figure in the avant-garde in early 20th-century Paris.

Jean Cocteau (1889-1963), French poet, novelist, dramatist, film director, and critic, and a leader of the modernist movement in art, literature, ballet, music, and the cinema.

Bergson's[1] philosophy and notion of time. Her revolutionary stylistic and literary theories are related to dadaism[2] (see her *Composition as Explanation*, 1926; and *Lectures in America*, 1935) and broke with traditional ways of narration and plotting. Stein suggested the use of a simple style, intentional monotony and repetition to express what she termed "immediacy" or the actual present. Her theories proved of greater influence than her novels (*Ida*, 1941; and the autobiographical *The Making of Americans*, 1925) which, given her theories and experiments, are difficult to read. A good access to her life and work is *The Autobiography of Alice B. Toklas* (1933), her own autobiography, written as though by her lesbian friend and secretary. Stein's idea that fiction should express immediate experience in a sober prose was taken up by Sherwood Anderson, Dos Passos, Fitzgerald, and Hemingway.

John Dos Passos (1896-1970) studied at Harvard and in Spain and took part in World War I in a volunteer ambulance corps. He recorded his growing disillusion and the inhumanity of the military machinery in his pacifist novel *Three Soldiers* (1921). Dos Passos's early novels give evidence of his leftist tendencies and of Gertrude Stein's literary theories. *Manhattan Transfer* (1925) was his first experiment in the novel. It tries to capture the vast variety and the pluralism of the world of the big city in a colossal portrait that involves some 50 characters in impressionistic and cinematic scenes. Similar in technique is his ambitious trilogy *U.S.A.*, consisting of *The 42nd Parallel* (1930), *1919* (1932), and *The Big Money* (1936). These novels combine narrative realism with biographies of contemporary public figures and such experimental elements as montages of newspaper headlines, musical hits, and "camera eye" semi-autobiographical impressions. They express his Marxist view of American society and his plea for a better social system. Although more concerned with social and economic forces than with individual characters, the series remains an impressive work. In his subsequent works (for example in *District of Columbia*, 1952) Dos Passos modified his political views and abandoned his experimental technique.

F. Scott Fitzgerald (1896-1940), another member of the "lost generation" and of Gertrude Stein's Paris circle, has gone down in literary history as the chronicler of the hedonistic Jazz Age (the 1920s). Fitzgerald wrote many excellent short stories and dealt with the frenetic and frivolous youth of the post-war years in *This Side of Paradise* (1920). His masterpiece is *The Great Gatsby* (1925).

Told by Nick Carraway, Gatsby's neighbour on Long Island, this novel tells the story of Jay Gatsby, who finances his huge mansion and fabulous entertainments by shady means. Gatsby's attempt to regain the love of his youth, Daisy, now married to a brutal man of wealth, ends in tragedy and murder. Fitzgerald draws a compelling picture of a society obsessed with money, and of an idealist forced to live a superficial life to make his dreams come true. The promise of the "American dream" is shown to be an illusion.

---

1. Henri Bergson (1859-1941), French philosopher and recipient of the Nobel Prize for literature in 1928. In his several books he opposed scientific materialism and positivism. He established the primacy of creative inner experience and distinguished between "real duration" and measured time. He also studied the aesthetics of comedy in *Le Rire* (1900).
2. See the note on page 232.

Fitzgerald provided a further fictional treatment of the theme of disillusionment in *Tender Is the Night* (1934), which traces the eventual failure of a psychiatrist, Dick Diver, who cures his wife Nicole from schizophrenia but spends his emotional energy in his multiple roles as doctor, lover, and husband. Fitzgerald's final novel, *The Last Tycoon* (1941) remained unfinished; it deals with Hollywood and the "American dream".

Ernest Hemingway's (1899-1961) fiction has been an influential source for European and American writers. With some guidance from Stein and Pound, and under the influence of sober and practical newspaper styles (Hemingway worked for several papers in America and as a correspondent in Europe), he developed a factual prose style that has remained connected with his name. Like Dos Passos, Hemingway served as a volunteer in an ambulance unit in Italy and was severely wounded. Between 1921 and 1927 he lived mainly in Paris and then in Cuba and Florida. In the Spanish Civil War, which he covered as a correspondent from 1936-1937, he sided with the republicans. In World War II he took part in the invasion of Normandy in 1944. Hemingway's themes are courageous endurance in the face of danger and death, and, increasingly toward the 1950s, an obsession with death. Ernest Hemingway tried to live his own fiction. He covered several wars as a journalist; he went on safaris in Africa and loved deep-sea fishing; he attended bull-fights (see *Death in the Afternoon*, 1932); he engaged in boxing and knocked out adversaries - and critics - in bars; he drank heavily and married four times. He was trying to prove his manhood, but his flirtations with death led to paranoia. And when he realized that he could no longer write with his former vigour and could no longer believe in his own act, he made a final gesture by blowing out his own brains with a shotgun in 1961.

Ernest Hemingway was a master of the short story, and he also wrote a few good novels on characters suffering bravely in a world without God. Hemingway gave great importance not to psychological analysis but to seemingly simple gestures and everyday speech. There is, however, a touch of romantic sentimentality in his lonely and disillusioned heroes. His first novel, *The Sun Also Rises* (1926; published in England as *Fiesta*), portrays the cynical disillusion of the "lost generation" in a group of hedonistic young people. They remain spiritually deficient as

Ernest Hemingway

they drown their disgust with life in alcohol and seek excitement in sex and bull-fights. *A Farewell to Arms* (1929) is set in World War I. Partly autobiographical, the novel is concerned with Frederic Henry, an American ambulance officer in the Italian army, and his love for the English nurse Catherine. The two escape the tragedy of war, but Catherine and her baby die during the birth of the child, leaving Henry alone in a strange land. The stoic Henry found a successor in Robert Jordan, the American volunteer in the Spanish Civil War and hero of *For Whom the Bell Tolls* (1940). Although Jordan knows that his mission is pointless, he does his duty and sacrifices his love and his life for the republican cause. He thus proves a heroic individual in a world of cynicism and chaos. The sentimental love story in this novel is balanced by realistic scenes of the inhuman war. When Hemingway received the Nobel Prize for literature in 1954, he had earned it with a number of excellent novels and short stories, and with a few less important works (e. g. *To Have and Have Not*, 1937; and *Across the River and Into the Trees*, 1950). His last outstanding piece of fiction was *The Old Man and the Sea* (1952). In this long tale or novelette, the Cuban fisherman Santiago loses the beautiful and huge marlin he has caught to the sharks. Santiago's courageous fight with the sharks lasts for two days and nights. In a symbolic contest with the inhuman elements and forces of nature, the poor fisherman emerges as the quintessential Hemingway hero. Proud in defeat and losing in style, the old man proves Hemingway's "macho" idea that a man may be "beaten but not destroyed". Hemingway's posthumously published *Islands in the Stream* (1970) is a variation on his major themes in the partly autobiographical story of an unhappy painter.

Several writers of the 1930s were dissatisfied with the "proletarian literature" as represented by Farrell, Dos Passos and Steinbeck, and with the tough personal realism of Hemingway. Writers such as Henry Miller, Nathanael West und Djuna Barnes went beyond protest and epic realism and found in a grotesque surrealism an adequate means of expression for their despair and devastating criticism of the false illusions generated by the "American dream". **Nathanael West** (1903-40) had an apocalyptic view of the world as hovering between dream and nightmare. He saw modern America as a doomed Babylon. West died at an early age in a car accident. His work, like that of Miller and the still vastly underrated and unknown Barnes, received little notice when it was first published; but his novels have gradually gained much positive critical attention. The son of Jewish immigrants, West spent some time in Paris in the 1920s and took a deep interest in surrealism and in Kafka. His first novel is the occasionally obscene fantasy *The Dream Life of Balso Snell* (1931). It was published in Paris and parodies literary styles and personalities while exposing human corruption. Yet West is best remembered for the three novels he published in the following years. *Miss Lonelyhearts* (1933) is a sad and bitter satire of a journalist who escapes into black humour in order to be able to bear the suffering of the people writing in response to his newspaper column. *A Cool Million* (1934), a parody of Voltaire's *Candide*[1], fiercely attacks the Horatio Alger rags-to-riches myth. West's most ambitious work, *The Day of the Locust* (1939), based on his knowledge of Hollywood as a film script writer, depicts in a surrealistic style the cruelty and the misery beneath the glittering surface of a city which, to West, represented everything that is sham and false in American society.

Djuna Barnes (1892-1982) was born in New York, but spent several decades of her life in Europe. She wrote two important experimental novels, *Ryder* (1928) and *Nightwood* (1935), portraying psychopathic characters and tragic horror in a complex fiction that was highly praised by T. S. Eliot and is being slowly recognized as a major contribution to American surrealism.

Henry Miller (1891-1980) explored another form of surrealism by pitting sensual life against the urban nightmare of the twentieth century and America as he described and assaulted it in *The Air-Conditioned Nightmare* (1945). In the 1930s Miller lived in Paris and then settled in California. His fiction is essentially autobiographical, expressing his individualism, his love of freedom, and his natural responses. Miller's books are marked by a lyrical prose, confessional passages with frank sexual descriptions, and obscene dialogue that caused his books to be banned in the United States up until the early 1960s. His novels were thus published in the USA with a time lag of some 30 years. *Tropic of Cancer* (Paris, 1934; USA, 1961) is an intense and sexually uninhibited fictional account of the life of an American expatriate in Paris, while *Tropic of Capricorn* (1939; USA, 1962) is concerned with Miller's life in New York in a satirical form. His final autobiographical and confessional series, *The Rosy Crucifixion* (made up of *Sexus*, 1949; *Plexus*, 1953; and *Nexus*, 1960), is less outrageously obscene and was written when Miller was partially reconciled with America. Also a prolific writer of stories and a critic, Henry Miller became one of the major sources for the Beat movement. The energetic and obscene vitality of his novels is balanced by his surrealistic and apocalyptic fantasy.

In addition to the realists, naturalists, and surrealists, a group of more traditional novelists wrote in a manner inspired by Henry James's psychological realism and Hawthorne's romances. The cultivated settings and laboured moral problems in almost all of **Edith Wharton's** (1862-1937) novels provide sufficient evidence of

---

1. Philosophical tale by Voltaire, written in 1759 against the optimistic teaching of Leibniz. Essentially, Voltaire's work attacks human utopias and illusions and warns against the dangers of imaginary paradises.

the thematic and stylistic influence of the cosmopolitan Wharton's great idol, Henry James (see her *The House of Mirth,* 1905; *The Custom of the Country,* 1913; and *The Age of Innocence,* 1920). **Ellen Glasgow** (1874-1945) deplored the end of the Southern aristocracy in her early sentimental novels but then found a more convincing ironic realism in *Barren Ground* (1925), a social satire in which the heroine, after the death of her father, restores the family's neglected farm. **Willa Cather** (1873-1947) was born in Virginia and grew up in Nebraska. She dealt with the hardships of men in a hostile environment and with the life of new settlers (see her *O Pioneers!,* 1913; and *My Ántonia,* 1918). Cather also wrote an outstanding historical novel on the work of the Catholic Church and of two saints in New Mexico: *Death Comes for the Archbishop* (1927).

Glasgow and Cather stand at the beginning of Southern literary realism. But there were also novelists in the South completely opposed to realism. One of them was **James Branch Cabell** (1879-1958). A Virginian and a belated romantic writer, Cabell created his own imaginary country and called it Poictesme, providing it with a history, geography, and mythology, and peopling it with characters descended from the country's ruler, Dom Manuel, a pessimistic comedian striving for unobtainable ideals in art and love. Among the many pseudo-scholarly romances dealing with Manuel *Jurgen* (1919) is perhaps the best known. It deals with a pawnbroker who becomes a duke, a king, and an emperor while visiting heaven and hell and meeting mythical and fictional characters in a number of partly erotic adventures. The pawnbroker finally returns to his former comfortable life.

Finally, **George Santayana** (1863-1952) and **Thornton Wilder** (1897-1975) remain to be mentioned as writers outside the current of realism. Santayana was a philosopher and critic who shared William James's idea of pragmatism while opposing German idealism. Santayana's novel *The Last Puritan* (1935) shows the gradual retreat of Calvinism in New England in an epic portrait of social and dramatic events. As a novelist, Wilder was indebted to James Joyce and Gertrude Stein. Wilder's *The Cabala* (1926) traces the growing corruption of the Italian aristocracy after World War I as seen by an ironic yet fascinated American. His novels are characterized by episodic structure and a mixture of classical-hedonistic and Christian backgrounds. They try to explore philosophical and metaphysical problems, such as the question of God's will in *The Bridge of San Luis Rey* (1927), or that of God's existence in *The Woman of Andros* (1930). *The Eighth Day* (1967) and *Theophilus North* (1973) are concerned with the meaning of man's life and future.

The two decades between the world wars also saw the first flowering of a Southern literature that was to produce a rich harvest after 1945. "Southern literature" is a rather complex term. It covers such movements as realism, the regionalism of the Southern "agrarians" John Crowe Ransom and Robert Penn Warren, and the symbolism and "Southern gothic" of William Faulkner, Eudora Welty and Flannery O'Connor; and it encompasses the work of such diverse writers as Thomas Wolfe, Erskine Caldwell, and Truman Capote. The extremes are marked by Ellen Glasgow and James Branch Cabell. The best of Glasgow's work, such as *Barren Ground,* is both regional and protest literature against social and economic

The Bootleggers
by Thomas Hart
Benson, 1927

injustice, while Cabell is an aesthetician who looks back to Poe and has fascinated contemporary Southern writers like Lytle and Walker Percy. Ellen Glasgow has found a successor in **Erskine Caldwell** (1903-87). A native of Georgia, he has described the plight and sorrows of poor whites and powerless blacks in a number of novels and short stories that have attracted a wide readership. In *Tobacco Road* (1932) and *God's Little Acre* (1933) Caldwell showed an ugly and degenerate rural world dominated by religious fanaticism, sadism, racism, sex and alcohol. *Tobacco Road* was dramatized and proved a great success on the New York stage. In many subsequent novels Caldwell has continued his fictional treatment of the South (see, for instance, *Trouble in July,* 1940; and *Jenny by Nature,* 1961). The elements of the grotesque and of horror relate these works to the fiction of Faulkner, McCullers and O'Connor.

There can be no doubt, however, that Thomas Wolfe and William Faulkner are the towering giants in the Southern fiction of the 1930s and, as far as Faulkner is concerned, even beyond 1945 and the limits of the Mason-Dixon line[1]. **Thomas Wolfe** (1900-1938) was born in Ashville, North Carolina, which was to become the "Altamont, Old Catawba" of his fiction. Wolfe studied at the University of North Carolina and at Harvard, travelled widely in Europe and died early of pneumonia. His epic and panoramic novels are autobiographical and confessional in character. They seek to capture the totality of the world – reality and imagination, people, events and moods – with an enormous vocabulary and styles that range from highly lyrical rhetoric to prosaic reporting. Wolfe's unrestrained formlessness

---

1. The boundary or line, first surveyed by Jeremiah Dixon and Charles Mason (1763-67), which later separated the Southern slave states from the free states. A related term is "Dixie", signifying the Southern states of the US.

led to huge sprawling manuscripts that his publishers reduced to an acceptable size. Thus *Look Homeward, Angel* (1929) began as a manuscript of some 800,000 words and covers the childhood and youth (1884-1920) of the hero, Eugene Gant, who gradually becomes aware of his ancestral roots and of the limits of the environment he intends to transcend. In the sequence to this work, *Of Time and the River* (1935), which covers the years 1920-1925, Gant leaves his native South, entering the world of urbanity and fast change in Boston, New York, Oxford, and France. When Wolfe died at a young age in 1938, several manuscripts were found which show his continued interest in covering the modern world through the mind of a fictional hero who closely resembles himself. In *The Web and the Rock* (1939), the protagonist George Webber searches for the "rock" of strength while trying to escape the "web" of heredity and environment. Like Wolfe, Webber travels to Germany. The continuation of this novel is *You Can't Go Home Again* (1940), which deals with Webber's life after his return to an America suffering from the Depression. Facing social and political problems abroad (Germany) and in America, Webber tries unsuccessfully to return to his home town, describes his career as a novelist and, finally, recognizes that "one cannot go home again", but that America could lead the way from decadence to a new beginning. Thomas Wolfe's epic narratives of himself, of America and life are very modern in their complex time scheme, incorporating the present, the past, and the experience of both. They are equally complex in their presentation of documentary and symbolic material.

Like Wolfe, **William Faulkner** (1897-1962) turned a part of his regional Southern background into the locale for much of his fiction. The son of a rich and reputable Southern family, Faulkner grew up in Oxford, Mississippi. He spent most of his life there, apart from serving briefly in the British Royal Air Force in Canada in 1918, some time spent as a reporter and bohemian in New Orleans and a brief visit to Europe in 1925. In New Orleans Faulkner became interested in poetry and avant-garde writers, such as Eliot and Joyce, and he met Sherwood Anderson, who helped him to publish his first novel. Faulkner was awarded the Nobel Prize for Literature in 1950. His novels achieve a unique combination of realism, symbolism and modernist techniques. In Faulkner's fiction the settings, the characters and their speech are distinctly Southern, but the suffering and the tragedy of his heroes point to a more general human level.

His first two novels show him in search of a modern style and a modern definition of literary art. *Soldier's Pay* (1926) is about a member of the "lost generation" returning from war, and *Mosquitoes* (1927) is a satire on the artists of New Orleans. With *Sartoris* (1929, published in its full text in 1973 as *Flags in the Dust*) he approached closer to his aim. It was for this novel that he first created his fictional Yoknapatawpha County and its capital, Jefferson, and introduced a complex group of characters he was to play with and develop through many of his subsequent works.

Sartoris has as its hero the disillusioned Bayard Sartoris, yet another representative of the "lost generation". Back from the war, he becomes estranged from his family in the process of experiencing the isolation of the individual, the influence of the past on the present, and the decay of the South's morality and traditions. Faulkner could use much of his own family background for the story of the three generations of the Sartoris family that is told here. Bayard finally seeks a manly death by testing an unsafe and new kind of aircraft. The novel contrasts the chivalric and cultured manners of the Sartoris family with the commercial self-interest of the newly-rich Snopeses.

After the completion of his great novels of the 1930s, Faulkner returned to the fictional exploration of the history of the Snopeses, a story of avarice, murder and perversion, told in the trilogy, *The Hamlet* (1940), *The Town* (1957), and *The Mansion* (1959).

In the late 1920s and 1930s Faulkner produced several magnificent novels in which his use of the literary methods of modernism (stream-of-consciousness, collage presentation, time shifts) helped to create some of the best fiction written in the twentieth century. The first of these works was *The Sound and the Fury* (1929).

This novel presents the degenerate and perverted life of the Compson family, formerly genteel Southern patricians, on their shrunken plantation near Jefferson, Mississippi. The first three parts are written in the stream-of-consciousness technique, showing the events of three days as reflected in the minds of three brothers: the idiot Benjy, who is 33 years old and incapable of speech; the introverted, sensitive and neurotic Quentin, who is in love with his sister Caddy; and the mean and dishonest Jason. The three interior monologues of the brothers are complemented by an objective report from an outsider, the simple and good-hearted black servant Dilsey Gibson, whose innocent character is set off against the perverted world of the whites.

The story, or rather the picture, that emerges after 106 fragments of recollection and monologues provides a panorama of the South and records the progress of moral and human corruption among the Compsons. Quentin, a student at Harvard, is obsessed by his incestuous love for his sister. When she is seduced by a stranger, he kills himself. Benjy is desolate when his sister is forced to marry and leave home. He plays with her illegitimate daughter until she grows up and runs away with a stranger. And Jason, proving the immorality of the Compsons, speculates with the money Caddy sends for her child.

The title of the novel, taken from Shakespeare's *Macbeth,* alludes both to Benjy's monologue, which is "a tale, told by an idiot, full of sound and fury, signifying nothing", and to the nihilistic mood of the whole work.

Joyce's influence on the technique in this novel is as remarkable as it is in *As I Lay Dying* (1930), set among the poor whites. Fifteen characters, with 59 interior monologues, make up the grotesque and tragi-comic tale of the transporting to Jefferson of the dead Addie Bundren in her coffin. This turns out to be a ten-day trek ending in a fire and, for Darl, one of the sons, in an asylum for the insane. With its numerous obstacles and bizarre events, the trek proves a sort of symbolic procession through life, a comic and grotesque dance of death and egoism around a coffin.

Faulkner's novels of the 1930s show a Southern world of hate, perversion, lust and obsession. This kind of fiction came to be known as "Southern Gothic". Its typical exploration of evil in historical, regional and moral dimensions has occupied a number of Southern novelists, notably Robert Penn Warren, Eudora Welty, Carson McCullers, and Flannery O'Connor. An example of such "Gothic" fiction is Faulkner's *Sanctuary* (1931). He wrote the book out of commercial interest, and its full text, with Horace Denbow as the central character, only appeared in 1981. It is a crime novel of murder, rape, prostitution, and lynching, and it found a sequel in *Requiem for a Nun* (1951), told partly in a dramatic form. Faulkner's two great novels from the Thirties, *Light in August* (1932) and *Absalom, Absalom!* (1936), again focus on human cruelty and perversion, but they also dramatize suffering and love. *Light in August* has three interlocking sub-plots concerned with the search of Lena Grove for the father of her child, with the tragic life and death of the mulatto and murderer Joe Christmas, and with the intellectual and idealist Reverend Hightower, who destroys his own life. With its mythical and biblical parallels, its complex treatment of racism and Puritanism, and its modern narrative techniques, this is one of Faulkner's finest works. It is matched by *Absalom, Absalom!*, also an extraordinary experimental novel which continues the history of Yoknapatawpha in the historical and gothic story of Thomas Sutpen. Sutpen is a poor white whose dreams of founding a rich and reputable family are destroyed by old tragedies, personal guilt and a cursed land. In this last of his modernist books Faulkner interweaves history and psychological disorientation and perversion in an ultimately symbolic panorama of sin and corruption in the South. Yoknapatawpha now had its dynasties and genealogies, its histories and crimes – and they occupied Faulkner in several subsequent novels: *The Unvanquished* (1938), *Intruder in the Dust* (1948), the Snopes trilogy mentioned above, his last picaresque novel, *The Reivers* (1962), and in numerous short stories.

Of Faulkner's contemporaries and successors in the South only a few can be mentioned here. **Robert Penn Warren** (born 1905) has written one outstanding novel, *All the King's Men* (1946). It deals with moral responsibility and political power and is superior to his more recent fiction. Among women writers, **Katherine Anne Porter** (1890-1980; see her novel *Ship of Fools*, 1962), **Caroline Gordon** (1895-1981), **Eudora Welty** (born 1909), and **Flannery O'Connor** (1925-64) are better known as short story writers. Nevertheless, Welty's *Delta Wedding* (1946), *Losing Battles* (1970), and *The Optimist's Daughter* (1972) provide sensitive portraits of families and individuals resisting change in the South, while the Catholic O'Connor's *Wise Blood* (1952) deals with disbelief and saving grace as God erupts into the lives of some Southerners. The most gifted novelist among the white women writers was **Carson McCullers** (1917-67). The tragic world and the neurotic characters of Faulkner also emerge in several of her works. *The Heart Is a Lonely Hunter* (1940), *Reflections in a Golden Eye* (1941), *The Member of the Wedding* (1946), and *Clock Without Hands* (1961) feature lonely and desperate adolescents, and eccentric and grotesque adults, all suffering as much from the dark corners of their minds as from their often frustrated attempts to establish human contacts. **Harper Lee's** (born 1926) *To Kill a Mockingbird* (1960) also belongs to this genre. It is concerned with the sensational trial of a black charged with raping a white woman, and is told from the point of view of the young daughter of the white defense lawyer. Gordon and O'Connor were both Roman Catholics, and their religious sensibility as well as their sense of tradition seem to be shared to some extent by other Catholic authors like the Alabama-born **Walker Percy** (born 1916; see *The Moviegoer*,1961; *The Last Gentleman*, 1966; *The Second Coming*, 1980) and **John William Corrington** (born 1932).

Many other writers continue to study the Southern consciousness as influenced by history and environment. Prominent among these are **Cormac McCarthy** (born 1933), **Reynolds Price** (born 1933) and the less known **Marion Montgomery** (born 1925) and **Andrew Lytle** (born 1902).

Other Southern novelists began as regionalists but have turned to more general subjects and other settings in their more recent works. To these belong **Elizabeth Spencer** (born 1921), **Calder Willingham** (born 1922), and **Shirley Ann Grau** (born 1929), who are less read outside the United States; **William Styron** (born 1925) and **Truman Capote** (1924-84). The South still occupies an eminent place in Styron's Faulknerian family tragedy *Lie Down in Darkness* (1951) and *The Confessions of Nat Turner* (1967), a fictional account of a slave rebellion in Virginia in 1831, in which Styron treats the race issue in what he terms a complex "meditation in history". *Sophie's Choice* (1979) has a narrator from Virginia but is concerned with a Polish Catholic woman who survives Auschwitz and later falls in love with an American Jew obsessed with the Holocaust.

Truman Capote was born in New Orleans and grew up on a farm in the South. He lived in New York and in Europe and travelled widely. Like Tennessee Williams, he held many jobs in his life and flaunted his Southern origin as well as his homosexuality. Capote was an unusually gifted writer of short stories and began his career with tales about the South. The novel *Other Voices, Other Rooms* (1948) is about a homosexually inclined boy trying to reach maturity, while *The Grass Harp* (1951) presents some eccentric outsiders escaping social restraint by living in a tree house. With his novella, *Breakfast at Tiffany's* (1958), of which a successful film was made, Capote left the South behind. This work is about Holly Golightly (a telling name), a charming and amoral playgirl of New York. *In Cold Blood* (1966) is Capote's experiment in the "nonfiction novel". It is an elaborately researched account of a murder in Kansas in 1959. Although this combination of documentary material and fiction can hardly be called a novelty (Dos Passos tried it before Capote), it is a compelling book and ushered in a brief wave of "nonfiction novels".

The past as legend, and the sense of a lost tradition, continue to fascinate such novelists as **David Madden** (born 1933), **Jesse Hill Ford** (born 1928), and **William Humphrey** (born 1924), while black writers, especially women, have made their native South the setting of their ethnic fiction.

Truman Capote

The post-war American novel is rich in genres, movements and names. It seems appropriate to divide the huge number of novelists into two recognizable movements: the Beats and experimentalists or metafictionists, and traditional writers in the realistic line, including novelists of manners, ethnic writers, such as blacks, Jews and Indians, and the increasingly important women authors with a distinct feminist viewpoint. The strain of realism in American fiction is most obvious in the war novels that appeared in the 1940s and 1950s. Whereas World War I generated works of great technical experiment, World War II produced mainly realistic or starkly naturalistic fiction reflecting the experience of young Americans on the European and Pacific battlefields. Remarkable examples are **John Hersey's** (born 1914) *A Bell for Adano* (1944) and *The War Lover* (1959), **Gore Vidal's** (born 1925) *Williwaw* (1946), **Irwin Shaw's** (born 1913) *The Young Lions* (1948), which portrays the fortunes of two American soldiers and a Nazi, **James Gould Cozzens's** (1903-78) *Guard of Honor* (1948), contrasting human and military values on an air force base, and **Norman Mailer's** (born 1923) *The Naked and the Dead* (1948), which employs modernist techniques and draws the picture of an American microcosmic male society on a South Pacific island held by the Japanese. There are also some explicitly realistic novels brimming with violence: **James Jones's** (1921-77) *From Here to Eternity* (1951) and **Herman Wouk's** (born 1915) *The Caine Mutiny* (1951). Exceptional novelists, such as **John Hawkes** (*The Cannibal*, 1949) and **Joseph Heller** (*Catch-22*, 1961), have covered grotesque and satirical aspects of the war experience. Among the younger realists, **Robert Stone** (born 1937) has dealt with the Vietnam war in *Dog Soldiers* (1974), a bitter tale of a morally corrupt American journalist who meets with destructiveness and egoism everywhere (see also Stone's *A Hall of Mirrors*, 1967, and *A Flag for Sunrise*, 1981, both concerned with individual and national corruption). Realism also marks the works of **James Dickey** (born 1923), who is also a poet, **Hubert Selby** (born 1928), and **Paul Theroux** (born 1941). Dickey's *Deliverance* (1970) tells of four men besieged by hillbillies in the backwoods of Georgia and became internationally known in its film version. Selby produced a vivid picture of corruption and violence in urban life with *Last Exit to Brooklyn* (1964) and explored sadistic and sexual fantasies in *The Room* (1971) and *The Demon* (1976). Theroux was born in Massachusetts but has spent most of his life in Africa, Eastern countries, and in Europe. His best fiction is concerned with Westerners caught in alien cultures, as in *Jungle Lovers* (1971), *Saint Jack* (1973), and *The Mosquito Coast* (1982), which is about a neurotic and self-sufficient Yankee engineer trying to build up a technical American nightmare in the Honduran jungle.

Another group of writers have distinguished themselves in the post-war novel of manners, which deals with the behaviour of the upper middle class and the urban upper class. The outstanding practitioners in this genre are, among older writers, **John P. Marquand** (1893-1960; see his *Point of No Return*, 1949; *Melville Goodwin, USA*, 1951; and *Women and Thomas Harrow*, 1958), **Louis Auchincloss** (born 1917; see his *The Great World and Timothy Colt*, 1956; *A World of Profit*, 1968; *The Dark Lady*, 1977; and *Watchfires*, 1982), the better known **John Cheever** (1912-82) and **J. D. Salinger** (born 1919), and, among the younger novelists, John Updike, Joyce Carol Oates, John Kennedy Toole, and J. P. Donleavy. **Cheever,** who also wrote many short stories, dealt with an affluent Massachusetts family in *The Wapshot Chronicle* (1957) and *The Wapshot Scandal* (1964), and satirized another suburban family in *Bullet Park* (1969). Cheever's last two works are among his best fiction: *Falconer* (1977) is largely told in monologues and is concerned with the imprisonment of an ex-professor for the murder of his brother, while *Oh What a Paradise It Seems* (1982) treats of the character of an aging man rejuvenated by a romance and his ecological work to save the landscape of his youth. **J. D. Salinger** shares with Cheever a preference for the short story. His *The Catcher in the Rye* (1951) remains his most important work and proved an influential novel for the generation maturing in the 1950s.

Like the best of American fiction *(Huckleberry Finn, Moby-Dick)*, Salinger's novel has a first-person narrator, the sixteen-year old Holden Caulfield, a lonely, slightly neurotic and sensitive boy from a rich family. Apparently recovering from a serious breakdown after being expelled from prep school, Holden addresses the reader as if he/she were a listening friend and tells his brief but compelling story about the expulsion and his picaresque adventures during two days in New York.

A novel of initiation, *The Catcher in the Rye* appealed to the readers of the 1950s because of the questions Holden asked and because of his rejection of what he considers the false world of the adults. Today, one is more impressed by Salinger's excellent ear for the jargon and speech of adolescents in the 1950s. Holden's imprecise and highly emotional slang proves a good means for Salinger's attempt to portray the painful transition of a youth from innocence to adult experience.

John Updike (born 1932) made his debut with short stories and has tried a variety of fictional techniques in his novels. He is most convincing as a novelist when he describes ordinary middle-class life, as in his *Rabbit* novels. His more unusual works include *The Poorhouse Fair* (1959), a parable about the individual and the welfare state; *The Centaur* (1963), which links the lives of an American teenager and his father to Greek mythology; *The Coup* (1979), a burlesque view of an African dictator and former student in Amercia now ousted by his supporters; and the comic descriptions of the problems of a successful Jewish novelist in *Bech: A Book* (1970) and its sequel, *Bech is Back* (1982). Updike will probably go down in literary history as the most talented chronicler of the American middle class. In dazzling style, he records his characters' waning religious beliefs, their experience of a hedonistic America, and their preoccupation with sex and the fear of approaching death. His novels also catch the spirit of the decades in which they were written. Thus *Couples* (1968), a bestseller that shocked many with its explicit sex scenes, covers the years of President Kennedy's administration. Sex as a means to achieve happiness, to escape the boredom of life, and to evade the idea of death, is also central to *A Month of Sundays* (1975) and *Marry Me* (1976). The three different endings of the latter imitate the literary fashion of the year. So far, Updike's best achievement as a novelist is his trilogy concerned with the life and thoughts of the former high-school basketball champion Harry "Rabbit" Angstrom. Magnificently rendering the political, economic and moral anxieties of three decades as seen by an ordinary and frustrated American, Updike has written a detailed and

Couple with Shopping Bags by Duane Hanson, 1976

vastly entertaining fictional history of modern middle-class America. *Rabbit Run* (1960) covers the early marital difficulties and frustrations of the young Harry, and *Rabbit Redux* (1971) picks up the story ten years later, as Harry temporarily loses his wife to a Greek car salesman, befriends two radicals, and gets a job in his father-in-law's car business. *Rabbit Is Rich* (1981) shows the Angstroms another ten years later. Now comfortably rich, "Rabbit" runs his father-in-law's business and enjoys the social and superficial atmosphere of the local country club. He meets his former lover, Ruth, has paternal problems with his son Nelson, and is increasingly plagued with visions of death. Even wild sex orgies cannot provide relief from this fear. Eros and Thanatas also emerge as leitmotifs in his novels *The Witches of Eastwick* (1984) and *Roger's Version* (1986).

In comparison with Updike's fiction, the novels and short stories of the very productive **Joyce Carol Oates** (born 1938) suffer from an excess of violence, horror and melodrama. Her works include *A Garden of Earthly Delights* (1967), *Wonderland* (1971), *The Assassins* (1975), *Bellefleur* (1980), and *A Bloodsmoor Romance* (1982). Oates has peopled her novels with demonic and obsessed characters. They are prevented from communicating by a violent Amercian society that, in turn, generates bloodshed.

Both **John Kennedy Toole** (1937–69) and **J. P. Donleavy** (born 1926) are representatives of the picaresque mode of the novel of manners. Toole killed himself before his first and only novel, *A Confederacy of Dunces* (1980) was published and recognized as a masterpiece. Its hero is Ignatius J. Reilly, a self-educated and self-defined young genius who intends to reform the twentieth century but refuses to accept work and responsibility. Set in the raffish French quarter of New Orleans, the novel justly won a Pulitzer Prize for its thoughtful critique of the shallowness of modern American life. Ignatius J. Reilly resembles Donleavy's heroes in their refusal to fit into the social fabric. Sebastian Dangerfield, an expatriate ex-soldier in Dublin and the dishonest American hero of *The Ginger Man* (1955), became the prototype for a series of similar selfish and roguish characters in Donleavy's *A Singular Man* (1963), *The Beastly Beatitudes of Balthazar B.* (1968), *A Fairy Tale of New York* (1973), which is a satire on contemporary America, and *The Destinies of Darcy Dancer, Gentlemen* (1977). Unlike the surrealistic *The Onion Eaters* (1971), these novels are too closely modelled on his *Ginger Man* and draw on his personal experience in England and Ireland, where he has lived since he renounced his American citizenship in 1967.

The novel of manners has also enjoyed a huge and lasting success in the more popular novels of **Sloan Wilson** (born 1920; see *The Man in the Gray Flannel Suit,* 1955) and **Alison Lurie** (born 1926; see *Love and Friendship,* 1962; and *The War Between the Tates,* 1974).

Post-war American fiction has seen the rise of two major schools, the brief neo-Romantic Beat movement and the experimental and self-reflective fiction (also called metafiction) that arose in the 1960s and is a dominant force today. Inspired by Whitman, Thoreau and Eastern philosophy, but also by the early work of Henry Miller, the Beats expressed in poetry and fiction an individualist view of life that celebrated, intensely and ecstatically, music, sex, alcohol and "fun". **William Burroughs** (born 1914) is the patron of the Beats. With his *Junkie* (1953) and *The Naked Lunch* (Paris, 1959; New York, 1962), partly autobiographical accounts of an addict's life and nightmares containing scenes of sadism and perversion, he opened the way for the Beat writers. Burroughs has meanwhile found his own territory in fiction, using the surrealist technique of cinematic cuts in further studies of apocalyptic hallucinations laced with social criticism of bourgeois America (see *The Soft Machine,* 1961; *Nova Express,* 1964; *The Wild Boys,* 1971; *Exterminator!,* 1973; the quasi-autobiographical *Port of Saints,* 1980; and the utopian *Cities of the Red Night,* 1981). The leader of the Beats in fiction was **Jack Kerouac** (1922-69). Trying to catch the "flow of the mind", he wrote what he termed "spontaneous prose" that gave expression to anarchic, mystical and ecstatic urges. *On the Road* (1957) remains his best novel. It is a description of picaresque scenes involving Beat people travelling around America in search of their own American dream. Less known Beat novelists are **Chandler Brossard** (born 1922) and **John Clellon Holmes** (born 1926).

Like Kerouac, **Ken Kesey** (born 1935) toured the USA in the 1960s on a trip with a bus-load of "merry pranksters". Kesey's fine novel, *One Flew Over the Cuckoo's Nest* (1962), was made into an excellent movie starring Jack Nicholson. It catches some of the hippie culture of the 1960s in the story of the lazy and funny Randle McMurphy, who finds himself locked up in a men-

Double Elvis by Andy Warhol, 1963

tal ward. He challenges the sadistic control of the head nurse in a symbolic rebellion against the "system". The narrator is an Indian chief who, like McMurphy, pretends to be insane. When McMurphy is almost reduced to idiocy by electric shock treatment and a lobotomy, Chief Bromden smothers him out of pity and makes his escape.

Various terms have been applied to the experimental novels that began to appear in the 1960s. They make use of absurd and surrealist as well as of self-reflective techniques while questioning the values of modern America and the meaning of history and literary forms. Some American writers have reacted to an international influence: the French nouveau roman, Beckett, and Latin American authors such as Borges and Marquez.[1] Other writers have given literary expression to an American counter-culture fed by the civil rights movement, the Vietnam war, and an awareness of the social and political violence done to humanity. Such expressions as postmodernism, nonfiction, metafiction and others attempt to describe the novels of a number of authors who have been as concerned with the impact of war and nihilism on modern man as with the meaning and form of their own writing. Names connected with this kind of fiction are Nabokov, Hawkes, Barthelme, Brautigan, Gass, Heller, Vonnegut, Gaddis, Pynchon, Barth, Vidal, Irving, and Purdy, and such younger authors as Sukenik, Abish, Federman, and Katz. Surveying the entire experimental field in 1967, John Barth spoke of a "literature of exhaustion", i. e. the exhaustion and uselessnes of older forms and of the referential text. Postmodernism thus rejected the meaningful realism in American fiction and considered the novel as experimental ground for the articulation of formal and epistemological questions. But in the late 1970s Barth began to perceive a "literature of replenishment", a pushing back to more conservative forms and self-conscious realism.

Vladimir Nabokov (1899-1977) was among the most significant experimentalists of the 1950s. He was the son of a distinguished Russian family and wrote his early novels in Russian and German in several European cities before moving to the United States in 1940. Nabokov's sources were Gogol[2] and European modernism. As a professor at Cornell, he influenced a number of younger writers. Nabokov's *Lolita* (Paris, 1955; USA, 1958) caused a scandal and has since been turned into a film with the late James Mason starring as Humbert Humbert. *Lolita* is a farcical and satirical novel on the erotic obsession of a middle-aged European man of letters, Humbert Humbert, with the twelve-year-old "nymphet" Lolita.

---

1. Jorge Luis Borges (born 1899), Argentinian writer and best known for his short stories portraying the fantastic in a realistic manner (magic realism).

Gabriel García Márquez (born 1928), Colombian novelist. Like Borges, he writes fiction in the tradition that has been termed "magic realism", treating supernatural and extraordinary events in a sober and realistic style (*A Hundred Years of Solitude,* 1967; *The Autumn of the Patriarch,* 1975). He received the Nobel Prize for literature in 1982.

2. Nikolai V. Gogol (1809-52), Russian writer and dramatist. A satirist, he is especially known for the short stories he wrote in St. Petersburg and which are set in a mad city where everything is strange, and for the comic epic *Dead Souls* (1842), of which he burned the second part.

Some of Nabokov's later works are translations of novels that were first written in Russian. They include *Pnin* (1957), about the comic experiences of an exiled Russian professor at an American college, *Pale Fire* (1962), *Ada or Ardor* (1969), which deals satirically with a man's love for his sister, *Transparent Things* (1972), and *Look at the Harlequins* (1974). Nabokov's amoralism, his comic games with literary forms, his preference for the double meaning, and his subversion of reality, are related to the grotesque humour and the absurd that emerged in American fiction in the 1960s.

Aspects of surrealism and the grotesque are essential elements in the novels of **John Hawkes** (born 1925), **Donald Barthelme** (born 1931) and **Richard Brautigan** (1935-84). A professor of English at Brown University, **Hawkes** has confessed his debt to the American gothic fiction of Faulkner, Djuna Barnes and O'Connor and to European surrealism. After his war novel *The Cannibal* (1949), a hallucinatory story of genocide and murder in Germany in 1914 and 1945, Hawkes developed his peculiar style of imaginative discovery in a series of novels that are less important for their plot and stress aesthetic impression and experience and artistic effect (see *The Lime Twig*, 1961; *Second Skin*, 1964; *The Blood Oranges*, 1971; *Death, Sleep and the Traveler*, 1974; *Travesty*, 1976; and *The Passion Artist*, 1980). This is most obvious in his novel *Virginie* (1982), which probes the effect of describing bizarre sexual scenes within the larger plot concerning a girl who has lived two previous lives in France, one in the eighteenth century and the other around 1945. Hawkes's *Adentures in the Alaskan Skin Trade* (1985) traces the picaresque travels in Alaska of the reckless John Deauville as seen through the eyes of his daughter Sunny. **Donald Barthelme** has written short stories and two grotesque anti-novels, *Snow White* (1967) and *The Dead Father* (1975). They suggest that both reading and our imagination are fiction and thus irrational. Barthelme destroys his own plot, characters and language, creating a new reality of absurd disorder. A new, if naive, reality was also the aim of **Richard Brautigan**. He came out of the Beat movement and wrote a substantial number of short novels parodying older textual patterns while trying to establish a modern text. Thus *Trout Fishing in America* (1967) makes fun of the fishing tale, *The Hawkline Monster* (1974) is a gothic "Western", and *Dreaming of Babylon* (1977) a "detective story". Brautigan made fun of ideologies and political systems in *A Confederate General from Big Sur* (1964) and implicitly criticized America in *In Watermelon Sugar* (1968). **William H. Gass** (born 1924), a professor of philosophy, has been preoccupied with the relation between language and reality, essentially asserting in his work that reality must be established with words (see *Omensetter's Luck*, 1966; and *Willie Masters' Lonesome Wife*, 1970).

Joseph Heller (born 1923) and **Kurt Vonnegut** (born 1922) have made the absurdity and the surrealistic humour of their fiction subservient to social criticism. Although Heller is an American Jew, his fiction is better understood when evaluated in the American mainstream rather than in a Jewish-American ethnic tradition. Thus the grotesque absurdity of Heller's war novel, *Catch-22* (1961), goes back to Melville's *The Confidence Man* and the surrealism of Nathanael West. Heller's *Something Happened* (1974) is a more pessimistic work about a business executive disgusted with his job and his life; but *Good as Gold* (1979) returns to the farcical vein in a comical treatment of Jewish family life and American politics. It is also a parody of the Jewish-American novel Heller had been expected to write by critics who stressed his "Jewishness". In *Honest to God* (1984), a delightful and comic "autobiography" of King David, Heller presents his hero in a human perspective.

Heller's view of man as a victim of history, and his assault on the historical and the real, relate his fiction to that of Vonnegut, Berger and Coover. **Kurt Vonnegut** is one of America's most popular authors. In his case, this is quite an achievement, for he has managed to combine the entertaining with the artistic and the critical without striking his readers as highbrow. Vonnegut began in a moralistic strain with a dystopian novel, *Player Piano* (1952), written in the vein of Orwell and Huxley. But he soon developed a literary cover for his experimental methods and social criticism by drawing on science fiction and the pulp novel. In such books as *The Sirens of Titan* (1959), *Mother Night* (1961), *Cat's Cradle* (1963), and *God Bless You, Mr. Rosewater* (1965), Vonnegut used science fiction concepts (apocalyptic situations, time relativity, sentimentalism) which he then undermined in satirical and compassionate studies of mankind and American society. Vonnegut's tragi-comic view of America is that of a country suffering from waste, decay and mind-lessness. One of his most studied books is *Slaughterhouse-Five* (1969). Inspired by his own experience of the bombing of Dresden, this novel plays with the displace-ment of the real horror of history by fantasy as the hero, who has survived the "slaughterhouse" of the war, is taken to the planet Tralfamadore. It is fiction and imagination, not real history, that render life humane, and Vonnegut's novels (see *Breakfast of Champions*, 1973; *Slapstick*, 1976; *Jailbird*, 1979; and *Deadeye Dick*, 1982) continue to confront representative, albeit eccentric, characters (several of them, such as Kilgore Trout, turn up in different novels and time periods) with a junked and mad America. His novel *Galápagos* (1985) seems to suggest that man is too mad to be saved from his own destruction and that animals know better how to lead a happy life. Vonnegut's seemingly naive literary forms appeal to many readers; but these forms have sophisticated functions and are employed to make his bitter message more palatable.

Thomas Berger (born 1924) has covered the period from 1945 to the late 1970s in his four novels about the former GI Carlo Reinhart: *Crazy in Berlin* (1958), *Reinhart in Love* (1961), *Vital Parts* (1970), and *Reinhart's Women* (1981). They play with historical myths, a method Berger also successfully applied to the Western in *Little Big Man* (1964), which became very well known in its film version with Dustin Hoffman. This novel parodies the myths and sagas of the Old West. Other popular forms Berger has exploited to show that myths no longer work in modern America include the detective novel *Who Is Teddy Villanova?* (1977), the Depression novel *Sneaky People* (1975), and the science fiction novel *Regiment of Women* (1973).

Like Vonnegut and Berger, **Robert Coover** (born 1932) has been concerned with the working of fantasy in the creation of myths in history, religion and politics. Coover uses familiar or historical forms, questions their content, and leads the reader to the recognition of the artificial and of myth (see *The Origin of the*

Brunists, 1965; *The Universal Baseball Association, Inc., J. Henry Waugh, Prop.*, 1968, in which a lonely accountant invents a baseball league and plays its games in his head; *The Public Burning*, 1977; *A Political Fable*, 1980; and *Spanking the Maid*, 1982). Similar literary aims – the play with the interrelation of fantasy, fiction, text, and history – characterize the work of the French-American **Raymond Federman** (see his *Take It or Leave It*, 1976), **Walter Abish** (see his *Alphabetical Africa*, 1974; and *How German Is It*, 1980), and **Steve Katz**, and the better-known experimental novels of **Gore Vidal** (born 1925). Vidal is not easy to be categorized as his fiction ranges from realistic war novels (see *Williwaw*, 1946) and historical novels (see *Julian*, 1964; *Burr*, 1973; *1876*, 1976; *Creation*, 1981; and *Lincoln*, 1983) to experimental works: *Two Sisters* (1970) merges fact and memoirs as well as past and present, and his "Hollywood novels", *Myra Breckenridge* (1968) and its sequel *Myron* (1974), trace the lurid adventures and the career of the transsexual Myra/Myron, who tries to save the film industry.

Self-conscious fiction, and the exploration of fiction and forgery in complicated encyclopedic structures, characterize the novels of **William Gaddis** (born 1922) and of the best-known contemporary experimentalists, **John Barth** and **Thomas Pynchon**. Gaddis's view of the novelist as "artificer" has found expression in *The Recognitions* (1955), which became a cult novel of metafiction. It shows a Yankee artist overwhelmed by his career as a forger of old Flemish painters. In *J R* (1975), a parodic novel on hypocrisy and corruption in the world of high finance, Gaddis plays with various styles and surreal situations.

The experimental novels of Barth and Pynchon make large demands on their readers. **John Barth** (born 1930) is from Maryland and is a university professor of English. He began his literary career with satirical novels on the comic aspects of existentialism (see *The Floating Opera*, 1956; and *The End of the Road*, 1958). With *The Sot-Weed Factor* (1960) Barth abandoned conventional forms and produced a comic-epic parody of eighteenth-century picaresque fiction and a very humorous satire of American colonial history. Alluding to a verse satire of the early eighteenth century, the novel provides a fictional biography of Ebenezer Cook, a "poet laureate" of colonial Maryland. The novel deals with Cook's thwarted incestuous relations with his sister Anne and his attempts to defend both his poetry and virginity. Barth's *Giles Goat-Boy* (1966), also a parody, is a complex and comical novel. It tells of the efforts of George Giles, the unnatural child of a woman and a computer, to convince an American college of his new philosophy, and of his fight with an evil and tyrannical computer. This work describes the modern world as a university campus

M-Maybe he became ill by Roy Lichtenstein, 1964

in allegorical terms. Barth has also written a number of short stories that exemplify his playful approach to fiction, and two more excellent novels. *Letters* (1979) parodies the epistolary novel as well as Barth's own fiction of the preceding years. The plot involves seven more or less parallel narratives, told in the form of correspondence between characters from his earlier novels and the "Author" as just another fictional character. Ironic self-parody is also an essential element in *Sabbatical* (1982), a "romance" about the adventures and ideas of a college professor and her husband, a former intelligence officer and an aspiring novelist, during a long cruise aboard a sailboat.

Thomas Pynchon (born 1937) has tried to wipe out all official records of himself and refuses to appear in public and to comment on his work. He studied engineering at Cornell, served in the US Navy and worked as a technician for Boeing Aircraft in Seattle before he became a full-time writer. Pynchon shares Barth's encyclopedic treatment, but he has different aims. The most radical explorer of the limits of modern fantasy, Pynchon has explained his view of history and fiction in *Entropy* (1960). His novels exemplify the thermodynamic law that all systems are bound to run down and that the world's energies will eventually disintegrate. Pynchon's novel *V.* (1963) demonstrates the eventual collapse of communication and reveals the human search for truth and reality to be useless and without meaning. The complicated plot mirrors Pynchon's idea of the disorganization of life and the world (entropy) in a story that follows the steps of two characters. One is the modern American "Schlemihl" (a reference to Adalbert von Chamisso's *Peter Schlemihls wundersame Geschichte,* 1814), Benny Profane, who hunts alligators in the sewers of New York and drifts through life like a yo-yo; the other is Herbert Stencil, who is determined to find V., a mysterious female spy representing Venus, Virgin or even Void (nothingness). Similarly, the plot of Pynchon's shorter novel, *The Crying of Lot 49* (1966), gradually dissolves in a series of grotesque and ambiguous episodes. Again, there is the general and symbolical theme of a search, which lies at the root of all his fiction. In this case Oedipa Maas tries to find the inheritor of a set of stamps (lot 49) in a world of conspiracy, secret organizations, and paranoia. These are also the major themes of *Gravity's Rainbow* (1973), in which dream-like fantasy, sexual allusions, and labyrinthine connections, together with detailed information on quantum physics, probability theory and ballistics, confuse the reader about the real and the imaginary in a story of plots and counterplots. The novel is set in post-war Germany, and its bizarre characters include the American lieutenant Tyrone Slothrop who is looking for a secret German V-2 rocket capable of breaking through the Earth's gravitational barrier. *Gravity's Rainbow* has been compared to Joyce's *Ulysses* and is considered by many critics as the exemplary postmodern novel: its complicated narrative structure, its numerous linguistic and literary codes, its ironic play with cybernetic and fictional forms, its massive accumulation of data and characters (about 400), all amount to the ultimate message that life and philosophy are basically without sense.

Thomas McGuane (born 1939), **Gilbert Sorrentino** (born 1929), and **Ronald Sukenik** (born 1932) are also experimentalists who have "exhausted" traditional literary forms while creating new satirical fiction. Outside the United States, however, Jerzy Kosinski, James Purdy, and John Irving are better known, perhaps because they are less boldly innovative. **Jerzy Kosinski** (born 1933) had had a brilliant career in Poland before he came to the USA in 1957. Most of his novels present lonely, sometimes desperate, psychopathic heroes or narrators trying to come to terms with evil in themselves or in society. Thus his partly autobiographical *The Painted Bird* (1965) is about a Polish boy's suffering and fight for survival during the German occupation. *Steps* (1968), *Cockpit* (1975) and *Blind Date* (1977) avoid sequential plot and present private views of diverse cruelties and the search for emotional and sexual intimacy of traumatized egos. Apart from *The Painted Bird,* Kosinski's best novels are *Being There* (1971), a satire of American society and politics that draws on Voltaire's *Candide* and was filmed with Peter Sellers starring as the hero Chance; and *Pinball* (1982), a treatment of sexual passion, seduction and crime. Like Kosinski, **James Purdy** (born 1923) has been fascinated by deviant behaviour in his fictional characters, who suffer violent and traumatic experiences and are deprived of love, (see, for instance, *Malcolm,* 1959; *Cabot Wright Begins,* 1964; *Eustace Chisholm and the Works,* 1967; *I Am Elijah Thrush,* 1972; the trilogy *Sleepers in Moon-Crowned Valleys,* 1970-81; and *Narrow Rooms,* 1978). **John Irving's** (born 1942) fiction, although highly successful with the reading public, is less convincing as literary art. Irving combines the conventional novel of character with melodramatic plots and metafictional elements that do not always produce the intended parody (see, for instance, *Setting Free the Bears,* 1968; and *The World According to Garp,* 1978).

Apart from these experimentalists, Jewish, black, and women writers have attracted much attention in contemporary American fiction. There is a remarkable numerical presence of Jewish novelists. Some, like Heller, Salinger and Irwin Shaw, write in the mainstream of American fiction, but Bellow, Malamud, Roth and, to a lesser extent, Doctorow are best understood when seen in the Jewish-American tradition. America has seen two great waves of Jewish immigration: that from Eastern Europe between 1881 and 1924, and that from Western Europe between 1930 and 1945. The first generation produced a rich literature in Yiddish, **Isaac Bashevis Singer's** (born 1904) works being outstanding examples; his books have meanwhile been translated into English. The Yiddish language and literature remain important sources for many Jewish writers, and also for those who stand at the beginning of a Jewish-American literature in English: the poet **Delmore Schwartz** (1913-66) and the novelists Bellow and Mailer. Those writers who consider themselves Jewish-American novelists - mainly Saul Bellow, Bernard Malamud, and Philip Roth (Norman Mailer and E. L. Doctorow hovering between the Jewish and the WASP traditions) - have been concerned with the alienation of Jews from, and their painful adaptation to, modern gentile America. The best of Jewish-American fiction goes beyond descriptions of, and lamentations on, various kinds of alienation and penetrates to a diagnosis of American society. **Isaac Bashevis Singer's** fiction, originally written in Yiddish and translated into English, has been concerned exclusively with Jewish settings and characters, first in Eastern Europe (see, for instance, *Satan in Goray,* 1935; *The Family Moskat,*

1950; *The Slave,* 1962; and *Shosha,* 1978), and, more recently, in New York (see *Enemies,* 1970). Singer is also an excellent writer of short stories and received the Nobel Prize in 1978. He is a masterful chronicler of the heritage, the religion, and the daily life of Jews in Eastern Europe.

Saul Bellow (born 1915) was awarded the Nobel Prize for his fiction in 1976. Bellow has repeatedly dealt with the dilemma of the Jew in modern America. Chicago provides the background for several of his novels. His early work reflects his reading of existential philosophers and of Kafka and Dostoevsky[1] as he explores questions relating to freedom and identity (see *Dangling Man,* 1944; *The Victim,* 1947; and *Seize the Day,* 1956). *The Adventures of Augie March* (1953) is Bellow's first successful attempt with realistic picaresque fiction and is concerned with the adventures of a young Chicago Jew. In *Henderson the Rain King* (1959) Bellow portrays a Connecticut millionaire in search of his identity on a journey in Africa. Problems of the middle-aged Jew are central in *Herzog* (1964), an autobiographical novel on the marital and emotional difficulties of a Jewish intellectual. This has remained Bellow's favourite subject. *Mr. Sammler's Planet* (1970) presents a cosmopolitan survivor of the Nazi concentration camps, now resident in the modern nightmare called New York but living in the imaginary world of religion and literature. *Humboldt's Gift* (1975) is a fictional portrait of the poet Delmore Schwartz and describes his assistance to the narrator, Charlie Citrine, who is plagued by women, success and the idea of death. The death motif is central to *The Dean's December* (1982), in which a Jewish university professor ponders death while in Chicago and Eastern Europe.

The tragi-comic aspects of the suffering Jew torn between his religious-cultural tradition and hedonistic America have been covered in several excellent and entertaining novels by Bernard Malamud and Philip Roth. **Malamud's** (1914-86) realistic and compassionate novels show outsiders distressed by the spiritual and moral poverty of their world (see *The Assistant,* 1957; *A New Life,* 1961; *The Fixer,* 1966; and *Dubin's Lives,* 1979). Malamud's *The Tenants* (1971) is a parable of moral failure, and his last novel, *God's Grace* (1982), mocks the idea of man as God's supreme creature in the story of the sole survivor of a nuclear war who starts a new civilization among apes. **Philip Roth** (born 1933), like Malamud a university professor, has written satirically on the Jewish libido, the constraints of the family, and guilt complexes (see *Goodbye, Columbus,* 1959; *When She Was Good,* 1967). *Portnoy's Complaint* (1969), a humorous psychoanalytical pseudo-study of the young Alexander Portnoy's sexual complexes and his struggle with his possessive mother, remains one of Roth's best books. He has also written witty satires on the Nixon administration, *Our Gang* (1971), and contemporary America, *The Great*

---

1. Fyodor M. Dostoevsky (1821-81), Russian writer and best known for his novels *The Insulted and the Injured* (1861), *Crime and Punishment* (1866), *The Idiot* (1868), and *The Brothers Karamazov* (1880). They discuss profound religious and political ideas and provide narrative tension and excellent characterization. Dostoevsky admired Dickens, and both authors share an interest in the city, in children, crime, and the suffering of the innocent. In the 20th century, he has become the most widely read Russian writer.

American Novel (1973); has explored with ironic humour the emotional and professional problems of a Jewish writer in the largely autobiographical trilogy entitled *Zuckerman Bound – A Trilogy and Epilogue* (1985), which brings together in one volume the previously published novels *The Ghostwriter* (1979), *Zuckerman Unbound* (1981), and *The Anatomy Lesson* (1983). He has treated in grotesque and farcical modes the sexual hang-ups of educated Jewish men in *The Breast* (1972), *My Life as a Man* (1974), and *The Professor of Desire* (1977).

E. L. Doctorow (born 1931) has been concerned more with American than with Jewish life. *The Book of Daniel* (1971) is a political novel concerned with the arrest and trial for espionage of the Rosenbergs, a Jewish couple, and *Ragtime* (1975) provides a fictionalized slice of life from the early decades of the century. It was sensitively filmed by Milos Forman. *Loon Lake* (1980) tries to reconstruct the world of capitalism and crime of the 1930s. The work of Jewish humorists and satirists – **Bruce Jay Friedman** (born 1930), **Wallace Markfield** (born 1926), and **Stanley Elkin** (born 1930) – and of such versatile novelists as **Chaim Potok** (born 1929; see *The Chosen,* 1967) attests to the continuing vigour of Jewish American fiction.

Like Doctorow, **Norman Mailer** (born 1923), as a writer, is more American than Jewish. Mailer has written a very successful war novel, *The Naked and the Dead* (1948), and has since tried a variety of fictional genres, never forgetting to dramatize himself. After his more conventional *Barbary Shore* (1951) and *The Deer Park* (1955) he abandoned traditional forms of the novel. *An American Dream* (1965) is Mailer's attempt at a psychoanalytical novel; *Armies of the Night* (1968) is his first nonfiction book with fictional passages. It was followed by *Miami and the Siege of Chicago* (1968), *Of a Fire on the Moon* (1970), which analyses the lunar landing, and *The Executioner's Song* (1979), which is indebted in its structure to Capote's *In Cold Blood* (1966) and discusses the events around the execution of the murderer Gary Gilmore. Among the numerous public statements Mailer has made about his life and fiction there are some that stress his need of money, and this would explain his more sensational works, written to become bestsellers in the market of popular fiction, such as *Ancient Evenings* (1983) and *Tough Guys Don't Dance* (1984), the speculative biography of Marilyn Monroe, *Marilyn* (1973), and a book on Cassius Clay, now Muhammad Ali, called *The Fight* (1975).

If black fiction is now a powerful voice in American literature, it is because its way was prepared by the Harlem Renaissance of the 1920s and the work of **Langston Hughes** (1902–67) and **James Weldon Johnson** (1871–1938), an educator and civil rights leader, and by the Civil Rights movement of the 1960s. Important novels written before 1960 include those of **Richard Wright** (1908–60), especially *Native Son* (1940), a naturalistic study of the tragic life of a black man in the Chicago slums, and *The Outsider* (1953), written in Paris and set in Chicago, and **Ralph Ellison's** (born 1914) superb *Invisible Man* (1952). Ellison's theme is the black hero's search for his identity and his gradual disillusionment with American capitalism, with socialism, and even with the black cause. Containing both realistic and expressionistic elements, this novel has exerted influence on several younger black writers. Ellison was followed by **James Baldwin** (1924–87). Baldwin's more recent fiction has not fulfilled the promise of his *Go Tell It on the Mountain* (1953), which is concerned with the frustrations of a young black and his relations to ecstatic religious fundamentalism. An expatriate in Paris for many years (Wright and Ellison went abroad, too), Baldwin has made his homosexuality as important a motif as the race issue, and both are prominent in *Giovanni's Room* (1956) and *Another Country* (1962). They were followed by *Tell Me How Long the Train's Been Gone* (1968), about an aging black actor, *If Beale Street Could Talk* (1974), about a pregnant young woman's courageous fight for her imprisoned fiancé, and *Just Above My Head* (1979), which returns to the setting of his early fiction, Harlem, and dramatizes the life of a Harlem gospel singer.

On 28 April 1963, 250,000 blacks, led by Martin Luther King, marched to Washington and demonstrated peacefully for their rights. In the wake of similar events and of the work of Baldwin and other writers, black literature has developed several impressive genres that include fiction and confessional or autobiographical writings, such as *The Autobiography of Malcolm X* (1965), written with the assistance of Alex Haley, **Eldridge Cleaver's** (born 1935) *Soul on Ice* (1968), **Bobby Seale's** (born 1936) *Seize the Time* (1970), **George Jackson's** *Soledad Brother* (1970), and the autobiography of **Angela Davis** (born 1944), published in 1974. **Alex Haley's** (born 1921) *Roots* (1976), a semi-fictional family chronicle, became internationally known when it was made into a TV series.

In the area of the novel, the most distinguished authors are Chester Himes, Toni Morrison, Alice Walker, and Ishmael Reed. **Toni Morrison** (born 1931) is an Ohio-born novelist who has written about the problems of black women in the North. Her major works are *Sula* (1973), about the friendship of two black girls, *Song of Solomon* (1977), in which a black man explores his family history and discovers how myth is created, and *Tar Baby* (1981), whose subjects are race and motherhood. **Alice Walker** (born 1944), who was born in Georgia, is one of several Southern black women writers. She started with aggressive novels of social criticism and has meanwhile turned to discussions and analyses of the specific problems of women and their relations with men. Walker's *Meridian* (1976) deals with a woman torn between the revolutionary Civil Rights movement and her love for the black people of the South. *The Color Purple* (1982) is largely written in the form of a diary. The novel depicts the lives of two devoted sisters, one of whom temporarily goes to Africa as a missionary, and their suffering in the South (Georgia). Although there is much to be said for Walker's detailed picture of black life, this novel suffers from an overdose of sentiment and flat characterization. Sentimentality and melodrama also dominate Steven Spielberg's film version of the novel, made in 1985. Other notable black women writers are **Lucille Clifton** (born 1936; *Generations*, 1976) and **Maya Angelou** (born 1928; *I Know Why the Caged Bird Sings*, 1971; *Singin' & Swingin' & Gettin' Merry Like Christmas*, 1976).

Finally, **Ishmael Reed** (born 1938) and **William Melvin Kelley** (born 1937) are two of several black experimental novelists (see also the works of **Ernest J. Gaines, Clarence Major, Charles Wright** and **Henry Van Dyke**). Reed has written a number of parodies and satires (see, for instance, *The Free-Lance Pallbearers,* 1967; *Yellow Back Radio Broke-Down,* 1969; *Mumbo Jumbo,* 1972; and

Koshare by Rafael Medina, 1968

Flight to Canada, 1976, the latter a parody of the slave narrative, which was popular in the nineteenth century).

Kelley studied creative writing at Harvard, where John Hawkes and Archibald MacLeish were among his teachers. His first novel, *A Different Drummer* (1962), portrays the exodus of the black population from a fictitious Southern state. Its scope and the use of frequent shifts of point of view are reminiscent of Faulkner. The experimental and surrealist style of John Hawkes has left its traces in Kelly's *dem* (1967), which is a scathing satire of "the ways of white folks".

American Indian novelists are not as strong in number as blacks. The poet and novelist **N. Scott Momaday** (born 1934) has recorded the legends of his Kiowa tribe in *The Way to Rainy Mountain* (1969) and won a Pulitzer Prize with his novel *House Made of Dawn* (1968). **James Welch** (born 1940) has written on the modern Indians' loss of identity in such novels as *Winter in the Blood* (1974) and *The Death of Jim Loney* (1979). **Leslie M. Silko's** (born 1948) *Ceremony* (1977) combines modern realism with traditional Indian forms, such as stories, songs, and myths. A younger Indian voice is that of **Louise Erdrich** (born 1954; see her *Love Medicine,* 1984).

Contemporary American fiction has become a battleground for movements. Various ethnic and social groups, including gays (homosexuals) and feminists, have caused and claimed public and literary attention. Supported by feminist publications, women writers have claimed that there is a specific female view and way of experience which a literature dominated by males has ignored. These writers see in women's literature a coherent body of fiction, with a (feminine) history that reaches from Gertrude Stein, Djuna Barnes and Edith Wharton to contemporary novelists such as Joyce Carol Oates, Alice Walker, and Erica Jong. The field, if field it is (there is still a lot of critical discussion about this point), is wide and encompasses **Mary McCarthy's** (born 1912) ironic and psychologically as well as socially interesting novels that go beyond the feminist viewpoint (see her *The Group,* 1963; *Birds of America,* 1971; and *Cannibals and Missionaries,* 1979), and the trendy "feminist" and shrill fiction of **Marilyn French** (born 1929; see her novel *The Women's Room,* 1977). Women and the way they cope with the modern world

281

have been treated in the satirical mode by **Lisa Alther** (born 1944) in *Kinflicks* (1976). The frankest expression of female sexuality can be found in the fiction and the journals of the French-born **Anaïs Nin** (1903-77; see her *Delta of Venus,* 1968) and in the partly autobiographical novels of the feminist liberationist **Erica Jong** (born 1942), such as *Fear of Flying* (1973) and *How to Save Your Own Life* (1977).

4.2 The Short Story

Brief, fast-moving, and offering the reader suspense, surprise and, often, literary art, the short story has become one of America's most popular forms of fiction. The reason for this may have something to do with the demand of newspapers, journals, and magazines for stories that fill only a few pages and attract readers. Such publications as *Harper's Bazaar* (founded 1929), *Atlantic Monthly* (founded 1857), and, above all, *The New Yorker* (founded 1925) have contributed to the variety and popularity of the short story by publishing experimental as well as traditional fiction. Writing, in America, is a tough, competitive job. Authors engage in highly publicized contests involving both critical esteem and financial success. And since many newspapers (the Sunday editions) and periodicals pay handsome fees for recognized celebrities, reputable short story writers such as Mailer, Updike, Vidal, Kesey and Theroux have published their fiction in *Esquire* and even in *Playboy.*

Short stories have been written in virtually all the genres and movements in which novels have also appeared, and most major novelists have produced short fiction. This holds true for naturalistic writers like **Jack London** (*Short Stories,* 1960) and **Theodore Dreiser** (*The Best Short Stories of Theodore Dreiser,* 1947), and the social criticism of **Steinbeck** (*The Long Valley,* 1938) and of Southern writers like **Erskine Caldwell** (*Complete Stories,* 1953). A few authors have proved masters of shorter fiction. One of them was **O. Henry,** the pseudonym of William Sidney Porter (1862-1910), who began his career while serving a prison sentence for embezzlement. His stories (see the collections *Cabbages and Kings,* 1904; and *The Four Million,* 1906) are humorous, sometimes sentimental, and highly ingenious in their use of coincidence and surprise, but they suffer from simplistic characterization that often leads to caricature. The satirical-humorous story was the special field of **Ring Lardner** (1885-1933), a sports journalist who published some of his stories in the *Chicago Tribune* and in *The Saturday Evening Post.* Held in colloquial speech and in slang, they expose the self-deception and vanity of a variety of ordinary characters (*The Collected Short Stories,* 1941). **James Thurber** (1894-1961) surpassed Lardner in public esteem. Many of his essays, stories and cartoons (some written in collaboration with **E. B. White**) first appeared in *The New Yorker,* including his much anthologized "The Secret Life of Walter Mitty" (1932), a hilarious description of the escapist fantasies of a hen-pecked husband (see also *Fables for Our Time,* 1940, and *The Thurber Carnival,* 1945).

Short stories with a stronger literary appeal came from the pens of **Sherwood Anderson** (*Winesburg, Ohio,* 1919; and *Short Stories,* 1962) and from those who profited from the psychological approach and the principles of composition of Henry James, such as **Edith Wharton** (*The Best Short Stories,* 1958). The principal authors who shaped the modern literary short story are Fitzgerald, Hemingway and Faulkner. All of them members of the "lost generation", they questioned the meaning of human existence and values. **F. Scott Fitzgerald's** stories about the Jazz Age demonstrate the degeneration of the American dream in a world of hypocrisy, materialism, and recklessness. These are the major themes in his story, "The Diamond as Big as the Ritz" (1922). Fitzgerald also covered the Hollywood world of make-believe he knew from personal experience as a screen writer (see *The Stories,* 1951). **Hemingway's** stories, written in the laconic and economical style for which he became famous, introduce characters in basic human situations that reflect both the nihilism of Hemingway's generation and his own preoccupation with courage in a cruel world without meaning and in the face of approaching death. Thus Nick Adams, the hero of several of his stories, must realize in "The Killers" how vicious and arbitrary life can be. "The Snows of Kilimanjaro" (1936) presents another disillusioned hero in an African setting: Harry, the novelist (a thinly disguised Hemingway), knows he must die, and as death approaches he recognizes that both love and happiness ceased to exist for him long ago - death will be a relief. It is this experience of recognition (the Joycean "epiphany") and the cruel surprise ending, borrowed from Ambrose Bierce, which the story has in common with Hemingway's other "African" tale, "The Short Happy Life of Francis Macomber" (1936). Hemingway's stories are collected in *The Fifth Column and the First Forty-Nine Stories* (1938) and *The Nick Adams Stories* (1972), which contains a number of posthumously published "Nick Adams" stories in addition to the ones contained in the previous collection. As a series, these stories were undoubtedly influenced by such earlier examples as Joyce's *Dubliners* and Anderson's *Winesburg, Ohio*. Hemingway's short fiction has proved influential for writers in America and Europe. This holds true for both his style and themes. His realistic, precise, and economical diction, his sparing and unobtrusive use of symbols, and his treatment of the issues that fascinated him most - violence, fear, courage, and death -

283

impressed numerous imitators and a number of contemporary authors. **William Faulkner's** short fiction is inspired by such motifs as the decay of the South and race relations (see *Collected Stories,* 1977). Like Hemingway, Faulkner wrote several stories combining a process of recognition with a realistic plot and symbolic events. One such story is "The Bear" (published in *Go Down, Moses,* 1942), in which Faulkner uses stream-of-consciousness techniques, thus achieving a fiction that is much more complex than Hemingway's. Told from the viewpoint of the rich landowner Isaac McCaslin, "The Bear" tells of the killing of Old Ben, a bear symbolizing the freedom of nature and the wilderness, and of the death of Sam Fathers, a half-blood. McCaslin's "epiphany" consists in the fact that he admits the guilt of his ancestors and is prepared to do penance by dispossessing himself of his land. Like his novels, Faulkner's stories are set in Yoknapatawpha, an imaginary Southern county he peopled with eccentric characters driven and motivated by myth, past crimes, and vengeance. The stories often refer to each other and, together, establish a convincing if partly grotesque picture of the South as Faulkner saw it (see, for instance, *The Unvanquished,* 1938, the first six chapters of which were originally published as short stories, and *Knight's Gambit,* 1949).

Between 1930-1960, the short story writers stood under the influence of Hemingway, James, and Faulkner. The psychological realism of James and the Southern Gothic of Faulkner are especially obvious in the work of such Southern writers as **Katherine Anne Porter** (1890-1980; see *The Collected Stories,* 1967), **Caroline Gordon** (1895-1981; *The Collected Stories,* 1981), **Eudora Welty** (born 1909; *Collected Stories,* 1981), **Carson McCullers, Flannery O'Connor** (*The Complete Stories,* 1971), and **Truman Capote** (*Tree of Night,* 1949; and *Music for Chameleons,* 1980). Although **Porter's** <u>"Flowering Judas"</u> (1930) is set in Mexico, the story is exemplary, much like the best fiction of Anderson, Hemingway, and Faulkner. Porter's story is about Laura, an American teacher, who has lost her Catholic faith and has become disillusioned with her revolutionary Mexican friends. Eventually, she realizes that she is a modern "Judas" in the sense that she is incapable of human love. **Truman Capote's** <u>"Children on Their Birthdays"</u> (1963) is an example of the typical Southern mixture of grotesque, humorous, and tragic elements, a mixture that also distinguishes some of the short fiction of Welty, O'Connor, Faulkner, and Porter. Capote's story, told by a thinly disguised "Mr. C.", brims with Southern colloquialisms and local colour. Without sentimentalism, it deals sympathetically with the essentially humorous behaviour, and the sudden tragic death, of a precocious and eccentric teenager, "Miss" Lily Jane Bobbit. Behind Capote's brilliant potraits of unforgettable characters and his charming views of the deep South one senses his profound love of a region where he spent most of his childhood.

The short stories written since the 1960s reflect the division of American fiction into traditional and experimental forms. J. D. Salinger, John Cheever, John Updike, James Purdy and many Jewish authors have preferred conventional forms in their short fiction. **Salinger** has often cast children and adolescents as heroes confronting the world of the adults. Typical examples are his *Nine Stories* (1953), the chronicle of the Glass family: *Franny and Zooey* (1961), *Raise High the Roof Beam,*

Carpenters, and *Seymour: An Introduction* (both in 1963) and his latest story, "Hapworth, 16, 1924", published in *The New Yorker* in 1965. **Cheever** was the chronicler of the upper middle class in which most of his novels and stories are set (*The Stories,* 1978). **John Updike** has fulfilled the same role a rung down in the social hierarchy: his stories about middle-class characters display a scintillating verbal virtuosity (*The Same Door,* 1959; *Pigeon Feathers,* 1962; *The Music School,* 1966; *Museums and Women,* 1972; and *Problems,* 1979). Updike's short fiction, much like his novels, is concerned with the issues he finds most interesting in American life: the overpowering influence of materialism, the individual's need for love, the omnipresent fear of death, and the futile attempts to overcome at least the fear by indulging in sex. He combined these themes with the treatment of marital love in "Wife-Wooing" (1960), a story that is also remarkable for its rich and evocative style. Written in the present tense, and from the point of view of a nostalgic husband recalling the time of honeymooning with his wife, the story records the almost "Joycean" disappointment of the man's lust and longing, and his "revenge" (a psychological reaction) as he recognizes his wife's physical defects brought on by her age. **James Purdy** has criticized the inhumanity of American society while demonstrating the perverse that lurks behind the ordinary in a number of his stories (*The Color of Darkness,* 1957; and *Children Is All,* 1962). Jewish writers who have produced remarkable studies of Jewish life and suffering in America include **Isaac Bashevis Singer** (*Collected Stories,* 1982), **Bernard Malamud** *(The Magic Barrel,* 1958; *Idiots First,* 1963; *Rembrandt's Hat,* 1973), and **Saul Bellow** (*Mosby's Memoirs,* 1968; *Him With His Foot in His Mouth,* 1984). Malamud belongs to the line of authors who have drawn on mythical and grotesque traditions reaching back to Irving, Poe, and Hawthorne. Malamud's story "The Jewbird" (1963), for instance, is a cruel modern fairy tale in which a persecuted Jew, in the shape of a bird, tries to find refuge in the home of a Jewish frozen-food salesman. When the "bird" is thrown out by the salesman, it/he is killed by anti-Semites.

Black and Indian authors have also produced a rich harvest of short fiction that includes the stories of **Langston Hughes** (*The Ways of White Folks,* 1934; *Something in Common,* 1963), **Arna Bontemps** (1902-73; *The Old South,* 1973), **James Baldwin** (*Going to Meet the Man,* 1965), **Alice Walker** (*In Love and Trouble,* 1973), **William Melvin Kelley** (*Dancers on the Shore,* 1964), and **Leslie M. Silko** (*Storyteller,* 1981).

The more distinguished short story writers among the experimentalists are **John Barth** (*Lost in the Funhouse,* 1968; *Chimera,* 1972), who has reserved the mode of the absurd for his short fiction; **Donald Barthelme** (born 1931), whose subjects are the loneliness of people in the grotesque and fantastic atmosphere of modern urban life (*City Life,* 1970; *Guilty Pleasures,* 1974; *Amateurs,* 1976); **Robert Coover,** who plays with myths and archetypes in equally grotesque settings (*Pricksongs and Descants,* 1969), and **Thomas Pynchon,** whose early stories have been collected in *Slow Learner,* 1984. In his "Entropy", first published in *The Kenyon Review* in 1960, Pynchon employs characters from Greek mythology in a story introducing people who live in three different apartments, and on different floors, in a house. The actions and conversations of the house dwellers essentially confirm Pynchon's conviction (which is based on the thermodynamic laws) that all "systems" are bound to run down and to produce chaos where there was order. As in his now much studied novels, he applies the laws of entropy to fiction and thus creates a new and fascinating combination of literature and science.

4.3 Popular Fiction, Crime Fiction, and Science Fiction

The novels of Norman Mailer, Erica Jong and Alice Walker are indicative of a phenomenon in American fiction that is not easily understood by Europeans who are used to distinguishing between "high" and "mass" culture and to dividing literature into slices labelled highbrow, middlebrow and lowbrow. But in America, more than in Europe, the writer and his literary product are subject to extreme commercialization by the publishing industry. This industry, in turn, has close links with the TV and film industry. Huge advances are sometimes paid for books that are not yet written; and books are often written with an eye to the possibility of making them into movies (Alice Walker's *The Color Purple*, 1982, seems to be such a work). Admittedly, this leads to a popularization of literary culture, a sort of middlebrow taste, that accepts a variety of genres, including the experimental, but does not discriminate sufficiently between the excellent, the mediocre and downright trash. However, what can be said in favour of contemporary American fiction is that it is always open to the innovative and very much aware of the present.

The market for popular fiction is enormous in the United States. On occasion, it absorbs bestsellers from such authors as Mailer, Updike and Vidal. Important names in the middlebrow market are **Margaret Mitchell** (1900–49), **Pearl S. Buck** (1892–1973) and the now very successful **James Michener** (born 1907). Mitchell's *Gone With the Wind* (1936) is a romantic-sentimental novel about the Civil War from the point of view of the Southern plantation owners. It sold 1,500,000 copies in its first year and many times that figure after the lavish motion picture (with Clark Gable and Vivien Leigh) was released in 1939. Pearl S. Buck was the daughter of a missionary and grew up in China. She popularized the East in such works as *The Good Earth* (1931) and many subsequent novels based on her personal experience. Michener has now become as popular as Buck. His successful recipe is the clever mixture of historical fact and fiction in works that deal with regions and countries, such as *Hawaii* (1959), *The Source* (1965, on Israel), *Centennial* (1974), which is a "faction" history of Colorado, *Chesapeake* (1978), and *The Covenant* (1980, on South Africa). One of Michener's latest works deals with America's last frontier (*Space,* 1982). Another typical popular novel written for the mass market is **Mario Puzo's** *The Godfather* (1969). Its mixture of crime and sex helped to make it a bestseller and an equally successful movie. A sequel exploited the popularity of the first film version.

After World War I, American crime fiction gained both a literary and sociopolitical dimension with the novels of **Dashiell Hammett** (1894–1961) and **Raymond Chandler** (1888–1959). They created realistic and disillusioned American

The 7 a.m. News by Alfred Leslie, 1976

detectives and provided some criticism of the greed and the false values of post-war society during the Depression. **Hammett** worked for eight years as a Pinkerton detective in San Francisco. He created the tough, "hard-boiled" private investigator Sam Spade. In his thrillers (see *The Dain Curse*, 1929; *The Maltese Falcon*, 1930; *The Thin Man*, 1932) there is a remarkable realism of subject and language. **Chandler** followed Hammet's lead with such bestsellers as *The Big Sleep* (1939), *Farewell, My Lovely* (1940), and *The Long Good-bye* (1953), distinguished by realistic scenes of the seamy side of Los Angeles and a laconic and melancholic detective, Philip Marlowe, who became a cult figure and was played by Humphrey Bogart in the film versions. **Earle Stanley Gardner's** (1889-1970) Perry Mason (see also the TV series of that title) is a more sophisticated and intellectual figure as he conducts his courtroom scenes as a lawyer-detective with an immense fertility of imagination (see, for instance, *The Case of the Sulky Girl*, 1933; and *Some Slips Don't Show*, 1957). Writers who have produced detective novels with special and genre-making characters include **Rex Stout** (1886-1975), creator of the gourmet detective Nero Wolfe (see *The Golden Spiders*, 1953, and the TV series), **John Dickson Carr** (born 1906), **Mickey Spillane** (born 1918), whose thrillers emphasize sadism more than mystery (see, for instance, *The Big Kill*, 1951), **Ed McBain**, and **Chester Himes** (1909-84). Himes was an expatriate black American who began his career after serving a prison term for armed robbery. He started with angry protest novels against racism in America (see *If He Hollers Let Him Go*, 1945; *Cast the First Stone*, 1952; and *The Primitive*, 1955). In the early 1950s Himes moved to France and there began writing detective novels set in Harlem and featuring two black police detectives, nicknamed Coffin Ed and Grave Digger Jones. Himes's best works, apart from a bawdy satire on the sexual relations between the races called *Pinktoes* (1965), are *The Real Cool Killers* (1959), *Cotton Comes to Harlem* (1965), of which there is a good film, *The Heat's On* (1966) and the outstanding *Blind Man With a Pistol* (1969).

Science fiction is an even bigger market than crime fiction. Novels and stories in this genre are published each day by the dozen – and most of them are quickly forgotten. A few authors, however, have written SF literature, as it is called in the USA, that is worth reading because it consciously avoids the stereotypes with which this kind of fiction seems particularly plagued. **Ray Bradbury** (born 1920) has produced a dystopian novel, *Fahrenheit 451* (1953), and many stories of the O. Henry type in SF settings. Among the 40 odd works to his credit, **Robert Heinlein's** (born 1907) most impressive novel is *Stranger in a Strange Land* (1961), a bitter satire on the failure of moral progress. **Isaac Asimov** (born 1920) is known for his huge output of novels and stories, not just SF; his outstanding work is the *Foundation* trilogy (1951-53), which assesses man's relation to history. Finally, **Ursula Le Guin** (born 1929) has written a fine SF novel, *The Left Hand of Darkness* (1969), which deals with a world where there is only one sex.

5. Nonfiction

H. L. Mencken (1880-1956) was beyond doubt the most gifted journalist and essayist in the first decades of the twentieth century. He attacked the imperfections of democracy in America as well as the alleged cultural superiority of Europe. Mencken encouraged and supported several major authors, such as Dreiser, Lewis and Anderson, and had a great influence on American public opinion with such publications as *The American Language* (first published in 1919 and revised several times), which deals with the development of the English language in the United States, and *Prejudices* (1919-27), a series of critical and iconoclastic essays on a wide range of topics, which had first appeared in newspapers and a selection from which was published in book form in 1927.

American nonfiction in the past decades has especially benefited from the deep interest several gifted authors have taken in politics and writing. The most obvious results of this dual interest are the movements called "new journalism" and "feminism". Both emerged in the 1960s. The term "new journalism" covers a new style of writing in non-fiction prose (not only journalism proper) that implies the writer's questioning of his own role and viewpoint and borrows techniques and elements from the novel: scenic construction, complete recording of dialogues, investigation of social mores, and even the stream-of-consciousness representation. Always ready to admit to their subjectivity, the "new journalists" have written about contemporary American culture, from its popular heroes to its alternative lifestyles. Among the "new journalists" - Tom Wolfe, Hunter S. Thompson, Seymour Krim, Jimmy Breslin, and Joan Didion - Wolfe and Thompson have been the leading exponents. The very titles of their books provide an impression of their uninhibited pop style. Of special interest are **Tom Wolfe's** (born 1931) *The Electric Kool-Aid Acid Test* (1968), which is partly about Ken Kesey and his fellow hippies, and satirical description of various social groups in *Radical Chic and Mau-Mauing the Flak Catchers* (1970). **Hunter S. Thompson** has freely admitted to his use of drugs in the composition of his reportorial works. The hallucinatory style remains his hallmark, from the early *Fear and Loathing in Las Vegas* (1971), concerned with narcotics and their various effects on those who take them, to his idiosyncratic coverage of the Honolulu Marathon in *The Curse of Lono* (1983).

As a reform movement aiming at the social and political equality of women, feminism has a long history going back to the Blue Stocking Ladies[1] of the late eighteenth century. In the United States, women gained suffrage (the right to vote) in 1920. Feminism received a new impetus in the 1960s with the creation of the National Organization for Women (NOW), and the cause of feminism came to be known as "Women's Lib", i.e. women's liberation. American feminist writers have drawn on the earlier work of Simone de Beauvoir (1908-86), especially on her *Le Deuxième Sexe* (1949). Works that were widely read and became best sellers include **Betty Friedan's** *The Feminine Mystique* (1963), **Kate Millet's** *Sexual Politics* (1970), and **Germaine Greer's** *The Female Eunuch* (1971). There are now many spokeswomen of feminism, and **Gloria Steinem's** *Ms.,* founded in 1971, is just one of many journals for women.

In the field of literary history the twentieth century has seen the completion of several multi-volume histories, of which *The Cambridge History of American Literature,* edited between 1917 and 1921 by a group of scholars, and **Robert E. Spiller's** *Literary History of the United States* (1948-1959) remain the most interesting, albeit now outdated, works. **Sacvan Bercovitch** is now preparing a new edition of the *Cambridge History.* Many critics have discussed literature in philosophical contexts. Important books include **Vernon Louis Parrington's** *Main Currents of American Thought* (1927-30) and the studies of American thought written by **Henry Steele Commager** (born 1902; see *The American Mind,* 1951) **F. O. Matthiessen** (1902-50; see *American Renaissance,* 1941), and **Perry Miller** (1905-63; see *The New England Mind,* 2 vols., 1939-1953).

In literary criticism the Marxist view was especially popular in the 1930s; it was later modified by **Kenneth Burke** (born 1897; see his *The Philosophy of Literary Form,* 1941) and **Edmund Wilson** (1895-1972; see *The Wound and the Bow,* 1941). The most influential movement was the New Criticism. It was by no means a unified theory, and there were always some differences of opinion between the various members of the movement. Yet they all subscribed to the need for structural analysis of works of art, stressing the form and make-up of texts (mostly poems) rather than their relations to the author or to history and politics. American writers associated with the New Criticism are the poets **John Crowe Ransom** and **Allen Tate** as well as **Cleanth Brooks** and **Robert Penn Warren** (see their book *Understanding Poetry,* 1938, reprinted and revised in many editions), **R. P. Blackmur** (1904-65) and **Yvor Winters** (1900-68). The work of these scholars and authors contributed to a re-evaluation of the autonomy of the literary work of art and to a recognition of its specific structural and formal aspects. But the heyday of the New Criticism did not last beyond the 1950s.

---

1. Also called Blue Stocking Circle or Blue Stocking Ladies, several intelligent and learned women met regularly in London in the second half of the 18th century. They were often ridiculed by male writers but were quite successful in their aims of furthering women's education and information. Their social gatherings became very popular and were also attended by men, such as Horace Walpole, Dr. Johnson, Boswell, and Samuel Richardson.

Not necessarily in opposition to the New Criticism, but advocating different principles of literary evaluation, the Chicago School of Criticism, led by **R. S. Crane,** wanted to revive Aristotelian principles (see Crane's *Critics and Criticism,* 1952). The latest movement in American criticism is the Yale School of critics. Since the 1970s the Yale professors Geoffrey Hartmann, Paul de Man, J. Hillis Miller, and Harold Bloom have assumed a dominating role. Like the New Critics, they do not stand for a closed system, although they share a common complicated rhetoric that is indebted to the work and style of the French psychoanalyst **Jacques Lacan** (1901-81) and the French philosopher **Jacques Derrida** (born 1930), both exponents of post-structuralism. The special kind of post-structuralism now in vogue (J. Hillis Miller, for one, has written on it) is called "deconstruction". It tries to show that any text (whether fiction or not) inevitably undermines its own claims to a definite meaning. The "deconstructionists" dismantle the meaning of texts by analysing the function of discourse and the role of the reader in the production of meaning.

In addition to these movements, several studies by independent critics have also gone down in literary criticism as seminal works. **Northrop Frye's** *Anatomy of Criticism* (1957) as well as his *The Great Code* (1982) stress the importance of symbols, myths, and archetypes in literary judgments. **Susan Sontag** (born 1933) has argued for a more emotive and less intellectual response in *Against Interpretation and Other Essays* (1966). **Leslie Fiedler** (born 1917) has made headlines with his lively and often witty criticism (see his *Love and Death in the American Novel,* 1960; and *What Was Literature?,* 1982). And **Lionel Trilling** (1905-75) insisted on seeing literature as social action (see his *Speaking of Literature and Society,* 1980).

Outside the fields of literary history and criticism, a few books had a profound influence on American intellectual life. In addition to the works briefly discussed in the introduction to this chapter, mention must be made of **Richard Hofstadter's** (1916-70) study of the role of the American intellectual in *Anti-Intellectualism in American Life* (1963) and of **Lewis Mumford's** (born 1895) critique of the American belief in technology (see *The Myth of the Machine,* 2 vols, 1967 and 1970; and *The Pentagon of Power,* 1970). There are also some magnificent histories, **Samuel Eliot Morison's** (1887-1976) *The European Discovery of America* (2 vols, 1971 and 1974) and **Sydney A. Ahlstrom's** *A Religious History of the American People* (1972) being two of the more prominent examples.

Glossary of Literary Terms

aestheticism   A movement during the last two decades of the 19th century which demanded "art for art's sake" and flourished in French, English, and American literature. It was also much ridiculed by contemporaries.

allegory   A manner of fictional representation in which events, settings, and characters have a second, symbolical meaning and also signify abstract ideas or moral qualities.

alliteration   A device used in poetry and sometimes in prose: the repetition of similar initial consonants, in a group of words or line of poetry.

ambiguity   The presence of more than one possible meaning.

analogy   A comparison between two essentially different things to show their similarity.

anapaest   A foot of three syllables, the first two unstressed and the third stressed.

archetype   Literally, A. means the first model or form from which subsequent forms are derived. In Jung's psychology, it refers to inherited ideas or ways of thinking that are present in the subconscious of the individual.

assonance   A device used in poetry and sometimes in prose: the repetition of similar vowel sounds.

ballad   A short and simple narrative poem written to be sung or recited. Folk ballads belong to the earliest forms of literature. The literary ballad imitates the anonymous popular form. The ballad stanza consists of four lines, with the rhyme pattern a b c b, and four stresses in the first and third and three stresses in the second and fourth lines.

baroque   Originally, the florid architecture from the mid-16th to the 18th centuries. The term is also used broadly for literature that is highly ornamented, exaggerated, and emotionally expressive.

beat generation   The writers coming of age after World War II who rejected the values of American society and used their writings as forms of protest. Loose structures and colloquial diction are hallmarks of their literature. "Beat" has been interpreted in musical terms (rhythm), in the sense of "beaten", and even in the context of "beatitude".

blank verse   Unrhymed verse with five stresses in each line and an iambic pattern (iambic pentameter). It has been a popular form of dramatic verse in English, and was used by Milton, Shakespeare, and Romantic writers.

blues   A sad or melancholy song of Afro-American origin. It usually consists of three-line stanzas, with the second line repeating the first.

burlesque   A literary or dramatic imitation intended to ridicule the original form by exaggeration. It usually implies the treatment of an elevated subject in a trivial way or of a low subject with mock dignity.

calligramme   Poems in which the arrangement of the typography underlines the theme. E. E. Cummings made use of this device. It is also referred to as concrete poetry.

canto   One of the sections of a long poem. Dante's *Divine Comedy,* Byron's *Don Juan,* and Pound's major collection of poems are arranged by cantos.

Cavalier poets   "Cavalier" refers to the followers of Charles I in his struggles with Parliament. The Cavalier poets include Thomas Carew (pronounced Carey) (1594-1640), Richard Lovelace (1618-58), and Sir John Suckling (1609-41).

classicism   A movement in art and literature representing the qualities for which the early Greeks and Romans were famous: clarity of expression, balanced and well-proportioned forms, and a concern for reason and universal themes. Ben Jonson, John Milton, and Alexander Pope are often cited as classicists.

cliché   A word, phrase, or idea that has lost its originality through constant use. The term is also applied to overused types of characters and ways of characterization.

closet drama   A play, often written in verse, more suitable for reading than for acting.

comedy   A literary work – usually a drama – that is humorous in its treatment of theme and character and has a happy ending.

comedy of manners   A humorous play making fun of the conventions and manners of the middle and upper classes of society.

conceit   A complicated or elaborate image or metaphor combining seemingly incompatible and vastly different things or ideas. The best conceits, such as those of the metaphysical poets, achieve a new meaning and insight that is often startling.

concrete poetry   See CALLIGRAMME.

connotation   Unlike "denotation", which signifies the accepted linguistic meaning of a word, "connotation" refers to all the meanings suggested by, or attached to, a word, i. e. the emotions and associations created by the sound or the look of a word. Poetry makes much use of connotations.

couplet   A pair of successive lines of poetry that rhyme. The English or Shakespearian sonnet closes with a couplet.

dactyl   A foot of three syllables, the first stressed and the others unstressed.

decadence   Term used for periods free from social, political and moral conventions. There were periods of decadence in all ages. The term is often applied to the 1890s (see also AESTHETICISM) when writers were trying to shake off the inhibitions and prohibitions of Victorianism.

deconstruction   A poststructuralist critical theory, inspired by the psychoanalyst Jacques Lacan (1901-81) and the philosopher Jacques Derrida (born 1930), which tries to prove that any kind of text, whether literary or non-literary, eventually undermines its own claims to a convincing logical meaning. The role of the reader is central to this theory, which has been popular in academic circles since the late 1970s.

doggerel   Badly written and trivial poetry, often very sentimental and monotonous. It is usually intentionally, and sometimes unintentionally, humorous.

dystopian   Term sometimes used to describe anti-utopian fiction, i.e. works presenting nightmare visions of the future.

dramatic poetry   Verse that uses dramatic form, such as the dramatic monologue, in which a character speaks to one or more listeners and reveals something about his/her personality. The term also refers to plays written in verse (see CLOSET DRAMA).

eclogue   A pastoral or idyllic poem in praise of country life.

elegy   A melancholy poem, usually mourning or lamenting a dead person or persons. An elegiac stanza is the quatrain (four lines of verse) in iambic pentameter rhyming alternately.

emblem   A sign or symbol representing an idea or a tradition of a society.

enjambement   A line of verse that is not end-stopped, i.e. has no logical pause at the close and runs over to the next line. Also called run-on line.

epic   A lengthy narrative poem and often concerned with heroes and courageous actions.

epigram   A brief and witty statement or saying, often in the form of a poem.

epigraph   A motto or quotation at the beginning of a literary work which provides a guideline for the work itself.

epitaph   An inscription on a tombstone; also a brief poem praising a deceased person.

epode   The third stanza of an ODE.

euphemism   An indirect word or expression used for one that is thought to be offensive or obscene.

euphuism   An affected and artificial style of writing that was popular in the 16th century. It implies the excessive use of alliteration, allusions, and conceits.

expressionism   In the fine arts, the term refers to techniques in which natural forms are exaggerated and distorted and in which colour is intensified. In drama, it means a style of writing and producing that stresses emotional concern, subjective reactions of characters, and symbolic representations of reality. In fiction, the term involves the representation of the world through the intensified impressions and reactions of characters. Generally, E. aims at a deliberate distortion of reality.

farce   A humorous, light play or comedy involving ludicrous action and dialogue, usually with stereotyped characters. The farce has much situational humour and slapstick.

fin de siècle   See AESTHETICISM and DECADENCE.

formalism   A critical theory of literature developed around 1915 by Russian philologists (W. Schklowskij, R. Jakobson) who considered it an "exact science" of literature as linguistic art. Formalists continually questioned their own aims and results and their theory later (1930s) developed into STRUCTURALISM.

free verse   Verse without regular metre or line length but relying upon the natural rhythm of language.

genre   A category or type of literature having a particular form or technique. The term is applied to such literary forms as the novel, the short story, the essay, etc., but also to types within these genres: thus there are lyrical and pastoral genres of poetry.

Georgian The term applied to authors during the later reign of George V (1910–1936), but (in historical literature) also to the reigns of the four Georges (1714–1830) and to the styles of architecture and art during that period.

Gothic A term with several meanings, including a medieval style in architecture, anything pertaining to the Middle Ages (and, by implication, considered barbaric), and, in literature, a style that is marked by gloomy settings, violent and bizarre actions, and a general feeling of decadence and decay. This third definition applies to the gothic novel of the late 18th and early 19th centuries.

graveyard school A group of 18th-century English poets who wrote sad and gloomy verse about death.

haiku A Japanese poetic form that is made up of three lines containing a set number of syllables. The haiku usually uses allusions and comparisons. It influenced European Imagism.

Harlem Renaissance The fiction and poetry of the 1920s, written by authors from Harlem, a section of upper Manhattan (New York City) inhabited mainly by blacks. Its leading figures were Langston Hughes, Countee Cullen, James Weldon Johnson, and Claude McKay.

heroic couplet A couplet in iambic pentameter (ten syllables with five stresses in each line). It was the most popular verse form of the 18th century.

hymn A lyric poem in verse form designed to be sung; also a song in praise of God.

iambus (iamb) A poetic foot of two syllables, of which the second is stressed. It is the most common metrical foot in English.

imagery The use of language to create actions, persons, and objects in the reader's mind. Imagery can be both literal and figurative, i. e. symbolical.

imagism The poetry and the theory of a group of early 20th-century poets in America and England who held that poetry should use everyday language and common themes, should create new rhythms, and present clear, precise, and concentrated images. Imagist poets included Ezra Pound, Richard Aldington, Hilda Doolittle (H.D.), and Amy Lowell.

impressionism A style of writing in which the author describes characters and scenes as they appear to him/her at a given moment rather than as they are (or may be) in reality.

intentional fallacy The error of critics and readers of judging the meaning of a literary work of art in terms of the authors's expressed purpose in writing it.

interior monologue A form of writing recording the inner thoughts and feelings of a character, usually using the tenses of reported speech. See also STREAM OF CONSCIOUSNESS.

Irish literary Renaissance The rise of Irish writers, mainly dramatists, in Dublin at the beginning of the 20th century. The writers who came to prominence then were George Moore, Lady Gregory, Edward Martyn, W. B. Yeats, and J. M. Synge.

Lake Poets (Lake School) A term applied to Samuel Taylor Coleridge, William Wordsworth, Robert Southey, and also to Thomas De Quincey, who all lived in the Lake District in Cumbria, England.

lampoon An aggressive satire, in verse or prose, against individuals or institutions. It ridicules the behaviour and the character of the attacked and was a popular form of satire in the 17th and 18th conturies.

limerick A form of light verse consisting of five lines rhyming aabba. The limerick is often naughty or obscene.

lyric A short, personal or subjective poem expressing the author's intense feelings. A lyric often has a melodic quality.

masque A theatrical form of entertainment that was popular in 16th and 17th-century England. It involved dancing, pantomime, songs, and dialogue.

melodrama A form of drama that exaggerates emotion, has stereotyped characters, and relates sensational events. Melodramas (from Greek "song" and "play") were originally plays with music. The modern kind developed in the 18th century, and melodramatic elements often dominate Gothic novels and 20th-century films.

metaphor A figure of speech by which one thing is imaginatively identified with another. These is no linking "like" or "as", as in a SIMILE. Thus, W. B. Yeats writes about an "aged man" who is "a tattered coat upon a stick".

metaphysical poetry Verse that is highly intellectual and philosophical, but also marked by verbal wit and imaginative images (conceits) and irregular metre. The outstanding metaphysical poet in English literature was John Donne, and in American literature, Edward Taylor.

metre The regular pattern or measure of stressed and unstressed syllables in poetry. The metrical units, or groups of syllables, most commonly used in English poetry are called IAMB(US), TROCHEE, ANAPAEST, and DACTYL. Each of these metrical units is called a foot. The number of feet in a line of verse determines its name: thus verse of five feet is called pentameter. The spondee is a rare form of foot: two stressed and successive syllables.

mimesis The Greek word for imitation. In literature, it refers to the attempt to "hold the mirror up to nature", as Hamlet puts it in act 3, scene 2.

mock epic (mock heroic) A long and comic poem in which a trivial subject is treated in the exalted style of the epic. Alexander Pope's *The Rape of the Lock* is written in this style.

modernism A general term for new developments in the arts and in literature in the first half of the 20th century. In English literature, it especially refers to the works of T. S. Eliot, James Joyce, Virginia Woolf, W. B. Yeats, and Ezra Pound; and in American literature, to the pre-modernists, Emily Dickinson, Walt Whitman, and the experimental and innovative authors who wrote after 1914 (Lowell, Pound, Williams, and Stevens). A main feature is the impact upon literature of the works and research of Freud and of a search for new forms of expression. Modernist literature rejected the procedures and values of the immediate past (Victorianism) and may be described as a literature of discontinuity.

montage In literature, the term means a series of rapidly presented impressions or observations that serve to create an atmosphere or to establish a theme.

myth A legendary story, usually dealing with supernatural events, and dating from ancient times. Myths arose out of man's need to give meaning to the mysteries of the world. Myths have been used in modern literature as a structural device (for instance, in Joyce's *Ulysses*).

narrative poetry   Verse that tells a story, such as the ballad or the epic.

naturalism   An extreme form of realism that rejects idealized portrayals of life and stresses the powerful influence, often tragic, of heredity and environment. Fiction in this movement emphasizes the animal nature of man and the coarse and cruel sides of life.

neoclassicism   A style of writing that emerged in the 17th and 18th centuries with the revival of classical standards of form, order, and harmony in literature. Neoclassicists advocated rationalism, logic, elegant diction, and emotional restraint.

new criticism   A form of literary evaluation that calls for a close and detailed analysis of language and form rather than a study of biography or the historical settings of works of literature. New Criticism was supported by such American writers as Allen Tate, R. P. Warren, Yvor Winters, and Kenneth Burke.

nouveau roman   A term applied to the work of a number of modern French novelists, including Claude Simon (who won the Nobel Prize for literature in 1985) and Marguerite Duras. They reject the traditional techniques of the novel (narrator, plot, time sequence) and create an intentional disorder that is meant to give collective significance to events.

novel   A form of fictional prose narrative that arose in the 18th century and was rapidly developed by Defoe, Richardson, Fielding, Smollett, and Sterne. Every novel involves characters, sometimes a dramatised narrator, action, settings, and theme.

ode   Originally, a poem meant to be sung. It now refers to a longer lyric poem in an elevated style and with a dignified theme. The Pindaric ode had several stanzas, each consisting of three sections (strophe, antistrophe, and epode), sung by a chorus.

ottava rima   A stanza form that has eight iambic pentameter lines rhyming abababcc.

pageant   An elaborate public event celebrating a date in history; also a theatrical outdoor performance.

panegyric   A solemn or dignified speech or work of literature (usually brief) in praise of someone or some achievement.

parody   The satirical, humorous imitation of a person, event, or work of literature. It achieves humour mainly by exaggeration, though good parody implies a sound and valid criticism of the original.

pastoral   A poem dealing with country life in an idealized way.

pathetic fallacy   Ascribing emotions and characteristics of human beings to inanimate objects.

pathos   The power of works of art to create strong feelings of pity and sadness for a character.

persona   In literature, the term refers to the person figuring in a poem or novel, serving as a "mask" (the meaning of the Latin word) for the author. Authors often invent a persona who narrates the events in a novel.

Petrarchan sonnet   See SONNET

Petrarchism   The style, introduced by the Italian poet and scholar Petrarch (1304-74), which is distinguished by its formal perfection, grammatical complexity, and elaborate imagery.

picaresque   A type of fiction in which the mostly humorous adventures of a character from low life are narrated. (The Spanish word "picara" means rascal or rogue.) The picaresque novel was popular in 18th-century England, and it was again revived in the 1950s.

plot   Sequence of events in a work of fiction, a play, or a narrative poem.

poet laureate   The title given to a poet who receives a certain amount of money (stipend), now very small and merely a token sum, as an officer of the Royal Household in London. His duty used to be to write poems for court festivities. The first modern poet laureate was Ben Jonson. 20th-century laureates: Bridges, Masefield, Day-Lewis, Betjeman, and, at present, Ted Hughes.

poetic diction   A style or way of writing that is different from ordinary speech and prose. An elevated style was especially popular in the 18th century; 20th-century poetry has generally tried to avoid it, arguing that there should be no differences between the language of poetry and that of speech.

poetic license   The liberty taken by a writer, usually a poet, in deviating from the rules of pronunciaton, grammar, and style to produce a desired effect.

poetics   Literary criticism dealing with poetry, or the art and technique of versification.

positivism   A philosphical movement that considers only facts and excludes speculation about causes and spirituality.

postmodernism   A term that is still vague. It refers to a new approach in the arts and in literature that began in the 1960s and implies the questioning of the meaning of history and of the real, an experimentalism that includes playing with forms and meanings, and a revolt against the seriousness of the modernists and their hope for formal coherence. In literature, some postmodernists are concerned with playful exercises in fantasy and grotesquery, others explore the process of writing and the formation of texts, and others again write fiction of excess and encyclopedic mass. One point all P.s have in common is the expression of formal and ideological questions about the nature of fiction.

Pre-Raphaelite Brotherhood   A group of English writers and artists who, around 1850, tried to revive the style and spirit of Italian art before the time of Raphael (1483-1520). Their poetry shows sensuousness, symbolism, and a preference for the exact depiction of the physical details of nature.

primitivism   This belief flourished in 18th- and 19th-century France and England. It holds that contemporary civilization is artificial and corrupt and suggests a return to nature. Rousseau in France, and Blake and Wordsworth in England, expressed primitivist views in some of their works.

prose poem   A section or passage of prose with poetic qualities, such as alliteration, rhythm, and rich connotations.

prosody   The study of verse structure, such as rhythm, metrical scheme, rhyme, stanza form, and metre.

quatrain   A poem or stanza of four lines.

realism   A way of writing, with respect to technique and content, in which the ordinary and familiar aspects of (everyday) life are shown in a straightforward manner. Realist writers usually depict the lives of the middle and lower classes, and many concentrate on the description of misery and decay.

regionalism   The literary description of a particular section or area of a country, with an attempt at accurate representation of the local speech, manners, and beliefs. In the USA the term has been applied to several authors from the West and from the South (another term used in this context is "local colour"); in England, the Wessex novels of Thomas Hardy are regional literature.

Renaissance   The period from about 1350 to 1650, when art, learning, and literature were revived in Europe. It marked the transition from the Middle Ages to the modern world. In literature, the works of classic authors were studied and translated, and many great works of fiction and poetry were written.

rhetoric   The theory and study of the effective use of language in writing and speaking. Modern rhetoric has been concerned with the methods of achieving literary quality.

rhyme   The repetition of the same or similar sounds in different words that appear close to each other. There are diffent kinds of rhyme: internal rhyme occurs within the same line of verse; end rhyme occurs at the ends of lines. Rhyme can be identical or approximate. One type of approximate rhyme is ASSONANCE, where the stressed vowels in the words agree but the consonants do not.

rhyme royal   A stanza of seven lines of iambic pentameter with the rhyme scheme ababbcc.

romance   Originally, this meant a medieval narrative in prose or verse about heroic persons and events. It now applies to any kind of fiction that deals with heroic achievements, passionate love, and supernatural experiences.

romanticism   A literary and artistic movement which considered imagination more important than formal rules and reason. It dominated European cultural life to a large extent between the 1780s and the 1830s. Romanticists rejected the ideas of classicism, emphasized the role of the individual, and were concerned with mystery, the supernatural, and feelings.

satanic school   A group of 19th-century English poets, including Byron and Shelley, who led unconventional lives and were at odds with contemporary society.

satire   The ridiculing in verse, prose, or drama of persons and institutions that the author considers foolish or bad. As a form or genre of literature, S. blends humour and wit with a critical attitude.

semiotics   The study of signs and symbols. This involves the theory of symbolism, including the meanings of words (semantics), structural relations (syntax), and the relations between behaviour and symbols (pragmatics).

sensibility   The responsive awareness and the emotionalism that characterizes an author and helps the reader to an emotional appreciation of a literary work of art.

sentimentalism   The excessive use of sentiment or emotion in literature.

simile A comparison in which two essentially different things are linked by the use of such words as *like, as,* and *than.*

sonnet A poem of 14 lines, normally in iambic pentameter, with rhymes arranged according to the Italian or Petrarchan manner (consisting of an octave, i.e. eight lines, and a sestet, i.e. six lines: for instance, abbaabba cdecde), the English or Shakespearean manner (consisting of three quatrains and a concluding couplet: abab cdcd efef gg), and the less frequent Spenserian manner (abab bcbc cdcd ee). The parts of the sonnet refer to each other in a variety of ways; Shakespeare's final couplet, for instance, allows a sort of general conclusion or a summing up of the argument.

Spenserian stanza A stanza of eight lines in iambic pentameter followed by a line of iambic hexamter (i.e. six stresses in a line); the rhyme scheme is ababbcbcc. It was invented by Edmund Spenser (1522-99) for his epic poem *The Faerie Queene* and was popular with the Romantic poets.

sprung rhythm A term invented by Gerard Manley Hopkins to designate a metre in which a stressed syllable may be followed by a number of unaccented syllables. All feet, however, are given equal time length in pronouncing. Poems which feature sprung rhythm have an irregular metre and resemble natural speech.

stanza Lines of verse grouped in a pattern. The most common forms are the couplet, tercet, quatrain, rhyme royal, ottava rima, sonnet, and villanelle.

stream of consciousness A way of writing that tries to record a character's ideas and feelings as they are experienced in the character's mind. This means that there is sometimes no logical sequence and no distinction between several levels of reality.

structuralism A continental European movement in the human sciences which has deeply influenced literary theory and criticism. It was developed by, among others, Roland Barthes (1915-80) and Claude Lévi-Strauss (born 1908), two brilliant French critics who drew on the work of the Russian formalists (Jakobson) and on the linguistic studies of Ferdinand de Saussure (1857-1913). Structuralists see any text, and even any cultural event, as the result of a system of signification, or code, and argue that the relations between the elements of such a system allow it to "mean" something, and that it is not the relationship between the system and reality which establishes meaning. They question the idea that a text reflects or holds a given reality, or that it expresses the self of an author. This implies an attack on the humanist ideas of traditional literary scholarship. The most radical challenge has come from the poststructuralist writers, such as Jacques Derrida (see DECONSTRUCTION).

surrealism A style in the arts and in literature that stresses the nonrational and subconscious aspects of man's personality. It sprang up in France at the end of World War I, with André Breton (1896-1966) as one of the leading figures. Surrealists were influenced by the theories of Freud and the inhuman brutality of war, which some painters and writers had experienced. One of the most distinguished surrealist painters is Salvador Dali; in literature, James Joyce's *Finnegan's Wake* demonstrates some aspects of surrealism.

syllabic verse   Poetry in which the lines are measured by the number of syllables rather than by accents. The American poet Marianne Moore has written syllabic verse.

symbol   Something or someone representing an idea. Usually, a symbol is a word or phrase with a complex of associated meanings or connotations. Thus a flag is a symbol of a nation.

symbolism   A literary movement in the art and literature of late 19th-century France, a revolt against realism. The symbolist poets used symbols and images to suggest life rather than direct statements of meaning. Baudelaire, Rimbaud, and Verlaine were the more influential writers in this movement.

synesthesia   The association (and poetic representation) of images and sensations perceived by different senses, e.g. sight and sound (as in "blue cry") or touch and sight ("cool red").

terza rima   A series of tercets (three lines of verse) with interlinking verse, with the rhyme scheme aba bcb cdc, etc.

tragedy   A literary work – usually a drama – with a sad or sombre theme that is carried to a disastrous end. It traces the downfall of a noble character who becomes a victim of fateful events he/she cannot control or of a flaw in his/her personality.

tragicomedy   A play combining elements of comedy and tragedy.

travesty   A form of satire which treats a dignified topic frivolously or absurdly. Unlike a PARODY, which changes the content of the object of literary ridicule, a travesty keeps the content of the satirical target and treats it in a new and ludicrous form.

trilogy   A series of three novels, plays, or operas.

trochee   A foot of two syllables; the stressed syllable is followed by an unstressed one.

utopian   Derived from a Greek word meaning "no place" or "nowhere". In literature, it is often applied to fiction showing an ideal society. Thomas More's book *Utopia* (1516) was the prototype of such works. The opposite of "utopian" is "dystopian".

villanelle   A verse form of French origin consisting of 19 lines on merely two rhymes. It has six stanzas, of which five have three lines, and the last four lines. The rhyme scheme is aba aba aba aba aba abaa. Certain lines recur in a fixed pattern. It was originally used in pastoral verse and for songs and has been put to a variety of uses by poets in the 19th and 20th centuries – e.g. Dylan Thomas ("Do Not Go Gentle Into That Good Night").

vorticism   An artistic movement related to cubism that began in the early 20th century. It favoured the imaginative reconstruction of nature in formal or mechanistic designs and related art forms to the machine and modern industrial society. Vorticists saw art as a vortex or whirl in which energy was transformed into forms. Wyndham Lewis, Ezra Pound, and T. S. Eliot were temporary supporters.

Chronological Tables

English Literature

Sovereign	Date	Political and Social History	Literature
	450	Invasions by Angles and Saxons	
	787	Invasions by Danes. England divided into five Kingdoms.	*Beowulf*
Alfred the Great 871–899	871	Alfred becomes King of Wessex.	*Anglo-Saxon Chronicle*
	878	Alfred defeats the Danes.	
Edward the Elder 899–924			
Canute 1016–35			
Harold I 1035–40			
Hardicanzte 1040–42			
Edward the Confessor 1042–66			
Harold II 1066	1066	The Normans defeat the English at Hastings.	

The Normans

Sovereign	Date	Political and Social History	Literature
William the Conqueror 1066–87		The feudal system begins.	
William II 1087–1100	1095	First crusade	

Sovereign	Date	Political and Social History	Literature
Henry I 1100-35			
Stephen 1135-54	1136		Geoffrey of Monmouth, *Historia Regum Brittanniae*

The Plantagenets

Sovereign	Date	Political and Social History	Literature
Henry II 1154-89	1146 1170	Second crusade Thomas à Becket murdered at Canterbury.	
Richard I 1189-99		Further crusades	
John (Lackland) 1199-1216	1205 1215	John signs Magna Carta.	Layamon, *Brut*
Henry III 1216-1272			*Roman de la rose*
Edward I 1272-1307		Edward conquers Wales and Scotland.	
Edward II 1307-1327		Hundred Years' War (1337-1453)	
Edward III 1327-1377	1346 1356 1362	The French are defeated at Crécy. The French are defeated at Poitiers.	Langland, *Piers Plowman*
Richard II 1377-1399	1386		Chaucer begins *Canterbury Tales*

Sovereign	Date	Political and Social History	Literature
Henry IV (Boling- broke) 1399–1413			
Henry V 1413–1422	1415	The French are defeated at Agincourt.	
Henry VI 1422–1461	1422 1431 1455	Henry becomes King of France. Joan of Arc executed. Beginning of the Wars of the Roses.	
Edward IV 1461–1483	1476	Caxton starts printing press.	
Edward V 1483			
Richard III 1483–1485	1485		Malory, *Morte d'Ar- thur*

The Tudors

Sovereign	Date	Political and Social History	Literature
Henry VII 1485–1509	1485 1492	End of the War of the Roses. Columbus arrives in the West Indies.	
Henry VIII 1509–1547	1516 1517 1534	Luther publishes his theses. Henry abolishes papal power in England.	More, *Utopia*
Edward VI 1547–1553	1553		Heywood, *Play of the Wether*
Mary 1553–1558			Udall, *Ralph Roister Doister*

Sovereign	Date	Political and Social History	Literature
Elizabeth I 1558-1603	1578 1582 1588 1590	Defeat of the Spanish Armada.	Lyly, *Euphues* Hakluyt, *Voyages* Sidney, *Arcadia*
The Stuarts			
James I 1603-1625	1611 1620 1621 1623	Pilgrim Fathers land in New England.	Authorized Version of the Bible Burton, *Anatomy of Melancholy* Folio edition of Shakespeare's plays
Charles I 1625-1649	1629 1633 1642 1645 1649	Charles dissolves the Third Parliament. The Civil War Execution of Charles I	Donne, *Poems* Milton, *Poems*
The Commonwealth			
1649-1658	1651 1653 1658	Charles II fails in his invasion of England and flees to France. Cromwell becomes Lord Protector of England. Death of Cromwell	Hobbes, *Leviathan*
The Restoration of the Stuarts			
Charles II 1660-1685	1667 1678		Milton, *Paradise Lost* Bunyan, *Pilgrim's Progress*

Sovereign	Date	Political and Social History	Literature
James II 1685–1688	1688	Protestants appeal to William of Orange for help against the Catholic James. William lands in England, James flees to France.	
The Hanoverians			
William and Mary 1688–1702	1690	William defeats James in Ireland.	Locke, *Essay Concerning Human Understanding*
Anne 1702–1714	1709 1711		Steele, *The Tatler* Addison/Steele, *The Spectator*
George I 1714–1727	1719 1726		Defoe, *Robinson Crusoe* Swift, *Gulliver's Travels*
George II 1727–1760	 1740 1749 1760	England at war with France, Holland and Spain. Conflicts between France and England in America and India.	 Richardson, *Pamela* Fielding, *Tom Jones* Sterne, *Tristram Shandy*
George III 1760–1820	1766 1768 1776 1786 1789	 American Declaration of Independence Beginning of the French Revolution.	Goldsmith, *The Vicar of Wakefield* Gray, *Poems* Burns, *Poems* Blake, *Songs of Innocence*

Sovereign	Date	Political and Social History	Literature
	1793	Execution of Louis XVI	
	1798		Wordsworth/Coleridge, *Lyrical Ballads*
	1804	Napoleon becomes Emperor.	
	1805	Nelson wins, but dies in, Battle of Trafalgar.	
	1812		Byron, *Childe Harold*
	1813	Napoleon defeated at Leipzig.	
	1816		Coleridge, *Kubla Khan*
George IV 1820–1830	1830	Louis Philippe becomes King of France.	
William IV 1830–1837	1833	Britain abolishes slavery.	
	1836		Dickens, *Pickwick Papers*
Victoria 1837–1901	1847		E. Brontë, *Wuthering Heights*
	1848	Revolutions on the Continent	
	1850		Tennyson, *In Memoriam*
	1855		Browning, *Men and Women*
	1859	Britain acquires colonies in Africa.	G. Eliot, *Adam Bede*
	1872		Butler, *Erewhon*
	1896	Industrial and colonial development	Hardy, *Jude the Obscure*
	1898		Plays by Shaw
	1900		Conrad, *Lord Jim*
Edward VII 1901–1910	1908		Bennett, *The Old Wives' Tales*
	1910		Wells, *Mr Polly*
George V 1910–1936	1912	China becomes a republic.	
	1913		Lawrence, *Sons and Lovers*
	1914	Beginning of World War I	

Sovereign	Date	Political and Social History	Literature
	1915		Maugham, *Of Human Bondage*
	1916		Joyce, *A Portrait of the Artist*
	1917		T. S. Eliot, *Prufrock*
	1922		T. S. Eliot, *The Waste Land*
			Joyce, *Ulysses*
	1932		Huxley, *Brave New World*
	1933	Hitler comes to power.	
	1935		Eliot, *Murder in the Cathedral*
Edward VIII 1936	1936	Edward abdicates in December.	
George VI 1936-1952	1939	Germany invades Poland: beginning of World War II.	Joyce, *Finnegan's Wake*
	1940		Greene, *The Power and the Glory*
	1945	End of World War II	Orwell, *Animal Farm*
	1947	Public welfare programmes introduced by Labour government.	Lowry, *Under the Volcano*
			Orwell, *1984*
Elizabeth II 1952-	1953		Amis, *Lucky Jim*
	1954		Golding, *Lord of the Flies*
	1955		Beckett, *Waiting for Godot*
	1957		Pinter, *The Dumb Waiter*
	1958		Burgess, *Malayan Trilogy*
	1960		Pinter, *The Caretaker*
	1962		Burgess, *A Clockwork Orange*
	1963	Britain is refused entry into the Common Market.	
	1964		Larkin, *The Whitsun Weddings*

Sovereign	Date	Political and Social History	Literature
	1965	Churchill dies.	Bond, *Saved*
	1968	Censorship of theatre is abolished in Britain.	Durrell, *Tunc*
	1970	British troops control Ulster.	Hughes, *Crow*
	1972		Stoppard, *Jumpers*
	1973	Britain joins Common Market.	
	1974	Labour government under Harold Wilson.	
	1975		Heaney, *North* Stoppard, *Travesties*
	1976	Wilson resigns; Callaghan becomes Prime Minister.	
	1977	Elizabeth II's Silver Jubilee	Tolkien, *The Silmarillion*
	1978	Great newspaper strike in Britain	Hill, *Tenebrae*
	1979	Mrs Thatcher becomes Prime Minister.	Golding, *Darkness Visible* Heaney, *Field Work* Raine, *A Martian ...* Shaffer, *Amadeus*
	1980		Brenton, *The Romans in Britain* Pinter, *The Hothouse* Burgess, *Earthly Powers*
	1981 – 1987	Race riots in several British cities.	Rushdie, *Midnight's Children* (1981) Boyd, *An Ice-Cream War* (1982)
		Arthur Scargill leads unsuccessful miners' strike. Rupert Murdoch buys several British and American newspapers and TV stations.	Fowles, *Mantissa* (1982) Greene, *Monsignor Quixote* (1982) Amis, *Stanley and the Women* (1984) Golding, *The Paper Men* (1984)
		Britain and France agree to build a tunnel linking the two countries.	Burgess, *The Kingdom of the Wicked* (1985)

American Literature

Date	Political and Social History	Literature
1585	Sir Walter Raleigh unsucessfully tries to found a colony in North Carolina.	
1607	Captain John Smith founds the Colony of Virginia at Jamestown.	
1608		Smith, *A True Relation*
1620	Plymouth Colony founded by the Pilgrim Fathers.	
1624		Smith, *The General History of Virginia ...*
1626	The Dutch establish New Netherland Colony on the Hudson River.	
1630	The Puritans found the Colony of Massachusetts.	
1640		*The Bay Psalm Book*
1662		Wigglesworth, *The Day of Doom*
1678		Bradstreet, *Poems*
1692	Witchcraft trials at Salem	
1702		C. Mather, *Magnalia Christi Americana*
1708		E. Cook, *The Sot-Weed Factor*
1732		Franklin, *Poor Richard's Almanack*
1741	Edwards initiates "Great Awakening" with his sermons.	
1754	Anglo-French War in America	
1770	Boston "Massacre"	
1773	Boston Tea Party	
1774		Woolman, *Journal*
1776	Declaration of Independence	Trumbull, *McFingal*
1781	General Cornwallis surrenders to Washington at Yorktown.	
1782		Crèvecœur, *Letters from an American Farmer*
1783	End of American War of Independence	
1789	Washington first President of the USA	
1791		Franklin, *Autobiography*

Date	Political and Social History	Literature
1798		Brown, *Wieland*
1803	Louisiana territory bought from France.	
1812	War between the USA and Britain	
1820		Irving, *The Sketch Book*
1823	Monroe Doctrine	Cooper, *The Pioneers*
1826		Cooper, *The Last of the Mohicans*
1827		Poe, *Poems*
1828		Webster, *American Dictionary*
1831		Poe, *Poems*
1835		Tocqueville, *Democracy in America*
1836		Emerson, *Nature*
1837		Hawthorne, *Twice-Told Tales*
1840	Meetings and publications of the Transcendentalists	Poe, *Tales* Cooper, *The Pathfinder*
1841		Emerson, *Essays*
1845	Annexation of Texas	Poe, *The Raven*
1846	Mexican War begins.	Melville, *Typee*
1848	End of Mexican War Beginning of California gold rush	Melville, *Omoo* Lowell, *Biglow Papers*
1850		Hawthorne, *The Scarlet Letter*
1851		Melville, *Moby-Dick*
1852		Stowe, *Uncle Tom's Cabin*
1854		Thoreau, *Walden*
1855		Whitman, *Leaves of Grass* Longfellow, *Hiawatha*
1856		Melville, *The Piazza Tales*
1860	Abraham Lincoln elected President.	
1861	Beginning of the Civil War	
1862		Whittier, *Snow-Bound*
1863	Lincoln proclaims emancipation of slaves.	
1865	End of Civil War Assassination of Lincoln	Whitman, *Drum-Taps*
1866	Ku Klux Klan founded in Tennessee.	
1867	Alaska bought from Russia.	Alger, *Ragged Dick*
1869	Completion of Union Pacific and Central Pacific Railroads	Twain, *The Innocents Abroad*

Date	Political and Social History	Literature
1876	Alexander Bell receives patent for his telephone; Edison invents phonograph.	Twain, *Tom Sawyer*
1884		Twain, *Huckleberry Finn*
1885		Howells, *The Rise of Silas Lapham*
1886		James, *The Bostonians*
1890		Dickinson, *Poems*
1892	Earthquake in California causes disaster.	Whitman, final edition of *Leaves of Grass*
1893		Crane, *Maggie*
1898	Spanish-American War	James, *The Turn of the Screw*
1899		Norris, *McTeague*
1900		Dreiser, *Sister Carrie*
1903		London, *The Call of the Wild*
1906	Earthquake in San Francisco	Sinclair, *The Jungle*
1909	Ford builds his Model T car. Freud lectures in the USA.	Pound, *Personae*
1913	Post-Impressionist exhibitions (Armoury Show) in New York and Chicago	Cather, *O Pioneers!*
1915		Masters, *Spoon River Anthology*
1917	The USA enters World War I.	Eliot, *Prufrock*
1919		Anderson, *Winesburg, Ohio*
1920	Period of prohibition of sales of alcoholic drinks starts (until 1933).	S. Lewis, *Main Street* O'Neill, *The Emperor Jones*
1922		Eliot, *The Waste Land*
1923		Stevens, *Harmonium*
1925		Dos Passos, *Manhattan Transfer* Fitzgerald, *The Great Gatsby*
1926	Execution of Sacco and Vanzetti	Hughes, *The Weary Blues*
1929	US stock exchange collapses; beginning of Great Depression.	Faulkner, *The Sound and the Fury* Hemingway, *A Farewell to Arms*
1930	Unemployment increases to four million.	Hart Crane, *The Bridge*
1932	Franklin D. Roosevelt elected President.	
1933	End of Prohibition	West, *Miss Lonelyhearts*
1935	"New Deal" era begins.	Steinbeck, *Tortilla Flat*
1936		Faulkner, *Absalom! Absalom!*

Date	Political and Social History	Literature
1938		Mitchell, *Gone With the Wind*
		Cummings, *Poems*
		Wilder, *Our Town*
1939		Steinbeck, *The Grapes of Wrath*
1940	Unemployment at over eight million	Hemingway, *For Whom the Bell Tolls*
		Wright, *Native Son*
1941	USA enters World War II after bombing of Pearl Harbor by Japan.	
1944		Bellow, *Dangling Man*
1945	Truman becomes President after death of Roosevelt.	Williams, *The Glass Menagerie*
	Japan surrenders after the USA drops atomic bombs on Hiroshima and Nagasaki.	Wright, *Black Boy*
1947		Williams, *A Streetcar Named Desire*
1948		Mailer, *The Naked and the Death*
1949		Miller, *Death of a Salesman*
1950	Beginning of the Korean War	
1951		Salinger, *The Catcher in the Rye*
1952	Eisenhower elected President.	Hemingway, *The Old Man and the Sea*
1953	End of the Korean War	Bellow, *The Adventures of Augie March*
	Senator McCarthy starts his hunt for communists in America.	Ellison, *Invisible Man*
		Miller, *The Crucible*
1954	Supreme Court orders desegregation of schools.	
1955	Beginning of black resistance to segregation in the South	Nabokov, *Lolita*
1956		Ginsberg, *Howl*
1957	Racial disturbances in Arkansas	Kerouac, *On the Road*
1958		Albee, *The Zoo Story*
1959	Alaska and Hawaii become 49th and 50th states.	Updike, *The Poorhouse Fair*
1960	John F. Kennedy defeats Nixon in presidential election.	Barth, *The Sot-Weed Factor*
		Updike, *Rabbit, Run*

Date	Political and Social History	Literature
1961	The USA assists exiles in attempt to invade Cuba.	
	A. B. Shepard is first American in manned space expedition.	Heller, *Catch-22*
1962	Confrontation over Soviet missiles in Cuba almost leads to war.	Albee, *Who's Afraid of Virginia Woolf?*
1963	President Kennedy is assassinated.	Pynchon, *V.*
	Civil rights march on Washington	Williams, *Paterson*
1964	The USA bomb North Vietnamese military bases.	Bellow, *Herzog*
		Berryman, *77 Dream Songs*
	Race riots in several cities	
1965	The USA engages openly in Vietnam War.	Plath, *Ariel*
	Race riots in Los Angeles	
	Assassination of Malcolm X	
1966	Further race riots	Capote, *In Cold Blood*
1967	Greatest race riots in American history	Baraka, *Black Magic*
	Demonstrations against the war in Vietnam	Brautigan, *Trout Fishing in America*
	Black power movement	
1968	Assassination of Robert Kennedy and of Martin Luther King	Updike, *Couples*
		Cleaver, *Soul on Ice*
	Nixon elected President	
1969	The USA is first nation on the moon.	Roth, *Portnoy's Complaint*
		Vonnegut, *Slaughterhouse Five*
1970	National guardsmen kill four student protesters at Kent State University in Ohio.	Lowell, *Notebook*
		Welty, *Losing Battles*
1972	Beginning of the Watergate affair	Barth, *Chimera*
1973	Ceasefire in Vietnam	Pynchon, *Gravity's Rainbow*
1974	Nixon resigns and is pardoned by his successor, Gerald Ford.	Heller, *Something Happened*
1975	Continuation of Watergate trial	Ashbery, *Self-Portrait in a Convex Mirror*
		Doctorow, *Ragtime*
		Gaddis, *JR*
1976	The USA celebrates Bicentennial.	Haley, *Roots*
	Bellow receives Nobel Prize.	
1977	James Earl Carter becomes President.	Coover, *The Public Burning*
1978		Updike, *The Coup*

Date	Political and Social History	Literature
1979	Sioux Indians receive financial compensation for the confiscation in 1877 of the Black Hills of Dakota.	Barth, *Letters* Roth, *The Ghost Writer*
1980	American hostages are held in Iran. Ronald Reagan is elected President.	Toole, *A Confederacy of Dunces*
1981	American hostages are freed by Iranians. Columbia space shuttle goes into orbit.	Updike, *Rabbit Is Rich*
1982		Bellow, *The Dean's December*
1983		Walker, *The Color Purple*
1986	Seven astronauts killed in explosion of space shuttle Columbia.	Updike, *Roger's Version*

Index

The index covers the main text (not the notes and appendices) and contains names and important subjects in literary history. Individual works are listed under the authors' names. Brief definitions of literary terms can be found in the glossary following the main text.